OPEN GRAVES, OPEN MINDS

MANCHESTER
1824

Manchester University Press

Open graves, open minds

Representations of vampires and the Undead from the Enlightenment to the present day

Edited by Sam George and Bill Hughes

Manchester University Press

Published by Manchester University Press
Altrincham Street, Manchester M1 7JA, UK
www.manchesteruniversitypress.co.uk

British Library Cataloguing-in-Publication Data is available

Library of Congress Cataloging-in-Publication Data is available

ISBN 978 1 7849 9362 7 *paperback*

First published by Manchester University Press in hardback 2013

This edition first published 2016

Printed by Lightning Source

Contents

List of figures

Notes on contributors

Dr Stacey Abbott is Reader in Film and Television Studies at Roehampton University. Her research covers developments within the horror genre, with a particular focus on the vampire film. She has published widely on cult and supernatural television and is the author of the seminal work *Celluloid Vampires* (2007). Her most recent work is *TV Horror: Investigating the Dark Side of the Small Screen* (I. B. Tauris, 2012), which she has co-written with Lorna Jowett.

Conrad Aquilina is Senior Lecturer in English at the Malta College for the Arts, Sciences and Technology and a visiting lecturer at the University of Malta. His main research interests range across the poetics and narrative strategies of the fantastic and horror, possible and alternative worlds ontology, and simulation theory. Conrad is currently a doctoral student at Durham University.

Dr Sarah Artt is Lecturer in English and Film at Edinburgh Napier University. Her work has appeared in the *Journal of Adaptation in Film and Performance*, and the edited collections *Reading Rocky Horror* (2008) and *Translation, Adaptation and Transformation* (Continuum, 2012). Her teaching and research interests focus on contemporary issues in screen adaptation, Hollywood cinema, women's writing and filmmaking and science fiction.

Malgorzata Drewniok is completing her doctoral studies in Linguistics at Lancaster University. She is examining *Buffy the Vampire Slayer*, and how the language of the series is manipulated to show the change in identity and historical setting among the vampires. Her research interests include stylistics, contemporary Gothic, popular fiction, television studies, popular culture, and gender and language.

Dr Sam George is Senior Lecturer in Literature at the University of Hertfordshire. She is the convenor of the *Open Graves, Open Minds* research project (including the 'Reading the Vampire' MA course). She is a frequent commentator on the contemporary vampire; her interviews have appeared in newspapers including *The Guardian*, *The Times* and *The Wall Street Journal*. She is co-editing an edition of *Gothic Studies* (May, 2013) on vampires with Dr Bill Hughes and contributing to a volume on teaching vampire fiction. She has published widely on literature and science. Her first monograph, *Botany, Sexuality and Women's Writing 1760–1820: From Modest Shoot to Forward Plant,* was published by Manchester University Press in 2007; a second, on entomology, is currently in preparation.

Dr Bill Hughes was awarded his PhD at the University of Sheffield on communicative rationality and the Enlightenment dialogue in relation to the formation of the English novel. His research interests are in eighteenth-century literature; cultural and literary theory; and Dark Romance. He has publications in print and forthcoming on Richard Hoggart; on Jane Austen, Bernard Mandeville, Maria Edgeworth and Frances Burney; and on intertextuality and the Semantic Web. He is co-editing with Dr Sam George a special edition of *Gothic Studies* on vampires (May, 2013).

Dr Lisa Lampert-Weissig is Professor of English Literature and Comparative Medieval Studies at the University of California, San Diego, where she also holds the Katzin Endowed Chair in Jewish Civilization. She has monographs on *Gender and Jewish Difference from Paul to Shakespeare* (2004) and *Postcolonial Studies and Medieval Literature* (Edinburgh University Press, 2010). She teaches a course on 'Vampires in Literature and Film' at UCSD.

Dr Kimberley McMahon-Coleman teaches at the University of Wollongong in the Faculty of Education. Her work has been published in a number of journals, and in R. K. Dhawan and Stewart Gill's book, *Canadian Studies Today: Responses from the Asia Pacific* (2009). With co-author Dr Roslyn Weaver, she has published *Werewolves and Other Shapeshifters in Popular Culture* (McFarland, 2012), focusing on the figure of the shape-shifter as a metaphor for difference. This marks a return to her early interest in vampires, werewolves and other things that go bump in the night.

Dr Ivan Phillips is Associate Dean of School (Learning and Teaching) and Award Leader for the MA Screen Cultures in the School of Creative Arts at the University of Hertfordshire. He completed a PhD on the poetry of Paul Muldoon in 1998, and his research interests span such subjects as Romanticism and its contexts, Gothic culture, modernism into postmodernism, twentieth-century poetry and poetics, and experimental fictions from Laurence Sterne to the Web. His most recent publications have included papers on Wyndham Lewis, David Jones and Dylan Thomas, and he is currently working towards studies on poetry and technology, and traditions of spectacle. He is an author of plays for stage and radio.

Dr Lindsey Scott is an Honorary Research Fellow in the Centre for Adaptations at De Montfort University. She currently teaches rewritings of classical mythology in the Department of English and Creative Writing and her work on adaptations has appeared in *Shakespeare Survey*, *Literature/Film Quarterly* and *Cinephile*. Her research interests include writing and screening the body, Gothic literature, horror cinema and Shakespeare on screen and she is currently reviewing the latest BBC film adaptations of Shakespeare's history plays.

Marcus Sedgwick has established himself as a widely admired writer of Young Adult fiction; his books have either been shortlisted for or won over thirty awards, including the Booktrust Teenage Book Award, the Carnegie Medal, the Edgar Allan Poe Award, and the Guardian Children's Fiction Prize. His novel *My Swordhand Is Singing* (2006) engages with the representation of the folkloric vampire of Eastern Europe and early seventeenth-century accounts of vampirism, and its sequel *The Kiss of Death* gives vampirism an eighteenth-century Venetian setting. His latest novel *Midwinterblood* (Indigo, 2011), features Viking vampires. He is currently working on a film and other projects with his brother, Julian.

Dr Michelle Smith is an Australian Research Council Postdoctoral Fellow in the School of Culture and Communication at the University of Melbourne. Her monograph *Empire in British Girls' Literature and Culture: Imperial Girls, 1880–1915* (Palgrave, 2011) won the 2012 ESSE Junior Scholar Book Award. Michelle has published widely in journals. She has forthcoming publications on 'Girl Crusoes', modern femininity and race in silent New Zealand film, colonial femininity in British girls' literature, and social Darwinism and masculinity.

Dr Catherine Spooner is Senior Lecturer in English Literature at Lancaster University and specialises in Victorian and contemporary literature and culture. Her research interests incorporate Gothic literature, film and popular culture, and fashion and dress in literature. Her books include *Fashioning Gothic Bodies* (2004), *Contemporary Gothic* (2006) and *The Routledge Companion to Gothic*, co-edited with Emma McEvoy (2007). Catherine is currently working on a new monograph entitled *Post-Millennial Gothic: Comedy, Romance and the Rise of Happy Gothic* (Bloomsbury, 2013). She is also co-editing two collections of essays with Fred Botting, *Monstrous Media/Spectral Subjects: Imaging Gothic from the Nineteenth Century to the Present* and *Gothic Bastards: Genre, Innovation and Contemporary Fictions*, to be published by Manchester University Press.

Dr Julieann Ulin is Assistant Professor of British and American Modernism at Florida Atlantic University. She has co-edited *Race and Immigration in the New Ireland* (University of Notre Dame Press, 2013). Her work has appeared or is forthcoming in *American Literature, Joyce Studies Annual*, *James Joyce Quarterly*, *Women's Studies Quarterly*, *Hungry Words: Images of Famine in the Irish Canon* and *Richard Wright: New Readings for the 21st Century*. She is currently completing a monograph which explores intersections between Ireland's medieval history and its modern literature.

Sara Wasson is Senior Lecturer in Literature and Culture at Edinburgh Napier University. Her monograph *Urban Gothic of the Second World War* (2010) examines how writing in the gothic mode subverts the dominant national narrative of the British home front; this book was co-winner of the Allan Lloyd Smith Memorial Prize of the International Gothic Association for advancing the field of Gothic studies. She is also co-editor with Emily Alder of *Gothic Science Fiction, 1980–2010* (Liverpool University Press, 2011), and her work on vampire fiction appears in *The Journal of Popular Culture* and the *Journal of Stevenson Studies*. She is particularly interested in intersections between vampire fiction and contemporary genetics.

Dr Jennifer Williams is Assistant Professor of English at Calvin College in Michigan. She is currently working on a project that investigates the intersection of consumer culture, religious discourse and identity in the works of Gertrude Stein, Mina Loy, Coco Chanel and Elsa Schiaparelli, and Simone Weil. She writes reviews and reflections on all things vampiric on her blog: www.thevampireblog.org.

Acknowledgements

WE WOULD LIKE TO THANK Dan Waters whose novel, *Generation Dead* inspired our use of the phrase 'Open Graves, Open Minds' in the title of the book and project. Dan has graciously allowed us to use this motto; his powerful, often funny, and moving novels explore with great intelligence many of the striking themes in fictions of the undead which have been explored throughout this project.

We are indebted to our families and friends for their support and to Bram Stoker for his legacy and inspiration. Sam would like to offer special thanks to Jonathan and to her father David George. A generous grant from SSAHRI at the University of Hertfordshire contributed to the costs of the book and its illustrations following the OGOM conference. We would like to express our gratitude to the University, to colleagues in Literature for their support and to Brandon Pazitka in Marketing for his work on the programmes and images for the conference and symposium.

Sam would like to acknowledge her appreciation of the artist David Reed, who inspired her discussion of vampire painting and who offered up a generous dialogue around vampires and non-reflection when she wrote to him explaining the project (like Harker at Castle Dracula, he entered freely and of his own will!). She is also indebted to John Rimmer, who introduced her to Reed and fired her discussion of aesthetics in relation to vampirism with his own work and commentary (it was a case of letting the right one in). She would like to thank the novelist Kim Newman for sharing his thoughts on the problem of photographing vampires which he continues to explore in his own writing; Stacey Abbott and Sir Christopher Frayling for their help with mirrors and shadows. She would also like to express her gratitude to

Catherine Wynne for providing the perfect Gothic moment at the centenary, tracing Lucy's sleepwalking steps in *Dracula* and eating fish, chips and mushy peas in Whitby with Dacre Stoker and Sir Christopher Frayling!

We, and the book, owe a great deal to those members of OGOM who have been there from the beginning: Ivan Phillips, Stacey Abbott, Catherine Spooner and Marcus Sedgwick. Special thanks are due to Stacey for kindly helping with frame grabs. Marcus has been a regular visitor to UH, inspiring students with his work, and he even wrote a special story for the centenary, 'Bram Stoker: Vampire', which he generously gave to all the speakers.

We would like to acknowledge various members of the press who have invited us to contribute to discussions around the project: Lucy Tobin in *The Guardian*, Simon Midgley in *The Times*, Tim Stanton at *The Sun*, Javier Hernandez at *The Wall Street Journal*. Thanks also to our editor at Manchester University Press, Matthew Frost, for attending the OGOM conference and for offering his expertise and advice.

Many friends have given Bill support during this project, but he would particularly like to mention his friends Liz Fox, Martin Green, Sarah and Dave Bartlett, and Kevin Jones, who have also contributed much intellectual dialogue; Mel and Pete Duxbury have provided warm friendship, plus cat-sitting during conference attendance; his family – Barbara, Caryl and Bob Hughes – have also been extremely supportive. He wishes to acknowledge the memory of his father, Bernard Hughes, whose influence on him was paramount and, above all, to commemorate his mother, Barbara, who was supremely inspirational and will be painfully missed. Bill is grateful, too, for the intellectual encouragement given him by Avril Horner, Angela Keane and Hamish Mathison, and could hardly avoid celebrating Spike, whose inspirational biting and vampiric typewriting spurred the editing process.

This book is dedicated to the memory of Buffy and Angel, two little souls who touched Sam deeply, and to the 'Reading the Vampire' MA students at the University of Hertfordshire (Lindsey, Sam, Adam, Beverley, Louise, Jo, Khamis, Lisa, Li-Anne, Sam, Kristin, Minal, Jennifer), together with Jillian who is embarking on a PhD on vampire texts. Thank you for accompanying us on this journey. It means a lot.

Preface

THE *Open Graves, Open Minds* project relates the undead in literature, art and other media to questions concerning gender, technology, consumption and social change. It also seeks to give prominence to writers who are contributing to Bram Stoker's legacy by resurrecting the Dracula myth in inventive new ways, such as Marcus Sedgwick, Kim Newman and Paul Magrs. OGOM was initiated by a prominent and exciting conference in 2010 when contributors came together for the first time to debate 'vampires and the undead in modern culture' and to interrogate these creatures in all their various manifestations and cultural forms. Following my interview with Lucy Tobin in *The Guardian*, the story was taken up by Reuters and soon went global, featuring in newspapers from the *Wall Street Journal* to the *Sydney Morning Herald* and *The Irish Times*.[1] News stories emerged that we were reacting against the Americanisation of the genre ('UK Bringing Vampires Back Home', 'University Rejects Americanization of Vampires', 'Cool Britannia for Vampires', and 'Bloody Hell: Brits Complain Yanks Are Stealing Their Vampires'), developing a vampire degree ('Coffin Boffin Syllabus', 'Twilight Gets Scholarly Treatment' and 'Wanna Study Edward Cullen') and eating food out of coffins (this part was true at least).[2] It was amusing but it also provoked some interesting debates about the canon and the study of popular literature in universities. We wanted to put vampires in the context of a rigorous academic conference to prove that you can study popular literature in a serious way. There was even a volcanic ash cloud – I wondered at the time if it was divine wrath brought about by our unholy celebration of the undead!

At this early stage, the plenary speakers were Catherine Spooner, Stacey

Abbott, and Marcus Sedgwick, all of whom have contributed chapters to this collection. Sarah Artt and Sara Wasson, Bill Hughes, Ivan Philips and Malgorzota Drewniok also gave papers at the conference and their work is represented here too. Other contributors, Conrad Aquilina, Julieann Ulin, Lisa Lampert-Weissig, Lindsey Scott, Jennifer Williams, Michelle Smith, and Kimberley McMahon-Coleman, responded to our call for papers and together they have helped to shape and define the project.

OGOM reconvened for a special symposium in the period setting of the Keats House in Hampstead to mark the centenary of Bram Stoker's death in April 2012. Keats explored vampiric pleasures in his *Lamia* (1819) and it has become synonymous with the female vampire,[3] and Hampstead features in the novel *Dracula*, most famously as the notorious setting of the 'bloofer' lady's vampiric crimes (Lucy roaming the Heath as a vampire). The symposium included a visit to the crematorium where Stoker's ashes are interred and a collection of artefacts, including a first edition of Polidori's *The Vampyre* from the archives. In the spirit of OGOM, there were Dracula canapés and vampire cup cakes (but without the oak coffins this time). The members of OGOM (myself, Stacey, Catherine, Bill, Marcus, Ivan) were joined by Dacre Stoker (great-grand-nephew of Bram), Elizabeth Miller, Sir Christopher Frayling, Kevin Jackson, Catherine Wynne, William Hughes, Peter Hutchings and the novelists Paul Magrs and Kim Newman. The talks and discussions were a testimony to the legacy of Bram Stoker. This legacy is evident in our research for the book, finalised as it was in Stoker's centenary year. Dracula can be seen to shape our narrative in all his various manifestations; 'he is known everywhere that man has been ... he lives on and cannot die by the mere passing of time'.[4]

OGOM is now firmly established as a research project at the University of Hertfordshire and the MA module, 'Reading the Vampire: Science, Sexuality and Alterity in Modern Culture', is approaching its third year. Bringing vampires into the curriculum has proved controversial for some and there have been detractors and scoffers, though these have not been without humour:

> Listen up, Lestat lovers: The University of Hertfordshire in England will be offering a master's degree in vampire lit, apparently the only one of its kind in the world. We imagine that the program, which begins this September, will cover all the bloodsucking basics, from Nosferatu to *Twilight* and of course Anne Rice. Extra credit for anyone who scores an interview with a vampire.[5]

Whilst Gothic courses have been popular for some time, it appears that vampire studies still require some explanation. I spoke to Simon Midgley in

The Times about vampires in academe and he even interviewed some of the MA students.[6] I get fan mail at the university now (I don't remember that happening with my book on eighteenth-century botanical literature!).

I am immensely proud of OGOM and what we have achieved. The project will continue to explore the vampire in all its vicissitudes and we now have a website to track that research and provide OGOM news (www.opengraveso-penminds.com). The chapters in this book are the living progeny of the undead project that began in 2010; they offer a lively commentary on the development of the genre, the emergence of dark romance and the rise of happy Gothic. Together, they are essential reading for anyone who wishes to explore open graves with an open mind.

Sam George

Notes

1 Lucy Tobin, 'University Conference Sinks Its Teeth into Vampire Fiction', *The Guardian* (6 April 2010), Education section, www.guardian.co.uk/education/2010/apr/06/vampire-conference-literature-hertfordshire.

2 Paul Casciato, 'Bringing Vampires Back Home – to Britain', *Reuters*, 6 April 2010, http://uk.reuters.com/article/2010/04/06/uk-britain-university-vampires-idUKTRE6352NP20100406; 'University Rejects "Americanisation" of Vampires', *NPR*, 7 April 2010, www.npr.org/templates/story/story.php?storyId=125660207; Karon Liu, 'Bloody Hell: Brits Complain Yanks Are Stealing Their Vampires', *Toronto Life* (7 May 2010), (online) www.torontolife.com/daily/hype/the-american-invasion/2010/05/07/bloody-hell-brits-complain-yanks-are-stealing-their-vampires/; 'Robert Pattinson, Kristen Stewart on Coffin Boffin Syllabus', *STV Entertainment News*, 7 April 2010, http://entertainment.stv.tv/showbiz/168301-robert-pattinson-kristen-stewart-on-coffin-boffin-syllabus; Mark Byrne, 'Vampire Lit Gets Its Scholarly Due', *Galleycat*, www.mediabistro.com/galleycat/vampire-lit-gets-its-scholarly-due_b11462; Chanel Lee, 'Wanna Study Edward Cullen', *Howstuffworks*, 9 April 2010, blogs.howstuffworks.com/2010/04/09/wanna-study-edward-cullen-and-eric-northman-head-to-england/.

3 See Twitchell, *The Living Dead*, p. 11

4 *Dracula*, ed. Luckhurst, p. 222.

5 'Vampire U', *Globe and Mail* (6 April 2010), www.theglobeandmail.com/life/style/tori-spellingvampire-uobama-jeans-wear/article1529173/.

6 Simon Midgley, 'Counting on Dracula', *The Times* (16 March 2011), p. 7.

I

Introduction

Sam George and Bill Hughes

'EACH AGE embraces the vampire it needs', says Nina Auerbach, famously.[1] Nowadays, those embraces are often very intimate; contemporary dark romances abound with couplings between vampire and human. No one can be unaware of the ubiquity of the undead in twenty-first-century culture – particularly, of course, since Stephenie Meyer's Twilight books and the film adaptations, with their fervid entwinings of human and sparkly vampire. Given the decade in which this volume has been produced, the shadowy presence of *Twilight* is inescapable. Many of the chapters below engage with *Twilight*, as book and film, or with affiliated Young Adult fictions; the humanised incarnation of the once-monstrous (such as Meyer's Cullen family) provides one of the themes that unifies this book. The vampire has long been fascinating, though, and many studies have appeared that have laid the foundations for this one. The narrative that emerges here, post-*Twilight* and in Bram Stoker's centenary year, takes vampire studies in a new direction for the twenty-first century whilst acknowledging its debt to the many scholars who first made the vampire an object of academic textual study.

Sir Christopher Frayling, in his introductory essay to *Vampyres: Lord Byron to Count Dracula* (1978), initiated the critical study of vampire texts and invited the undead into the academy. Frayling pays particular attention to the eighteenth-century origins of the literary vampire – an attention which we share. We are also indebted to his identifying the dominant archetypal vampires as they emerge in fiction: the Byronic vampire (or 'Satanic Lord'), the Fatal Woman, the Unseen Force, the Folkloric Vampire, the 'camp' vampire and vampire as creative force.[2] When we asked him recently if another strand had since emerged, he made reference to the vampire with a conscience. We are fortunate in being the first book-length study to analyse and comment on this new strand of sympathetic vampire as it appears in the twenty-first century.

Another work, Ken Gelder's *Reading the Vampire*, is seminal in its decipherment of the vampire in its cultural context from a range of theoretical perspectives (appropriately open-minded for such an elusive creature), but it appeared in 1994, necessarily excluding recent avatars of the humanised vampire in paranormal romance and Young Adult fiction. Equally seminal and much cited is Nina Auerbach's *Our Vampires Ourselves* (1995). Auerbach charts the progress of vampires through the nineteenth and twentieth centuries as far as the 1980s, focusing on US culture during the Reagan years. These two monographs pave the way for our publication, which continues to document the interest in vampires within academic circles; however, we are in the position to respond to more recent developments.

James Twitchell's *The Living Dead* (1981) shares our text-based approach and survey of different genres. Twitchell traces the vampire through its manifestations in Romantic-period literature and nineteenth-century works of a post-Romantic sensibility, notably identifying Wilde's Dorian Gray as vampiric. Written over fifteen years ago, these studies leave ample scope for expansion and new directions; we (that is, ourselves and our contributors) cover more recent manifestations of the undead and aim to trace a narrative of how they mediate contemporary political and epistemological concerns. We also revisit earlier, more familiar texts ('Carmilla' and *Dracula*, for instance) via this new perspective. Our approach is dominated by the figure of the undead as political metaphor in the realm of identity and difference, the trope of reflection and the sympathetic vampire. The chapters below reveal in various ways the persistence of Enlightenment concerns with knowledge and doubt and with transformations of genre. The emergence of Young Adult undead fictions forms a crucial part of this story.

Existing collections of essays on the vampire include *Blood Read: The Vampire as Metaphor in Contemporary Culture*, edited by John Gordon and Veronica Hollinger (1997) and *Draculas, Vampires and Other Undead Forms*, edited by John Edgar Browning and Caroline Joan Picart (2009). The first of these has some excellent essays but was published too early to offer analyses of recent texts such as *Twilight*, *True Blood*, *The Vampire Diaries*, and *My Swordhand Is Singing*. The second of these is a recent text which, while offering a useful transnational perspective, concentrates on cinema and revolves around the figure of Dracula. There are also important anthologies of key vampire texts, often with an ethnological bent.[3] Our volume supplements film and TV studies with a literary and cultural critique that engages with but is not restricted to ethnology. It is also unlike other collections of essays as it has a strong connecting narrative (which yields the incidental virtue that the book can be used as a course text), one which builds upon but in some ways moves away from the now conventional 'Gothic studies' approach in that the vampire, following Frayling, Gelder and Auerbach, forms its own tradition and discipline.[4] In addition, this book has developed from an innovative and highly successful collaborative research project, one that has inspired attention worldwide and generated over forty media stories, and which has become far more than the conference that launched it.

Since the millennium, Erik Butler's *Metamorphoses of the Vampire in Literature and Film* (2010) gives special prominence to French and German texts produced between 1732 and 1933. Unavoidably, this must treat other cultures, notably that of the United States, with some brevity; our book discusses European and transatlantic texts and continues debates around vampirism beyond the 1930s, covering the mid- to late twentieth-century and the twenty-first century too. Butler invokes the Enlightenment and vampires with great theoretical depth – an approach which informs our narrative. Milly Williamson's *The Lure of the Vampire* (2005) and Susannah Clements *The Vampire Defanged* (2011) both attempt to account for the appeal of the vampire in different ways. Williamson does this through an analysis of gender and fandom, of vampires and vampire fans; Clements looks at the temptations of the sympathetic vampire through Christian values and symbolism, addressing a committed Christian readership. Williamson concludes with Anne Rice and *Buffy the Vampire Slayer*; we have covered more recent texts, contextualising them in a variety of ways. Clements's study begins with *Dracula* whereas we look back to Enlightenment thought and belief systems around vampires prior to *Dracula*.

Perhaps the most significant feature of these studies has been their focus on the development of the humanised vampire in fiction. It is here, of course, that we return to the vampire romance of *Twilight*; the prominence of this text in late twentieth-century and twenty-first-century narratives of the undead partially triggered our project and is an important concern of many of our chapters. Gordon and Hollinger's collection, and Auerbach's book in particular, explore the first stirrings of the sympathetic vampire in their analyses of a handful of significant texts from the 1970s onwards which lay claim to inaugurating the sympathetic revenant and the vampire as lover.[5] Of crucial interest are Fred Saberhagen's Dracula series, beginning with *The Dracula Tape* (1975); Chelsea Quinn Yarbro's *Hôtel Transylvania* (1978) and its sequels; and Suzy McKee Charnas's *The Vampire Tapestry* (1980). In *The Dracula Tape*, Dracula's self-justifying (and perhaps highly unreliable) retelling of Stoker's narrative voices his yearning to assimilate to human society, raising doubts about narrative evidence along the way. In *Hôtel Transylvania*, Saint-Germain is not only a sympathetic vampire, a lover and an agent of righteousness and of female emancipation, he is an Enlightenment rationalist (drawn with a convincing attention to his eighteenth-century context). Wayland in *The Vampire Tapestry* is still a predator, but the reader gains intimate acquaintance with his complex subjectivity. Charnas shows us not a humanised vampire but a vampire being tempted into becoming human; we see the domestication of the monster in process. A less recognised precursor is in a different medium – the Marvel comic, Marv Wolfman and Gene Colan's *The Tomb of Dracula* (1972–1979), which shows Dracula in love, married and smitten by tragedy.[6] It has often been remarked that Stoker's Dracula has mainly been denied a voice;[7] these vampires are different: the narrative is focalised through them, sometimes autodiegetically (as with Saberhagen).[8] It may be more than coincidence that, as the vampire gains a voice, it often gains a reflection too. Thus, the trope of the vampire in the mirror which the chapters explore gains new significance with the focus on the subjectivity of the undead. Many of our contributors seek to explore the various ways in which the undead have become sympathetic or even tamed in later texts, taking Anne Rice's *Interview with the Vampire* (1976) and Coppola's *Bram Stoker's Dracula* (1992) as starting points, though we acknowledge those highly significant literary precursors of the 1970s.

As the studies above are inevitably exclusive, we too must be selective, and adopt some rationale for the creatures, texts and genres that are covered. Definitions are troublesome; especially so with the vampire, where much of the appeal for both reader and writer lies in its multifarious nature and the variety of forms it can take. On the other hand, in our choice of undead figures, we do not want to succumb to the flaw of over-inclusivity. Accordingly, we have avoided mythical archetypes and confined ourselves to vampires consciously created as artistic productions and who originate in that eighteenth-century European moment of fictionalising folklore.

Provisionally, let us restrict the term 'vampire' to those who return from death in palpable form to sap the life of others and who can trace their ancestry through literary transformations to those blood-sucking creatures originally designated *vampyr*. But our title talks of the Undead, too, though space allows us only a passing glance at other revenants and it is predominantly vampires who inspire the most fascination. So we have chosen creatures who show an affinity with, or allow a constructive comparison with, the vampire of Eastern Europe as absorbed by literary texts. Marcus Sedgwick tackles the problem of definition from the point of view of its challenges to a writer of fiction, consciously defining his vampires against the domesticated Cullens and returning to their East European ancestors from the early eighteenth-century. Sedgwick wittily verifies or demolishes the received conventions of what characterises the vampire, such as their lack of reflection, casting no shadow, aversion to garlic and holy emblems, and their inability to cross a threshold uninvited. In turn, our contributors examine the significance of these motifs and how vampire fictions transform them in order to probe the unsettled definition of the vampire.

The second criterion is one of restriction rather than definition; the vampire has had many incarnations and, inevitably, not every significant text could be covered in depth. We have chosen avatars of the undead who aptly illustrate our themes of reflection, political metaphor, identity and difference, and the transformations of genre and knowledge. Thus, following Twitchell, we have included the parasitical and ageless Dorian Gray, who is involved in aesthetic arguments over reflection and representation that link to the trope of non-reflection in vampire narratives.[9] We also considered that Viereck's psychic vampire, Le Fanu's leech-like parasitic lodger and Daniel Waters's sympathetic undead teens were significant figures that illustrated well our themes.

Similarly, there is no vampire fiction genre as such; vampire narratives too are infected by these metamorphoses, and mutate and cross-breed between genres. As we move from the eighteenth century to the present day, we see not only, as Auerbach shows, how each age resurrects the vampire for its own purposes but how the vampire materialises through a transformation of genres – literary kinds fuse promiscuously with others, embed themselves in others and so on. Genres can themselves be seen as perspectives and a collision of genres may thus often express a situation where fixed perspectives are questioned. Hence we see a parallel adaptation to different kinds of knowing, often accommodating to particular epistemological crises. (Arguably, even the foundational shift from ethnology to fiction at the end of the eighteenth century was one such crisis.)

The chapters below trace several strands in the post-*Dracula* narrative, all found in that seminal text: ways of knowing and doubting; a politics of otherness, with a direction towards humanising and acknowledging the alien, but with frequent reversals; a mixing and cross-fertilisation of genres – currently, an engagement with romantic fiction – like the forbidden commingling of blood in *Dracula* (the book is itself notoriously hybrid).[10]

Contemporary vacillations in vampire fiction between science fiction and horror, detective fiction and fantasy, and the appearance of parody and mash-ups seem again to dramatise an epistemological uncertainty.

And such themes as the hesitation between scientific rationalisation and supernatural credulity play the same part – for various ends, however. Often in contemporary fiction, this seems to demonstrate a postmodern suspicion of Enlightenment, with all the political ambivalences that stem from that.

In considering what texts are to be discussed, the problem of value is inevitably raised. Romance, in its laxer sense, gets a bad press from feminism, and the heavily romanced Gothic of *Twilight* has invoked much disapproval for what has long been seen as the deleterious effects of romantic fiction on young women's minds (Wasson and Artt give a less mechanistic account in Chapter 11 below). *Twilight* has also been seen by horror fans and stalwarts such as Stephen King as having been far too diluted by the genre of romance; modern vampires are just not scary enough. It may be that the heavy dose of romance in *Twilight* brings a kind of certainty that renders it less interesting than other, more questioning fictions.

. But horror, and the adjacent and mixed genres involved in vampire stories, are also disparaged. At this point, those questions of value appear: why study these texts? Why have conferences and generate collections of essays on them? Our quick answer is that, without becoming relativists, a concern for such popular and widely disseminated narratives, and the longevity of its central figure, is worth analysing in its own right. This, perhaps, puts our objects in the realm of cultural studies rather than literary or film studies *per se*. But we also believe that, among those we have sampled (a tiny fraction of this massively prolific area), there are some – sparkly – gems. Some vampire fictions have a stylistic competence and ingenuity and a certain daring that raises them above many contemporary 'literary novels'. Often, intriguingly, it is among the Young Adult novels of the undead that these are to be found. Why this is so may be worth further investigation, though there is not space to do so here; perhaps reader expectations are less ossified and commercial constraints less determining. Whatever the case, Young Adult fictions receive due attention below, with chapters covering *Twilight* (of course), L. J. Smith's *The Vampire Diaries*, Daniel Waters's *Generation Dead* and the writer Marcus Sedgwick discussing the composition of his own *My Swordhand Is Singing*.

Having outlined the scope of this book, we will now fulfil the promise of part of our subtitle by describing the seeds of this genre (or series of generic transformations) in the eighteenth century. In this brief return to origins we will also see that the themes announced above are very much implicated in Enlightenment discourse on vampires.

Reflections upon vampires: Enlightenment and the Undead

The vampire was born in the early eighteenth century. From Montague Summers on, many have universalised the creature out of concrete existence; such revenants as lamia from ancient Greece, Assyrian ghosts and Arabian ghouls are all named 'vampires', broadening the term beyond usefulness.[11] But the vampire was originally, and for a short while only, an East European folk panic which came under critical scrutiny by *philosophes* of the metropole, was adapted by them in turn as critical metaphor; then rose again as a literary motif, an inhabitant of Gothic fictions reacting against Enlightenment.[12] Therefore, we give here a brief account of the rise of the eighteenth-century literary vampire, where the dominant themes of fictional vampires discussed below were foreshadowed. Having established its immense adaptability, the vampire becomes reborn in successive incarnations, shape-shifting, inviting contradictory passions, remaining ever enigmatic but for diverse reasons, and reshaping the genres it inhabits. Thus its history amply demonstrates Auerbach's by now well-worn (yet still valid) claim which opens our introduction.

Beginnings are always problematic, but we have chosen to begin our narrative in the early eighteenth century (around when the word 'vampire' enters into English).[13] A particular phenomenon did trigger off a bout of frenzied devouring of vampire texts – and it is this entry of vampires into the world of letters and print media that interests us. Thus, this study is primarily literary and textual criticism (including film and TV studies for later manifestations), rather than folkloric or anthropological (though not unresponsive to these spheres).

In Goya's paradigmatically Enlightenment etching, 'The sleep of reason produces monsters' (1797), 'the author is asleep on a desk bearing the inscription "universal language"' (Figure 1.1).[14] The caption reads: 'His only intention is to banish those prejudicial vulgarities and to perpetuate with this work of *caprichos* the sound testimony of truth'.[15] Goya's *Caprichos* suggestively connect the demonic with political evils and with an irrationality that Enlightened thought can unmask.[16] In this famous engraving, the fantastic, uncorrected by reason, generates monstrous figures, among them bats (the vampire bat had been named as such by Buffon in 1774, establishing the link).

Goya's monsters are not simply the degenerate fancies that are born when reason lapses; two plates later, in 'There is plenty to suck', these bats figure as vampiric emblems of an atomised and mutually parasitic society where, in Goya's caption, 'Those who reach eighty suck little children; those under

Figure 1.1.   Francisco Goya, 'The sleep of reason produces monsters',
from *Los Caprichos*

eighteen suck grown-ups. It seems that man is born and lives to have the
substance sucked out of him' (Figure 1.2).[17]

So, for Goya, the pathological imagination, unsupervised by reason,
breeds the bloodsucking vampire, and an irrational society is vampiric.
And, in various ways, this is how the Enlightenment thinkers of Western
Europe saw the vampire – either in their ethnological analysis of the craze
that inundated the fringes of Europe or in their employment of it as critical
social metaphor. Goya's image, citing 'universal language', suggests, too, that
vampiric unreason gnaws away at the dream of universal communication and
common humanity. This connects with the shifting metaphor of the vampire
as Other that resonates with twenty-first-century discourses of identity.
Chapters below pursue this theme through analyses of racial and sexual
otherness in contemporary texts such as *True Blood* and *Generation Dead*.

The vampire first entered Western European letters through the reports
of 'vampire outbreaks erupting across Eastern Europe in the early decades of

Figure 1.2.   Francisco Goya, 'There is plenty to suck',
from *Los Caprichos*

the eighteenth century'.[18] This became textual when 'the Austro-Hungarian
authorities … enacted legislation to quell the situation, conducted official
investigations into the matter and documented their findings'.[19] It is not our
purpose in this section to chart the nature of folk panics or the causes of this
one, but to examine the textual adventures of the vampire as examined by
eighteenth-century investigators and later fictionalised.[20] Erik Butler warns
us against an ahistorical archetype of the vampire.[21] Of course, folkloric and
mythical revenants and bloodsuckers loom from antiquity, but these are only
assimilated to the vampire proper through a progressive series of unwarranted
abstractions that strip the creature of all regional and historical particularity.
David Keyworth, too, argues for vampires as a distinctly eighteenth-century
phenomenon. He compares them with other folkloric avatars of the undead,
noting they are uniquely marked by their 'all-consuming thirst for blood'.[22]
It is a mistake to suppose that even the folkloric vampire is timeless. The
vampire quickly became diversified by '"daemonic contamination", whereby

the distinguishing characteristics of one type of folkloric being ... merge with
that of other folkloric kinds of beings', just as it would by more conscious
generic transformations in literature and, later, other media.[23]

The eighteenth-century responses to vampirism were, at first, primarily
ethnographical. They commonly depict the peasantry as deluded by
superstition, with priests often cast as a harmful and venial source of this
contagion. Yet the portrait is not necessarily disparaging; often the people
have all the ambiguous integrity and simplicity of the 'noble savage'. In these
accounts, the vampire – almost always itself a peasant – becomes a figure in
Enlightenment discourse of all that is premodern and regressive, thus linked
to the feudalism from which it emerges on the fringes of modernising Europe.
As is well known, later literary vampires are frequently metonymous with
feudalism but this time as aristocrats. Perhaps personal animosity triggered
Polidori's transposition of folkloric qualities on to a thinly disguised Lord
Byron, activated by his subordinate position as a petty bourgeois professional,
but it initiated a long line of haughty aristocratic bloodsuckers, tinged with
ancient and decadent grandeur.[24] Though in Polidori and *Varney* and Le Fanu,
the vampire crosses from the villages of Middle Europe to be invited in over
the threshold of the polite drawing room, in Stoker's *Dracula* he truly enters
modern urban life.[25] Confusingly, as Moretti points out, by this stage, in
the late nineteenth century, the vampire here is both a nobleman from an
underdeveloped region yet represents, in a displaced way, modern capital.[26]

The dominant impulse in these responses was to give an enlightened account
of the bizarre uprisings of unreason that reached the ears of intellectuals in
the more developed areas of Europe. The explanations advanced are mostly
in either physiological or cultural terms. Thus in Jean-Baptiste de Boyer,
Marquis d'Argens's epistolary novel *The Jewish Spy* (1735?–1742), Aaron, in
correspondence with Isaac, reproduces from the official accounts the story of
Arnold Paul, a Serbian peasant who supposedly returns from the dead to prey
on his fellow villagers.[27] For Isaac, an explanation of these phenomena 'by
physical Causes' rules out 'all Necessity of having recourse to Miracles' (130).
Isaac establishes a rationalist explanation based on physical or physiological
factors (such as the tendency for blood in the corpse to remain liquid) and
psychology, where these phenomena interact with a cultural, textual situation
where the peasantry have 'their Heads full all Day of these strange Stories'
and succumb to their own 'epidemick Fanaticism' (127). This psychological
perspective reaches into the sexuality of the vampire, which is suggested
even in this early account; there is a buried vampire seduction story here, at
least in d'Argens's (or Isaac's) interpretation of it. The '*Heyduke*'s daughter'
had been thinking of 'a certain dead Person', imagined an attack by him,

and 'continued in a languishing Condition for some Days, and then died ... of Terror, Apprehension and Melancholy' (128) – a mixture of repulsion and love-sickness. This ambivalence towards the vampire is prominent in twenty-first-century vampire fiction and becomes one of the motifs explored below.

Dom Augustin Calmet compiled many of these accounts into his *Dissertations* (1746), which became one of the most widely known source of vampire narratives (drawn on by Le Fanu among others). Calmet is not as gullible as many have claimed; his treatment of vampires (as distinct from other cases of resurrection) is sceptical rather than credulous. However, for an orthodox Catholic, *some* kinds of resurrection are obviously not impossible or irrational – vampiric narratives are to be measured against doctrine. Within his own theist paradigm, he employs a rational and critically exegetical approach to the reports he examines. Calmet is thus an Enlightenment sceptic to some degree – yet not enough of one to his contemporaries who, taking a stricter, Humean epistemology, deride his credulity. Calmet himself stresses the uniqueness of the eighteenth-century vampire scare (180), equating it with the fashion for novelty, particularly in religion, thus positing cultural factors as primary.

For Calmet, accounts of revenants, when observed 'before a whole congregation ... cannot be denied, or even disputed' (243). There are none of Hume's strictures here.[28] In the section, 'Reflections upon vampires. Whether they are really dead or not' (LVIII: 289–93), he dismisses hypotheses that vampire stories are 'fancy or whim' or 'a disorder in the brain' because of observed 'real and substantial effects' (289). However, he does suggest an explanation which combines naturalist and cultural explanations, resting on the disjunction between West and East. In the unenlightened regions of Europe, the irrational contagion of 'epidemical disorders' are frequent, where 'coarse food' renders people 'susceptible of certain indispositions, which take their rise from a bad climate, and unwholesome nourishment, but are prodigiously encreased by prejudice, fancy, and fear' (289). This is a paradigmatically Enlightenment approach, discerning a materialist causality co-determined by cultural factors. Intriguingly, the sexual vitality of the vampire appears again in the story of Peter Plogojowitz who, on being staked, apparently has an orgasm (287) in a male inversion of the dubiously ecstatic staking of *Dracula*'s Lucy. However, Calmet's ultimate authority, despite his careful probing and weighing of evidence, is not human reason but Christian doctrine and the textual weight of the Church fathers and Classical authors.

Alberto Fortis, the Venetian physician and naturalist, whose *Travels into Dalmatia* (1774) were hugely popular, is more sceptical, and adopts what will become a frequent strand of anti-clerical critique. In his account, priests disseminate superstitious tales of vampires among the peasants, for whom

'the ignorance of their teachers daily augments this monstrous evil' (61).
Fortis's sympathy is with 'the innocent manners of these good people' (63)
from whom the priests 'draw illicit profits' (63). Set out here is a connection
between vampirism and political exploitation which Voltaire and then Marx
will elaborate and which lives on in the postmodern vampires of our own
period.

A report for the Manchester Literary and Philosophical Society by
John Ferrier, the reforming physician, is a model of sober Enlightenment
methodology, carefully examining evidence and establishing rational grounds
for probability. Considering vampires among other superstitions, he wants
'to shew, by unquestionable facts, how such delusions *have* taken place';
to 'unveil their origin'.[29] He notes the exceptional nature of the vampire
panic and that 'the triumph of this absurdity was reserved for an advanced
period of the eighteenth century' (96). But rather than pathologising these
delusions, which should not glibly 'be ascribed to the occasional workings
of distempered minds' (24), he historicises them, discovering at work the
cultural distortion of an innate and reasonable 'restless curiosity' (25) about
the natural world. Verification and doubt are central topics in the story of the
vampire's involvement with literature.

Rousseau continued these sophisticated, cultural emphases on the origins
of the vampire myth, taking up strands that appear in both Fortis and Ferrier.
He has a Humean scepticism towards testimony: 'if there is in the world an
attested history, it is just that of vampires ... Nothing is lacking – depositions,
certificates of notables, surgeons, curés, and magistrates. ... Yet with all this,
who actually believes in vampires?'[30] Yet the ironic tone here has been much
misread; over-enthusiastic websites frequently cite this as support for the
existence of vampires, revealing the postmodern doubts about Enlightenment
that have permeated our culture. According to Frayling and Wokler, 'The
essential point [for Rousseau] was that neither the exegesis of Scripture nor
the rationalists' attempts to explain paranormal phenomena could really teach
us anything about the nature of vampires, or about the manifest nightmares
those perhaps mythical creatures represented to us' (117). Instead, the reports
of vampires alert us to 'the nature of authority in civilised society' (116), and
'the relation between vampires and their prey are an extremely potent symbol
for characterising even the ordinary ties of dependence that bind individuals
together in civilised society' (118). Thus, as Goya shows, we all suck from
one another; the vampire serves as a powerful image of the rapaciousness of
modern society.

The political metaphor of vampirism was employed very early on, in
The Craftsman's article 'Political Vampires' of 1732, an interpretation of the

vampire scare in Eastern Europe as a response to tyranny. Thus Enlightenment scepticism is linked to its own emancipatory urges, demonstrating the generic shift from cultural aetiology to satiric metaphor while maintaining its critique of irrationalism. In this example, the peasantry are not dupes but conscious agents, employing the vampire narrative as subterfuge; a political critique necessarily allegorical under conditions of oppression: 'This account, of *Vampyres*, you'll observe, comes from the Eastern Part of the World [where] The States of *Hungary* are in subjection … and govern'd by a pretty hard Hand; which obliges them to couch all their Complaints under *Figures*.' The article then slyly appropriates this figurative vampirism for use against Walpole's England, where 'Private Persons may be *Vampyres*, or *Bloodsuckers*, i.e. *Sharpers, Usurers, and Stockjobbers, unjust Stewards and the Dry Nurses of the Great Estates*; but nothing less than the Power of a *Treasury* can raise up a compleat *Vampyre*'.[31]

Thus for many Enlightenment commentators, the traditional intellectuals of the ancient regime, its priests and other hangers on, are vampiric. The Enlightenment vampire presages Marx's capitalist bloodsucker; the monsters let loose during the sleep of reason are symbols of feudal power who prey on the vulnerable. Voltaire (in 1764) contrasts the vampires of Eastern Europe with the 'stock-jobbers, brokers, and men of business, who sucked the blood of the people in broad daylight' (270) in London and Paris. And, with his usual irreverence, recalling Fortis, he claims 'the true vampires are the monks' (272). Pointing to the transience of the vampire panic, whereby 'Europe has been infested with vampires for five or six years, and … there are now no more', he makes connections with other focuses of superstitious power which have vanished through enlightened progress: 'we have had Jesuits in Spain, Portugal, France, and the two Sicilies, but that we have them no longer' (272).

Typical, too, of this political use is the radical Thomas Holcroft's play *The Deserted Daughter* (1795), with its 'human vampire, the attorney'; or Charles Forman, praising the Dutch Republic, where paying taxes does not go 'to indulge the Luxury, and gratify the Rapine of a fat-gutted *Vampire*'.[32] Frayling has some fine pictorial examples of the vampire as social-critical symbol: Marie Antoinette was a popular target; and Goya employs vampires once more to dramatise the horrors of war.[33] In the nineteenth century, avatars appeared in socialist or anticolonial propaganda (though they would, too, be used for reactionary ends, notoriously against Jews). Marx develops Enlightenment critique beyond Voltaire, and discovers that parasitism in the new economic order that the latter had celebrated in its progressive phase. In one of several examples of this figure, he says 'Capital is dead labour which, vampire-like, lives only by sucking living labour, and lives the more, the more labour it sucks'.[34] Marx is probably recalling the aristocratic Varney and similar incarnations in mass fiction (but bear in mind that in Britain a unique alliance had formed between land-owning aristocrat and capitalist).[35]

There are some interesting eighteenth-century variants on these literary appropriations of the vampire. In an account which should whet the appetites of Foucauldians, Jeremy Bentham brings optics (the science which haunts vampire narratives) into conjunction with an exoneration of vampirism. In his *Panopticon* (1791), vampires appear in the, by now, very common metaphorical sense of those who prey on other people's wealth and labour, or even freedom: 'a contracting manager of the imprisoned and friendless poor, against whom justice has shut the door of sympathy, must be the cruellest of Vampyres'.[36] But some ironies emerge. Bentham argues that penal institutions should be managed by the self-interested; but with the managers under constant public surveillance that their vampirism might be disciplined.[37] Bentham does not attempt to disguise the vampiric nature of capitalism; somewhat like Mandeville before him, he believes the private vice of bloodsucking can yield public benefits and invigorate the body politic.[38]

One other curious Enlightenment manifestation of vampirism is as metaphor for disease – a transformation of the original physiological rationalisations in ethnographical accounts, and not unrelated to its power as a political symbol. In *The Loves of the Plants* (1791), his botanical verse epic, the polymath Erasmus Darwin figures malaria as vampire: 'Fierce from his fens the Giant Ague springs/ And wrap'd in fogs descends on vampire-wings' (lines 359–60).[39] This rises again in the suggestion of AIDS metaphors in late twentieth-century vampire texts, and in Anne Rice's sublimation of the death of her child from a blood disease.[40] More recently, in the spirit of postmodernism, the disorder of vampirism itself demonstrates epistemological uncertainties about science: Charlaine Harris's Southern Vampire series, for instance, hesitates over whether vampirism is virus or curse, natural or supernatural.

Alexander Pope, in a letter of 1740, inverts the political metaphor ironically, making the satirist himself vampiric; he imagines himself '(like the Vampires in Germany) such a terror to all sober & innocent people, that many wish a stake were drove thro' him to keep him quiet in his grave'.[41] Pope's self-dramatisation has the satirist as the lone outsider who stalks the complacent community, announcing one potentially subversive motif in vampire narratives. Here Pope recalls our attention to the generic and textual issues involved with the vampire.

Thus eighteenth-century vampire narratives were at first ethnography, whether rationalist but somewhat credulous as in Calmet, or more fully in the Enlightenment spirit. Then, of their diagnoses, the seeds of a new genre are sown – from the manipulative strategies of priests, accounts of vampires move to the genre of satire, and the political metaphor of vampirism emerges. The vampire very quickly becomes a symbol of political tyranny, and its metaphorical powers are awakened. This sense is still with us, and has also been employed in fiction, albeit often inverted into reactionary uses against outsiders, as with the racist undercurrents often discerned in Stoker's *Dracula*.[42] From Romania's Ceauşescu to the crises of the twenty-first century, the metaphor is revitalised.[43] The supernatural can (and the undead do indeed today) figure as economic as well as political allegory (to the extent that these are separable, of course); thus we read: 'Neoliberalism is like the undead, marching on as it decomposes. Yet we can regain control of our limbs'.[44] There is some confusion over agency in this image, but this does reveal the power that the undead retain to represent the political (and other) forces that escape our control. It draws, too, on the fascination of the parasitical revenant. It should be noted here that fiction of the undead has proved a powerful medium for the exploration of issues of autonomy and agency; this is another concern of the chapters below.

But, of course, such dry themes do not fully explain why the appropriation of folkloric accounts should have engendered the still-fascinating literary vampire. Emma Clery shows the importance of the moment when the supernatural became material for Gothic fiction, '[f]or the now all-too-familiar repertoire of spectres, sorcerers, demons and vampires was not from the first unproblematically available as a resource for writers of fiction'.[45] Likewise, in the early eighteenth century, there was a brief moment when, as news or rumour, the supernatural had the narrative excitement that Gothic fiction would later offer. This exploitation of supernatural resources occurs earlier than the phase which Clery depicts, yet a similar process is at work, whereby 'the compulsive element of fascination' is aroused despite 'the ridicule of scepticism' which dominates Enlightenment critique.[46] This book explores those intermingled strands of narrative fascination and figuring of oppressive forces and their interaction with belief and doubt.

Vicissitudes of the vampire

The story of vampires since their discovery in eighteenth-century Europe is one of transformations and interbreedings of genre, which mediate shifts in ways of knowing and doubting, and is marked by metamorphoses of the vampire itself – from monstrous to sympathetic, but always fascinatingly Other. Certain tropes, such as optical figures, and particularly that of reflection, recur throughout, calling attention to the preoccupation with epistemology in vampire narratives. Our contributors below each focus on various aspects of these themes as the story unfolds to the present day.

With the Romantic reaction against Enlightenment, a new epistemology – doubting universal certainties, centred in individual experience – issued in new genres as embodiments for the vampire. This initiates a sequence of shape-shifting through genres and ways of knowing to the amiable or amorous vampire of today, which has also demanded new styles and sensibilities, culminating in a new genre of paranormal romance. This is the story our book traces in part. By the early nineteenth century, the creatures now roam entirely within the fictional realm, losing their peasant attributes and much of their monstrosity, acquiring humanity and possibly sexuality, and recorded in the novel (and poetry) rather than ethnography or satire. Conrad Aquilina, in Chapter 2, shows how the persona of Byron became the effective vehicle for the vampire of fiction as a transformed Gothic mode. Born out of class antagonism, Polidori's Lord Ruthven marks a severance between Byronic hero and folkloric monster and initiates a sequence of aristocratic vampires who alternate between the monstrous and the sympathetic.

Juliann Ulin in Chapter 3 engages with one of the earliest texts that demonstrate the vampire as lover and as Other – and to present-day sensibilities a somewhat sympathetic one. She analyses Le Fanu's 'Carmilla', with its seductive lesbian vampire, alongside his vampiric tale 'The Mysterious Lodger'. But, for Ulin, it is the Irish context of Le Fanu that is important, as is another of the recurring tenets of vampire lore: the famous rule that vampires must be invited over the threshold (which Ivan Phillips will analyse as interface in Chapter 14).[47] Here, the invitation is the highly ambivalent one extended by Ireland to its vampiric, colonial neighbour, revealing the persistence of the vampire as political metaphor.

The shadow of Dracula looms over this book, completed as it was in the centenary year of Bram Stoker's death. The sympathetic vampire we are familiar with today was already present in its tortured Byronic avatar. But in *Dracula* there is a return to monstrosity (though something of the demon lover must have lingered in order for subsequent vampire lovers to have been reborn from this narrative). There is a rejection, too, of the epistemological certainties of the Enlightenment. Themes of knowing – forms of reflection – draw our attention to another famous axiom of the vampire lore we are familiar with (which Marcus Sedgwick dismantles below), one apparently invented by Stoker.

Thus Sam George, in Chapter 4, grapples with the figure of the non-reflecting vampire who casts no shadow, moving deftly between *Dracula* and Wilde's *Dorian Gray* and the 'vampire painting' and installations of the contemporary artist David Reed. Anxieties over new technologies of mass reproduction and the loss of aura identified by Walter Benjamin are linked to the absence of the soul that Darwinism seemed to suggest and doubts over what it is to be human; the soulless essence of the vampire cannot be discerned through reflection. Via a reflection on Wilde's aesthetic questions over realism, George sees Reed's practice as representing the twenty-first-century manifestation of these problems through his homage and citation of Stoker's notes for *Dracula*.

In *Dracula*, Van Helsing calls upon his 'Crew of Light' to reopen their minds to the magical, complaining of 'this enlightened age, when men believe not even what they see'.[48] However, he is more nineteenth-century than he thinks; his combination of positivist and naturalist explanations of human behaviour, coupled with a turn to mystical pseudoscience, is almost mainstream. His retreat from Enlightenment rationalism is in tune with much *fin-de-siècle* thinking.[49] Yet there were more genuinely subversive counter-currents. Oscar Wilde, as George shows with *Dorian Gray*, engages with vampiric motifs in a critical engagement with mimesis and realism. Wilde's scepticism (although his worldview is notoriously difficult to pin down) is not in the more dominant spirit of counter-Enlightenment; if anything, he is counter-Romantic, with his privileging of art and human critical rationality over Nature.

Yet if vampire fiction explores the shadows of the Enlightenment, and if National Socialism is capitalism's dark underside, erupting at a juncture when Enlightenment liberalism collapses, then Marx's image of capitalism as vampiric becomes horrifyingly even more appropriate.[50] In Chapter 5, Lisa Lampert-Weissig performs a case study of two paradoxical writers who wrote vampire novels amidst this darkness. Wilde's vampiric aesthetic came to be appropriated by the self-styled philo-Semitic, yet Nazi sympathiser George Sylvester Viereck in *House of the Vampyr* (1907). Viereck's hero feeds off the energies of artists to produce his own work, justifying his vampirism as a collective process nurturing a greater good. For Viereck, Hitler's Germany was akin to such a work of art, built on collective sacrifice. The Nazi writer Hanns Heinz Ewers also claimed sympathy with Jews; his Jewish heroine sacrifices her blood for the greater good, feeding her German lover with the artistic energies that enable him to stir up the nation with rhetoric.

Reflection and shadows are associated optical phenomena, figuring heavily amidst the epistemological instability dramatised in Stoker's *Dracula*. Concealed among all the other recording media that fascinated Stoker is that technology which was just emerging: cinema. Stacey Abbott, in Chapter 6, gives a luminous account of early vampire cinema as a 'Kingdom of shadows', digging up lost cinematic texts which should be better known. Abbott demonstrates how ours is never a monolithic narrative; conflicting epistemological statuses and genres coexist in early cinema. Two different modes of early twentieth-century vampire film oscillate between different ways of knowing: one, in Todorov's terms, partakes of the marvellous, succumbing to the supernatural worldview; the other is in the mode of the uncanny, where mysteries are ultimately resolved by meeting scientific and empirical criteria.[51] So epistemology and genre are again intimately connected with the evolution of the vampire.

Stephenie Meyer's *Twilight*, its sequels and cinematic adaptations inevitably overshadow this discussion. Vampires are more lovable than ever before, but may have lost their bite. However, many attribute this supposed decline not to Meyer but to Francis Ford Coppola's 1992 film *Bram Stoker's Dracula*.[52] In Chapter 7, Lindsey Scott seizes on Dracula's exclamation 'I, too, can love', and examines the complex intertextuality involved with *Dracula* and *Twilight*, via Coppola and Anne Rice, drawing on adaptation studies. Scott attempts a rehabilitation of the Coppola film, adopting a more nuanced view, and charting the rise of vampire as lover along the way.

Shifts of genre take place alongside the linguistic shifts analysed by Malgorzata Drewniok in Chapter 8 as she looks at the transformations of states of being in *Buffy the Vampire Slayer* – from good Angel, the archetypal romantic vampire, to evil, monstrous Angelus; from romance to horror. Her stylistic analysis reveals these metamorphoses and the instability of perception of another's identity dramatised there. Linguistic heterogeneity reveals the generic hybridity of vampire texts. And the mirroring theme is discovered again through the stylistic analysis of the speech of Willow and of her evil vampiric *doppelgänger*.

Catherine Spooner engages in Chapter 9 with the most recent of sympathetic vampires – the sparkly ones – via the ostinato line of undead as Other that is never absent from this narrative. *Twilight*'s Edward Cullen and his like have attracted much disapproval yet the humanised vampire is, Spooner argues, an intriguing cultural phenomenon. Cullen is, in some sense, anti-Gothic; ordered rather than barbaric and no longer transgressive. There is considerable interplay between vampire imagery and the style of Goth subculture; in her exploration of the dialectic between these, Spooner reveals how an oppositional youth culture yearns to transform itself into an assimilationist one in response to moral panics over its perceived association with violence.

In Chapter 10, Jennifer H. Williams is concerned with the autonomy of the Undead (as are Chapters 11 and 15 in their own ways), plotting an unusual argument drawing on theology and linking the monstrous with ideas of human agency and moral responsibility. She examines the shifts in ideas of redemption and the cultural shifts in religious feeling that have taken place from *Dracula* to *Twilight*. She suggests, too, a utopian dimension of human transcendence – utopian in Jameson's sense; that is, as opposed to the ideological, which is where most attention on *Twilight* has been focused.[53]

And the much-maligned *Twilight* receives a different treatment in Chapter 11 from Sara Wasson and Sarah Artt, who draw on psychoanalytic theories of masochism and the gaze to explore the pleasures of a suspect text in a way that grants its readers interpretative autonomy rather than, as too often, casting them as mindless zombies whose flesh and spirit may be corrupted by malign fictions. Artt and Wasson acknowledge the violence against women in the *Twilight* texts (books and films) but eschew a simplistic reading that sees them purely as reactionary and anti-feminist. Instead, they ask the important question of why women would take pleasure in the spectacle of women suffering and the 'broken body', and find an answer that rests on more than a masochistic false consciousness.

In Chapter 12, Michelle Smith is concerned with the sympathetic Other and the relationship of the Undead with subcultures that Catherine Spooner explores. She sees the HBO TV series *True Blood* as a postmodern Gothic narrative in an allegedly 'post-racial' USA. Here, the suspicion of grand narratives raises up vampires who dissolve the boundaries of good and evil and blur racial and sexual differences. Ethnic identities are allegorised as supernatural beings in order to critique oppression and remind us of its persistence, while homosexual rights are defended through the metaphorical difference of the vampire.

Kimberley McMahon-Coleman (Chapter 13) takes up the reflection trope again but in a transposed form – that of the double (but this hints back, too, to motifs contemporaneous with Victorian Gothic and Stoker, in Wilde, R. L. Stevenson and Poe). She analyses the doubling – of the twin brothers and the mirrored female leads – of the books and TV series *The Vampire Diaries* in its Southern US setting against a background of unstable family structures. This splitting and doubling itself involves an epistemological confusion over identity and questions the boundaries of humanity and monstrosity

Ivan Phillips in Chapter 14 explores the undead at the interface, where knowing becomes problematic – 'unsettlement', in his terms. From recalling his childhood fright at the subversion of domesticity induced by the appearance of the child vampire at the window in *Salem's Lot*, he explores how vampires lurk on the threshold in *Doctor Who*, Dreyer's *Vampyr* and Coppola's *Dracula*. The vampire is an unsettled and unsettling creature who must be invited through the interface. Lindqvist's *Let the Right One In* and its film adaptations meet Stoker's *Dracula* as paradigmatic instances of vampires at such interfaces, which may be mirror, doorway, window, page or screen. The anxieties of cultural change provoked by the emergence of new media have frequently been mediated by the figure of the vampire on the boundary.

In Chapter 15, Bill Hughes, following Catherine Spooner, explores the undead as subculture. The Undead, as many have noted (see Michelle Smith's Chapter 12 once more), stand in for otherness, for deviant subcultures of various kinds. Our focus has been on the fascination of the vampire but, in a gesture of tokenism, Hughes turns to the zombie (who may be undergoing something of a revival – perhaps to fill the need for monstrosity that the sparkly vampire no longer supplies).[54] Among the uncountable hordes of paranormal romances and dark fantasies of the past two decades, Young Adult fiction often stands out as having a certain literary value. Hughes analyses Dan Waters's *Generation Dead* as a witty and moving mediation of our current period's approach to otherness and assimilation via identity politics. He argues that Waters reasserts an Enlightenment humanism with his sympathetic Others.

In the final chapter, Marcus Sedgwick turns full circle, demonstrating in the actual practice of fiction the cyclical story that Aquilina outlined at the beginning, with a self-conscious return to the folklore that eighteenth-century scholars sought to demystify. Sedgwick narrates his unearthing of the folklore roots of vampire fiction, in his quest to revivify what he sees as a somewhat moribund genre. This led to his powerful melding of fantasy, historical novel and folklore in *My Swordhand Is Singing* (2006) and subsequent Young Adult novels.[55] He gives us a glimpse of how contemporary writers adapt the perennial figure – a contrast with our collective critical attempts to dissect the vampire text from the outside as it were. In doing so, he performs some surprising debunking of myths about the vampire myth itself. From the raw materials of folklore, Sedgwick selects the motifs that serve his fiction best, resurrecting an avatar of Otherness that is pure monstrosity but not this time projected onto alienated sectors of humanity – this is the absolute Otherness of everything that degrades the human strivings for love and family; ultimately, Death itself. Here, a fiction writer lays bare the conscious strategies of writers that lie behind this story of protean others, genres and ways of knowing.

Notes

1 Auerbach, *Our Vampires*, p. 145.
2 Frayling, *Vampyres*, p. 62.
3 Anthologies of texts and extracts: Christopher Frayling, *Vampyres: Lord Byron to Count*

Dracula (first pub. 1978); *The Penguin Book of Vampire Stories*, ed. Alan Ryan (1987); *Vampires: Encounters with the Undead*, ed. David Skal (2006); *Dracula's Guest: A Connoisseur's Collection of Victorian Vampire Stories*, ed. Michael Sims (2010); *Dracula's Precursors: The Mysterious Stranger and Other Stories*, ed. David Annwn (2011). Anthropological and folkloric studies of vampires and zombies: Paul Barber, *Vampires, Burials and Death* (first pub. 1988); *The Vampire: A Casebook*, ed. Alan Dundes (1998); Matthew Beresford, *From Demons to Dracula: The Creation of the Modern Vampire Myth* (2008).

4 General books on the Gothic which cover vampires: *A Companion to the Gothic*, ed. David Punter (2001); *The Routledge Companion to Gothic*, ed. Catherine Spooner and Emma McEvoy (2007). The former has chapters by William Hughes on nineteenth- and twentieth-century fictional vampires. There is now also *The Encyclopedia of the Gothic*, ed. William Hughes, David Punter and Andrew Smith (2012).

5 Carole Senf's detailed account of the twentieth-century vampire is invaluable here, too; see 'Blood, Eroticism, and the Twentieth-Century Vampire', in Senf, *The Vampire*, pp. 1–16.

6 We could not cover every significant or interesting text, but among other crucial literary moments in the evolution of the sympathetic vampire is certainly, still from the 1970s, Angela Carter's tale 'The Lady of the House of Love' in *The Bloody Chamber* (1979) (derived from her 1976 radio play *Vampirella*). Following this are Whitley Strieber, *The Hunger* (1981), George R. R. Martin's *Fevre Dream* (1982), Jewelle Gomez's *The Gilda Stories* (1991), Poppy Z. Brite's *Lost Souls* (1992), Kim Newman's *Anno Dracula* (1992), and Octavia Butler's *Fledgling* (2005).

7 Notably, by Auerbach, *Our Vampires*, p. 82.

8 'Autodiegetic', for Gérard Genette, is more precise than 'first person', and indicates the voice of a 'narrator who is the hero of his narrative' (*Narrative Discourse*, p. 245).

9 Twitchell, *The Living Dead*, pp. 171–8.

10 *Dracula*'s narrative appears as a 'mass of typewriting' (*Dracula*, ed. Luckhurst, p. 351), but this is only the final transcription of a heterogeneous mass of documents and genres – all of which affirm or cast doubt on ways of knowing. Apart from the incorporation of folklore, there is the travel journal (which as anthropological study enables the former incorporation); touches of the Gothic as reinvented by Byron's circle; diary; and the celebrated employment of new media.

11 Summers, *The Vampyre*.

12 For accounts of the eighteenth-century vampire, see Frayling's *Vampyres*, pp. 3–36; see also Dimic, 'Vampiromania', and Erik Butler, *Metamorphoses*, pp. 27–82. Butler also covers here the transformation of the vampire in European Romanticism. The significant contributions made by the likes of Tieck, Hoffmann and Goethe are, unfortunately, outside the scope of this book. For vampires and British Romanticism, see Twitchell, *The Living Dead*. But, again, Twitchell's vampires are sometimes simply *too* ubiquitous for our account (though his account of how Romantic and post-Romantic writers have drawn on the vampire is illuminating).

13 The *OED* records the first use in 1745 in 'The Travels of Three English Gentlemen … in the Year 1734'; Katherina M. Wilson, in 'The History of the Word "Vampire"',

suggests it was already well known in 1688 (though she is herself mistaken in saying that the *OED* has too early a date for 'The Travels').

14 Tomlinson, *Goya*, p. 132.

15 *Ibid.*

16 It is common to claim that Goya here, in a kind of postmodernism *avant la lettre*, is demonstrating the inevitable irrational undercurrent to Enlightenment; see Hoy and McCarthy, *Critical Theory*, p. 1. Dimic's interpretation of the vampire panic rests on a similar notion of the repressed unconscious of Enlightenment.

17 Goya, *Los Caprichos*, caption to plate 45 [n. p.].

18 Keyworth, 'Was the Vampire', p. 241.

19 *Ibid.*

20 Marie-Hélène Huet seeks to explain, not the panics themselves, but the anxieties behind the excited response to the panics ('Deadly Fears').

21 Erik Butler, *Metamorphoses*, pp. 3–4.

22 Keyworth, 'Was the Vampire', p. 251. Even the Greek *vrykolakas* of Tournefort's much-cited *Voyage* (1717) were not bloodsuckers, Keyworth points out (p. 253).

23 *Ibid.*, p. 256.

24 See Conrad Aquilina's Chapter 2 below.

25 Among the first prominent vampire fictions in English were John Polidori's *The Vampyre* (1819), James Malcolm Rymer's *Varney the Vampire* (1845–1847), and Sheridan Le Fanu's 'Carmilla' (1872).

26 Moretti, 'A Capital *Dracula*', pp. 90–104.

27 The story had already been reported in English in the *London Journal* (March 1732).

28 See Hume's 'Of Miracles', where even the most respectable of testimonies are suspect if not in conformity with reason.

29 Ferrier, 'Of Popular Illusions', p. 88. The search for origins – of language, of society, of political economy – was a common eighteenth-century concern, and unveiling was a frequent Enlightenment metaphor for demystification, contrasting with the shadows and other optical obscurities which signify the vampire's epistemological elusiveness.

30 *Letter to Christophe de Beaumont*, cited in Frayling and Wokler, 'From the Orang-utan', p. 116.

31 'Political Vampires', *The Gentleman's Magazine* (May 1732), cited in Dimic, 'Vampiromania', pp. 7–8.

32 Holcroft, *The Deserted Daughter*, 1.3, p. 9; Forman, *Second Letter*, p. 38.

33 Fig. 2: 'Marie Antoinette as a vampire'; fig. 4: Goya, *The Consequences*, in Frayling, *Vampyres*, facing p. 214.

34 Marx, *Capital*, 1, p. 342 (Ch. 10).

35 James Malcolm Rymer's hugely popular 'penny dreadful', *Varney the Vampyre, or, The Feast of Blood* was serialised from 1845 to 1847.

36 Bentham, *Panopticon*, p. 381.

37 *Ibid.*, pp. 383–4.

38 Bernard Mandeville's *Fable of the Bees* (1705–1734) scandalously suggested that the

well-being and prosperity of the public depended upon the vices of individuals. Bentham's questions on the management of public bodies are, incidentally, quite fascinating in the light of the present-day privatisation and radical reorganisation of public services in the UK, particularly the rumoured privatisation of blood donation.

39 In Darwin, *The Botanic Garden*, p. 75.

40 For AIDS, see, for example, Auerbach, *Our Vampires*, pp. 7, 175–81; Gelder, *Reading*, p. 143; Nixon, 'When Hollywood Sucks', pp. 117–19. For Rice, see Wadler and Greene, 'Anne Rice's Imagination'.

41 Letter to Dr William Oliver, February 1740, cited in Brownwell, 'Pope', p. 96.

42 For a concise, but comprehensive, summary of the many discussions of race in *Dracula*, see William Hughes, *Bram Stoker*, pp. 77–102.

43 For Ceauşescu as vampire, see Glover, *Vampires*, pp. 136–52.

44 *Guardian* (5 August 2011), p. 37. On zombies and vampires in predominantly economic discourse, note the similar response to the South Sea Bubble, discussed by Clery, *The Rise*, p. 7.

45 *Ibid.*, p. 1.

46 *Ibid.*, p. 27.

47 Plenty has been written on gender and sexuality in 'Carmilla'; Ulin's approach is interesting for its deliberate focus elsewhere, on this particular employment of the vampire as political figure.

48 Stoker, *Dracula*, ed. Luckhurst, p. 298. The 'Crew of Light' – Van Helsing and his band of vampire hunters – are never named as such by Stoker; this widely adopted phrase was first coined by Christopher Craft in '"Kiss Me with Those Red Lips"' (see note 7, p. 130).

49 The Enlightenment, in its late Victorian configuration as liberalism and positivism, was in crisis, as Glover shows through Stoker's response (see, in particular, *Vampires*, Chapter 3, pp. 58–99).

50 See Marcuse, 'The Struggle Against Totalitarianism'.

51 See Todorov, *The Fantastic*, pp. 41–2.

52 Though, as we have said, there are literary precedents for the humanised vampire in Saberhagen, Yarbro and Charnas.

53 Jameson, 'Utopia and Ideology'.

54 See Tenga and Zimmerman, 'Vampire Gentlemen and Zombie Beasts'.

55 There is a sequel, *The Kiss of Death* (2008), and one of the embedded narratives in *Midwinterblood* (2011) concerns vampires.

2

The deformed transformed; or, from bloodsucker to Byronic hero – Polidori and the literary vampire

Conrad Aquilina

A N E I G H T E E N T H - C E N T U R Y V O Y A G E from France to the Levant by Joseph Pitton de Tournefort proved to be auspiciously influential as in Greece he would witness a classic case of vampirism attributed to a *vroucolacas*, a peasant superstition which would be assimilated by the Romantics a century later as exotic material for fiction. Tournefort's account, *A Voyage to the Levant* (1702), is anthropological and critical, and dismissed such incidents as mania, 'an epidemical disease of the brain, as dangerous and infectious as the madness of dogs' (89).

Yet such mania fed the Gothic imagination, and Tournefort's voyage to the Levant served to transport the Greek vampire legend into British Romantic literature. Sir Christopher Frayling identifies several archetypes of the literary vampire; one of these, the Byronic, though born in that Romanticism, is still very much a presence in contemporary vampire texts. In this chapter I will show the evolution of the Byronic vampire as it mutated from its folkloric roots, as documented in the ethnography of the likes of Tournefort, into a powerful literary figure. I will also show that, as this archetype evolved, it did so through an interplay with the actual (or imagined) persona of Byron. Thus this rise owes much to the representations and self-dramatisation of Byron's own life, particularly as mediated through the rivalry of his one-time companion, John Polidori. This archetype is in perpetual tension with another archetype – the folkloric, bloodsucking monster. The humanised vampire (whose current incarnation in *Twilight*, it seems, has almost erased those roots) alternates with its bestial ancestor over the course of vampire fiction, leading to a crucial encounter between the two in Anne Rice's *Interview with the Vampire* (1976) which I will turn to at the end of the chapter.

It is likely that Byron came across Tournefort's account via Robert Southey's notes to his *Thalaba the Destroyer* (1801), an epic poem which exemplifies the kind of pretentiousness that Byron loved to mimic and deflate.[1] The *enfant terrible* of British Romanticism also possessed a copy of the 1813 French translation of the *Phantasmagoriana* (1811–1815), a collection of German ghost tales, which inspired the well-known ghost story session in Geneva of 1816 and which, too, made reference to Tournefort. It also inspired John Polidori, Byron's private physician and another vital participant in the parlour game which spawned a literary archetype. In introducing his *Vampyre* (1849), Polidori alludes to 'the veracious Tournefort', and also 'Calmet, [who] in his great work upon the subject put forth some learned dissertations'.[2] Furthermore, he mentions Southey's *Thalaba* as well as *The Giaour* (1813), the only poem by Byron to feature the vampire of peasant folklore, and from which Polidori quotes extensively.

Many of the writers who incorporated Eastern European revenant folklore into their works felt the need to resort to often pedantic paratexts in an attempt to authenticate the same phenomena from which they drew their dark inspiration. Southey's copious end-notes in *Thalaba* are exemplary, and Book VIII digresses into a lengthy commentary on vampirism, reproducing Tournefort as well as mentioning the notable case of the Serbian *heyduke* 'Arnold Paul', one of the most widely documented cases of vampire epidemics.[3] Similarly, the 'Argument' preceding John Stagg's decidedly bloodier poem *The Vampire* (1810) sacrifices brevity for pseudo-medical bombast – the vampire's victims are drained of their blood while sleeping by 'suckosity', then they are 'phlebotomised'.[4] Stagg, an obscure Romantic poet whose *Vampire* may indeed be his best known work, derived his vampire from the folkloric stereotype of the cadaverous relative who returns from the grave to enervate its victims by draining their blood, this plague to be finally dealt with by impaling the clotting blood-smeared body 'deep in the earth' (line 148).[5] The details in such early literary representations are derived from the records of vampire infestations in the Slavic countries in 1730, which provoked exhumations and the defiling of corpses. Despite the apparent barbarism of these practices, however, the vampire became simultaneously repulsive and fascinating.

In *The Living Dead*, James B. Twitchell observes how the Romantic successors to the age of Enlightenment turned their eyes towards 'monkish darkness, mesmerism, Satanism, and deviancy of all sorts [while embracing] the vampire [as] an artistic figure of some complexity' which became a highly malleable metaphor.[6] Thus, Calmet's shambling village folk who return to feed on their blood relations, usually their spouses, find their way into Continental Romantic literature.[7] Vampirism in British literature becomes a voracious theft of blood and spirit, moving from faintly detectable to plainly perceptible leeching. In their poetry, Stagg, Byron and their successors endowed their vampires with sadism, blood-thirst and the parasitical qualities of the leech, psychic and actual. This process from enervation to blood-letting is quite clear in Stagg's poem, where Herman first informs his preoccupied wife that 'In spite of all [his] wonted strength ... / The dreadful malady at length / Will drag [him] to the silent tomb' (lines 29–32). The cause of Herman's 'sad pant[ing] and tug[ging] for breath' (line 18) is revealed to be his friend Sigismund, newly deceased, yet now 'suck[ing] from [his] vein the streaming life' (line 73) and 'drain[ing] the fountain of [his] heart' (line 74).

Southey's *Thalaba* never reveals the full sordidness of vampiric defilement, nor the violence required to end it. By contrast, Stagg's description of Sigmund's walking corpse, with 'jaws cadaverous', 'besmear'd / With clotted carnage o'er and o'er' (lines 125–6) and with body bloated after having drunk his fill, is exceptionally gory for this period of English vampire literature, recalling the graphic chronicles of Calmet. Stagg's vampires are indisputably folkloric and both have the mandatory 'sharpen'd stake' (line 148) driven through their bodies, pinning them forever to their 'slumb'ring tomb' (line 152). In Southey's poem, the same method is employed, with Thalaba ordered to 'strike' the vampire Oneiza with his 'lance'; however, here the damaging blow is cathartic, releasing her spirit.[8]

Composed as a *Fragment of a Turkish Tale*, *The Giaour* is Byron's only incontestable direct contribution to vampire literature. Byron roots his vampire within the peasant folklore of the Levant (rather than that of Eastern Europe), having travelled to Athens on his Grand Tour between 1809 and 1810. In many ways, Byron's representation of the vampire whose 'corse shall from its tomb be rent' (line 756) and 'At midnight drain the stream of life' (line 760) is akin to Stagg's Sigmund, the 'goblin' who in an act of unholy procreation creates more of his kind and in his blood-matted image.[9] But Byron's *Giaour* is more than a mere continuation of the folkloric vampire superstition. Byron's poem attributes to the vampire the tragic quality which would become one of the trademarks of the new strain of vampires modelled on Byron's own persona. The fate laid upon the Giaour is that he should 'ghastly haunt [his] native place / And suck the blood of all [his] race' (lines 757–8).

Byron's Giaour is cursed with 'a fire unquench'd, unquenchable' (line 751) so that 'Nor ear can hear, nor tongue can tell / The tortures of that inward hell!' (lines 753–4), this hell being the 'banquet which perforce / Must feed [the Giaour's] livid living corse' (lines 761–2). Previously, few had aimed at understanding – or justifying – the demon's own torments, since vampiric defilement was a scourge to be dealt with promptly and mercilessly; the victim's plight was what mattered. In a departure from Southey and Stagg, Byron's vampire is both victimiser and victim. This banquet consists of the Giaour's own flesh and blood, with the 'youngest – most belov'd of all' (line 768) providing the most agonising feed as his daughter blesses him.[10] Byron's Giaour, essentially the *vroucolacas* found in Tournefort, Calmet and others but refitted in Oriental garb, points the genre towards a new direction, that of the ancestral curse, while retaining the trappings of folklore. Beyond this, there is little proof that Byron's interest was sufficiently piqued to pursue the vampire legend further, as his letters to his publisher Murray were to show.

However, Byron, or rather his many incarnations in literature and art, remains crucial to the evolution of the fictional vampire. In this respect, we must perforce note the shift from depicting the vampire as a shambling blood-drinking revenant to representations of the vampire as irresistible Byronic hero. Byron's *Giaour* aside, the archetypal 'Byronic' vampire was firmly established only as a result of Byromania, the notoriety that effused from the poet's dramatic life and works and which permeated social consciousness in the nineteenth century. In this, Polidori's *Vampyre* was to play a functional role.

On a stormy evening in the summer of 1816, two monsters were born. Not the unclean offspring of the Eastern European vampire but an original product of Romanticism in the West, *Frankenstein* became an instant success, even though its author, the then Mary Godwin, was till then virtually unknown. More ironic is the fate of the other monster, the first aristocratic vampire, who made his mark on high society only by a curious combination of events in which was involved the most colourful, mysterious, and maligned figure of British Romanticism itself – Lord Byron.

Apart from the forty-odd lines of this passage in *The Giaour*, Byron's association with and unconcealed aversion towards the folkloric vampire was decidedly uncanny. He was born with a caul and a deformed right foot – the latter associated with the Devil's chosen while the former was, according to Moldavian folklore, reputed to turn a person into a vampire after death. Byron often sarcastically quipped that he had been predestinately cursed at birth.

Simultaneously revered and reviled, both society's darling and demon, bisexual and profligate, brooding and melancholic, Byron's tempestuous career was to prove both short and scandalous.[11] For the real Childe Harold, life was to become one long cathartic pilgrimage in search of a self now entirely constructed by others. Ghislaine McDayter identifies Byron's 'commodification of personality', noting how 'The Byronic had come to take precedence over Byron, the creation over the creator'.[12] Being sexually initiated at the age of ten by a family servant girl; acquiring poetic fame overnight with *Childe Harold's Pilgrimage*; acquiring celebrity status and then forced into self-exile away from British soil following a number of sordid affairs and allegations of incest and homosexuality, Byron is the obvious model for the new strain of post-Romantic vampires who would feature in the genre from then on.[13] No other personage, however colourful or distinguished, could have contributed to such excess all the necessary requisites which make up the Byronic hero, a figure of mythic proportions akin to Milton's Satan or Marlowe's Faustus.

The Byronic hero bears the dual markings of both villain and victim. He is a fallen creature in his own right; a dark angel bringing both love and death, yearning for redemption and ultimately finding none. His is a tragic mind which 'in itself / Can make a Heaven of Hell, a Hell of Heaven'.[14] Byron's description of his eponymous hero in *Lara* (1814) is thus both archetypal and solipsistic: 'In him inexplicably mix'd appear'd / Much to be loved and hated, sought and feared' (XVII.289–90) and 'There was in him a vital scorn of all ... He stood a stranger in this breathing world / An erring spirit from another hurl'd; / A thing of dark imaginings' (XVIII.313, 315–17).[15]

Lady Caroline Lamb, an ardent and jilted lover of Byron, was to write as much. Forced to commit shameful public acts of love to win him back, Lamb had her revenge on the poet by defaming him in her novel *Glenarvon*, which was published in May 1816 shortly after Byron left England for Geneva. John Cam Hobhouse, Byron's travel companion, was to write about Lamb's 'impudence to send a ... paragraph to some paper hinting that the whole novel is from the pen of Lord B'.[16] Nonetheless, Lamb's portrait of rakish Lord Glenarvon is not just Byronic but unmistakably that of Byron himself:

> It was one of those faces which, having once beheld, we never afterwards forget ... The eye beamed into life as it threw its dark ardent gaze, with a look nearly of inspiration, while the proud curl of the upper lip expressed haughtiness and bitter contempt; yet ... an air of melancholy and dejection shaded over and softened every harsher expression.[17]

This Byronic image shares with the Romantic vampire a love of darkness, a hypnotic gaze and a paradoxical obsession with destroying the object of his desire. Transgressing all social and ethical boundaries, the Byronic hero is therefore always an outcast, living in perpetual exile on the fringes of society, on the run from persecution and persecuting others in turn.

Ironically, Byron claimed to have 'a personal dislike to "Vampires"', admitting that the 'little acquaintance' he had with them 'would by no means induce [him] to reveal their secrets'.[18] In the context of his antagonism with Polidori and the genesis of *The Vampyre* (1819), to which we now turn, Byron's words become less cryptic.[19]

Byron himself had little to do with the vampire's humanisation; yet his physician and rival John Polidori would appropriate his aura of melancholic broodiness and reputation of nocturnal lover and destroyer in *The Vampyre*. Polidori had read *Glenarvon* and glutted upon its many revelations. Polidori's was the first story to feature the Byronic vampire, a Lord Ruthven possessing 'irresistible powers of seduction [rendering] his licentious habits more dangerous to society'.[20] It was the result of a long-drawn feud between the two in which the doctor's jealousy of his employer's notoriety would be quite palpable. Byron in turn fuelled Polidori's resentment by dismissing his authorial attempts with contempt.[21]

Mary Shelley's (as Mary Godwin had become) account of the storytelling which led to *The Vampyre* was published as her 'Introduction' to the third edition of *Frankenstein* (1831), fifteen years after the event supposedly happened. By this time, the depressed Polidori had already published *The Vampyre* and had committed suicide two years later. According to Mary Shelley, after a night of reading from Byron's copy of the *Phantasmagoriana*,

> [t]he noble author began a tale, a fragment of which he printed at the end of his poem 'Mazeppa'. Shelley … commenced one founded on the experiences of his early life. Poor Polidori had some terrible idea about a skull-headed lady, who was … punished for peeping through a keyhole … The illustrious poets also, annoyed by the platitude of prose, speedily relinquished their uncongenial task.[22]

Mary Shelley's reminiscing, if accurate, is both revealing and significant. For one, it indicates that only Mary herself seems to have been committed to finishing her story. 'Poor Polidori['s]' idea was presumably belittled beyond repair; Byron's tapered to inconclusiveness, and Shelley's remained unnamed and unrecorded. Percy Shelley himself wrote that *Frankenstein* was the only tale to have been completed.[23]

Polidori's revelations about Byron's narrative that stormy evening are more telling. Apparently it involved two characters, travelling from England into Greece, where

> one of them should die, but before his death, should obtain from his friend an oath of secrecy with regard to his decease. Short time after, the remaining traveller returning to his native country, should be startled at perceiving his

former companion moving about in society, and should be horrified at finding
that he made love to his former friend's sister. Upon this foundation I built
the Vampyre.[24]

What emerges from Byron's *Fragment of a Story* (1819) is, however, only
nominally faithful to Polidori's testimony. The nameless narrator accompanies
Augustus Darvell, 'a man of considerable fortune and ancient family' and
'a being of no common order' (126) on a tour of the Continent.[25] Voyaging
towards the East, the narrator notices Darvell 'evidently wasting away'
(128). Resting in a Turkish cemetery in Greece, Darvell asks his companion
to swear that 'on the ninth day of the month' (129) he should fling Darvell's
ring into the Bay of Eleusis. While he says this, 'a stork, with a snake in her
beak' (130) is seen nearby. Darvell dies in the narrator's hands, and is buried
in the Muslim burial ground. So ends Byron's odd and decidedly un-vampiric
Fragment.

That the *Fragment* is a semi-biographical account of Byron's prior adventures
with Hobhouse in Greece, drawing on the events and settings so hauntingly
described in *Childe Harold*, is indubitable. The fact that Byron vests Darvell
in his image is also to be expected. Yet nowhere do we see any reference to
vampirism or vampires. Twitchell argues that 'the central image in Byron's
story – the stork with the snake in her beak – is nowhere to be found in
vampire lore', and that 'the most crucial bit of evidence that Darvell is not a
vampire is the rapid decomposition of his body'.[26] Moreover, Polidori gives us
a different plot for the story in the Introduction to his novel *Ernestus Berchtold*
(1819). Are we to suppose that Byron *altered* his *Fragment* on publication? If
so, to what purpose?

Frayling believes that the vampire elements were present in the original
Fragment but that Byron omitted most of them in 1819, when *Mazeppa* was
published concurrently with *The Vampyre*, Polidori's 'usurped' version of
Byron's 1816 tale.[27] This was falsely attributed to Byron himself, with Goethe
going as far to praise it as Byron's best work to date; the poet decided he had
had enough nonsense about vampires and Polidori and denied authorship.
Byron, however, secured authorship rights to his *Fragment* by having it
immediately published, albeit in a slightly altered form from the 1816 original,
so that his dissociation with any tales of vampirism would be complete.
Polidori could face public ridicule alone.

Born out of revenge, *The Vampyre* became involved in a dubious mistake
which, however, entangled Byron with the vampiric. Polidori explains how
'the tale … to which his lordship's name was wrongfully attached' was
written at the 'request of a lady' and 'over the course of three mornings'.

Polidori cannot explain how the story ended up in the hands of Henry Colburn, nor does he reveal the name of the person whose words left doubt 'whether it was his lordship's or not' (63). Dismissed by Byron shortly after they left Geneva, Polidori returned to England embittered and poor, but still bent on pursuing his literary ambitions. He also had in his possession Byron's personal notebook which he had stowed away. By then, Byron's caustic and witty retorts against Polidori had intensified and become public. Taking his cue from Lamb, Polidori got his own back by satirising Byron and the Byronic in *The Vampyre* which, while expropriated from Byron's *Fragment*, reveals notable extensions to the genre, these principally involving aristocracy, itinerancy, seduction and dominance.[28]

Above everything else, Polidori made the vampire dignified, in a perverse kind of way. The vampire, Lord Ruthven, appears as a 'nobleman, more remarkable for his singularities, than for his rank', and while seemingly unable to participate 'upon the mirth around him', he still induces 'a sensation of awe' (39) in those he meets. He also possesses a 'winning tongue' (40) and 'irresistible powers of seduction' rendering his 'licentious habits more dangerous to society' (43).[29] Byron and the Byronic thus pervade Polidori's 'Vampyre' to saturation point. Polidori's and Byron's mutual dislike becomes narrative, with both roles clearly distinguishable. In this biographical vampirism, the aristocratic status of Polidori's Byronic villain remains clear. Here Nina Auerbach notes a 'class antagonism' that characterised the Byron/ Polidori relationship.[30]

To all extent and purposes, Polidori did not seek to impersonate Byron but merely wanted to deface an all too recognisable portrait of his rival. Byron's tenancy of ancestral Newstead Abbey in 1808, in the course of which he had unearthed a skull which he reputedly drank hot wine from, is shamelessly transmuted in Lamb's *Glenarvon* into a John de Ruthven drinking 'hot blood from the skull of his enemy'.[31] This blood-thirst is replicated by Polidori's Ruthven. One can only speculate why he resorted to representing Byron as an aristocratic blood-drinker. Perhaps his slander was intentionally further reaching, extending to the aristocracy which he came to regard with antipathy. Ken Gelder notes one particular dissimilarity between Polidori's vampire narrative and Byron's only poetic contribution to the genre: whereas *The Giaour* 'remove[s] [Byron's] characters from socialised contexts, Polidori's characters are immersed in them'.[32] Gelder observes that Ruthven moves freely around society, 'unnoticed', because vampirism is already present in high society, 'the fashionable leisured classes' that Byron frequented; a society whose 'aristocratic representatives prey upon 'the people' wherever they go'.[33]

Further compounding the Byronic vampiresque, we find Annabella Milbanke's complaint about Byron's inner conflicts and how 'he would be most unkind to those he loves best, suffering agonies at the same time for the pain he gives them'.[34] Byron's grandson would also similarly reveal how Byron's 'dramatic imagination resembled a delusion; he would play at being mad, and gradually get more and more serious, as if he believed himself to be destined to wreck his own life and that of everyone near him'.[35]

History may have been hard on 'Poor Polidori', for, although managing to exonerate himself of any charges of authorial plagiarism, his story and vampire would long be associated with Byron. True to his fictional *alter egos*, Byron played out these literary roles with mock indifference. In fact, an intriguing entry in Byron's private journal tantalisingly hints at a dark secret which Byron kept hidden from all, promising to reveal why he 'omitted all the really consequential & important parts – from deference to the dead – to the living – and to those who must be both'.[36] As Twitchell perceptively notes, 'Life had become theatre'.[37]

Vampire literature remains indebted to Polidori for ushering in a new archetype, one that would be further embellished and revised by his many successors. The most important distillation perhaps occurs with the victim's sexual awakening. Bloodletting is not explicitly coupled with lust in *The Vampyre* as in later vampire texts. Yet, though it is not made clear in the story, the vampire's victims (all noticeably female) are won over by seduction to the point where they desire corruption. The vampire's bite does not merely drain but it also infuses. Sustenance is taken out and degeneration is injected. Ruthven's victims are defiled both physically and psychologically; their repressed sexuality is exhumed, their fall is complete. Such sexual motifs would pervade the literature of vampirism from then on.

Polidori's little vendetta against Byron was minimal compared to what various plays, stories and operas by authors such as Bérard, Nodier, Planché, Rymer and Dumas did to his own *Vampyre*, which was ruthlessly fed upon.[38] In mass-producing his inconsistent and interminable *Varney the Vampyre* (1845–1847), James Malcolm Rymer borrowed many plot ideas from Polidori yet still made crucial innovations in this evolving genre, many of which find their way into the seminal *Dracula* and beyond: an Eastern European vampire; a scientific investigation of vampirism; the initiation of the heroine through the blood-rite; the vampire's projecting fangs and long nails (used to great filmic effect in Murnau's *Nosferatu* in 1922) and finally the vampire's destruction by a lynch mob, which has become an enduring image in monster movies since.[39]

While vampire literature remains indebted to Polidori for creating a new archetype, to be further embellished and revised by his many successors, one

wonders whether the vampire of folklore would have naturally evolved into
the sullen aristocrat with open shirt and fervid eyes in the absence of Byron's
notoriety. 'Aristocratically aloof, unfailingly elegant, and invariably merciless'
is how Anne Rice's Lestat describes Byron's descendants; very different
from the folkloric vampires who never stray from their birthplace, they are
itinerant and questing, touring the Earth in search of other immortals like
themselves.[40] (Stoker's vampire Count assimilates both types, in travelling
from Transylvania to London with its teeming crowds but still confined to
his boxes of native earth.)

The contemporary vampire's journey is, however, ultimately one of self.
Burdened by the weight of immortality and the prospect of ennui, the Byronic
vampire contemplates his presence as outsider in the fleeting world of mortal
time, and finds solace in autobiography and parody, two forms vampire
narratives would take following Anne Rice's popular Vampire Chronicles
series. The passive observer of human history would become its contestant;
the spoken object a speaking subject. Once we get a vampire to tell the tale
instead of a tale being told about a vampire, we can expect creative dissension
and inversion of vampire 'laws'.[41]

This postmodern conceit allows certain innovative liberties within the
genre. Fred Saberhagen rewrites *Dracula* from the Count's point of view in
The Dracula Tape (1975), setting the record straight by giving his own version
of events. Taking the cue, Rice was to adopt Saberhagen's focal inversion of
Stoker's narrative and develop vampire autobiography as an entire subgenre,
from *Interview with the Vampire* to *Blood Canticle* (2003). Rice's vampires possess
Byron's narcissism and fatalism and question their existence both within the
text and outside it. 'What are thou, who dwellest / So haughtily in spirit,
and canst range / Nature and immortality – and yet / Seem'st sorrowful',
asks Cain of Lucifer.[42] In a like manner, in their struggle to break free
from their monstrous history, postmodern Byronic vampires agonise over
their lost humanity, which may have been limiting once, but to which they
nostalgically return in order to mitigate their fall. They also seek to justify
their depredations, and they must do so in their own voice. Such demands
are stylistically and structurally met by vampire autobiography, where
Dr Seward's phonograph in *Dracula* has been superseded as the medium
of transcription by the tape recorder, but with the vampire's own voice
dictating (*The Dracula Tape*, *Interview with the Vampire*). Byronic vampires have
proliferated: Saberhagen's Dracula, Lestat and Armand, Saint-Germain, Don
Sebastian and Tsepesh,[43] and Tom Holland's own Byron; Holland, in playful
tribute, turns the poet into one of the Undead in his novel, *The Vampyre: The
Secret History of Lord Byron* (1995). Explicitly forbidden to reveal the truth about

his race, Rice's Louis deigns to give an interview while Lestat, ever more flamboyant and reckless, another Byron, goes fully public and even becomes a rock star.

Byron's dark sons and daughters ponder the prospect of perpetual immortality in the light of the ambivalent gift that has been given them, and which they must now bestow on others if they are not to remain alone. Such moral conflict interferes with the basic urges of self-preservation – Louis initially refuses to drink human blood, with Lestat angrily reminding him that they cannot cheat their predatory nature: 'God kills, and so shall we; indiscriminately He takes the richest and the poorest, and so shall we; for no creatures under God are as we are, none so like him as ourselves'.[44]

Yet if we recall Annabella Milbanke's words about her husband, Byron, suffering agonies while giving pain, we might empathise with the conscientious Louis, now torn between his new-found dual nature of god and man; in his own eyes, a monster. In another postmodern incarnation of the Byronic vampire, Tom Holland's novel draws its power from the premise that Lord Byron was an actual vampire, fusing biographical and poetic material to immortalise the poet beyond his own texts. Drawing inspiration from the events which succeed Byron's *Childe Harold* and the eventual appearance in London society of a Lord Ruthven (Holland's homage to Polidori), Byron joins the ranks of the decadent undead in fiction who chronicle their own tragic fall while seeking to justify their complex existence.

Having sampled new pleasures, sensations and delights, the Byronic vampire soon finds immortality to be as exhausting as it is intoxicating. In Holland, the 'aching lust for blood' of his fictional Byron becomes a lust for all life.[45] The object of desire and sensation must be either assimilated or abandoned. Yearning to be part of an eagle which soars above him, Byron shoots the majestic bird, claiming that 'it was so alive – and in killing it, I destroyed what attracted me' (181).

Byron's twentieth- and twenty-first-century successors rejoice in their vampiric Otherness, reaffirming themselves against that which they are now not, the deformed transformed. Shunning their distasteful ancestors, which they now hold in contempt, Byronic vampires might be accursed but they are also sensually and morally irresistible. Having ventured into Transylvania, Rice's Louis and Claudia come across the folkloric vampire:

> The two huge eyes bulged from naked sockets and two small, hideous holes made up his nose; only a putrid, leathery flesh enclosed his skull, and the rank, rotting rags that covered his frame were thick with earth and slime and blood. I was battling a mindless, animated corpse. But no more.[46]

Symbolically dissevering themselves from the vampires of Tournefort and Calmet, Byron's modern descendants proceed to kill it in disgust.

However, despite Louis and Claudia's attempt to wipe out the East European plague after over two hundred years of superstition, the monster survives. Vampire literature may well have taken the Byronic legacy from Polidori's Ruthven to a phase of reaffirmation, particularly with Rice, Yarbro and Holland, transfiguring the monstrous revenant into a seductive anti-hero, yet this evolution is periodically interrupted and challenged. Bram Stoker, Richard Matheson, Stephen King have each resurrected the monstrous vampire; more recently, Marcus Sedgwick, whose vampires are a far cry from the aristocrat with open shirt and fervid eyes, takes the vampire back to its roots in eighteenth-century Romania.[47]

Driven underground and appropriately confined to boxes of earth, dank sarcophagi or forgotten crypts, the folkloric vampire reluctantly concedes its territory to the urbane and sophisticated libertine who mixes freely in society and walks its gas- or neon-lit streets, an object of desire, demonic but also human. Rice's Lestat, that exemplary culmination of the tradition, muses:

> Maybe we had found the perfect moment in history, the perfect balance between the monstrous and the human, the time when that 'vampire romance' born in my imagination amid the colourful brocades of the ancient regime should find its greatest enhancement in the flowing black cape [and] the black top hat.[48]

Thus transfigured, the vampire has certainly come far and has climbed his way up the social ladder. Following the period of Byron and *The Vampyre*, the bloodsucker had left the graveyard and entered the drawing-room. Groomed and debonair, now he mingles within high society and is often invited into the bedroom. Through compulsion he is still a killer, yet one to whose allure his victims meekly respond. Polidori's Ruthven assimilated a number of Byron's conflicting but arresting qualities, and while the notion of the vampire as introspective tragic hero appears only in several later and postmodern incarnations, Polidori was responsible for detaching the vampire from his folkloric roots and rendering him solely Byronic. The conceit seems to have lent itself wonderfully to the genre, since the Byronic vampire as established nearly two centuries ago remains a dominant archetype in its own right, putting less seductive, more monstrous representations into the shadows, from which they periodically emerge to reclaim lost ground.

Notes

1 See Southey's notes to *Thalaba the Destroyer*, *Volume the Second*, VIII, pp. 102–12. In his notes to *The Giaour*, Byron writes that 'The Vampire superstition is still general in the Levant. Honest Tournefort tells a long story, which Mr. Southey, in the notes on Thalaba, quotes about these "Vroucolachas", as he calls them' and 'The stories told in Hungary and Greece of these foul feeders are singular, and some of them most *incredibly* attested' (notes to lines 755, 781, *The Giaour*, in Byron, *Works*, ed. McGann and Weller, III: pp. 420–1).

2 Introduction to Polidori's *Vampyre* in the *New Monthly Magazine*, April 1819 (cited in Frayling, *Vampyres*, p. 19). Dom Augustin Calmet's *Treatise on the Appearance of Spirits and on Vampires* (1746) was possibly the first scholarly attempt at making sense of alleged vampire epidemics (there is an extract in Frayling, *Vampyres*, pp. 92–103).

3 For Arnold Paole, see Barber, 'Forensic Pathology', p. 110.

4 Stagg, Argument, *The Vampire*.

5 Stagg, *The Vampire*, lines 1–41.

6 Twitchell, *The Living Dead*, p. 33.

7 Notably, Ossenfelder's *The Vampire* (1748), Goethe's *The Bride of Corinth* (1797), Tieck's *Wake not the Dead* (1800), and Hoffman's *Aurelia* (1820); the latter three show that the first literary vampires were generally female and exemplify what Frayling, identifying another archetype, calls 'The Fatal Woman' (Frayling, *Vampyres*, p. 62).

8 Southey, *Thalaba*, VIII.11.124–5, p. 82.

9 Byron, *Works*, ed. McGann and Weller, III, p. 64.

10 Byron's *Gaiour* recalls Southey's *Thalaba*, who is doomed to attack his next of kin, and has been seen as Byron's veiled attempt at coming to terms with society's allegations of sexual predation and incest with his half-sister Augusta. See Woolley, *The Bride of Science*, p. 61. Twitchell argues that this blood-relation aspect of the vampire myth may have been important for the Romantics but that it has been lost in our twentieth-century retelling of the myth (*The Living Dead*, p. 83). Nevertheless, Tom Holland's historical fictions *The Vampyre* (1995) and *Supping with Panthers* (1996), and Jeanne Kalogridis's *The Diaries of the Family Dracul* (*Covenant with the Vampire* (1995); *Children of the Vampire* (1996); *Lord of the Vampires* (1997)) trilogy resuscitate this motif. Holland has his vampire Lord Byron feed on 'golden blood': his own offspring's.

11 See MacCarthy, *Byron*, pp. 60–1.

12 McDayter, 'Conjuring Byron', p. 56.

13 See MacCarthy, *Byron*.

14 Milton, *Paradise Lost*, 1.254–5.

15 Byron, *Works*, III, ed. McGann and Weller, pp. 224–5.

16 See MacDonald's account of the Polidori–Byron exchange and the Glenarvon influence in *Poor Polidori*, p. 96.

17 Lamb, *Glenarvon*, p. 31.

18 Byron, letter dated 27 April 1819 to Jean Antoine Galignani, editor of the *Messenger*,

who printed an announcement linking Byron's name with Polidori's *Vampyre* (in
Letters and Journals. Supplementary Volume, ed. Marchand, p. 50).

19 Polidori's story is reproduced, with accompanying contemporary reviews, in *The
Vampyre*, ed. Macdonald and Scherf, p. 43. Further references are taken from this
edition; this is based on Polidori's final amendment to the text, which replaces
'Ruthven' with 'Strongmore', perhaps as a means of shaking off the undue attention
to Byron it generated in its first print run.

20 The name is, like many elements of *The Vampyre*, directly plagiarised from previous
sources. In *Glenarvon*, the Byronic villain is named Clarence de Ruthven, Lord
Glenarvon. This was Caroline Lamb's deliberate slander of the man who had used
and rejected her. Byron had confided to her sordid secrets about a Lord Gray de
Ruthyn whose tenancy of Byron's ancestral home had led to Byron's early loss of
sexual innocence. See MacCarthy, *Byron*, pp. 36–7.

21 Byron's undisguised antipathy towards his physician is evident in his frequent
altercations with 'Child and Childish Dr. Pollydolly'. See Twitchell, *The Living Dead*,
p. 105.

22 *Ibid.*, pp. 170–1.

23 Percy Bysshe Shelley, Preface to *Frankenstein*, p. 6.

24 See Polidori, Introduction to *Ernestus Berchtold*, in *The Vampyre*, ed. Macdonald and
Scherf, p. 63, n. 1.

25 Byron's *Fragment of a Story* is reprinted in Frayling, *Vampyres*, pp. 126–30.

26 Twitchell, *The Living Dead*, p. 15.

27 Frayling, *Vampyres*, p. 126.

28 See Macdonald and Scherf, 'Introduction: The Modern Vampire', in Polidori, *The
Vampyre*, ed. Macdonald and Scherf, pp. 11–17.

29 *Ibid.*, pp. 39–43.

30 Auerbach, *Our Vampires*, p. 15.

31 Lamb, *Glenarvon*, p. 37.

32 Gelder, *Reading the Vampire*, p. 34.

33 *Ibid.*, p. 34.

34 Lady Byron's statement to a doctor on the supposed insanity of her husband
(epigraph to Holland, *Vampyre*, Ch. 10, p. 263).

35 Milbanke, *Astarte*, p. 117.

36 Byron, *Letters and Journals*, ed. Marchand, 1, p. 22.

37 Twitchell, *The Living Dead*, p. 104.

38 Polidori's Ruthven inspired several dramatic adaptations in the 1800s, chief of
which was *Le Vampire* (1820) by Charles Nodier. James Planché adapted this work
into English as *The Vampire, or the Bride of the Isles* (1820). Cyprian Bérard freely
used Ruthven for a two-volume novel in 1920 while Alexandre Dumas also used
the character in an 1852 play. See Skal's marginal note, 'Theatre of Blood: "The
Vampyre" On Stage' to Polidori, *The Vampyre*, in Skal (ed.), *Vampires*, pp. 37–51
(p. 47).

39 For Stoker's use of Rymer's motifs, see Frayling, *Vampyres*, pp. 400–41.

40 Rice, *The Vampire Lestat*, p. 545.

41 That is, the conventions that have accumulated which define the vampire, such as the lack of a reflection, the malign effects of sunlight, the aversion to garlic, and so on, and which Marcus Sedgwick explores and exposes in Chapter 16 below.

42 *Cain: A Mystery*, in Byron, *Works*, ed. McGann and Weller, VI, II.1.85–8.

43 In *The Dracula Tape*; Anne Rice, The Vampire Chronicles (1976–2003); Chelsea Quinn Yarbro, The Saint-Germain Cycle (1978–); Les Daniels, The Don Sebastian Vampire Chronicles (1978–1991); and Jeanne Kalogridis, The Diaries of the Family Dracul (1995–1997) respectively.

44 Rice, *Interview*, p. 98.

45 Holland, *The Vampyre*, p. 181.

46 Rice, *Interview*, pp. 191–2

47 Matheson, *I Am Legend* (1954); King, *Salem's Lot* (1975) and, more recently in an apparent response to *Twilight*, his collaboration with Scott Snyder and Rafael Albuquerque in *American Vampire: Volume 1* (2010); Sedgwick, *My Swordhand Is Singing* (2006).

48 Rice, *The Vampire Lestat*, p. 545.

3

Sheridan Le Fanu's vampires and Ireland's invited invasion

Julieann Ulin

He cannot go where he lists; he who is not of nature has yet to obey some of nature's laws – why we know not. He may not enter anywhere at the first, unless there be someone of the household who bid him come; though afterwards he can come as he pleases. (Van Helsing)[1]

Recent scholarship has situated the vampire within the discourses of colonialism and empire more broadly, and with respect to Bram Stoker's *Dracula*, specifically within an Irish colonial context. Representative work by critics such as Stephen D. Arata, Seamus Deane and Michael Valdez Moses offered readings of Count Dracula as enacting the horror of reverse colonialism, as emblematic of the Irish Famine and absentee landlords in nineteenth-century Ireland, or as allegorical representations of Irish political figures such as Charles Parnell.[2] Indeed, such readings became commonplace enough that Joseph Valente would open his own full-length study in 2002, *Dracula's Crypt: Bram Stoker, Irishness, and the Question of Blood*, with the declaration that the 'decade of the Irish *Dracula* ended in 2000'.[3] Given the subject matter, it is somewhat fitting that Valente's declaration of the death of the Irish *Dracula* was premature; in the decade since the publication of Valente's study, not only has the Irish *Dracula* been resurrected by Sarah Goss but its counterparts have multiplied in critical readings extending its presence to texts ranging from Yeats and Gregory's *Cathleen ni Houlihan*, through *Bowen's Court* to *Buffy the Vampire Slayer*.[4]

In general, critical readings of the Irish vampire have, first, focused primarily on Stoker's *Dracula* and offered a more scant treatment of the work of Sheridan Le Fanu; and, second, have limited their reading of the vampire's Irishness to the racial, political and national discourses of nineteenth-century

Ireland. This chapter concentrates on two of Le Fanu's vampires, arguing that
they enact not only a spatial invasion but a temporal one that brings Ireland's
medieval history to bear on Le Fanu's nineteenth-century texts. As a writer,
Le Fanu was never concerned only with contemporary Irish events. He begins
as an Irish historical novelist with *The Cock and the Anchor* (1845), *The Fortunes
of Colonel Torlogh O'Brien: A Tale of the Wars of King James* (1847) and the later
The House by the Church-Yard (1863), works which explore seventeenth- and
eighteenth-century Irish history. For critics such as W. J. McCormack, this
period defines the limit of Le Fanu's historical interest in Ireland's past: 'One
further feature of this oft-remarked Irish gothic tradition which distinguishes
it from the school of Walpole is its pronounced lack of interest in the medieval
period; nothing earlier than the seventeenth-century wars of religion ever
really gripped the imaginations of Maturin, Le Fanu or Stoker'.[5] My own
reading rejects this claim that Le Fanu's evinced a 'pronounced lack of interest
in the medieval period'. In what follows, I will concentrate on two works
of Le Fanu which deal specifically with a vampire's presence in the house,
the short story 'The Mysterious Lodger' (1850) and the novel 'Carmilla'
(1872). My analysis attends to the resonances among these texts and Ireland's
medieval history, reading that history as available for continual resurrection.
I wish to posit that the great attraction between Irish writers and vampire
narratives lies in the striking correspondences between the twelfth-century
colonial origin story of Ireland's relationship with England and the key
structural elements of vampire narratives.

Toward the end of Le Fanu's 'The Quare Gander' (1840), the Catholic
priest Francis Purcell surveys the desolate Irish landscape marked by the
remnants of a 'once noted and noticeable town' which is 'now a squalid
village' and thinks:

> Alas, my country! what a mournful beauty is thine. Dressed in loveliness
> and laughter, there is mortal decay at thy heart: sorrow, sin, and shame have
> mingled thy cup of misery. Strange rulers have bruised thee, and laughed thee
> to scorn, and they have made all thy sweetness bitter. Thy shames and sins
> are the austere fruits of thy miseries, and thy miseries have been poured out
> upon thee by foreign hands … there for thee, my country, a resurrection?[6]

Here we have a depiction of death-in-life, the appearance of life corrupted
with a 'mortal decay at thy heart'. There is a clear sense of the Irish landscape
invaded by a foreign and threatening element; the land is the victim of abuse
by 'strange rulers' and 'foreign hands' and recovery and 'resurrection' are in
doubt. The passage invites a return to a prelapsarian time before the arrival
of these 'strange rulers' and 'foreign hands', and indeed the trope of a house

or land destroyed by a strange invading presence will be repeated throughout Le Fanu's fiction. While not always overtly linked to the Irish landscape as above, the motif structurally reproduces the initial invasion of Ireland and the 'mortal decay' and death which follow. As McCormack and Walton have argued, Le Fanu's hauntings 'represent the consequences of an "original" sin historicized as a "criminal inheritance"'.[7] But the story of this 'original sin' and the entrance of the 'strange rulers' predates the nineteenth-century history that so dominates Le Fanu criticism. As Siobhán Kilfeather has argued, 'There is another – more political – dimension to the repetition of Gothic plots. It represents a formal enactment of one of the major Gothic themes of particular significance in Ireland, namely that history is repeating itself and that its victims cannot stop themselves banging on about the same old story.'[8] That 'old story' in Irish medieval history is one of an *invited invasion*.

In Irish writing since the twelfth century, the 'stranger in the house' figure has appeared as a colonial allegory for the English presence in Ireland. The presence of the stranger in the house forms the basis of a number of horror 'invasions' by Le Fanu in texts such as 'The Mysterious Lodger' and 'Carmilla'. A central convention in these stories, and one to which both Le Fanu and Bram Stoker adhere, is that the invitation must precede the entrance of the vampire into the home. Among his working papers for the novel *Dracula*, Bram Stoker writes that the vampire 'must be carried, led, helped, or in some way welcomed over the threshold'.[9] A key element in vampire lore, the dependence of the vampire upon the invitation to cross the threshold has a strong link to medieval Irish history and to Ireland's colonial origin story. In 1167, Diarmuid Mac Murrough of Leinster was driven from his land and banished from Ireland by a cohort of Irish leaders for a lengthy series of offences. Furious at his dispossession, Mac Murrough elected to seek aid from King Henry II to regain his position in Ireland. The twelfth-century historian Giraldus Cambrensis records Mac Murrough's invitation to King Henry II:

> [Mac Murrough] crossed the sea with a favourable wind, and came to Henry II., king of England, for the purpose of earnestly imploring his succor … [The king] granted him letters patent to the following: 'Henry, king of England, Duke of Normandy and Aquitaine, and count of Anjou, to all his liegemen, English, Norman, Welsh, and Scots, and to all other nations subject to his dominion, Sendeth, greeting, Whensoever these our letters shall come unto you, know ye that we have received Diamitius, prince of Leinster, into our grace and favour, – Wherefore, whosoever within the bounds of our territories shall be willing to give him aid, as our vassal and liegemen, in recovering his territories, let him be assured of our favour and licence on that behalf'.[10]

Armed with these letters, Mac Murrough formed several key alliances through promises of territories in Ireland. Richard Fitzgilbert de Clare, a Norman warrior known as Strongbow, agreed to assist Mac Murrough in exchange for territories in Ireland and marriage to Mac Murrough's daughter Aoife. Mac Murrough's invitation to these foreign forces to come to Ireland and the subsequent landing of the Anglo-Normans is written into history as the origin story of the struggle between England and Ireland. In the aftermath of the military success of Mac Murrough and his foreign forces, Giraldus's history records the depiction of Ireland as a land under attack by the 'invasion of the strangers'.[11] On 18 October 1171, unnerved by the military successes of Strongbow, King Henry II landed in Ireland. In the literary and historical record, Mac Murrough's invitation to King Henry II precipitates the violent and destructive presence of a 'stranger in the house'.

The vampire narrative structurally resonates so deeply with medieval Irish history because of the nature of the *invited invasion*. Both Le Fanu's 'The Mysterious Lodger' and 'Carmilla' are preoccupied with the horror, violence and death that follow the invitation to the stranger. Le Fanu's structure of an invaded house in which invitations are extended to a stranger who cannot be convinced to leave and who brings about the eventual destruction of the house re-enacts the Irish colonial narrative. Indeed, both in 'The Mysterious Lodger' and in 'Carmilla', Le Fanu's characters will be preoccupied and horrified by their own guilt in inviting the destructive element into the house. In 'The Mysterious Lodger', the narrator and his wife attribute the death of their child to 'the mysterious and fiendish agency of the abhorred being whom, in an evil hour, we had admitted into our house', the presence of the 'malignant agent who haunted, rather than inhabited our home'.[12] The narrator is consumed with the 'dreadful sensation' and 'apprehension that I had admitted into my house the incarnate spirit of the dead or damned, to torment me and my family' (358). The word 'admission' functions on two levels here; it is both a confession of guilt by those who have invited the stranger into the house and a signal of the inability to banishing that which has been 'admitted' into the house. In 'Carmilla', the narrator Laura's father invites Carmilla's mother to 'entrust her child to the care of my daughter', to 'Permit her to remain as our guest, under my charge' and to 'confide this young lady to our care', thus extending the opening necessary to the vampire.[13] In General Spieldorf's letter to Laura's father, the General identifies the vampire Carmilla as 'The fiend who betrayed our infatuated hospitality' (249). In addition to this emphasis on the invitation, Le Fanu repeatedly uses the term 'stranger' in both texts to identify the figure of the vampire. The lodger is 'the dreaded stranger' (359) and the narrator recognises his precarious positing as 'a man who, for the first time, invites a stranger into his house, on the footing of a permanent residence' (338). Carmilla is 'the stranger' (256), 'the young stranger' (256), 'the beautiful stranger' (260) to whom Laura acts 'in the vein which hospitality indicated, to bid her welcome' (259). The designation of the invading presence as the 'stranger', a word with such currency in anti-colonial Irish narratives, links the presence of the vampire to Ireland's medieval history of invasion. Structurally, the historical and literary narratives demonstrate the calamities and the irreversible dispossession which result from this bidden presence; the vampire embodies the nightmare of history from which Ireland cannot awake.

The short story 'The Mysterious Lodger' appeared in *Dublin University Magazine* in 1850, in the midst of the Irish Famine. W. J. McCormack's analysis of the story in *Sheridan Le Fanu and Victorian Ireland* rests primarily on the role of religion in the story and on intersections between the domestic crisis in the story and incidents in Le Fanu's own life.[14] McCormack neglects a critical dimension of the stranger in the house framework that Le Fanu invokes through his continual use of language that suggests not a domestic but a national conflict. Le Fanu's notebook in the National Library of Ireland includes the following story outline: 'Hints for the story. A person supposed to be most harmless taken in from charity, turns out to be the dreaded enemy of the House, & becomes its cruel tyrant. Old Mr Beaufort is rich and severely virtuous. Has been in commerce – is a member of Pt not a speaking but a voting one.'[15] McCormack notes the thematic connection between this fragment and 'The Mysterious Lodger', but continues to interpret is as an 'attempt to relate the Great House and marital distress'. Yet this fragment's inclusion of commerce and Parliament suggests that the story is not confined to interpretation as a purely domestic narrative. McCormack's brief analysis obscures not only the story's potency but the continuing return to the trope of the invading houseguest for Le Fanu.[16]

From the opening, 'The Mysterious Lodger' reveals a compromised border between Ireland and England and directs itself to an Irish audience:

> About the year 1822 I resided in a comfortable and roomy old house, the exact locality of which I need not particularise, further than to say that it was not very far from Old Brompton, in the immediate neighbourhood, or rather continuity (as even my Connemara readers perfectly well know), of the renowned city of London. (332)

The narrator's address from London to 'my Connemara readers' links the framed story to Irish emigration; the imagined reader in the rural west of Ireland who nonetheless has an intimate knowledge of London neighbourhoods introduces the history of Irish exile and depopulation into this vampire story with its strong parallels to Irish history.

In debt for two hundred pounds, the narrator and his wife decide to advertise for a lodger, whose room and board will allow them to repay their debt. The newspaper advertisement goes unanswered, but the narrator's young daughter meets a strange man who agrees to send a lodger to their home. The man is very well-dressed and well-off, and, though his manner frightens the child, the financial terms that he and the narrator exchange in letters prove very agreeable. There is a structural correspondence here with Mac Murrough's solicitation of aid from King Henry II, who also uses letters to mediate between Mac Murrough and the Norman soldiers who respond to his invitation. The narrator and his wife, in fact, seem pleased that the man has 'taken a decided fancy' to their daughter and the narrator 'thought of the magnificent, though remote possibilities, in store for her' (339). Here the narrator hints that his daughter and indeed the daughter's hand are part of the negotiated transaction, another resonance with Diarmuid Mac Murrough's contract with the foreign invader. The narrator pronounces himself 'on the whole, very well pleased with my bargain' and awaits with waning hopes the stranger he believes will restore his position (341): 'I awaited the issue of the affair with as much patience as I could affect ... Days passed away – days of hopes deferred, tedious and anxious. We were beginning to despond again' (337). He thinks later, 'When will he come? Yellow waistcoat promised *this evening*! It has been evening a good hour and a half, and yet he is not here. When will he come? It will soon be dark – the evening will have passed – will he come at all?' (339). Urging Strongbow to keep his promise and defer his arrival in Ireland no longer, Diarmuid Mac Murrough writes to him in a tone similar to that of Le Fanu's narrator:

> We have watched the storks and swallows; the summer birds have come, and are gone again with the southerly wind; but neither winds from the east nor the west have brought us your much desired and long expected presence. Let your present activity make up for this delay, and prove by your deeds that you have not forgotten your engagements, but only deferred their performance.[17]

Despite the narrator's confidence that the presence of the stranger will restore his position and secure his possession of the house, the story will instead end in death and dispossession.

When the lodger eventually arrives, his clothing evokes a military presence as he begins to slowly contaminate the house. The stranger wears a mechanical apparatus surrounding his eyes and mouth, perhaps recalling the well-armoured Normans:

> a sort of white woollen muffler enveloped the lower part of his face; a pair
> of prominent green goggles, fenced round with leather, completely concealed
> his eyes; and nothing of the genuine man, but a little bit of yellow forehead,
> and a small transverse segment of equally yellow cheek and nose, encountered
> the curious gaze of your humble servant. (339–40)

Under the muffler 'was a loose cravat, which stood up in front of his chin
and upon his mouth, he wore a respirator – an instrument which I had
never seen before, and of the use of which I was wholly ignorant' (340).
This 'piece of unknown mechanism upon his mouth, surmounted by the
huge goggles which encased his eyes' contributes to the *'tout ensemble* of the
narrow-chested, long-limbed, and cadaverous figure in black' (340). The
narrator later encounters the lodger 'in precisely the costume in which I
had left him – the same green goggles – the same muffling of the mouth,
except that being now no more than a broadly-folded black silk handkerchief,
very loose, and covering even the lower part of the nose, it was obviously
intended for the sole purpose of concealment' (341). This repeated emphasis
contributes to the growing sensation that the narrator has installed within
his own house some military presence. The stranger's regular and sudden
appearances at windows and doors signify his breaching of thresholds and
the narrator's inability to physically control or contain the stranger to whom
he has granted admission.[18]

In addition, the presence of the stranger initiates religious conflict and
brings turmoil into the house. The lodger visits his landlady and questions her
religion. The narrator finds her 'shocked and horrified at the doubts which
this potent Magis had summoned from the pit – doubts which she knew not
how to combat, and from the torment of which she could not escape. "He has
made me very miserable with his deceitful questions. I never thought of them
before; and, merciful Heaven! I cannot answer them! What am I to do? My
serenity is gone; I shall never be happy again"' (346). The stranger's influence
destroys her ability to worship:

> She had, however, scarcely assumed the attitude of prayer, when somebody,
> she said, clutched her arm violently near the wrist, and she heard, at the
> same instant, some blasphemous menace, the import of which escaped her the
> moment it was spoken, muttered close in her ear … [S]he became literally
> afraid to pray, and her misery and despondency increased proportionately.
> (347)

As in Irish history, the invited invasion brings in its wake religious restrictions
and measures which make worship impossible.

In addition to the religious turmoil occasioned by the lodger, the narrator begins to feel a sort of 'superstitious misgiving' that stranger is not operating in isolation but is rather the agent of another malevolent and more powerful being (342). Another presence is consistently heard within the room, one which indicates that there is now another dark force lodged within the house:

> Meanwhile, the unaccountable terror which our lodger's presence inspired *continued to increase*. One of our maids gave us warning ... that Mr. Smith seemed to have constantly a companion in his room; that although [the maids] never heard them speak, they continually and distinctly heard the tread of two persons walking up and down the room together, and described accurately the peculiar sound of a stick or crutch tapping upon the floor. (353; italics mine)

Here the Irish medieval history of the twelfth century is evoked in that the presence invited into the house to secure it is not in fact an independent agent, but 'continue[s] to increase' in league with a powerful entity that will bring about the destruction of the house.

The diction of the story now shifts away from the domestic, with the terms of the narrator's description suggesting national and military oppression as he discovers the impossibility of ridding the house of the presence he has invited in: 'I would have made any sacrifice short of ruin, *to emancipate* our household from the odious mental and moral thraldom which was invisibly *established over us*' (351; italics mine). When the narrator offers to return the money in exchange for the lodger abandoning their agreement, he describes the lodger as armed, 'fully *equipped* with goggles and respirator, and swathed, rather than dressed, in his puckered black garments' (349; italics mine). The stranger refuses to vacate the house: 'But who on earth said that I was going away so soon? ... I have not said so – because I really don't intend it; ... I have no notion of vacating my hired lodgings, simply because you say, *go* ... I can't do this; here I am, and here I stay' (350). Rather than the restoration of his supremacy through the gains afforded by the lodger, the narrator discovers instead the impossibility of emancipating his household from the foreign element within.

Too late, the narrator realises that the taking in of the stranger and the contract negotiated with the wealthy old man has been a literal 'dead bargain,' a deal with the Devil. The narrator's wife declares that 'I never ... could understand till now the instinctive dread with which poor Margaret, in Faust, shrinks from the hateful presence of Mephistopheles. I now feel it in myself ... I never knew what anguish of mind was until he entered our doors; and would to God – would to God he were gone' (347). The house is utterly transformed by the presence of the stranger. It is 'pervaded with an atmosphere of uncertainty and fear' (350), its inhabitants 'unhappy, dismayed, DEMON-STRICKEN' (358). No protection is possible against an enemy 'so unearthly and intangible' (358). Around the lodger's door 'an atmosphere of death and malice hovered ... and we all hated to fear or pass it' (362). In one of the more revealing passages, the narrator states that: 'so far from courting a collision with the dreaded stranger, I would have recoiled at his very sight, and given my eyes to avoid him, such was the *ascendency* which he had acquired over me, as well as everybody else in the household, in his own quiet, irresistible, hellish way' (359; italics mine). Le Fanu's use of the term 'ascendancy' here is significant, as it imbues the story with the Irish landowning tensions of the period. Appearing at the time of the Irish Famine, a story structured upon an invitation to a demonic stranger who gains the ascendancy and brings tyranny, death and religious turmoil to the inhabitants of the house would have strong resonances.

Death comes to the house as the lodger-vampire literally sucks the life out of both the narrator's children, transforming the home into 'a house of mourning' and 'of sorrow and of fear' (357). The infant son dies shortly after the daughter sees the lodger remove his respirator, lie upon the child's bed and kill him (355). The daughter's death is particularly gruesome. The narrator returns home one day to find her seated on the lap of the lodger, whose goggles and muffler have been removed. The child unable to speak, can only 'put her hand to her throat, as if there were some pain or obstruction there' (364). The daughter dies shortly after this encounter and, in the middle of the night, the narrator visits her coffin only to discover the lodger and his cat 'Perched upon the body of the child, and nuzzling among the grave-clothes with a strange kind of ecstasy' (368). After the daughter's burial, the lodger tells the narrator that the child has been accidentally buried alive, an account verified when the narrator frantically exhumes the coffin and body: 'There was the corpse – but not the tranquil statue I had seen it last' (370). Tortured by 'the presence in my house of the wretch who had wrought all this destruction and misery', the narrator follows the advice of a spiritual gentleman who instructs him that the only solution is to abandon the house entirely, for its repossession is impossible (365): 'But leave the house as soon as may be yourself; you will scarcely have peace in it. Your own remembrances will trouble you *and other minds have established associations within its walls and chambers too*' (371; italics mine). Here again, Le Fanu underscores the multiplication of evil influences, an indication that the lodger is never operating alone but is himself the agent of a more penetrating, powerful and immovable force. The references throughout the story to 'establishments', 'ascendancy' and 'emancipation' support a reading of the vampire's threat not in exclusively domestic terms but through the framework of Ireland's colonial and national conflict.

At the conclusion of 'The Mysterious Lodger', the narrator returns to the opposition sent forth in the story's opening, between urban London and rural Connemara. Walking past the site of the house, the narrator notices that it has since been torn down and replaced with two new houses featuring tranquil gardens. No such easy eradication of history is possible, he hints to his readers, in the west of Ireland: 'In a country village there is no difficulty in accounting for the tenacity with which the sinister character of a haunted tenement cleaves to it. Thin neighbourhoods are favourable to scandal; and in such localities the reputation of a house, like that of a woman, once blown upon, never quite recovers' (371). Le Fanu's return to the vampire in 'Carmilla' locates the vampire narrative in just such a rural and remembering landscape. As in 'The Mysterious Lodger', a stranger will enter the house as an invited presence, initially seen as an aid to those within the house. Again, the transaction that results in the arrival of the stranger will occur through a third party, this time not a man but the vampire's mother. And once more, the presence of the stranger will evolve into a corrupting influence which will threaten the destruction of the house. While Le Fanu resurrects the structure of 'The Mysterious Lodger' in 'Carmilla', he deploys the vampire in this novella to disrupt clear demarcation of identity. If 'The Mysterious Lodger' concludes with the destruction of the house and the suggestion that its history has been comfortably laid to rest, 'Carmilla' offers no such resolution. Le Fanu's return to the structure of the invited invasion suggests the impossibility of purging its history in Styria/Ireland. In his transplantation of the vampire narrative from urban London to rural Styria, Le Fanu indicates that not only the legacies of invasion and conquest but also the campaigns to repel them retain a continual capacity for resurrection.

In *Aisling Ghéar*, Breandán Ó Buachalla identifies persistent and long-standing fears of Catholic communion as blood-drinking and of Catholics depicted as 'Romish wolves, which would [Protestants] soon devour'.[19] In another early text, Protestants are warned of a time when they might see

> your wives prostituted to the lust of every savage bog-trotter, your daughters ravished by goatish monks ... whilst you have your own bowels ripped up ... and holy candles made of your grease (which was done within our memory in Ireland), your dearest friends slaving in Smithfield, foreigners rendering your poor babes that can escape everlasting slaves, never more to see a Bible, nor hear again the joyful sounds of Liberty and Property. This, this gentlemen is Popery.[20]

Writing in the *Dublin Evening Mail* in 1840, Le Fanu himself described Daniel O'Connell, whose 'monster' rallies were aimed at securing Catholic Emancipation, in terms that evince a vampire. O'Connell, Le Fanu wrote:

> has achieved his own political elevation at a sacrifice of human life, greater than any mortal pestilence has caused, and at an expense of human crime which must be slowly paid for [by] ages of national degradation – and one who, having seen the victims of his hatred laid in the graves of martyrdom, and those of his perfidy and cajolery exposed upon the gibbets of their country, now approaches the verge of his iniquitous existence, unaffected by the visitings of remorse, with a soul in which every passion, but that of unquenchable malignity had perished, and a heart which so far from being touched by the awful approaches of death and judgment, seems not to anticipate the coldness and corruption of the grave.[21]

Arguing that the presences which haunt Le Fanu's fiction usually appear 'to right some wrong connected with the ownership of real estate',[22] Robert Tracy has read the vampire Carmilla as emblematic of the Catholic dispossessed:

> Many of [Le Fanu's] stories, supernatural or otherwise, portray the dispossessed Catholic gentry of Ireland after the Williamite triumph … As Le Fanu contemplated his own class's loss of power in the aftermath of Daniel O'Connell's successful campaign for Catholic Emancipation (1829), and increasing Catholic political and economic power, he seemed to imagine the Ascendancy's future by examining the Catholic gentry's dispossessed past, to recognize that the Williamite revolution, which had given the Le Fanu family lands and prestige, was being altered by another revolution which would reverse the earlier one.[23]

In his approach, Tracy echoes readings of *Dracula* that view the vampire as enacting the horror of reverse colonisation; Carmilla in this formulation takes revenge upon an Anglo-Irish ascendancy that had robbed her.

The vampire Carmilla certainly carries with her a memory of dispossession and a fear of invasion. She tells her host Laura, 'I am haunted with a terror of robbers. Our house was robbed once, and two servants murdered, so I always lock my door' (261). She shares an incredible likeness with a portrait of one Mircalla Karnstein painted in 1698 (272). In Irish history, 1698 marks the time when many of the Penal Laws and their injunctions against Catholics came to be enforced. As does the stranger in 'The Mysterious Lodger', Carmilla's presence occasions religious strife (266, 277). One might read Mircalla/Carmilla, who even in the painting 'seemed to live' and who in the present is one of the undead, as a Catholic presence feared to be unextinguishable, personified by a woman whose house has been robbed, and who may yet rise to rob in turn. The imagining of Catholic Ireland restaging and reversing the original invasion makes for a possible horror story indeed. Carmilla hints at just such a possibility of an uprising when she declares that 'People say I am languid ... I am very easily set up again; in a moment I am perfectly myself. See how I have recovered' (274).

Yet to read Carmilla solely as the representation of the dispossessed neglects the ways in which she herself re-enacts the invited invasion of Ireland's medieval period even as she embodies its destabilising aftermath. McCormick identifies Le Fanu's work in 1868–1870 as exhibiting an 'awareness of history's multiple levels' and 'a pattern and structure which reveal and openness to interpretation'.[24] In operating both as dispossessed and invader, the vampire in 'Carmilla' disrupts the binaries between native and stranger delineated in 'The Mysterious Lodger'. If that earlier text lends itself to an allegorical reading of the origin story of Ireland's colonial narrative, Le Fanu's reconstruction of the stranger in the house in this later novella would seem to gesture towards the complex history of its aftermath. 'The Mysterious Lodger' ends first with the narrator ceding the house to the stranger, and then with the house's destruction; 'Carmilla' allows for no such clear-cut resolution. In her duality, the vampire Carmilla reveals the disparate presences coexisting within the house. In 'Carmilla', the vampire signifies not solely the spilled blood of colonial history but its mixed bloodlines as well. In this, Carmilla indicates both a hybridity and the immortality of a conflict continually resurrected from the 'blood-stained annals' of history (305). Carmilla resists attempts to read her in a clear allegorical sense – she is neither exclusively a dispossessed Catholic nor a landed aristocrat but rather emblematic of these dualities locked in a seemingly immortal conflict that began with an invited invasion.

'Carmilla' contains a number of echoes of Ireland which emphasise the conflict within the landscape and also point to the title character's multiple and shifting identities. Le Fanu's London publisher Richard Bentley discouraged Irish settings,[25] and Matthew Gibson has pointed out the intersections between the Protestant and Catholic conflicts in Ireland and 'Carmilla''s setting in Styria, suggesting that Le Fanu's Irish reader would have assumed a substitution of colonial Styria for Ireland.[26] In landscapes oscillating between the well-manicured and the wild terrain, Styria evokes the duality of Ireland within and beyond the Pale. The journey into Carmilla's territory is a journey 'westward, to reach the deserted village and ruined castle of Karnstein' (292). In the twin symbols of the evacuated village – with what Laura calls 'its quaint little church, now roofless'– and the castle, Le Fanu evokes Ireland's own architectural remnants of ruling powers and the dispossessed (244). Upon entering the Karnstein territory, Laura reflects that the grounds are 'totally destitute of the comparative formality which artificial planting and early culture and pruning impart' (292). Laura's reading of the Karnstein land as lacking in 'early culture', as destitute, and as antithetical to formality echo the views of the Irish as barbaric and uncultivated savages espoused by their colonisers. The reference to 'artificial planting' evokes Ireland's colonial history of settler plantations.[27]

Yet in spite of the seemingly obvious oppositions within the landscape and between Laura and Carmilla, the vampire Carmilla continually resists being pinned to a fixed allegorical identity. When Carmilla is assured of her welcome by Laura's father, she states, 'Thank you, sir, a thousand times for your hospitality' (275). There is an echo here of the Irish *céad míle fáilte* (one hundred thousand welcomes) which suggests that Carmilla is perhaps both invited guest and host. Martin Willis notes that

> Laura's mother was descended from the Karnstein family, as was General Spielsdorf's wife, meaning that Laura, and potentially General Spielsdorf's ward (his niece), were also descendants of that same ancient Styrian family. The vampire, Carmilla, is not only a Karnstein but the original Countess from whom these mothers and their daughters are descended.[28]

Thus in the vampire Carmilla, Le Fanu offers not a distant stranger invited into the house as in 'The Mysterious Lodger', or strictly an emblem of dispossession as Tracy argues, but an embodiment of both the initial invasion and the mingled and spilled blood of its aftermath.

Whereas 'The Mysterious Lodger' depends upon a binary opposition between the stranger and the narrator, in 'Carmilla' identities are fluid. Laura believes she and Carmilla share 'a like temperament', she finds Carmilla's identity 'infectious' and cannot help but 'imitate' it (277): 'I had adopted Carmilla's habit of locking her bed-room door, having taken into my head all her whimsical alarms about midnight invaders and prowling assassins. I had also adopted her precaution of making a brief search through her room, to satisfy herself that no lurking assassin or robber was ensconced'. The word 'ensconced' appears, like Carmilla's fears, to have been 'taken into [Laura's] head'. Laura begins a slow decline in which she increasingly begins to resemble Carmilla physically (287). The physical, mental and linguistic synergy between Laura and Carmilla resists a reading of the vampire or her victim as representing one side or the other of the binaries set forth in

'The Mysterious Lodger'; indeed, the fact that Carmilla's language appears to be overtaking Laura's own would make a reading of Carmilla as Catholic dispossessed difficult.

Indeed, rather than seeking any clear possession of the house as a means to right a historical wrong, the vampire Carmilla appears more interested in the acquisition of blood. At times, Carmilla's language seems to echo the demands of the Irish Shan Van Vocht, who demands blood sacrifice to restore the house or nation. She urges Laura 'You must come with me, loving me, to death … Love will have its sacrifices. No sacrifice without blood' (276–7). But her shifting identity suggests that Carmilla is less representative of one side of the conflict or the other, but of the demand and thirst for bloodletting. As the General states of the Karnsteins, 'It was a bad family, and here its blood-stained annals were written … It is hard that they should, after death, continue to plague the human race with their atrocious lusts' (305). With this in mind, the continued existence of the vampire, emerging out of the 'blood-stained annals' of history, points less to a clear allegorical correlation and more toward the continuous capacity for the resurrection of the historical past and its 'atrocious lust' for blood in the present.

In the duality of his construction of Mircalla/Carmilla, Le Fanu deploys the vampire not simply to evoke an initial invasion but to embody the hybrid identities and histories that exist now within the same house. Carmilla's haunting declaration to Laura, 'I live in you', is perhaps the most direct recognition of the irreversibility of the initial invasion and the immortality of its legacy (274). Elizabeth Bowen stated of Le Fanu himself that he sprang from 'a race of hybrids' which made it 'necessary for him to invent nothing' but to be aware only of 'his own heredity'.[29] The vampire Carmilla's major departure from the deadly invited stranger in 'The Mysterious Lodger' is in her ability to embody not exclusively the spilled blood of the colonial invasion but the mixed blood of its legacy. Carmilla is both the invading and colonising stranger and the disparate hybrid populations now contained within the house. When Laura dreams that her mother appears to her 'to beware of the assassin', the warning is accompanied by an image of Carmilla 'bathed, from her chin to her feet, in one great stain of blood' (283). Carmilla appears here as both victim and perpetrator; Laura is the warned of the 'assassin', yet Carmilla herself appears assassinated. She confesses as much to Laura earlier in the novella: 'I was all but assassinated' (276). Though the portrait she resembles dates from the seventeenth century, Carmilla is discovered floating in seven inches of blood, a mixture and measure which may recall the seven centuries following the Anglo-Norman invasion and the landing of Henry II in Ireland.

Despite McCormack's claim that 'Le Fanu is concerned with space rather than time', Le Fanu's vampires signify not only a spatial invasion but a temporal one.[30] Carmilla's presence, like that of the lodger, signals a temporal crossing of boundaries, bringing Ireland's medieval memory forward to bear upon the present and infecting the text with the very history the vampire carries. In 'Carmilla', Laura's shock at hearing General Spielsdorf's story of the vampire Mircalla's destruction of his niece is the shock of having her own personal narrative reflected back to her: 'having just listened to so strange a story, connected, as it was, with the great and titled dead, whose monuments were mouldering among the dust and ivy round us, and every incident which bore so awfully upon my own mysterious case – in this haunted spot, darkened by the towering foliage that rose on every side, dense, and high above its noiseless walls – a horror began to steal over me' (311). That horror is the recognition that history – whether that of Mircalla as related by the General or that of the 'great and titled dead' – is not in fact 'mouldering' but is, as the General puts is 'not so dead as you fancy' (306). The vampire narrative achieves a similar effect, structurally re-enacting Ireland's colonial origin story of an invited invasion through a figure that embodies mixed and spilled blood.

Even as the novella's conclusion suggests that Carmilla's presence has been extinguished, Baron Vordenborg issues the following caveat: 'One sign of the vampire is the power of the hand … But the power is not confined to its grasp; it leaves a numbness in the limb it seizes, which is slowly, if ever, recovered from' (319). The grasp of the vampire, like that of colonialism, retains its hold on the present. The continued influence of Carmilla may be seen in the temporal confusion left in her wake. Even after the spectre of Carmilla has been banished, the boundaries of time in the narrative remain compromised. Laura concludes her narrative with the claim that 'it was long before the terror of recent events subsided', a grammatically and temporally confusing syntax which operates simultaneously in both past and present. If the vampire is extinguished at the conclusion of Carmilla, the end of the text suggests that what is truly immortal is the bloodshed and the conflict of which her current incarnation is but a symptom. Carmilla returns to Laura's memory 'with ambiguous alternations', recalling Carmilla's capacity to reinvent herself. One of Carmilla's few limitations has to do with her name, 'which, if not her real one, should at least reproduce, without the omission or addition of a single letter, those, as we say, anagrammatically, which compose it. Carmilla did this; so did Mircalla' (317). So too, then, does Ill Carma, a diseased cycle of retribution and bloodshed which continues to reproduce and can never be fully eradicated.

Notes

1 Stoker, *Dracula*, ed. Ellman, p. 240.

2 Arata, 'The Occidental Tourist'; Seamus Deane reads the soil in which Dracula resides as 'a literal version of a coffin-ship – that resonate image from Famine times' (*Strange Country*, p. 89); Moses, 'The Irish Vampire'.

3 Valente, *Dracula's Crypt*, p. 1.

4 See Goss, 'Dracula and the Spectre of Famine'; Merritt, '"Dead Many Times"'; Ingelbien, 'Gothic Genealogies'; Potts, 'Convents'.

5 McCormack, 'Irish Gothic and After', p. 832. The 'school of Walpole' refers to Horace Walpole, the author of the 1764 novel *The Castle of Otrano*, viewed as having initiated the Gothic tradition in fiction.

6 Le Fanu, 'The Quare Gander', p. 390.

7 Walton, *Vision and Vacancy*, p. 3; McCormack, *Sheridan Le Fanu*, pp. 86, 244.

8 Kilfeather, 'The Gothic Novel', p. 82.

9 Frayling, 'Bram Stoker's Working Papers', in *Dracula*, ed. Auerbach, p. 343.

10 Giraldus Cambrensis *et al.*, *The Historical Works*, pp. 185–6.

11 Barnard, *Strongbow's Conquest of Ireland*, p. 24.

12 Le Fanu, *Ghost Stories and Mysteries*, p. 357. Additional references will be cited parenthetically in the text.

13 Le Fanu, *In a Glass Darkly*, ed. Robert Tracey, pp. 253, 254. Additional references will be cited parenthetically in the text.

14 The religious crisis within the text has by far dominated the scant critical analysis the story has received. In addition to McCormack's emphasis, Ivan Melada, for example, notes that the story 'puts its author squarely into the mainstream of the Victorian crisis of faith' and notes that it is ultimately 'an exploration into the wages of unbelief' (*Sheridan Le Fanu*, pp. 117, 119). McCormack concludes that 'If we are to take the evidence of letters and diaries seriously, we can hardly avoid the conclusion that the domestic distress depicted in "Richard Marston" and "The Mysterious Lodger" has a bearing (however oblique) on life in the author's home' (p. 134). While McCormack notes that the identity of the guest 'is at times nearly confused with that of the master of the house', he reads this destabilisation as primarily a reflection of Le Fanu's own domestic distress (p. 118).

15 McCormack, *Sheridan Le Fanu*, p. 246.

16 *Ibid.*, p. 120.

17 Giraldus Cambrensis *et al*, *The Historical Works*, p. 205.

18 For more on the vampire at the threshold, see Ivan Phillips's Chapter 14 below.

19 Ó Buachalla, *Aisling Ghéar*, p. 150.

20 *Ibid.*, pp. 150–1.

21 Cited in McCormack, *Sheridan Le Fanu*, p. 84.

22 Tracey, Introduction, in Le Fanu, *In a Glass Darkly*, p. viii.

23 *Ibid.*, p. xvii.

24 McCormack, *Sheridan Le Fanu*, p. 252.

25 *Ibid.*, p. 140.

26 Gibson, *Dracula and the Eastern Question*.

27 'Plantation' refers to the seizure of Irish land and the re-granting of that land to English, Irish or Scottish settlers loyal to the Crown.

28 Willis, 'Le Fanu's *Carmilla*', p. 125.

29 Cited in McCormack, *Sheridan Le Fanu*, p. 141.

30 McCormack, *Sheridan Le Fanu*, p. 252.

4

'He make in the mirror no reflect': undead aesthetics and mechanical reproduction – *Dorian Gray, Dracula* and David Reed's 'vampire painting'

Sam George

IN DEVELOPING the *Open, Graves, Open Minds* project, I was struck by the irony of creatures with no reflection becoming such a pervasive reflection of modern culture. My research here has developed directly out of this meditation on the vampire's reflection or shadow. Bram Stoker's Dracula famously 'throws no shadow' though he has long been associated with darkness and shade ('I love the shade and the shadow').[1] In the former Yugoslavia, certain Muslim gypsies are said to believe that a vampire *is* a dead person's shadow.[2] 'Shadow traders' were common in Romania, according to Emily Gerard, writing not long before Stoker's novel. They traded shadows to architects who attempted to secure and wall up a person's shadow to ensure that their buildings were durable, with the result that after death that person would become a vampire.[3]

Shadows are inextricably linked to superstitions about vampires but they are equally associated with myths around the origins of art, and with broader notions of reflection and reproduction, as I will show. The term 'shadow' can be applied to 'a portrait as contrasted with the original' and to 'an imitation, copy; a counterpart'.[4] Pliny even identified the birth of artistic representation in tracing an outline around a man's shadow.[5] Here, the dark shape or outline confirms an absence, but there is a presence too, a representation, of self or soul. In the eighteenth century, it was the shadow of the face, not the face itself that was the soul's true reflection, according to Lavatar's theory of physiognomy.[6] In the nineteenth century, Stoker showed the soulless vampire to be 'an unmirrorable image', a creature virtually beyond representation, assuming multiple forms. Without his mirror image, Dracula becomes 'physiognomy's true vanishing point', a profoundly unsettling figure.[7]

In this chapter I attempt to uncover the origins of the non-reflection motif and interrogate the vampire's complex relationship to this optical phenomenon. I focus, to begin with, on Stoker's handwritten notes for *Dracula* where the vampire's lack of a reflection or shadow is first located and where this conceit is extended to include its image in photography and painting.[8] From this, I develop the notion of 'vampire painting' in the writings of Pater and Wilde, and interrogate *Dracula* and *Dorian Gray* in relation to the idea of reproduction, and tensions around realism and mimesis, drawing on Benjamin's analysis of art in the age of mechanical reproduction and his theorisation of the outmoded. I conclude with a discussion of the contemporary artist David Reed whose abstract painting is offered up as another version of non-reflection. Reed has responded directly to Stoker's *Dracula* notebooks in his own 'vampire painting', creating a compelling homage to the unmirrorable figure of the vampire.

The vampire's lack of a reflection, the 'unseen face in the mirror',[9] is first revealed to us in *Dracula* (1897). On arriving at the castle, Harker is quick to observe that 'in none of the rooms is there a mirror' (21); as he gets the little shaving glass from his bag and hangs it by the window, he is approached by the Count:

> Suddenly I felt a hand on my shoulder, and heard the Count's voice saying to me, 'Good morning.' I started, for it amazed me that I had not seen him, since the reflection of the glass covered the whole room behind me. In starting I had cut myself slightly, but did not notice it at the moment. Having answered the Count's salutation, I turned to the glass again to see how I had been mistaken. This time there could be no error, for the man was close to me, and I could see him over my shoulder. But there was no reflection of him in the mirror! The whole room behind me was displayed; but there was no sign of a man in it, except myself. (27)

Dracula reacts violently to this 'foul bauble of man's vanity' (28), the mirror, which has betrayed his secret, hurling it out of the window where it smashes it into a thousand pieces on the stone courtyard below. The trope of the vampire's non-reflection has always intrigued scholars. Critical approaches to this phenomenon in fiction have tended to draw on Freud's 'uncanny', Otto Rank's theory of the *doppelgänger* or double, or Lacan's 'mirror phase'.[10] My aim in this chapter is to take this phenomenon back to its beginnings, to examine the *Dracula* Notebooks in the Rosenbach museum (Stoker's research notes for the novel) and simply to pose the question: did Stoker sit down at his desk one day and invent the mirror non-reflection motif?

Tellingly, there is no mention of mirrors in relation to vampires in any of Stoker's folkloric sources – Emily Gerard's *Transylvanian Superstitions* (1885) or *The Land Beyond the Forest* (1888), for example – nor is there any material on this phenomenon in 'Vampires in New England', the article Stoker found during a trip to New York in 1896, or in the entry on 'vampires' in the *Encyclopedia Britannica* of 1888 which he had consulted.[11] Dracula's literary precursors, Polidori's *The Vampyre* (1819), Rymer's *Varney the Vampire* (1847) and Le Fanu's 'Carmilla' (1872), similarly lack any reference to this particular aspect of vampire lore (though Le Fanu's collection of tales *In a Glass Darkly* (1872), where 'Carmilla' appeared, points to reflection as a motif). The truth is that despite much speculation that the silver in mirrors is repellent to the vampire – a trait borrowed from werewolves – we are still no closer to understanding how the non-reflection motif came about.[12]

Stoker picked up a few details from Sabine Baring-Gould's *The Book of Werewolves* (1865) which elaborates on the werewolf's relationship to the vampire and how it loses its soul: 'The Greek werewolf is closely related to the vampire. The lycanthropist falls into a cataleptic trance, during which his soul leaves his body, enters that of a wolf and ravens for blood … after death the lycanthropists become vampires.'[13] In the light of this, and of Lavatar's shadow-soul, I begin to wonder, as others have, if Stoker's imagining of the vampire casting no reflection is an elaborate metaphor for its lack of a soul.[14] Dracula throws no shadow and casts no reflection; he has no soul, as physical existence and appetite are all that concern him. Paul Barber's work on the folkloric vampire sheds some further light on this, documenting the importance of mirrors as soul traps. They can contain the soul of the dead in the form of a reflection, hence they are turned to the wall when someone dies or when a corpse is in the room.[15] In many cultures the shadow and the mirror image are both unmistakably associated with the soul. Shadowy images (including the photograph) are seen as part of a person and not just optical phenomena.[16]

Shadows are undoubtedly connected to superstitions about vampires; the role played by mirrors is harder to gauge with any certainty.[17] Casting around, I seized on the idea that mirrors were used to create the vampire on stage in the early nineteenth century, a technique developed for early melodramas, such as Planché's *The Vampire, or Bride of the Isles*, staged at the Lyceum in London in 1820.[18] Phantasmagoria saw the raising of the dead on stage in productions such as *Pepper's Ghost* where mirrors and reflections were again used.[19] These vampiric theatricals predate *Dracula* and it seems

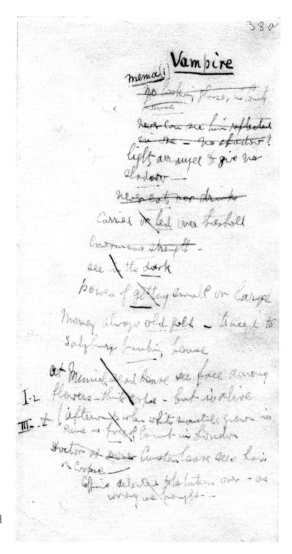

Figure 4.1. Bram Stoker's notebook entry on mirrors and reflection

plausible that Stoker would have been aware of earlier optical effects and the 'vampire trap', immersed as he was in the culture of the nineteenth-century theatre.[20] I wondered if the *Dracula* notebooks contained evidence of this. Leafing through the handwritten pages, I stumbled immediately on a reference to mirrors (see Figure 4.1). As early as page three, Stoker writes 'No looking glasses in Count's house never can see him reflected in one – no shadow?'[21] Then, on page four, he elaborates further: 'painters cannot paint him – their likeness always like someone else'; 'Could not codak him [*sic*] – come out black or like skeleton corpse' (see Figure 4.2). What I found in the

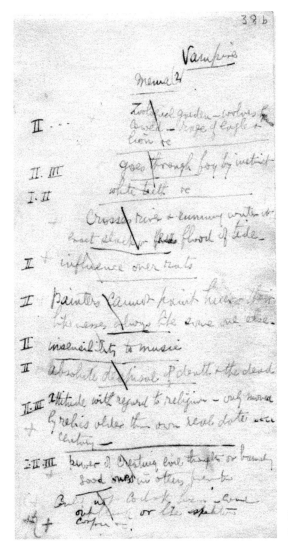

Figure 4.2. Bram Stoker's notebook entry on Kodak

notebook entries was surprising: emerging from all the drawings and notes was a unique record of developing theories of mechanical reproduction. In writing the novel, Stoker's research was not confined to folklore; it extended to aesthetic debates and ideas around new technology, in particular the birth of photography.

The rise of photography was propelled by the innovations in 1884 of George Eastman, who replaced the photographic plate with dry gel on paper, or film. Photography immediately became more appealing and accessible to the amateur. Eastman began selling his Kodak camera in July 1888 with the slogan 'You press the button, we do the rest'. Now, anyone could become a photographer, and photography became available for the mass-market soon after via the Kodak Brownie.[22] There are multiple references to new recording technologies in *Dracula*: the camera, phonograph, typewriter – all of these are used by the 'Crew of Light' in an attempt to track down and document the non-reflecting vampire. '*Dracula* and its media' have been well documented by Jennifer Wicke, but she does not make any reference to the notebook entry on Kodak in relation to the Count.[23] 'Everyday the urge grows stronger to get hold of an object at very close range by way of its likeness, its reproduction', argues Benjamin.[24] What results is 'a tremendous shattering of tradition'.[25] These processes are 'intimately connected with contemporary mass movements'.[26] Harker's use of the camera in the novel can be seen to demonstrate these processes. It marks a new vogue for photo consumerism. He takes 'views' of the Carfax estate 'from various points' (25) and uses his Kodak in the service of real estate (but he never attempts to photograph the Count).

The vampire's lack of a reflection or image in a photograph is symbolic of a tension whereby premodern worldviews collide with contemporary modes of production in the novel, and, as Wicke points out, the 'snapshot camera so many people were wielding at the time is really also a celluloid analog of vampirism in action, the extraction out of an essence in an act of consumption'.[27] 'The mirror with a memory' is a term used for photography in Rosalind Krauss in her analysis of new media; inviting us to see photography in *Dracula* as an extension of the non-reflection motif.[28] Stoker's ancient, shadowless Count does not show up on a photograph; he 'come[s] out black or like a skeleton corpse'. We are nearer to the X-ray than the photograph in Stoker's imagining of this image. In 1896, close to the date of the novel's publication, Röntgen made a picture of his wife's hand, formed through X-rays, on a photographic plate. This was the first ever photograph of a human body part using X-rays. On seeing the picture Frau Röntgen believed that she had seen her own death.[29] This whiff of the grave is evocative of the figure of the vampire and indicative of wider fears over the new medium of photography. In 1902, Van Negelein noted that farmers in the north of Greece were afraid of the photograph (their souls might be captured if their pictures were taken),[30] and Benjamin cites 'a chauvinistic rag' to show the reactionary attitudes to photography in nineteenth-century Europe: 'To try to capture fleeting mirror images … is not just an impossible undertaking … the very wish to do such a thing is blasphemous. Man is made in the image of God, and God's image cannot be captured by any machine of human devising.'[31] Unease over new technologies is wedded here to deeper anxieties around scientific

Figure 4.3.   Darwin and an ape looking at their likeness in a mirror

discovery and its challenge to Christian doctrine. A satirical cartoon from the nineteenth century shows Darwin and an ape looking at their likeness in a mirror (see Figure 4.3). Stoker's refusal to allow us to acknowledge our likeness to Dracula (we cannot see a reflection) is symptomatic, perhaps, of wider anxieties around our kinship with the soulless 'Other' brought about by Darwin's evolutionary theories.[32] Renfield, the maniacal character controlled by Dracula, is the vehicle for these Darwinian ideas in the novel ('I want no souls, life is all I want' (250)).

Van Helsing perpetuates the myth of non-reflection, informing his associates that the vampire 'throws no shadow; he make in the mirror no reflect' (223). A scientist, philosopher and metaphysician (106), he must explain the existence of vampires 'for [in] this enlightened age when men believe not what they see, the doubting of wise men would be his [the vampire's] greatest

strength' (298). 'I have trained myself to keep an open mind' (220), reports
Van Helsing (in sympathy with our *Open Graves, Open Minds* project). Dracula
has no likeness, no shadow, and no photographic image, and he cannot be
tracked by these means. He 'can grow and become small; and he can at times
vanish and come unknown' (221). He is timeless, 'he is known everywhere
that man has been', 'he cannot die by the mere passing of time' (222). Despite
such advantages, he is destroyed at the end of the novel, but the new recording
technologies have failed to document the history of this ancient creature with
any authenticity:

> I took the papers from the safe where they have been ever since our return
> so long ago. We were struck with the fact that, in all the mass of material
> of which the record is composed, there is hardly one authentic document!
> Nothing but a mass of typewriting. (351)

Benjamin demonstrates how in the age of mechanical reproduction 'authenticity and authority' are lost: 'Since the historical testimony rests on the
authenticity, the former, too, is jeopardized by reproduction … And what is
really jeopardized when the historical testimony is affected is the authority of
the object.'[33] This loss seems to occur in *Dracula*, and the witnesses return to
word-of-mouth testimony or storytelling to record and give authenticity to
their encounter with the vampire. Faith in modernity, in new technologies,
has been tested and the reader is encouraged to acknowledge that 'The old
centuries had, and have powers of their own which mere modernity cannot
kill' (37). An anti-Enlightenment narrative is emerging, but it is ambiguous.
Even the smallest of innovations, such as the shorthand used by Mina, is a
manifestation of mechanical reproduction; it is such as this that creates the
contradictions around modernity and new technologies in the novel. Dr
Seward's phonograph diary, recorded on to wax cylinders, is listened to by
Mina and transcribed on to her typewriter. Her account of these processes
reveals something of what has been lost:

> That is a wonderful machine … it told me in its very tones, the anguish of
> your heart. It was like a soul crying out to almighty God. No one must hear
> that spoken ever again! See I have tried to be useful. I have copied out the
> words on my typewriter and none other need hear your heart beat, as I did.
> (207)

The authenticity of the experience, its rawness, cannot be reproduced when
transcribing between different media and the typewritten words are instead
another 'analog of vampirism in action'. Benjamin argues 'that which withers
in the age of mechanical reproduction is the aura of the work of art. This

is a symptomatic process whose significance points beyond the realm of art'.[34] Here its loss is made manifest in literature through the medium of typewriting. Though Benjamin sees revolutionary potential in this stripping away of aura, it unsettles Stoker. Intriguingly, though, in the first stage of the recording processes, the authenticity is emphasised, rather than it withering, highlighting the novel's ambivalence towards technological transcription.

Stoker himself was a painter and a founding member of the Dublin Sketching Club, as it was known when it was set up in 1874.[35] A painter whose vampire did not have a likeness, he says of the creature that 'painters cannot paint him – their likeness always like someone else'.[36] I now want to broaden my approach to include painting and ideas that surface in relation to the figure of the vampire in works of art, both real and imagined, beginning with the writings of Oscar Wilde.

There is a passage in 'The Critic as Artist' (1891) where Wilde imagines the *Mona Lisa* as a vampire, following its description in Pater:[37]

> Mr Pater has put into the portrait of the Monna Lisa [*sic*] something that Lionardo [*sic*] never dreamed of? The painter may have been merely the slave of an archaic smile, as some have fancied, but whenever I pass into the cool galleries of the Palace of the Louvre and stand before that strange figure 'set in its marble chair in the cirque of fantastic rocks, as in some faint light under sea', I murmur to myself, 'She is older than the rocks on which she sits; like the vampire she has been dead many times, and learned the secrets of the grave' … and so the picture becomes more wonderful to us than it really is, and reveals to us a secret of which, in truth, it knows nothing.[38]

Pater's description of the *Mona Lisa* as a vampire fired Wilde's imagination, and *Dorian Gray*, in turn, allows discussions of vampirism in the *fin de siècle* to map on to wider aesthetic debates and cultural fears around the relevance of painting in an age of mechanical reproduction. The theme of mirroring, of doubling, is extended to include uncanny or vampiric portraits in *Dorian Gray*.[39] The nature and function of art is a central concern in this cautionary tale; Dorian's living portrait enacts a decadent rejection of the act of mimesis, of art imitating life. The artist, Basil Hallward will not exhibit the painting of Dorian because he is afraid he has put too much of himself into it and because he has 'shown in it the secret of his own soul'.[40] Dorian, in turn, is disturbed by the portrait's vampiric qualities: 'every moment that passes takes something from me and gives something to it. Oh, if it were only the other way! If the picture could change, and I could always be what I am now!' (26); 'I would give my soul for that' (25). His wish granted, the portrait lives and is mutable whereas Dorian has the fixity and permanence of a work of art; he has 'become the spectator of [his] own life' (94) – he is nothing but a pallid mask of chalk with leaden eyes (91). Following his corruption by the 'yellow book', Dorian becomes a creature of the night, a vampiric seducer, a Lord Ruthven, with a Mona Lisa smile.[41]

It is after the suicide of one of his conquests, the actress Sibyl Vane, that he first notices the change in the portrait, where 'the quivering, ardent sunlight showed him the lines of cruelty round the mouth as clearly as if he had been looking into a mirror after he had done some dreadful thing' (78). The vampiric portrait is for Dorian 'the most magical of mirrors. As it had revealed to him its own body, so it would reveal to him his own soul' (91). His narcissism is such that he is often pictured standing 'with a mirror, in front of the portrait … looking now at the evil and aging face on the canvas, and now at the fair young face that laughed back at him from the polished glass' (109). [42] Dorian is too enamoured of his resemblance, presented without 'mist or veil' in the portrait (98). In the 'Decay of Lying' (1891), Wilde argues that Art 'is not to be judged by any external standard of resemblance. She is a veil, rather than a mirror.'[43] Yet *Dorian Gray*'s preface contrasts this anti-realism with the bourgeois monster, Caliban's aversion to seeing himself reflected: 'The nineteenth-century dislike of Realism is the rage of Caliban seeing his own face in a glass. The nineteenth-century dislike of Romanticism is the rage of Caliban not seeing his own face in a glass.'[44] Wilde, the master of paradox and contradiction, indulges in some Hegelian dialectics, rejecting the narrow instrumentalism demanded of realist art and advocating aestheticism, yet simultaneously defending a critical realism that exposes the vices of the bourgeoisie (indeed, there is evidence that he had read Hegel).[45] He uses this device to explore and satirise the relationships in realism between artist, subject and audience/viewer.[46]

The portrait's undead subject, Dorian, is driven to destroy his own image after stabbing the artist in the neck – gestures reminiscent both of the staking of the vampire and the act of vampirism. The palette knife that had created the portrait is now used to destroy the artist; 'as it had killed the painter, so it would kill the painter's work, and all that that meant' (187). It would kill the 'monstrous soul-life' (187) of the painting. A man, 'loathsome of visage', is found in front of the portrait with a knife in his heart. It is perhaps worth noting that Dracula, similarly, is killed not by a stake but by a knife that is plunged into the throat and through the heart. James Twitchell's analysis of the 'artist as vampire' is illuminating here. 'For just as the vampire enervates his victims, so too does representational art, art that attempts literally to "hold a mirror up to nature", drain metaphorical energy or attention from the artistic experience.'[47] The notion of vampiric painting is a response to

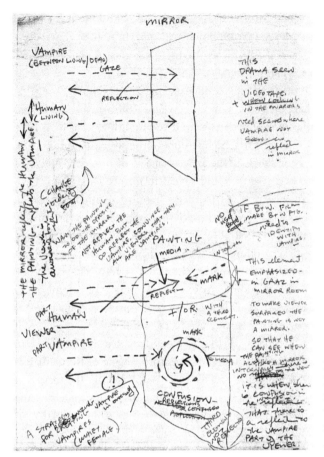

Figure 4.4. David Reed's notebooks on reflection: an homage to Bram Stoker's research notes for *Dracula*

the precarious future of painting following the birth of photography and foreshadowing the development of film.[48] The image of the artist as vampire can be used in relation to David Reed's practice, for, as Stephen Berg says, all painting is essentially 'reliant on an act of vampirism – vampirism towards reality, or as in Reed's case, towards what we are accustomed to calling its image, that is toward, itself'.[49]

David Reed was born in San Diego, California, in 1946. He has been a resident of New York since the 1970s. A practising artist for over forty years, Reed has developed an *oeuvre* that, with all its concentration on forms of painting, also maintains relationships to other, more recent image media, especially to film and video art.[50] In a reversal of the perspectives of abstract expressionism (whose subjective pathos refers back to the artist), his paintings directly address the effect on the viewer. In short, he invites us to explore the 'non-reflective' nature of abstract painting: 'It is conceivable that Reed's

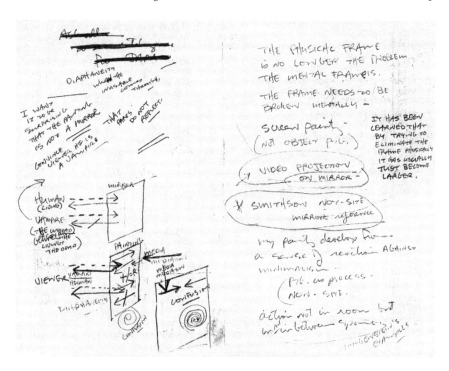

pictures [like the vampire] themselves have no looking-glass images and can only come into your life if invited'.[51]

Such an invitation came to me, via the artist John Rimmer.[52] John sent me some images of Reed's paintings and introduced me to the artist's 'vampire journal'.[53] Reed exhibited 'New Paintings for the Mirror Room and Archive in a Studio off the Courtyard' at the Neue Galerie in Graz in 1996. It contained a 'mirror room for vampires'. 'Painting: Motion Pictures' at the Museum of Contemporary Art in San Diego followed in 1998, and the 'Painting/Vampire Study Center' at the Goldie Paley Gallery at Moore College of Art and Design, Philadelphia, was developed in 1999. I wrote to Reed, explaining the *Open Graves, Open Minds* project and my research into non-reflection. He responded by sending me a supplement to his earlier works. This consisted of a series of notes, diagrams, reproductions and paintings, and contained excerpts from Bram Stoker's notes for *Dracula*, as well as stills from Tod Browning's 1931 film *Dracula*. When I examined the papers, I found the artist's notes and diagrams were a homage in the style of Bram Stoker's journal (see Figure 4.4). And I saw my own research questions writ large: 'Did Stoker ... invent the mirror non reflection motif? Are the notes from the Rosenbach Museum and Library evidence of this? Or, is there evidence that he came across the motif in his research of vampire legends?

I like to think that he did invent the motif. Then there is a specific insight from which all variations are derived.'[54] Reed was continuing the theme of vampire paintings which began for him in Graz. Thinking back to the installations for the mirror room for vampires, he asks, 'Is our experience of looking at an abstract painting like the vampire's experience when looking in a mirror? Does looking at an abstract painting allow us to see the vampire in ourselves?'[55] The *Dracula* notebooks marked a particular historical moment when vampirism in literature responded to mechanical reproduction and the new media of photography and film. In an attempt to find out how these ideas resonate in contemporary painting, I examined Reed's journal:

> May 20th: [T]he painter Dona Nelson ... spoke about how abstract painting reflects not the actual appearance of our body but a distorted body, a body closer to the way we actually experience it. We are not simply the body form we see reflected in the mirror but a strange amalgam of our actual experience and distortions. Many of these distortions are caused by our experiences of photography, film and video. These mediated distortions of our body mean that like the vampire we are both alive and dead. We are each part machine. Like the vampire's stare our gaze can be as mechanical as the view through the lens of a camera.

Reed's thoughts turn from abstract painting to vampirism and technology and back again before focusing on the non-reflection scene in Browning's *Dracula*. In the film, Dracula is detected because he casts no reflection in Van Helsing's cigarette case. Reed re-imagines this as a laptop computer:

> July 8th: [T]he cigarette case ... looks like a laptop computer in Tod Browning's film, which was made in 1931, many years before there were any laptop computers [see Figure 4.5]. When Dracula knocks down the reflecting cigarette case (for fear of his non reflection becoming apparent in it) it is as if he is trying to destroy future technology. One could make a chart: more anxiety about technological changes, more vampires.[56]

Some insightful theorising around the vampire's reflection from the perspective of a painter develops from this:

> August 20th: Several years ago Frank Owen, a painter friend of mine spoke of a theory he developed about the vampire's reflection. He said that a reflection in a mirror is half the size of what is reflected. Perhaps a vampire reflects back a reflection. So the reflection is reflected back and forth an infinite number of times becoming infinitely small. Perhaps that is what Count Dracula sees when he looks into the cigarette case ... Or perhaps for a vampire the image is doubled instead. Then the vampire sees his image reflected back and forth

Figure 4.5. Dracula is detected because he casts no reflection in Van Helsing's cigarette case (reimagined as a laptop computer in David Reed)

doubling in size until it is infinitely large. Perhaps that sight is what scares the vampire. That seems to be what the media is doing to us.[57]

Inspired by Reed's discussion of reflection and non-reflection, I gave some consideration to his question, 'what does Dracula see?' Given the folklorist accounts of mirrors as soul traps, it is not inconceivable that Dracula does see something, or, like Dorian Gray, is confronted with his own blackened soul trapped there. Hence his violent reaction; he knocks the mirror to the floor. Kim Newman addresses this very idea of what the vampire sees in *Anno Dracula* (1992); his character Lord Ruthven claims that 'it is untrue that vampires lack a reflection. It is just that the reflection invariably does not *reflect*, as it were, what is out here in the world.'[58] The problem of photographing vampires is also given some creative consideration through Newman's Lord Godalming: 'some disappeared completely while others saw an apparently empty suit of clothes'; this is explained at the expense of modern technology as 'only a painter can capture the inner man ... human genius shall always be superior to mechanical-chemical trickery'.[59] Newman's vampire can be painted, whereas Dracula shows no likeness in any media.

I decided to expand my research to include painting in relation to vampirism in a number of texts. Van Helsing's 'he make in the mirror no reflect' is a useful metaphor for Reed's relationship to his own paintings (and

Figure 4.6.   David Reed, 'Installation of Mirror Room. On-screen scene from
The Brides of Dracula, Terence Fisher, 1960

possibly to the viewer of them). John Rimmer tells me that 'like the helluloid [*sic*], there are no shadows in abstract painting; if there are, the work is moving towards verisimilitude, which is where Reed hovers, maybe'.[60] Reed's painting practices are as elusive as the vampire, despite our exchanges and the explanations in his journals.[61] Here, Reed responds playfully to the vampire through gesture, because the vampire 'has no presence, his body is defined by motifs and constructed through devices'; he is, in short, 'Van Helsing's bag of tricks bought to life'.[62] In the installation of the 'Mirror Room for Vampires', a number of Reed's vampire paintings are displayed on mirrors and there is a video screen playing a compilation of scenes involving reflection from thirty-five vampire films (see Figure 4.6).

In the Goldie Paley Gallery,

> [w]hile thinking about his installation for the museum's spectacular mirror room, Reed was struck by the way that light was refracted through the prisms of its twenty crystal chandeliers 'Light was everywhere – spectral light, flashing on and off; always changing, depending on where you were standing in the room'. He also noted that sometimes he could see his reflection in the room's

elaborate Baroque mirrors, but sometimes he could not. He remembered as a
child, seeing a film about a vampire that was detected because its image was
not reflected in a mirror. There, in Graz (home to several famous vampires)
surrounded by spectral light and his own reflection and non reflection, David
Reed discovered a new line of inquiry – Vampire Painting.[63]

The notion of 'vampire painting' is not new; as my discussion of Wilde and
Pater has shown, in fact, it predates Stoker. In the preface to *Dorian Gray*,
Wilde argues that 'it is the spectator and not life that art really mirrors';
this is complicated by abstract painting.[64] Without a likeness reflected in a
painting, does the onlooker become in some way a vampire? Or, as Reed puts
it, 'is looking at an abstract painting similar to a vampire not reflecting in a
mirror?'[65] Reed's paintings are both veil and mirror, elongated like celluloid
they are revived and animated by the 'vampire's kiss' of photography. Reed's
'Vampire Study Center' is a fitting homage to *Dracula*, developed as it is
from the phenomenon of non-reflection and its metaphorical resonances for
abstract painting. In the conclusion to the notes Reed sent me, I discover the
following epigram:

> The death of painting has been announced for at least a hundred years. David
> Reed makes vampire paintings to extend the limits of the medium and to
> ensure that painting, like the creature itself, will endure until the end of
> time.[66]

Reed's work shows non-reflection in painting in the present where it is in
dialogue with other visual media such as photography, video and film.

In the twentieth century, the figure of the non-reflecting vampire was to be
transformed and reanimated by its appropriation in film. Stacey Abbott recalls
that in 1896 Maxim Gorky described the effect of the newly invented cinematograph itself as 'entering the Kingdom of Shadows'.[67] German expressionist
filmmakers used the shadow metaphorically to give added, often uncanny
meaning to the nature of projection; the vampire's shadow was restored via
these techniques.[68] Many of the unsettling effects in early vampire film (for
example, Murnau's *Nosferatu* (1922) and Dreyer's *Vampyr* (1932)) come from
making play with the fiend's menacing shadow (despite Dracula's lack of one).
Kim Newman implies that the 'old not-visible-in-a-mirror trick' is perhaps an
outmoded conceit, following the development of film:

> It used to be among the most commonplace of undead traits – like drinking
> blood [or] sleeping in a coffin … even more arcane lore about not being able
> to cross a threshold unless invited is now (thanks to *Let the Right One In*) more
> common in film and fiction. If you're trying to fit vampires into something

resembling our universe – representing vampirism as a blood disease, a
lifestyle choice, a sexual kink or a parasitic species mimicking humanity –
then the mirror thing is embarrassing magic.[69]

The mirror motif is 'hard to square with practicalities, especially if extended
to photography in all its forms,' Newman continues, 'so Anne Rice's vampires
can be seen in a looking-glass, and that runs into many recent vampire
franchises'.[70] Kimberley McMahon-Coleman observes too that 'televisual
vampires post-*Buffy* are often reflected in mirrors and can be photographed
… reflecting the trends of domestification and normalisation'.[71] Vampires
in *Buffy* and *Angel* don't cast reflections but they can be photographed and
recorded on video.[72]

Despite the 'domestification' of the contemporary vampire figure, *I*
see the non-reflection trope being continually reborn. Rice spectacularly
debunked such lore in *Interview with the Vampire* (1976), but Stephenie Meyer
has reimagined it in the Twilight saga.[73] In *New Moon* (2006), Bella has a dream
in which she thinks she is meeting her long-dead grandmother.[74] Then, behind
her, she sees the beautiful Edward. Only then does she realise 'There was no
Gran. That was *me*. Me in the mirror. Me – ancient, creased and withered.
Edward stood behind me, casting no reflection, excruciatingly lovely and
forever seventeen'.[75] In this female-centred narrative, Edward is the one
'casting no reflection'; he will neither age nor experience the overbearing
strangeness that Walter Benjamin identifies as 'the estrangement felt before
one's own image in the mirror', a strangeness akin to that felt by an actor
'before the camera'.[76] The mechanical portraiture of film makes of the actor's
soul a transferrable commodity; Edward's non-reflection may liberate him
from this market. A vampire Adonis who remains 'Forever seventeen', he
is perhaps more Dorian Gray than Dracula, though he has not paid Dorian's
price.[77]

Wilde's themes around mirroring, reproduction, reflection and a lack of
soul find their way into the supernatural machinery of *Dracula*, in the motif
of the soulless vampire not reflecting in a mirror. Mirrors are undoubtedly
connected to the soul in Wilde, and Dorian reacts violently to them at
times in the novel, foreshadowing Dracula: 'flinging the mirror on the floor
[he] crushed it into silver splinters beneath his heel' (185). It does not seem
far-fetched to see Dorian, who shares the protagonist of the yellow book's
'grotesque dread of mirrors' (108), as influential on Stoker's representation
of Dracula.

Following Auerbach's assumption that 'Dracula has no voice' and that
his story is entirely constructed by others, we might assume that as the

vampire gains a voice it also gains a reflection.[78] This is only partially true; the non-reflection motif is still a prominent and enigmatic device. I have departed from current debates around the subjectivity and humanisation of the vampire, tracing the elusive origins of the non-reflection motif in the references to contemporaneous technology in Stoker's *Dracula* notebooks. I have argued that *Dracula* and *Dorian Gray* mark a unique historical moment when vampirism in literature surfaces in response to mechanical reproduction and the new media of photography and film. Superstitions around vampires and myths about the shadowy origins of art converge in the vampiric portrait of *Dorian Gray*. The anxieties that occur around realism and mimesis in this text, following the birth of photography, show vampirism to be firmly bound to notions of reflection in art and fears over new technologies. Painting's relationship to new media in the present has again been illustrated through vampirism in an analysis of David Reed's 'vampire painting'. And there's a *'Twilight* connection': rather than killing painting, the 'vampire's kiss of photography' has made it the 'immortal beloved'.[79] Reed has allowed us to come full circle, gesturing back to the *Dracula* notebooks that were our starting point, and where the origins of the myth were first uncovered, whilst exploring non-reflection in abstract painting and video art. I began at the outset of the project with the thought that the vampire not reflecting in a mirror may have fallen out of favour. But the vampire still refuses to show a likeness of its own; yet, holding a glass up to ourselves, it perpetually mirrors modern culture.

Notes

1 Stoker, *Dracula*, ed. Luckhurst, p. 223, p. 26. All further references are to this edition and in parentheses.

2 Barber, *Vampires*, p. 188.

3 Gerard, *The Land Beyond the Forest* (1888), II, p. 18. Shadow trading also features in Adelbert von Chamisso's story *Peter Schlemihls wundersame Geschichte* (*Peter Schlemihl's Miraculous Story*) (1814). The story was widely circulated in English when it was illustrated by George Cruikshank (1827).

4 '"Shadow", ME. b. Applied rhet. to a portrait as contrasted with the original –1679. c. an obscure indication; a symbol, type; a prefiguration, foreshadowing. late ME. d. Something of opposite character that necessarily accompanies or follows something else, as shadow does light 1830. e. An imitation, copy; a counterpart 1693. ... 4. A spectral form, phantom'. late ME' (*Shorter OED*).

5 '[T]he origin of painting ... began with tracing an outline around a man's shadow ... pictures were originally done in this way' (Pliny, *Natural History*, Book XXXV, p. 15, cited in Stoichita, *A Short History*, p. 11).

6 '[T]he author of *Essays on Physiognomy* makes an important conceptual leap. In fact,
   according to him, it is not – as was accepted by tradition – the human face that is the
   reflection of the soul, but the shadow of this face', Stoichita, *A Short History*, p. 157.
   Lavatar's *Essays on Physiognomy* (Leipzig and Winterthur, 1776) was translated into
   English and published in London in 1792. Stoker owned an edition of it (see 'Bram
   Stoker's Library' in *Bram Stoker's Notes*, p. 313).

7 David Glover claims that Stoker's novel is 'beset by the difficulties that haunted
   physiognomy, the fear that things are not always what they seem … the Count
   himself often seems to occupy a space that is virtually beyond representation, an
   unmirrorable image, a force able to assume a multiplicity of forms, physiognomy's
   true vanishing point' (*Vampires*, p. 74).

8 Bram Stoker's handwritten research notes for *Dracula* (1890–1897) are housed in the
   Rosenbach Museum and Library in Philadelphia. The museum acquired them only
   in 1970. They were originally sold at Sotheby's by Stoker's widow Florence in 1913.
   Sir Christopher Frayling was the first scholar to have access to the newly recovered
   notes; he used them to research his seminal work *Vampyres* (1978). The notes were
   eventually transcribed and edited by Robert Eighteen-Bisang and Elizabeth Miller
   and published in facsimile in 2008.

9 As in the subtitle of Senf's 'Dracula' article.

10 I am thinking in particular of Ken Gelder's application of the 'uncanny' to the theme
   of doubling in 'Carmilla' in his seminal study *Reading the Vampire*, pp. 42–64; see
   also Martin, 'The Vampire in the Looking Glass'. Andrew Butler's current work
   in *Solar Flares* draws on Otto Rank's three types of double in relation to vampires.
   Senf's 'Dracula: The Unseen Face in the Mirror' is more broadly psychoanalytic in
   its approach.

11 Both sources are in *Bram Stoker's Notes for Dracula*. This comprehensive work
   reproduces the handwritten notes both in facsimile and in annotated transcription.

12 There is a huge amount of confusion in popular culture about the origins of this. See,
   for example, 'Why Does Silver Kill Werewolves?'; and 'Silver Bullet', in Wikipedia.

13 Baring-Gould, *Werewolves*, p. 87. Stoker's use of this book is well known; see, for
   example, 'Bram Stoker's Nonfiction Sources for *Dracula*', in *Bram Stoker's Notes*, p. 4;
   and Luckhurst's introduction to Stoker, *Dracula*, p. xvii. Elsewhere, Paul Barber
   asserts that 'among the Slavs, the werewolf typically turns into a vampire after its
   death' (*Vampires*, p. 96), and Alan Dundes claims that 'in Yugoslavia the vampire has
   merged with the werewolf (usually called '*vukodlak*', and only occasionally '*vampir*')'
   (*The Vampire*, p. 51).

14 As Dundes says, 'The vampire is "dead" and soulless it has no reflection' (*The Vampire*,
   p. 145). Erik Butler is in agreement: 'a missing reflection is functionally identical to
   a missing shadow – that is, a missing soul' (*Metamorphoses*, p. 56).

15 Barber, *Vampires*, p. 182.

16 Notably in Northern Eurasian cultures, according to Barber (*Vampires*, p. 188).
   It seems that reflecting water can also act as a convenient soul receptacle (there
   is the belief that spirits cannot cross water). Dracula can cross water only at the

slack or flood of the tide (a motif that is frequently taken up in the Hammer
Horror Christopher Lee films). See Hutchings, *Dracula*, for discussions of Dracula's
attributes in such films (pp. 34–42).

17 There is an obvious connection between the two phenomena as the *Shorter OED*
illustrates: '"Shadow" II. 2. A reflected image ME'.

18 For Planché, see McFarland, 'The Vampire on Stage', pp. 29–32.

19 For the influence of this on vampire cinema, see Stacey Abbott's Chapter 6 below.

20 Stage effects, including those of the phantasmagoria, are discussed more broadly
in Roxana Stuart, *Stage Blood*. Auerbach describes the function of the vampire
trap thus: 'Depending on its placement, the vampire trap allowed the actor to be
alternately body and spirit; the trap in the floor catapulted him back and forth,
between hell and heaven, while the trap in the flats endowed him with the semblance
of immateriality as he moved in and out of walls' (*Our Vampires*, pp. 6–7). For Stoker
and the theatre more generally, see Wynne, *Bram Stoker and the Stage*.

21 Stoker, *Bram Stoker's Notes*, pp. 3, 4.

22 'History of Kodak', Kodak website. See also Teukolsky, 'Picture Language' and
Walter Benjamin, 'A Small History of Photography'.

23 Wicke, 'Vampiric Typewriting'. For compelling discussions around 'unsettlement',
contemporary technology and vampirism, see Ivan Phillips, Chapter 14 below.

24 Benjamin, 'The Work of Art', p. 225.

25 *Ibid.*, p. 223.

26 *Ibid.*, p. 223.

27 Wicke, 'Vampiric Typewriting', p. 472.

28 Krauss, 'Reinventing the Medium', p. 295.

29 Assmus, 'The Early History of X-rays'. 'Frau Röntgen was taken aback and somewhat
frightened by the first x-ray plate of a human subject which enabled her to see her
own skeleton. The feeling … was [of a] vague premonition or death': Calarco, 'An
Historical Overview'.

30 Cited in Barber, *Vampires*, p. 180.

31 The *Leipziger Stadtanzeiger*, cited in Benjamin, 'A Small History', p. 241.

32 This denial of our kinship with the soulless or animal 'other' (through the figure of
the vampire) may reveal Stoker's response to Darwinism. The unsettling Darwinian
idea that species are not fixed and are fluid is dramatised in Dracula's metamorphosis into lower animals (bats, dogs etc.) in the novel. One of the vampire's
most vulnerable victims is Renfield, a weak-minded maniac whose bizarre mental
condition, 'Zoophagia', means he has a compulsion to devour ever more evolved
animals – the fly, then the spider that catches the fly, then the bird that catches the
spider. This apt Darwinian metaphor is developed by Stoker in the novel.

33 Benjamin, 'The Work of Art', p. 223.

34 *Ibid.*, p. 223.

35 See Sweeney, '*Dracula* Creator Bram Stoker'.

36 Stoker, *Bram Stoker's Notes*, p. 4.

37 Pater, 'Leonardo Da Vinci', in *The Renaissance*, p. 80.

38 Wilde, 'The Critic as Artist', Part 1, pp. 213–43 (pp. 238–9).

39 For doubling in *Dorian Gray*, see Craft, 'Come See about Me'. For the relationship between *Dracula* and Wilde's novel, see Schaffer, '"A Wilde Desire Took Me"'.

40 Wilde, *The Picture of Dorian Gray*, ed. Bristow, pp. 6, 8. All further references are to this edition and in parentheses. Kim Newman has a character called 'Basil Hallward' exhibit with Whistler and Sickert in his novel; a wonderful conceit (see *Anno Dracula*, p. 158).

41 The significance of the yellow book should be noted here. *Dorian Gray* features a French novel (most probably Huysmans's *A Rebours* (1884)) with a yellow cover to which its hero is attracted; the literary magazine of Beardsley was called *The Yellow Book*; Oscar Wilde is carried off to prison holding a book with a yellow wrapper; Constable issued *Dracula* in a bright yellow cover in May 1897.

42 'The vampire is the nameless counterpart of Narcissus' (Weibel, 'Phantom Painting', p. 56).

43 Wilde, 'The Decay of Lying', in *The Soul of Man Under Socialism*, pp. 163–93 (p. 178).

44 Preface, *Dorian Gray*, p. 3

45 Wilde cites 'Hegel's system of contraries' in 'The Truth of Masks', p. 304. Linda Dowling confirms that 'Wilde became familiar with Hegelian philosophy at Oxford, where a powerful school of English expositors of Hegel established itself by the 1870s' (*The Soul of Man*, n. 78, p. 377). For further reading, see Smith, 'Protoplasmic Hierarchy'.

46 Themes of creativity and painting continue in Viereck's 1907 novel *The House of the Vampire*. Here Wilde himself is recast as an undead vampire figure and art has become the province of a master race of vampires (see Lisa Lampert-Weissig's Chapter 5 below). Other supernatural tales with themes of vampiric portraiture include Poe's 'The Oval Portrait' (1842) and Hume Nisbet's 'The Old Portrait' (1900). Christopher Frayling notes that the vampire as 'metaphor for the creative process' makes 'an occasional appearance' in nineteenth-century fiction (*Vampires*, p. 62).

47 James Twitchell includes *Dorian Gray* in a study of 'The Artist as Vampire', in *The Living Dead*, pp. 142–91.

48 Interestingly, Wilde has Basil Hallward state 'there are only two eras of any importance in the world's history. The first is the appearance of a new medium for art, and the second is the appearance of a new personality for art' (*Dorian Gray*, p. 12).

49 Berg, 'Technicolor Vampires', p. 68.

50 Sixty works by the artist have recently been exhibited at Kunst Museum in Bonn in a show entitled 'Heart of Glass' (June to October 2012).

51 Reed in correspondence, 8 May 2011. Critical material on Reed in relation to vampirism has included, but is not limited to, the following: Madore, 'Sixty Fractions of Wegohn', Weibel, 'Phantom Painting', Loreck, 'Some Reflections on David Reed's Paintings', all in Reed, *New Paintings*, pp. 4–11, pp. 49–55, pp. 56–62; Berg, 'Technicolor Vampires', in Reed, *You Look Good in Blue*, pp. 58–68.

52 'John Rimmer is an artist who trained as a painter and is currently working on a project employing digital technologies "as painting", co-opting the visual language of painting into digital video making. John's research ... developed out of his training in philosophy and fine art ... he has exhibited both nationally and internationally and recently curated *Digitalis*, a touring exhibition that was hosted in Transylvania' (John Rimmer in correspondence, 20 March 2012).

53 The 'Vampire Journal' records Reed's thoughts as he embarks on a journey through vampire film and listens to a recording of Stoker's novel *Dracula*. It is reproduced in full in David Reed, *New Paintings*, pp. 12–23.

54 Reed, notes from the artist's journal, 6 July 1999, 'Painting/Vampire'.

55 Reed, 'Painting/Vampire', 12 April 1999.

56 The cigarette case image is shown on a laptop computer photographed alongside the film stills in the notes.

57 Reed, 'Painting/Vampire'; select entries in the artist's journal for the year 1999.

58 Newman, *Anno Dracula*, p. 158. In Newman's alternative history, historical and fictional characters (such as Ruthven) mix freely.

59 *Ibid.*, p. 158. 'In the TV series *Ultraviolet*, vampires don't show up in any mechanical media – they can't use telephones, for instance. In the *Anno Dracula* piece I'm writing at the moment, I'm exploring the difficulty of photographing vampires as a minor theme', Kim Newman in correspondence, May 2012.

60 John Rimmer in correspondence, May 2011.

61 'I have mixed colors for the horizontal bands that will be under the brush marks of the paintings for the mirror room. The color sequence from top to bottom is: rose/ paler red/white/pale green/blue. These colors will be barely visible when the brush marks are cut out and surrounded by white. They cause a subliminal suffusion, like the sparkling prismatic flash of the chandeliers' (Reed, *New Paintings*, p. 13).

62 Reed, *Vampire Journal*, p. 16.

63 Longhauser, Foreword, Reed, 'Painting/Vampire', p. 1.

64 Preface, *Dorian Gray*, p. 3.

65 From the title-page to Reed, 'Painting/Vampire'.

66 Longhauser, Foreword, Reed, 'Painting/Vampire', p. 2.

67 See Stacey Abbott's Chapter 6 below (p. 94). All the optical effects of cinema are already there in the novel despite the absence of the cinematograph itself.

68 See shadow and projection in Stoichita, *A Short History*, p. 148. Stacey Abbot's and Ivan Phillips's Chapters 6 and 14 below are similarly insightful on the use of shadow and projection in vampire film.

69 Newman, 'Why Don't Vampires Cast Reflections?'.

70 *Ibid.*

71 Kimberley McMahon-Coleman, pp. 221 (Chapter 13) below.

72 I am grateful to Stacey Abbott for clarifying this via correspondence.

73 See Rice, *Interview*, p. 27.

74 Meyer, *New Moon*, p. 3

75 *Ibid.*, p. 5

76 'The Work of Art', p. 232. Benjamin is referring to the experience of the actor transcending self here so it seems fitting to use it for *Twilight*, where Robert Pattinson has become the commodity 'Edward Cullen' through the medium of film.

77 David Skal draws some useful comparisons between Wilde and Stoker biographically and thematically in terms of their work in *Hollywood Gothic*, pp. 59–65; and Christopher Frayling comments on their Anglo-Irish connections, their friendship and shared intellectual and literary circles (*Vampyres*, pp. 65–6).

78 Auerbach, *Our Vampires*, p. 82.

79 'Thank you for reviving my thoughts about non reflection. I recently had an exhibition of my painting with the photographs of Wiliam Eggleston at Peder Lund in Oslo. I discovered that painting and photography look especially good together at the moment because both are freshly outmoded media – there's a *Twilight* connection. Rather than killing painting, the vampire's kiss of photography has made it the immortal beloved. I hope there are more shows combining photography and painting' (David Reed in correspondence, 8 May 2011).

5

The vampire as dark and glorious necessity in George Sylvester Viereck's *House of the Vampire* and Hanns Heinz Ewers's *Vampir*

Lisa Lampert-Weissig

Evil has its right to live, just like everything else – only the petty are hateful/ ugly.[1]

Vampires embody paradox: they are simultaneously living and dead, attractive and repulsive, immortal yet still vulnerable. It is perhaps fitting, then, that the figure of the vampire can help us to understand the intertwined stories of two equally paradoxical humans, George Sylvester Viereck (1884–1962) and Hanns Heinz Ewers (1871–1943). Each openly supported the National-Socialist regime in Germany while simultaneously maintaining that he was 'philo-Semitic'. How can one be a 'pro-Jewish' Nazi? The cognitive dissonance required to maintain such self-deception could be seen as the psychological equivalent of the liminal vampire state. I want to suggest that the portrayals of vampires by Viereck and Ewers provide some insight into how they could support Hitler's brutal regime.

Ewers, a German, and Viereck, a German-born US citizen, came to know one another in New York while working together for the German cause prior to the American entry into the First World War. The two prolific and prominent men of letters had much else in common. Both styled themselves as literary provocateurs whose works included explorations of sexuality and 'perversity', features included in the vampire novels each penned, Viereck's 1907 *House of the Vampire* and Ewers's 1920 *Vampir: ein verwilderter Roman in Fetzen und Farben* (*Vampire: An Overgrown Novel in Scraps and Colours*). Viereck and Ewers were also both admirers of Swinburne, Wilde and Poe. The Satanist Alesteir Crowley and the sexologist Magnus Hirschfeld were among their shared associates.

My approach to the vampires of Viereck and Ewers follows the work of critics such as Nina Auerbach, Erik Butler, Jeffrey Jerome Cohen and Ken Gelder in examining the vampire as a culturally specific representation that embodies the political and historical contexts in which it is created.[2] Viereck and Ewers create vampires whose superiority to those around them justifies the 'collateral damage' they cause in the name of higher principles of genius and nation.[3] In *House of the Vampire*, Viereck's charismatic vampire, Reginald Clarke, sucks the creativity and even the sanity from his victims, but this parasitism allows him to create powerful and immortal works of genius. Ewers's *Vampir* portrays vampirism as serving the cause of German nationalism: Frank Braun's blood drinking propels him to oratorical heights for his country. Those from whom Braun draws blood become necessary sacrifices to a great nation, whether they wish to sacrifice themselves or not. Viereck's and Ewers's portrayals of the necessity of doing evil in the cause of something beyond good and evil provide, I believe, some clues as to how these 'philo-Semitic' writers could support Hitler despite awareness of the brutal anti-Semitism of National Socialism.[4]

House of the Vampire

Like Elizabeth Braddon's 'Good Lady Ducayne' (1896) or Harriet in Florence Marryat's 1897 *The Blood of the Vampire*, Reginald Clarke saps his victims' energy rather than their blood. Clarke draws talented male and female artists into erotically charged relationships and then slowly drains his protégés' creative essences in order to create brilliant works of art that he claims as his own. After the gifted young writer Ernest Fielding moves into Clarke's house, Clarke slowly robs the young artist first of his ideas and then of his sanity. Fielding finally exits Clarke's doors as 'a dull and brutish thing, hideously transformed, without a vestige of mind' (189).

As the novel progresses Ernest gradually becomes aware of his impending ruin. Through a relationship with one of Clarke's former lover-victims, the painter Ethel Brandenbourg, Ernest learns Clarke's true nature. As the two contemplate their mutual fates, Ethel describes to Ernest the traditional myth of the blood-sucking vampire: 'They are beings, not always wholly evil, whom every night some mysterious impulse leads to steal into unguarded bedchambers, to suck the blood of the sleepers and then, having waxed strong on the life of their victims, cautiously to retreat' (144). Ernest cannot believe that such beings can exist in modern times. He points out to Ethel that vampires prey on the body rather than the soul, asking '"How can a man suck from another man's brain a thing as intangible, as quintessential as thought?"' She replies: "'you forget, thought is more real than blood"' (147–8).

When Ethel asserts that 'thought is more real than blood', she advances the novel's portrayal of creative genius as a kind of natural force. Clarke sees himself as a 'chameleon' that absorbs 'the special virtues of other people' (112). Ethel imagines him as a 'sea-monster … whose thousand tentacles encircled her form' (103). He is like a 'snake' (109), a 'carnivorous flower' (126) and 'charged with the might of ten thousand magnetic storms that shake the earth in its orbit and lash myriads of planets through infinities of space' (184). He is also 'the reverse of radium, with unlimited absorptive capacities', a quality Edith directly equates to Clarke's ability to drain creativity from others (117). By depicting Clarke as a force of Nature, Viereck relieves his character of much responsibility for his actions; Clarke operates in a natural realm beyond human morality.

Perhaps more significantly, Viereck's vampire does not only evil but also good. He does not simply absorb what he takes from his prey; he makes this energy and talent into something truly transcendent. He is driven to do so like '[t]he high-priest of some terrible and mysterious religion, demanding a human sacrifice to appease the hunger of his god' (114). His absorptive genius makes Clarke part of a pantheon of great men. As Ernest Fielding stands in Clarke's study, he is struck by a 'curious family resemblance' between Clarke and the busts of Shakespeare, Balzac and Napoleon that adorn the space. All exhibit 'the indisputable something' that marks those who are chosen to give ultimate expression to some gigantic world-purpose … They seemed to him monsters that know neither justice nor pity, only the law of their being, the law of growth' (162). While *House of the Vampire* vividly portrays the turmoil and suffering that Clarke inflicts on Ernest, Ethel and others, it simultaneously emphasises Clarke's greatness. The works Clarke creates elevate his vampirism into the necessary mechanism of genius.

For his part, Clarke sees himself not as a vampire or a thief but as a vessel for a greatness that flows through him. He lectures Ethel about 'giants who attain greatness' (117) and when accused by Fielding of stealing others' art Clarke responds: 'You err. Self-love has never entered into my actions. I am careless of personal fame. Look at me, boy! As I stand before you I am Homer, I am Shakespeare … I am every cosmic manifestation in art. … I have a mission. I am a servant of the Lord. I am the vessel that bears the Host!' (183). Clarke makes his lovers into unwilling acolytes of the cult of genius, an initiation for which he believes that they should be grateful: 'It is through me that the best in you shall survive, even as the obscure Elizabethans live in him of Avon. Shakespeare absorbed what was great in little men – a greatness

that otherwise would have perished – and gave it a setting, a life' (183). Clarke
sees his cultural vampirism as a gift of immortality to his victims and believes
that they understand on some level the larger enterprise of which they have
become a part: 'The very souls that I tread underfoot realize, as their dying
gaze follows me, the possibilities with which the future is big ... Eternally
secure, I carry the essence of what is cosmic ... of what is divine' (185).

Clarke is Viereck's vampiric version of Nietzsche's *Übermensch*.[5] Creating
a version of the *Übermensch* that likely would have been unrecognisable
to Nietzsche, Viereck portrays Clarke as a figure whose ability to achieve
greatness can justify the sacrifice of lesser beings in the name of a higher
cause. Viereck expressed his theories about genius not only in *House of the
Vampire* but also in essays, arguing that genius is 'primarily a collective
function'.[6] 'The mind of the man of genius', he argues, 'differs from others
by its extraordinary developed power of absorption'.[7] Viereck saw this kind
of genius as specifically vampiric:

> The vampire mind appears in all branches of life. Rockefeller possesses the
> genius of absorbing gold even as Napoleon possessed the genius of absorbing
> power. The founders of the great world-religions have never been what is
> commonly known as original thinkers. Messiahs have come and gone and the
> same message has been reiterated again and again in the flights of the eons.[8]

Viereck's novel, inspired by Oscar Wilde's tale of decadence and creative
destruction, *The Picture of Dorian Gray*, centres on art and aesthetics. This
artistic focus reflects the early part of Viereck's career as a writer; he had
been hailed as a *Wunderkind* in both the US and Germany with the 1906
publication of his first book of poems, *Nineveh*. But, as his references to
Rockefeller and Napoleon show, Viereck's conception of genius extends far
beyond the artistic realm, reflecting his later sense that he lived in 'a political,
not a literary age'.[9] Viereck later came to see Hitler as a genius of this age.

Viereck's 1930 *Glimpses of the Great* collects interviews he conducted with a
range of prominent figures, including Bernard Shaw, Sigmund Freud, Henry
Ford, Benito Mussolini and Albert Einstein. In the collection's introduction,
entitled 'To What Tune Danceth The Immense?', Viereck describes himself
as a 'Lion-Hunter', a bold collector of the greatest specimens of his age (p. 1).
Notably absent from the book, however, is Viereck's 1923 interview with Adolf
Hitler.[10] As numerous of his writings attest, Viereck was clearly 'dazzled'
by Hitler and saw him as a messiah for Germany after its crushing defeat in
the Great War.[11] Viereck had long been a prominent pro-German activist,
following in his father's footsteps by editing the journal *Fatherland*, which had
65,000 subscribers in 1914. Viereck worked tirelessly to rally support for the

Germans in the lead-up to the USA's entry into the First World War.[12] These wartime activities greatly damaged his reputation and nearly ruined him financially.[13] Viereck's subsequent work for the National Socialists can be in part attributed to financial causes, but his motivations were also ideological.[14] He saw the rise of National Socialism as a movement essential for restoring the German nation after the calamitous end of the Great War.

When criticised for his vigorous support of Hitler's regime, Viereck responded that 'I did not, then, and do not, now, conceal my admiration for the epoch-making genius of Adolf Hitler', whom Viereck credited with 'astonishing achievements'.[15] In an article entitled 'Hitler or Chaos', Viereck writes that the National Socialist's 'methods are, at times, a trifle rough. But who can make a revolution with bon-bons? With bon-bons you cannot even win a woman.'[16] He concludes by asserting that 'even his foes realize that there is no choice for Central Europe save Hitler or Chaos'.[17] Viereck's portrayal of the vampire Reginald Clarke and his defence of Hitler are strikingly similar: Clarke reduces Ernest Fielding to a 'gibbering idiot', but in doing so he creates magnificent art (*House* 190). Similarly, Hitler's methods are a 'trifle rough', but they create a 'New Germany' from the ashes of the First World War.[18]

In a private letter of 1939, Viereck bemoans the fact that Germany has lost its colonies and argues in favour of Hitler's leadership: '[i]t is not a question of ethics; a great nation must live ... Hitler, whether he wills it or not, is the heir of the Hapsburgs as well as of the Hohenzollern. He out-Napoleons Napoleon, but he does so without shedding a drop of blood.'[19] Viereck's linkage of Hitler to Napoleon is reminiscent of the pantheon of genius adorning Reginald Clarke's study. Viereck portrays both as men of genius who, almost in spite of themselves, must inflict some damage the service of a great cause. The idea that some causes can transcend the 'question of ethics' also echoes the novel's defence of Clarke and his pursuit of genius.

Viereck was well aware, though, of the anti-Semitism of Hitler's regime and treated this topic in numerous writings, always from a defensive posture. As evidence that he is not an anti-Semite, Viereck references *My First Two Thousand Years*, a novel he co-wrote with Jewish author Paul Eldridge about the legendary Wandering Jew, proclaiming that 'I am not, nor ever will be, an anti-Semite'.[20] Viereck saw Nazi anti-Semitism as 'only one phase, to my mind, a regrettable one, of Germany's resurrection', again drawing on the idea of necessary damage for a greater good.[21] His evocation of German 'resurrection' recalls his quasi-mythical portrayal of Clarke's cult of genius and indeed, Viereck's political writings praise Hitler's 'new mystical conception of the state of which he is the spokesman'.[22]

Viereck continually maintained that he did not want a totalitarian regime in the United States, as demonstrated in his 1937 allegory of *The Temptation of Jonathan*, in which a typical American man is tempted by both Communism and Fascism, but ultimately chooses democracy. The tract's treatment of Germany features a schoolroom scene in which Jewish children 'sit listlessly'[23] in a corner, ostracised solely because of their race:

> 'What have these poor kids done?' Jonathan asked.
>   The stranger replied: 'They have Jewish parents.'
>   'Oh,' said Jonathan, but he did not understand. 'Where I come from we all played together and went to school together and nobody bothered much if we were Jews or Gentiles.'
>   'That,' the stranger replied icily, 'is race pollution'.[24]

Viereck did not always figure the Jews as hapless victims, however. Writing critically of international Jewish boycotts of Germany, he blamed these actions for inflaming German hatred.[25] Following the end of the war and his 1947 release from prison, he sometimes referred to what he called 'professional Jews', and 'internationalists', groups he maintained had destroyed his career.[26] (He was convicted as a Nazi agent in 1942 and was in prison from 1942 to 1947.)

Viereck once wrote of himself: 'I fought for what I deemed the right. / I saw the Truth. I was her knight.'[27] Viereck's contemporary, the writer Upton Sinclair, saw Viereck very differently. In an open letter in *The Nation*, Sinclair charged that Viereck must have, on some level, realised that he had killed his own literary legacy.[28] Sinclair sums up Viereck's hypocrisy:

> Somewhere in the deeps of your perverted soul hides a shy and sensitive poet – for you were a real poet, even though you chose to embrace 'the roses and raptures of vice.' That poet is sitting in contemplation of what you are and what you are doing, and shudders with horror at what you have become. That poet knows that if there is anybody in America who is doing Satan's work you are the man. (551)

Viereck's support of Hitler and National Socialism despite its evils forever shattered any aspirations he had to join the vampire Clarke's pantheon of great men. A biographer concludes that 'the record of his life's work betrays a pattern of self-diffusion and moral anarchy'.[29] Viereck's portrayal of Clarke provides some insight into how he might have been able to sustain a belief that, far from doing 'Satan's work', he was rather serving a noble cause, despite public and private criticism and ample contradictory evidence.

Vampir

Because he was a German national living in Germany, Ewers's support for
Hitler might not seem as challenging to understand as Viereck's. Given,
however, Ewers's frequent declarations of philo-Semitism and his controversial, provocative writings about sexuality and the occult, his embrace of
the National-Socialist regime and his belief that the Party would accept him
in return still seem surprising. Ewers was widely known in Germany for his
work in literature, film, cabaret and travel literature. *Vampir* is a *Zeitroman*
(period novel) of the First World War, loosely based upon Ewers's own
experiences. Frank Braun, a German who is in the United States as the First
World War breaks out, becomes an activist for the German cause. Viereck
appears to have been the inspiration for the character of Tewes, an editor
who directs Braun's activities. After being released from his US imprisonment
for wartime activities, Ewers returned to Germany and became increasingly
involved in politics. He renewed contact with the German-Jewish nationalist
Walther Rathenau, whose politics resonated with the idea of German-Jewish
union celebrated in *Vampir*. Rathenau's 1922 assassination led to Ewer's
move away from support of the Weimar Republic and increasingly toward
right-wing politics and eventually National Socialism.[30]

Ewers joined the Nazi Party in 1931, despite the reluctance of some Party
functionaries, and threw his talents into developing the myth of Nazi 'martyr'
Horst Wessel. However, as Party members delved into works like *Vampir* and
Fundvogel, a novel about a sex-change operation, most of Ewers's work was
banned and he was expelled from the Party despite his protestations. He died
in obscurity from illness in 1943. Like Viereck's, Ewers's legacy has been
permanently stained by his support for National Socialism.

Vampir is the last part of a trilogy that also includes *Der Zauberlehrling* (*The
Sorcerer's Apprentice*) (1910) and *Alraune* (1911), Ewers's best-known novel. In
Der Zauberlehrling, Braun conducts a 'will to power' experiment on a tiny
mountain village. He purposefully encourages the villagers to form a fanatic
religious cult that ends in the crucifixion of Braun's young lover, who is
carrying their unborn child. In *Alraune*, Braun and his uncle experiment,
again capriciously and wilfully, with artificial insemination. They impregnate
a prostitute with the sperm of a condemned criminal to create a beautiful but
deadly woman. Her lethal sexuality threatens even the formidable Braun, but
does not ultimately conquer him.

Throughout the trilogy, Braun flouts conventional morality, always seeing
himself as above the crowd and acting accordingly. As Ulrike Brandenburg has
asserted, Ewers believes that history can be shaped by the power of thought,

a perspective that echoes Viereck's view of the importance of the intellectual realm (36). Braun has always viewed himself as part of an elite group of talented and cultivated individuals, as a member of an elite 'Kulturnation' ('nation of culture') rather than as a patriotic German.[31] This 'Kulturnation', however, has never required anything of him. Braun's awakened patriotism at the end of *Vampir* parallels Ewers's own story. *Vampir* chronicles the change in Braun from one who serves only his own interests to one who harnesses his powers in the service of a greater calling, the future of Germany.

The novel begins with Frank Braun voyaging from South America on a ship ravaged by yellow fever. Braun finally makes entry into the United States just as Germany and England have declared war. Braun chooses not to travel home to Germany, believing this can only lead to death or imprisonment at British hands. He instead becomes an activist for the German cause in the US, speaking at rallies, travelling to Mexico to try to manipulate Francisco 'Pancho' Villa to German advantage, and also courting American debutante Ivy Jefferson in order to keep her fortune away from the British.

Throughout his adventures Braun suffers from a strange malady that often saps his strength. The illness remains incurable despite medical intervention and Braun's frequent recourse to drugs such as arsenic, opium and peyote. Braun experiences relief from his symptoms only through close human contact, especially with his German-Jewish mistress, Lotte Lewi. Mysteriously, Lotte's state of health always seems the inverse of Braun's: when he improves she exhibits weakness and pallor and vice versa. Braun suspects that Lotte is draining him of blood, but it turns out that just the reverse is true: Braun is the vampire. Lotte has been giving him blood, not only out of devotion to him but, more significantly, out of her devotion to the German cause. Other women involved with Braun, Ivy, a young dancer, and an opera diva, reject him once they discover that he drinks blood. Lotte, in contrast to all of the others, sees Braun as a hope for Germany and willingly sacrifices herself to keep him fit for the task of helping his country. She is ultimately responsible for transforming him from an individual adrift and irresponsible into a devoted supporter of the German cause.[32]

This transformation is at the centre of the novel. At the beginning of the novel, as his fellow Germans attempt to return to Germany to enlist, Frank Braun holds back. While those around him are willing to sacrifice themselves to the last drop of blood, Braun remains unmoved by feelings of patriotism.[33] He does not see himself as German and does not want to become a small gobbet of flesh in the giant body of the *Volk*.[34] To do so would be to join the herd, a move that would rob him of everything and 'would make him – like all the others – into a fleck of dust, into a pitiful, tiny scrap of flesh in the bleeding body of the *Volk*. Death was to him – what life was to the others.'[35] Braun sees himself as not simply different from others, but as opposed to them as life is to death. Others are willing to be part of the body of the people (*Volk*) and to shed blood for it. Braun cannot surrender to this fate, and, indeed, he will transcend it even as he works for the German cause. As a *völkischer* vampire he will literally take others' blood in order that he might serve the nation with his rousing words, giving speeches he experiences as coming from somewhere beyond himself.

Braun's transformation into a champion of his nation is the result not of his vampiric disease but of its management by Lotte Lewi. Lotte sees herself as absolutely bound to Germany and the German cause, despite the fact that she is an American citizen and despite her Jewish heritage. In fact (and this is surely part of what disturbed the Nazis about Ewers's writings) Lotte is devoted to Germany *because* she is Jewish. Lotte explains that she is a 'half-blood' (Halbblut) devoted to two *Völker*; her awakened sense of being German comes from the war (128). She invokes Disraeli as a great believer that the world belongs to her two peoples, 'both together, closely united, the Germanic and the Jewish'.[36] Two bloods flow through her veins, mixed together; she is German and Jew alike. Braun's vampirism causes him to consume the potent German-Jewish essence contained in Lotte's blood and it is this essence that allows him to reach oratorical heights for Germany.

In *Vampir*, identity is consistently expressed through the language of blood and through a blood mythology that links Germans and Jews.[37] Lotte asserts, 'Through my veins flow, well mixed together, both bloods. I am simultaneously German and Jew. And I, I found the prophecy of my people's mission for this time – long live my German, long my Jewish *Volk*!'[38] Lotte, who is extremely wealthy, possesses the original breastplate of Aaron, the story and meaning of which she has been studying diligently. She has determined that the original colours of the flag of the ancient Israelites are the same as that of the German flag – black, white and red. This is no coincidence, but a sign that informs her fervent belief that Germans and Jews have a shared destiny that justifies any sacrifice (133).

At the novel's end Lotte allows Braun to drain her of blood almost completely. Indeed, she orchestrates this dangerous move in order to cure Braun of his vampirism. She does this, she tells him, not only because she loves him but also because she believes firmly that he can be a saviour for the German cause. She has set up his work as a spokesman for Germany from the beginning (93). When Braun returns from prison he goes to her. She has been slowly recovering from loss of blood, but is still weak. Braun, in contrast, is fully recovered, his healthful appearance has returned despite his imprisonment. What's more, Lotte tells him, his appearance has changed in other ways; he seems more German: 'German! You took the path I led you – the path home [*Heimat*]. Took it – with me – for me. You became German: my blood flows in you.'[39] Lotte Lewi's German-Jewish blood has cured Braun of a disease that she believes not only he, but the entire world suffers from during the world war (605). Throughout the novel the war has been discussed in terms of blood, a metaphoric connection goes beyond the fact that combatants are willing to shed blood for their cause. The war itself is a '*Blutwahn*' (606), a coinage that could be translated as 'blood frenzy' and that implies a sense of the nightmarish, a blood mania void of reason, a nightmare of blood akin to Braun's own attacks of vampirism, which come upon him in a kind of dream state and which he cannot later recall.

Ewers brings this blood and war imagery together with notions of disease to form a unique depiction of vampirism. His vampirism is a type of malaria. Braun discusses his symptoms with a doctor who is struggling to diagnose Braun's illness. The doctor has read in a scientific journal of the spread of a '*Kannibalenmalaria*' ('cannibalistic malaria') transmitted through bat bites. Braun, the doctor suggests, may have been so infected while he was visiting the South Seas, where, it is stressed, cannibalism is practised. The doctor suggests that Braun should seek treatment at the renowned Hamburg Institute for Tropical Diseases, the only place that might be able to help him. Braun denies having a taste for human flesh but finally concedes that the Institute might be able to help him if only he could travel to Germany. Then he adds:

> Don't you think that all of Europe is stricken with this disease, and a good part of the rest of the world to boot? ... How about disclosing your theory to the *Völker* of the world ...? To make known to the Germans and English, Russians, French, Turks and all of society that all of this was merely a regrettable error, only the resulting symptoms of a highly infectious South-Sea illness, which awakens cannibalistic desires and would force them to devour each other? If the *Völker* realized that, the war would end tomorrow.[40]

Braun speaks in a jesting way, but when pressed, he says his joking is based in truth. His suggestion that the whole world is infected with a raging bloodlust again touches on the novel's central metaphor: the Great War is a form of vampirism.

The tropical origins of this disease are part of Ewers's imperialist view of the world. Through contact with 'primitive savagery' in places such as Haiti, where the novel depicts Braun as having witnessed ritual child sacrifice, Europe and then the entire world have become infected with '*Blutwahn*'. The depiction of *Tropenkoller* ('tropical madness') is a recurring theme in German popular literature at the turn of the century which depicted 'superior' Germans becoming infected through contact with colonial 'primitives'.[41] Braun originally journeyed to the tropics to cure his European 'malaise', but instead he becomes infected with a tropical 'disease of impulsiveness', bringing it with him to the metropole.[42] Lotte Lewi turns the potentially disastrous consequences of this infection into a boon for her beloved Germany. In this way we can see Ewers's representation of vampirism as part of his racialised understanding of the world and its peoples. This disease that comes from the tropics to infect 'superior' cultures can be managed and defeated only through co-operation by two 'superior' peoples, the Germans and the Jews.

Lotte's heroic sacrifices for her two peoples are revealed only at the novel's end. Despite this exchange with the doctor and numerous other clues, Braun does not realise that he himself is the vampire until the novel's last scenes. He suspects Lotte of draining his blood, wondering if she is the embodiment of the bloody goddess, Astarte, connected in the novel's mythology with the Haitian priestess who sacrifices her own child. Instead it turns out that Lotte is making herself the sacrificial victim. In the rather confused Christian imagery of the novel, Lotte is both Virgin and Christ. Lotte refers to herself as a both a mother and lover to Frank at numerous points.[43] Finally when Braun almost drains Lotte of blood and she lies near death she tells him, 'I am your wine – you drank so much milk, by dear boy. So much red milk'.[44] She is like a mother, feeding her child, but also like Christ, whose blood and body nourish through the eucharist. To emphasise this, there are several references to Lotte's antique signet ring, which bears a medieval symbol of Christ, a pelican opening its breast to feed its young.

Lotte Lewi may have been based on Ewers's lover Adèle Guggenheimer-Lewisohn, to whom the book is dedicated, but Lotte is also a literary type, a *'schöne Jüdin'* figure.[45] The *'schöne Jüdin'* or 'beautiful Jewess' type, the lovely Jewess who falls in love with a Christian man, dates back into medieval narrative, but is perhaps best known through characters such as Shylock's daughter, Jessica, in Shakespeare's *Merchant of Venice* or Rebecca of York in Sir Walter Scott's *Ivanhoe*. As this type developed over centuries it divided into what Charlene Lea has called *'la belle juive'*, the good Jewess, and *'la juive fatale'*, the Jewish *femme fatale* (61). The sensual attractions of the latter, like those of Ewers's deadly Alraune, are deadly for her conquests. The novel continually plays with the dichotomous tensions inherent in the *'schöne Jüdin'* figure. Is Lotte a *'juive fatale'*, a figure with strong affinity to literary depictions of the deadly, seductive female vampire? Or is she instead a lovely

prize for her Christian lover, like Shakespeare's Jessica, additionally endowed
with the maternal and sacrificial instincts of the most famous Jewess of them
all, the Virgin Mary?[46]

Despite the 'philo-Semitic' assertion of a mythic connection between
Germans and Jews, the novel taps into anti-Semitic myth to develop the
suggestion that Lotte is a vampiric *'juive fatale'* who aims to suck him dry.
Near the novel's end, as Braun struggles to grasp what is happening to him,
he recalls visiting Lincoln Cathedral as a boy and learning there the medieval
tale of 'The Jew's Daughter', who uses an apple to lure a little Christian boy
into a tower, where she then stabs him to death. [47] While elsewhere in the
novel Ewers has presented a very dramatic picture of Slavic anti-Semitism
and pogroms and the Russian/Slavic use of ritual murder accusation, here
he himself draws upon the image of the bloodthirsty Jew, linking Jew and
vampire as Braun struggles to figure out what has been happening to him
(136–7).

In *Vampir*, Jews can either be bloodthirsty, vampiric murderers or sacrificial
victims. Finally, though, Lotte is not a *juive fatale*, but a *belle juive* with Marian
overtones. She is both mother and lover to Braun and literally gives him her
blood – her red milk – by extension giving this milk to Germany. If Lotte
represents the Jews, then these good German-Jews are willing to sacrifice
everything, body and life for Germany. The Jew is, for Ewers, like all other
non-Germans, a type of Other with both good and evil aspects. Lotte is
associated with the ancient Israelites, a great beauty linked to occult icons,
like the breastplate of Aaron, and to the frequently misspelled Hebrew
lettering that adorns the chapter headings. These numerous misspellings
reveal more than Ewers's pretension.[48] More significantly, they show that
Hebrew as a functioning language is not important for Ewers; Hebrew is used
to signify magic and exoticism. Likewise, Jews and Judaism on their own
terms are not of importance; they are symbols for the author to manipulate
as much as vampires are. Lotte the Jewess is a sacrificial victim to Braun the
vampire; both serve the cause of Germany.

This instrumental use of the Jew as symbol, as well as the novel's depiction
of sacrifice for a higher cause, helps us to understand how Ewers could
eventually support National Socialism despite his self-proclaimed 'philo-
Semitism' and despite close ties to individual Jews. And, of course, his
'philo-Semitism' should be understood not as the opposite of anti-Semitism
but as part of a larger system that connects them both to each other and to
other forms of racism. Ewers's views on the Jewish *Volk* are based not on
recognition of human equality or universal human rights but on generalised
conceptions of Jews and Judaism. As Marco Frenschkowski has put it, Ewers

was 'ein massiver Rassist'.[49] This is made clear through not only his fiction but such declarations on 'racial equality' as this:

> Thus appears to me the closest possible assimilation of these two races as highly desirable, for us Germans as well as for the Jews. I recognize in no way the equal rights of all races in general[;] I am, on the contrary, quite aware of the full superiority of my race. I treat the Yellow and especially the Nigger as something beneath my standing[;] yes, I don't even recognize the Latin as of equal rights, unless he has, like the French or the Northern Italian, a very strong dash of Germanic blood. I am by no means a chauvinist, I have rather only purchased my patriotism during long voyages to all parts of the world[;] yes, I must say that I only fought my way through ingrained [*eingefleischte* – which invokes the body] 'humane thoughts of mankind' to my Germanness over years. The only race, however, which I have to recognize as equal to mine is the Jewish one – if I disregard small splinters like Basques, Celts, Finns, and so on. [50]

For Ewers, some Jews are worthy equals because, using terms that connect to the depiction of a '*Kulturnation*' in *Vampir*, the Jews are a '*Kulturvolk*'.[51] Not all Jews, however, fall into this privileged category. Ewers considered the so-called '*Ostjuden*', recent immigrants to Germany from Eastern Europe, to be a 'lead weight' around the feet of German-Jewry, or 'our Jews' as he refers to them.[52] Therefore not only is Ewers's seeming elevation of the Jewish *Volk* part of a broader hierarchy but Jews themselves are divided into levels within this larger racist scheme that is ultimately readily compatible with the white supremacist ideology of Nazism.

Conclusion

Nina Auerbach has observed that 'every generation creates and embraces its own' vampires.[53] Ewers and Viereck created the types of vampires they seemed to need, figures that justified the superiority of some humans over others, a strategy in keeping with their views on colonialism, nationalism and the '*Gleichberechtigung aller Rassen*' ('the equality of all races').[54] If every age gets the vampires it 'deserves', then we could also say that Ewers and Viereck have got not only their justly deserved vampires but also the tarnished literary legacies that go with them. The vampires Clarke and Braun believe that they can justify evil not only because of their connection to a superior calling but also because of their own superiority. It is in this way that these vampires perhaps most resemble their respective creators. The published and unpublished writings of Viereck and Ewers reveal the deeply self-aggrandising

postures that each adopted toward himself and his work. The sense each had
not only of belonging to a superior group but of being himself a figure of
genius and greatness comes out strongly through their vampire characters.

   These vampire avatars could be seen merely as exercises in egotism, but,
when examined alongside their creators' support of Hitler's murderous
regime, they seem to be much closer to Upton Sinclair's charge of 'Satan's
work'. Sinclair expresses certainty that Viereck 'shudders with horror' at
what he 'has become', a sentiment that calls to mind Anne Rice's portrait
of Louis, the self-loathing vampire. Ewers died before the end of the Second
World War, but he does appear to have had some remorse over his past.
His last recorded words were apparently spoken to his secretary, *'Jennylein,
was war ich für ein Esel!'* ('Little Jenny, what an ass I was!').[55] It is not clear,
however, exactly what he regretted. Viereck, who was released in 1947 from
a US prison for his wartime activities, remained defensive about his past.
Likewise, Ewers's and Viereck's vampires also do not 'shudder' at their own
deeds. Clarke revels in his and any doubts Braun experiences are washed away
by Lotte's interpretations of her own blood sacrifice. Viereck's and Ewers's
vampires provide insight, however, into how an individual could justify a
recognised evil in the name of a mythical greater good, an insight relevant not
only to the generation of Ewers and Viereck but to our own as well.

Notes

1 'Das Böse ... habe sein Recht zu leben, wie alles andere auch – Nur was klein ist, ist
   hässlich' (Ewers, *Der Zauberlehrling*, p. 27). I am grateful to Sören Fröhlich, who was
   invaluable in assisting with research and translation. I also thank Kathryn Hodson of
   the University of Iowa Library and Bruce Kirby of the Library of Congress for their
   help in accessing unpublished materials.
2 Auerbach, *Our Vampires*; Butler, *Metamorphoses*; Cohen, 'Monster Culture'; Gelder,
   Reading the Vampire.
3 The question of nation in these novels is a complex one, potentially complicated
   by the idea of a vampire nation that would create tension between figures such as
   Frank Braun and his German *Vaterland*. Both Viereck and Ewers, however, focus on
   the vampire as a singular individual and do not follow through the implications of
   vampires creating their own nation within their respective novels.
4 Numerous scholars have noted literary and political connections made between the
   figure of the vampire and representations of Jews and Judaism. My forthcoming
   book, *The Once and Future Jew: Anti-Semitism in Medieval and Modern Narrative*, will deal
   with the medieval roots of these connections as well as modern manifestations.
5 David Skal calls *House of the Vampire* 'a delirious love note to the ghosts of Wilde
   and Nietzsche, in which art itself was presented as the vampiric province of a

master race' (*Hollywood Gothic*, p. 62). On Viereck's acknowledgement of Friedrich
Nietzsche's influence, see Johnson, *George Sylvester Viereck*, pp. 10, 130, 144, and
also Viereck's own *Confessions of a Barbarian*, p. 132. On Ewers's 'Nietzscheanism'
in the Frank Braun trilogy, see Layne, 'Uncanny Collapse', pp. 144–5, and
Ruthner, 'Andererseits', p. 175. See also Kugel, *Der Unverantwortliche*, *passim*. Ewers's
contemporary Soergel refers to Frank Braun's 'Nietzschean tone' in his 'Siebentes
Kapitel', p. 820. Ewers's short story 'Der Tod des Barons Jesus Maria von Friedel'
references Nietzsche's sister, Elisabeth. On interpretations of Nietzsche and National
Socialism, I have found Penzo useful: 'Zur Frage der "Entnazifizierung" Friedrich
Nietzsches'.

6 Viereck, 'The Absorptive Nature of Genius', p. 53.

7 *Ibid.*, p. 54.

8 *Ibid.*

9 Viereck, 'Letter to Elmer Gertz', 29 March 1939.

10 Viereck, 'No Room for the Alien'.

11 See Keller, *States of Belonging*, p. 176.

12 See Kupsky, '"The True Spirit of the German People"', p. 91.

13 On Viereck's early fame, see Keller, 'George Sylvester Viereck', p. 70. For
biographical information on Viereck, I have found Neil Johnson, 'Pro-Freud and
Pro-Nazi'; Keller, 'George Sylvester Viereck'; and Kupsky, '"The True Spirit"'
especially useful.

14 On Viereck's financial ties to Nazi Germany, see 'Viereck Got $2000 from Nazi
Consul', and Keller, *States*, pp. 179–81.

15 Viereck, 'Mr. Viereck Protests'; 'Letter to the Editor', *New York Times* (7 June 1934),
p. xi.

16 Viereck, 'Hitler or Chaos', p. 11. Kupsky dates this document to early 1934 ('"The
True Spirit"', p. 73).

17 *Ibid.* See also discussion in Kupsky, '"The True Spirit"', p. 73.

18 Viereck, 'Mr. Viereck Protests'.

19 Viereck, 'Letter to Elmer Gertz', 29 March 1939.

20 Viereck, 'Mr. Viereck Protests', p. 111. The fact was not lost on his contemporary
critics, however, that Viereck did not protest when this book was banned in
Germany. See 'Viereck Kisses the Rod', p. 460.

21 Viereck, 'What I Saw in Hitler's Germany', p. 9.

22 *Ibid.*, p. 4.

23 Viereck, *The Temptation of Jonathan*, p. 15.

24 *Ibid.*, pp. 15–16.

25 Viereck, 'The German-Jewish War'. He references a 'Jewish-Communist reign of
terror' in the United States in his 'Letter to Elmer Gertz', 5 November 1938.

26 Kupsky, '"The True Spirit"', p. 91.

27 Viereck, *Spreading Germs of Hate*, p. xiv.

28 Sinclair, 'To George Viereck (Personal)', p. 551.

29 Keller, *States*, p. 186.

30 On Ewers's politics, see Kugel's immensely detailed biography, which is excellent for providing background despite its apologetics: *Der Unverantwortliche*, pp. 262–5 and 398–400.

31 'Aber es gab über allen Völkern ein anderes Volk, höher, edler und grösser. Die Kulturnation hatte er es genannt – ihr gehörte alles an, was hinausflog über die Massen. Und er kannte sie gut, fand ihre Bürger überall in der Welt. Es war da, dieses Volk, ganz gewiss, ohne jeden Zweifel' ('But there was, above all *Völkern*, a different *Volk*, higher, nobler and greater. He had dubbed it the "nation of culture" – to it belonged all that, which outshone the masses. And he knew it well, found its citizens everywhere in the world'), p. 26. See also pp. 426–7.

32 The novel refers to Frank Braun as 'the irresponsible one' ('Er war der Unverant-wortliche'), p. 109, which is also the title of Kugel's biography.

33 ('bis zum letzten Blutstrophen'), p. 47.

34 ('kleinstes Teilchen nur in dem Riesenleibe des Volkes') (48). The German '*Volk*' can be translated as 'people', but the concept is far more complex. See Mosse, *The Crisis of German Ideology*, pp. 13–30.

35 The English translation is deliberately stilted here to try to capture the feel of Ewers's prose: 'Würde ihn – wie die andern alle – zu einem Stäubchen machen, zu einem jämmerlichen Fleischfetzchen im blutenden Leibe des Volkes. Tod war für ihn – was für die andern Leben war' (pp. 47–8).

36 'beiden zusammen, eng vereint, dem germanischen und dem jüdischen' (p. 133).

37 Ewers is by no means alone among his contemporaries in this understanding of blood. See Biale, *Blood and Belief*, pp. 123–61.

38 'Durch meine Adern fliesst, gut vermischt, beider Blut, ich bin Deutsche und Jüdin zugleich. Und ich, ich fand die Deutung von der Sendung meines Stammes für diese Zeit – lange lebe mein deutsches – lange lebe mein jüdisches Volk!' (p. 134).

39 'Deutscher! Du gingst den Weg, den ich dich führte – den Weg zur Heimat. Gingst ihn – mit mir – für mich. Deutsch wurdest du: mein Blut fliesst in dir' (p. 605). Like the concept of '*Volk*' the German concept of '*Heimat*' has a complex history. See Blickle, *Heimat*.

40 '[D]eucht Sie nicht, dass ganz Europa von dieser Krankheit befallen ist und ein gutter Teil der andern Welt noch dazu? ... Wie ware es, wenn Sie Ihre Theorie den Völkern der Erde bekannt gäben ...? Den Deutschen und Engländern, Russen, Franzosen, Türken und der ganzen Gesellschaft kund und zu wissen täten, dass das alles nur ein bedauerlicher Irrtum sei, nur die Folgeerscheinung einer sehr ansteckenden Südseekrankheit, die kannibalistische Gelüste erwecke und sie zwänge, sich gegenseitig aufzufressen? – Wenn die Völker das einsehn, ist morgen der Krieg zu Ende' (pp. 290–1).

41 Poley, 'Ant People', pp. 83–5.

42 *Ibid.*, pp. 74, 83. Poley has also convincingly argued that *Vampir* represents a reaction to 'colonial loss', the same loss to which Viereck also reacted, p. 121. See also Arata, 'The Occidental Tourist'.

43 See pp. 77, 86, 586.

44 'Ich bin dein Wein – trink – so viel Milch trankst du, mein lieber Junge? So viel rote Milch' (p. 593).

45 Soergel in his critique of the first Frank Braun novel, *Der Zauberlehrling*, in which Lotte first appears and expresses a desire to have Braun's child ('Siebentes Kapitel', p. 820). For background on the '*schöne Jüdin*', see Lampert, '"O My Daughter!"'.

46 I am researching connections on the deadly vampiric seductress and the figure of the Jewess as part of a larger project. For an introduction into the vampire seductress in the late nineteenth century, I have found Bram Dijkstra, *Evil Sisters*, extremely illuminating.

47 Ewers, *Vampir*, pp. 572–4. The Scottish version of the ballad appears in the 1934 American edition, pp. 334–7. On the American translation of *Vampir*, see Wikoff, 'Hanns Heinz Ewers' *Vampir*'. There is a substantial literature on the 'Jew's Daughter' ballad. For a version of the ballad, see Child, *Popular Ballads*, vol. 3, pp. 233–54. On ritual murder and child sacrifice in Ewers's work, see also Poley, 'Ant People', pp. 147, 154.

48 The novel is divided into fifteen chapters titled with the names of stones that roughly correspond to the twelve stones on the breastplate of Aaron that Lotte possesses. Each chapter heading includes the name of the stone in Hebrew and also features an image of a sign of the zodiac and an astrological glyph although an exact system of symbolism remains unclear. The chapter headings and their obscure epigraphs are amusingly skewered in Reimann's 1922 parody of *Vampir*, which names each chapter after a type of cheese.

49 Frenschkowski, 'Von Schemajah Hillel', p. 145.

50 'So erscheint mir die möglichst enge Assimilation dieser beiden Rassen sehr erwünscht, sowohl für uns Deutsche, wie für die Juden. Ich erkenne in keiner Weise die Gleichberechtigung aller Rassen überhaupt an, ich bin mir im Gegenteil der völligen Ueberlegenheit meiner Rasse durchaus bewusst. Ich behandle den Gelben und gar erst den Nigger als etwas unter mir Stehendes, ja ich erkenne nicht einmal den Romanen als gleichberechtigt an, sofern er nicht, wie der Franzose oder der Norditaliener einen sehr starken Schuss germanischen Blutes hat. Ich bin durchaus kein Chauvinist, ich habe vielmehr meinen Patriotismus erst auf langen Reisen in allen Weltteilen erworben, ja ich muss sagen, dass ich mich gegen eingefleischte "humane Menschheitsgedanken" erst in Jahren zu meinem Deutschtum durchgekämpft habe. Die einzige Rasse aber, die ich der meinen als gleichberechtigt anerkennen muss, ist die jüdische – wenn ich von kleinen Splittern wie Basken, Kelten, Finnen usw. absehen will.' 'Judentaufe', p. 37. Cited in Frenschkowski, 'Von Schemajah Hillel', pp. 145–6.

51 Ewers, 'Die Lösung der Judenfrage', p. 33.

52 Ewers, 'Judentaufen', pp. 37–8.

53 Auerbach, *Our Vampires*, p. vii.

54 Theweleit, *Male Fantasies*, pp. 87–8.

55 Kugel, *Der Unverantwortliche*, p. 379.

6

The Undead in the kingdom of shadows: the rise of the cinematic vampire

Stacey Abbott

You have only to freeze a film image and then set it in motion again to appreciate the difference. A photograph embalms the ghosts of the past; film brings them back to life.[1]

Photography is an uncanny medium, capturing and freezing moments in time. We change and age but our images are immortalised. Where photography provides a haunting image of the past, however, film infuses the image with life through the illusion of motion. In 1896, Maxim Gorky described the experience of watching the newly invented cinematograph as entering 'the Kingdom of Shadows', explaining that 'as you gaze at it, you see carriages, buildings and people in various poses, all frozen into immobility … But suddenly a strange flicker passes through the screen and the picture stirs to life … It is terrifying to see, but it is the movement of shadows, only shadows.'[2] Gorky astutely observed that this was life but not as it was once lived, rather existing more like an echo. Tom Gunning similarly described filmmaking as 'creating ghosts', explaining that these images, like ghosts, are 'forced to repeat the same gestures over and over again … condemned to an eternal repetition'.[3] Cinema, therefore, has much in common with the vampire, which can also be seen as a shadow of life, famously represented as such in F. W. Murnau's *Nosferatu* (Germany, 1922).[4] Vampirism causes the dead to be revived but then trapped in an ever-repeating cycle of behaviour, defined by their need to sleep and feed. Cinema is undeath and therefore it is an ideal place to find vampires.

Ken Gelder extends this analogy by highlighting the inherent internationalism of both the cinema and the modern vampire. From the early

Figure 6.1.   The shadow of the vampire – *Nosferatu*

showmen who brought films to local communities to the digital distribution
of films around the globe, cinema's nomadic qualities have led to it becoming
'an internationalised medium', mirroring the evolution of the vampire.[5]
Similarly, the nineteenth-century literary vampire, from Lord Ruthven to
Count Dracula, sought to extend its influence beyond its own borders,
insinuating its presence within new modern communities. In the twentieth
century, the vampire followed cinema in its move toward globalisation and
became the centre point for the popular consumption of the vampire myth.
The cinematic Dracula came to dominate the modern understanding of the
vampire, providing a face, costume and voice that are still recognisable today.
Pale skin, dark lips, widow's peak, tuxedo, cape, mannered performance,
and Hungarian accent are the characteristics around which Bela Lugosi, star
of Tod Browning's *Dracula* (USA, 1931), constructed his interpretation of
Bram Stoker's infamous literary vampire. These elements have now become
the blueprint for many cinematic vampires in films such as *Dracula's Daughter*
(Lambert Hillyer, USA, 1936), *The Return of Dracula* (Paul Landres, USA,
1958), *Count Yorga Vampire* (Bob Kelljan, USA, 1970), *Andy Warhol's Dracula*
(Paul Morrissey, USA, 1974), *Love at First Bite* (Stan Dragoti, USA, 1979),
and *My Grandfather Is a Vampire* (David Blyth, New Zealand, 1992). Since the
1970s, the vampire in film has increasingly diversified but Lugosi's image still
maintains its recognisability through Grandpa from *The Munsters* (1964–1966),

the Count von Count in *Sesame Street* (1969–), *Count Duckula* (1988), 'Buffy vs
Dracula' (*Buffy the Vampire Slayer,* 5.1, 1997–2003), contemporary advertising,
Hallowe'en costumes, and a vast array of vampire-related merchandise.
While the twenty-first-century vampire shows its predilection for both old
and new technologies through its presence in literature, television, video
games and online role-playing games (RPGs), cinema still remains one of
the most visible locations for the vampire.

Not only did Tod Browning's *Dracula* introduce, in Bela Lugosi's
performance, the formulaic appearance of the vampire but its success spawned
a wave of horror films initially produced at Universal but very quickly
spreading to other studios. This emerging horror genre has been described
by David J. Skal as 'Hollywood Gothic', a union of Gothic literature with
the visual style of German Expressionism, while Andrew Tudor describes it
as a period of 'secure horror' in which society 'can be protected against all
manner of threats'.[6] A monster may be unleashed upon society but audiences
can rest assured that it will be destroyed and normality will be restored by
the film's end. *Dracula* also established the generic formulae and iconography
for the vampire film, including studio-bound location, a timeless setting and
a mixture of folklore superstition and religious iconography, that would, with
some variation, be consistently used until the horror genre underwent its own
process of modernisation in the 1960s.

The success of Browning's *Dracula* did, therefore, have a lasting impact
upon the genre but filmmakers did not settle upon this formula overnight.
Rather it developed over years from the dawn of cinema at the end of the
nineteenth century and continuing beyond the release of *Dracula* as other
studios such as MGM sought to replicate Browning's success with their
own generic formula.[7] In this chapter, I will demonstrate that the vampire
film underwent a process of experimentation wherein vampire imagery was
used across a wide range of genres and to convey diverse meanings before it
became consolidated into a recognised horror formula. As a result this period
of 'secure horror' includes a diversity of approaches to the vampire that is
usually associated with the contemporary vampire film. While the modern
horror genre from the 1960s onward presents the vampire as a product of
modernity 'born out of the processes of change within the modern world',
it is my contention that in the first half of the twentieth century the vampire
film demonstrated a greater ambivalence toward modernity, marking a
transition between premodern and modern sensibilities.[8] Repeatedly harking
back to vampire folklore and nineteenth-century literature, these films betray
a nostalgia for the security of the past versus the uncertainty of the modern.
However, I will consider how the reimagining of the vampire through the

technological language of cinema also serves both to celebrate modernity and to bring the vampire 'up-to-date with a vengeance'.[9]

Despite the connection between film and vampirism, the cinematic vampire did not appear in full flourish until the 1920s with the release of Károly Lajthay's *Drakula halála* (Hungary, 1921) and F. W. Murnau's *Nosferatu* (Germany, 1922), both loosely based upon Stoker's novel.[10] Prior to these films, the vampire appears more as metaphor than monster. George Méliès's *Le manoir du diable / The Haunted Castle* (France, 1896), drawing upon well-established Gothic imagery, features much of the iconography that would become key components of the cinematic vampire genre: a devilish figure in black with the ability to transform into a bat, a Gothic castle, a coven of female followers who torment the male hero, and the use of a crucifix to ward off the devil/vampire. This film presents the clear opposition between good and evil that would be an intrinsic element of Stoker's novel, published a year later, but the film is fundamentally a trick film, a spectacle of cinematic magic, and the villain of the piece is primarily a devil figure, with vampiric overtones suggested through the presence of the bat and the crucifix. While Méliès's film melds the conventions of the trick film with Gothic imagery to present a fantastic realm of the supernatural, Louis Feuillade's serial *Les vampires* (France, 1915–1916), draws upon vampiric imagery to convey the near supernatural skills and ingenuity of a gang of master criminals operating in Paris. In particular the imagery, consolidated in the gang's signature use of black body stockings and masks, is used to highlight the transgression of the female criminal in the form of the character Irma Vep (an anagram for vampire). As Vicki Callahan argues, Irma Vep is the 'central figure of crime and evil' in the series and, while she is linked romantically with the leaders of the gang, 'the frequent change of leadership and her ability to quickly realign her romantic attachments suggest that Irma's emotional investments in the leaders are primarily founded on expediency and self-interest'.[11] As a result, Irma Vep is the most vampiric of 'les vampires', whose transgression lies in the manner in which she uses men for her own aims.

The sexually predatory and manipulative woman, embodied in Irma Vep, was in fact most common representation of the vampire in American silent cinema, usually described as a 'vamp'. According to Janet Staiger, a vamp was 'a woman gone astray, a parasite woman who could feed off the solid stock of America, destroying the vital future it should have'.[12] In this they have much in common with the psychic vampires that, according to Nina Auerbach, rose to prominence in twentieth-century literature and who 'feast on the horror inherent in friendship and intimacy. They refuse blood, but they grow fat on human fellowship.'[13] The cinematic vamp persona was initially based upon the actress Theda Bara, whom Jeannine Basinger describes as 'the original vamp' because her stardom grew from her successful performance in *A Fool There Was* (Frank Powell, 1915), based upon Rudyard Kipling's poem *The Vampire*.[14] Bara's vamp takes Kipling's sexually predatory vampire and presents it as a metaphor for the modern world, rather than Victorian anxieties about female sexuality. Thus, while Bram Dijkstra argues that the nineteenth-century female vampire 'had come to represent woman as the personification of everything negative that linked sex, ownership, and money',[15] Janet Staiger points out that *A Fool There Was* is more critical of the male victims than the vamp herself. The men suffer while the vamp, in this period of cinema at least, is rarely punished for her actions. As Staiger explains,

> the character of the vamp seems almost to be merely a foil for an extensive examination of the power of sex, women's rights in this new age, and the crumbling belief in the assertion that some nineteenth-century notions of the family's behaviour were still pertinent for twentieth-century America.[16]

The success of Bara's vamp led to numerous subsequent on-screen vamps, such as Gloria Swanson and Pola Negri, whose exotic images made them both 'desirable' and 'dangerous', betraying an ambivalence toward these modern women, and modernity itself.[17]

Yet another silent screen vamp emerges in F. W. Murnau's *Sunrise* (USA, 1927), made five years after *Nosferatu*, when a woman from the city seduces a humble farmer with the promise of excitement and glamour, causing him to neglect his farm and family while he becomes consumed with her allure. The Woman is equated with the vampire – or vamp – when in one scene, dressed in a clingy, black silk dress, she lures the Man away from his family home for a clandestine meeting in the marshes. Holding the Man in her arms, she leans over him, in a sexually dominant pose reminiscent of Edvard Munch's 1896 painting *The Vampire*, and kisses him before quietly whispering in his ear that his Wife might drown, thus releasing the Man from his country entrapment. When he recoils in horror at the suggestion of murder, she overwhelms him with kisses until he succumbs to her charms, and then gently convinces him to kill his wife by describing the wealth, speed and scale of what the city has to offer. In this manner, she is presented as a poison that, like the vampire, infects the man's system and causes him to consider evil actions. The vamp in silent cinema, therefore, came to represent the attraction and danger of modernity, luring men into forsaking traditional values in favour of modern ambitions, prioritising technological progress, financial gain and sexual liberation.

This use of vampire imagery stands in contrast to the more common association of the vampire with notions of the premodern and the primitive through their association with the Gothic. Fred Botting, for instance, argues that 'Gothic figures have continued to shadow the progress of modernity with counter narratives displaying the underside of enlightenment and human values', while David Punter clearly interweaves the vampire into his definition of the Gothic when he explains that it is 'the fiction of the haunted castle, of heroines preyed on by unspeakable terrors, of the blackly lowering villain, of ghosts, vampires, monsters and werewolves'.[18] The Gothic traditionally creates an opposition between the realms of the day and night, in which the day represents the rational, the modern and the civilised, and the night, the world of the vampire, embodies the irrational, the primitive and the unconscious. As the world moved into twentieth-century notions of modernity, however, the night came to represent the epitome of the modern through the invention, and the spectacular display, of the electric light as evidenced at international expositions around the world at the end of the nineteenth century, which positioned the city as the icon of progress. The *New York Times*'s review of the opening night of Coney Island's Luna Park amusement park in 1903 specifically describes those who attended as being 'dazzled by Electric City' and highlights the 'beauty of the place under its extraordinary electrical illumination' as being its 'primary feature'.[19] The vamp in *Sunrise* is presented as embodying this image of the night, not primitive but vibrant and electrifying, as the screen dissolves from her image to a dazzling montage sequence of the bright lights and musical splendour of the city. Through her association with the modern city, the vamp prefigures a series of vampire films from the 1990s in which the female vampire was re-imagined as a *flâneuse* at home in New York, the city that never sleeps.[20] In 1867, when Karl Marx described capital as 'dead labor, which, vampire-like, lives only by sucking living labor', he used the vampire as a metaphor for the perils for capitalism.[21] In much the same way, modern cinema has, through the vamp, appropriated the image of the vampire, not to oppose but to embody modernity in all its wonder and horror.[22]

The ambivalence towards modernity embodied in the vamp continued to be a key component of the cinematic vampire as the genre developed beyond pure metaphor in which the vamp is presented as vampire-like and into a genre about vampires, drawing upon nineteenth-century precursors. In this period between the 1920s and the 1930s, the genre, however, became split between two strands of vampire film best explained through Tzevetan Todorov's distinct categories of fantasy literature: the marvellous, in which the supernatural exists as a part of the natural landscape, and the uncanny, stories that suggest the supernatural but where a rational explanation is eventually revealed.[23] Films such as *London after Midnight* (Tod Browning, 1927), *The Vampire Bat* (Frank Strayer, 1933) and *The Mark of the Vampire* (Tod Browning, 1935) draw upon the conventions of Gothic literature to suggest the intrusion of vampires within the modern world, thus undermining rational scientific thinking, before, in the tradition of Todorov's uncanny, restoring normality by revealing that the murderer is in fact human.

Each of these films begins with a series of murders that show the signs of vampirism, usually two pin-prick marks on the victim's neck and the loss of blood, and an investigation takes place that creates a conflict between premodern and modern beliefs. In *The Vampire Bat*, the town council's conviction that they have been targeted by a vampire is based upon superstition about bats and the Devil, as well as the civil registers of documented cases of 'vampirism' in their community, much like the numerous recorded cases across Europe in the seventeenth and eighteenth centuries as discussed by Christopher Frayling.[24] In contrast, the modern-thinking police inspector, played by the film's star Melvyn Douglas, is convinced that he is looking for a human murderer and begins his investigation accordingly. While his perspective is challenged by the supernatural-seeming events of the film, his view is eventually upheld when the murderer is revealed to be a scientist recreating the appearance of a vampire attack.

The Mark of the Vampire, set in Prague, similarly situates its narrative within a superstitious environment by opening with an establishing shot of a cross on top of a cathedral. This shot is then followed by a tilt and vertical wipe to a shot of the base of the church where a group of gypsies are setting up camp below. A Gothic atmosphere is created as the light from their fire flickers and creates shadows while the gypsies say prayers and hang bat-thorn, a local plant that grows in graveyards, around their camp as protection from the vampires. This is followed by a scene in a local inn in which the owners explain their belief in vampires to their British guests who scoff at the superstition. This confrontation between East and West deliberately evokes Jonathan Harker's disregard for local warnings, describing them as 'all very ridiculous', before going to Dracula's castle in Stoker's novel, which has subsequently been repeated in Murnau's *Nosferatu* and Browning's *Dracula*.[25] Whereas in *Dracula* and its adaptations this scene prepares the reader/audience for the unravelling of Harker's beliefs when he comes face to face with the vampire, in *The Mark of the Vampire* Browning designs the scene to parody his earlier film by virtually remaking the scene from his version of *Dracula* – even casting the same actor (Michael Visaroff) as the innkeeper. It also establishes two ways of looking at the world, represented in the film by folklorist Dr Professor Zelen (Lionel Barrymore) and police inspector Neumann (Lionel Atwill), that will come into conflict when the body of Sir Karell Borotyn is found with two seeming vampire bites on his neck and the investigation into his murder begins.

The earlier *London after Midnight* (Tod Browning, 1927),[26] while still exploring the clash between the modern and the premodern, takes a different tack, set as it is in modern London and beginning with the apparent suicide of Sir Roger Balfour, albeit under suspicious circumstances. Five years later, a vampiric-looking man, with hollowed eyes, razor-sharp teeth and sporting a top hat and cape, moves in to the supposedly haunted Balfour house and signs Balfour's name to the lease. Superstitious belief in ghosts and vampires erupts in the neighbouring household, first with the servants and then eventually among the upper-class friends and family of Balfour. Eventually, however, it is revealed that the vampire is actually detective Burke investigating Balfour's death in costume as part of an elaborate ruse to discover the murderer. Furthermore, the focus on vampire folklore in the film, along with the Gothic art-direction of Balfour's ghostly mansion, is a smokescreen for a scientific experiment to test whether a murderer can be hypnotised into repeating their crime. While this film wallows in the unsettling atmosphere of the Gothic and the fantastic, made particularly horrific by Lon Chaney's monstrous appearance as the vampire, the revelation that the murder was committed in order to acquire both Balfour's money and his daughter locates horror within comparatively mundane preoccupations with greed and lust. Each of these films, *London after Midnight*, *The Vampire Bat* and *The Mark of the Vampire*, reveals a human monster at the centre of the narrative, effectively disproving a belief in the supernatural but at the expense of revealing an even more horrific truth about humanity. The vampire, therefore, becomes a means of exposing the monstrosity of modern humankind, prepared to commit murder for financial or scientific gain.

In contrast, films such as *Nosferatu* and *Vampyr* (Carl Dreyer, Denmark, 1932) present the vampire genre as a confrontation between premodern and the modern in which modern man becomes engulfed in a supernatural landscape from which there is no escape. In these films, there is no rational explanation for the presence of the vampire. Rather, as in Stoker's novel, the supernatural quickly undermines modern rationalism as the protagonists, Hutter in *Nosferatu* and Allan Gray in *Vampyr*, are confronted by visions that defy their modern sensibilities. While Hutter initially scoffs at peasant superstition about ghosts and vampires, once he crosses the bridge into the Carpathian mountains on his approach to meet Count Orlok's carriage, he is, according to the intertitles, 'seized by sinister sights', while Allan Gray is described as being so overwhelmed by his study of superstition and folklore that he has become 'lost at the border between reality and the supernatural'. In the tradition of the Gothic, both films suggest the existence of a boundary between the worlds of the rational and the irrational, but, notably, they also blur the distinction between these worlds through the technology of cinema. In both cases, as Hutter and Gray cross into this netherland of the supernatural, it is through the language and techniques of cinema that the uncanniness of this world is conveyed, not in a Todorovian sense – this is most definitely a world in which the supernatural exists – but rather in the Freudian approach in which the familiar is made unfamiliar.[27] In *Nosferatu*, Orlok's coach is filmed in fast-motion to suggest preternatural motion and then later, as the coach carries Hutter to Orlok's castle, the sequence cuts to negative footage of the coach travelling through the forest which, when mixed with the blue tinting that was commonly used in the silent era to suggest nightfall, creates an unsettling image as if the carriage were, quite literally, entering the land of shadows. In *Vampyr*, it is the film's aesthetic design that suggests the uncanny. Shot as a silent film, with selected dialogue and sound effects post-synchronised, creating a disjunction between sound and image, the film uses a roving camera and unsettling compositions to suggest the disturbing and dream-like atmosphere into which Gray has entered. In this film, the line between dream and reality is not blurred but invisible. In both films the supernatural is made manifest through technology.

This duality, in which superstition and technology are merged, calls to mind the duality in Stoker's own representation of Dracula as both animalistic – through his association with wolves and rats, as well as his ability to scale down the wall of his castle head first like a lizard – and an embodiment of modern business practices and technologies. The Count buys his way into England, conceals his whereabouts through paper trails of lawyers and leases, and communicates with Mina via telepathy, in the same way that the Crew of Light – the team of gentlemen who work together to destroy the vampire – communicate via telegram. Furthermore, his story emerges through the collection of written documents accumulated by Mina and the others, making Dracula a product of the modern archive and conveying Stoker's own ambivalence to modernity, in which he highlighted the wonders and the weakness of the modern age. Murnau's vampire, Count Orlok, is similarly marked as a hybrid of primitive and modern. His animalistic appearance, with pointed ears, rat-like teeth, and long elongated fingers, evokes the primitive, while early special effects, such as dissolves, superimpositions, stop-motion and changes in film speed are used throughout the film to present the vampire as a spectral creature – a product of technology.[28]

Figure 6.2.   The looming female vampire in *Vampyr*

Vampyr uses similar optical trickery to present a dynamic spectral landscape of dancing shadows and ethereal visitations in which the shadows, controlled by the vampire, come to life to do her bidding. In one scene, Gray follows the shadow of a peg-leg soldier as it scampers along the shore of a lake, reflected in the water, and passes the shadow of a grave digger, digging a grave, filmed in reverse in order to exaggerate the shadow's uncanny movements. These spectral moments stand in contrast to the vampire who is presented as a slow-moving, but commanding and decidedly physical old woman. While she evokes the archaic, the shadows suggest the modern. Furthermore, the film possesses a distinctively grainy or murky aesthetic, particularly in the scene where the vampire is found looming over the collapsed figure of her victim Leone. These visuals are painterly in their design, as the vampire pauses over her unconscious victim in a pose reminiscent of nineteenth-century paintings such as *The Vampire* (1897) by Philip Burne-Jones (son of Edward Burne-Jones) while the grain of the image suggests the visible brush strokes of Impressionism. This painterly quality is, however, achieved through modern technological means as outlined by David Rudkin:

> *Vampyr* legend tells of a shot accidentally marred during early filming, when unwanted light had shone into the lens. Maté [the cinematographer] and

Dreyer were so taken with the resulting blurred quality that they set about recreating the effect by intentionally reflecting light into the camera from a sheet of gauze.[29]

Like Stoker's *Dracula* and Murnau's *Nosferatu*, *Vampyr* captures a tension between the past and the present, the supernatural and the technological. In this manner, the cinema celebrates the wonders of modernity but also posits its downfall through the intrusion of a vampire.

A major distinction between Stoker's novel and these two early vampire films is their exclusion of science as a defence against the vampire. In the character of Van Helsing, the learned scholar in *Dracula* schooled in folklore, philosophy, law and medicine, Stoker fused folkloric and scientific beliefs, recognising that the supernatural of today is but the as-of-yet unexplained science of tomorrow. It is Van Helsing's willingness to believe in Dracula that enables him to eventually destroy the vampire, for, as Van Helsing explains in Browning's film, 'the strength of the vampire is that people will not believe in him'. That Van Helsing both believes and can make others recognise the relationship between superstition and science, in the novel and repeatedly in most adaptations of the novel and their sequels, is his power (see *Dracula's Daughter* (Lambert Hillyer, USA, 1936) *Horror of Dracula* (Terence Fisher, UK, 1958), *Brides of Dracula* (Terence Fisher, UK, 1960) and *Bram Stoker's Dracula* (Francis Ford Coppola, USA, 1992)). In contrast, both *Nosferatu* and *Vampyr* look to folklore for authority rather then science. In both films, the protagonists find or are given a book of vampire folklore that explains to them the characteristics of the vampire and outlines the methods for its destruction. The knowledge that is of value, therefore, stems from the old world, whereas science is presented as at best ineffectual and at worst demonic. In *Nosferatu*, the scientist Bulwer lectures to his students about the existence of vampires in nature by looking at carnivorous polyps and plants but never recognises the presence of a vampire in his own community.[30] In *Vampyr*, the village doctor betrays his scientific background as he is shown to be in league with the vampire, assisting her in gaining access to her victim, Leone, and concealing her actions. He is a monstrous presence in the film, feigning authority over Leone's condition while undermining her recovery.[31] Here science facilitates the vampire rather than opposing it. As a result, his violent death, buried alive in a flourmill, is the climax of the film.

Furthermore, in the novel *Dracula* the fatal blows to the vampire are delivered by two of the young male heroes: Jonathan Harker, encapsulating the efficiency of modern business and law, and Quincey Morris, embodying the New World action-man – together representing the triumph of modernity. In contrast, in Browning's *Dracula* it is Van Helsing who delivers the fatal blow to Dracula, off-screen, but in this action he is representing not modern science but rather old-world authority embodied in his own status as a 'foreigner' like Dracula. As Nina Auerbach observes, Van Helsing 'is a pale parody of Lugosi, even, like him, shunning daylight: at the end, he stays in the crypt with the dead Dracula, directing the young lovers [Mina and Jonathan] as they walk somnambulistically up a huge staircase toward the light'.[32]

In Murnau's and Dreyer's films, however, it is not the young male protagonists who destroy the vampire. Hutter and Gray are in fact ineffectual. Nor is it a figure of authority like Van Helsing. Instead, the knowledge is used by Hutter's wife Ellen and, in *Vampyr*, one of the servants, each of whom reads the books and intuitively understands what must be done. The choice of a woman and a servant as vampire slayers is quite unique in this period of vampire film. The use of the servant in *Vampyr* aligns the film with traditional folkloric beliefs more common among European peasant classes. This familiarity enables the servant to act when faced with the actions of a vampire, in contrast to Allan Gray, the middle-class intellectual who is overwhelmed by his confrontation with the supernatural and therefore unable to do more than observe. In *Nosferatu*, Hutter is equally paralysed by his encounter with Orlok and, when he returns to Wisborg, ignores the correlation between the sudden deaths within the community and his experiences with Orlok. Ellen's ability, however, both to recognise the truth and to decide to act is both forward- and backward-thinking in its representation of women. It does position a woman as having the strength of mind to save her community from the monster and in this she has much in common with Stoker's new woman Mina, who is equally perceptive and decisive. However, Ellen's only means of action is to lure the vampire to her bedroom, emphasising her sexuality rather than intelligence, and give herself over to the vampire in order to keep him by her side until sunrise. To save the day the woman must die, which alludes to nineteenth-century depictions of women as maternal, self-sacrificing saviours.

Furthermore, the conclusion in which Orlok fades away in the rays of the sunlight, while seemingly steeped in folklore, is inherently cinematic. Most folkloric stories of vampires simply describe the vampire as emerging at night (with no specific mention of an aversion to sunlight) while, in Stoker's novel, Dracula is simply trapped in his physical form with the rise of the sun. In contrast, Orlok's demise in sunlight is a nod to the significant role of light in cinema, used to burn an image on to film stock and later to project it on to a screen. In *Vampyr*, the servant tracks down the grave of the vampire and, in true folkloric fashion, hammers a stake through her heart but, in a cinematic flourish, the body of the vampire dissolves into the image of

Figure 6.3.   Death of the vampire in *Nosferatu*

a skeleton to convey the destruction of the vampire. This recalls Stoker's assertion (as discussed by Sam George) that Dracula would not appear truly in a photograph, instead 'com[ing] out black or like a skeleton corpse'. This trope would be repeated in numerous other films including two sequels to Universal's *Dracula*: *Son of Dracula* (Robert Siodmak, USA, 1943) and *House of Dracula* (Eerle C. Kenton, USA, 1945). These conclusions both hark back to the past through references to folklore and the notion of purity being able to destroy evil but the spectacle of cinema celebrates the modern through the emphasis on optical effects.

As I have demonstrated, the vampire genre of the 1920s and 1930s served as a transition point between nineteenth- and twentieth-century traditions, drawing upon an amalgamation of conventions from folklore and Gothic literature, while also infusing the genre with new representations of the vampire drawn from the media's technological origins. It is this hybridity that encapsulates the genre's conflicting relationship with modernity. As the genre moved into the 1950s, with Riccardo Fredo and Mario Bava's *I vampiri* (1956) and Hammer Studios' first foray into the vampire genre with *Horror of Dracula* (1958), the genre continued to demonstrate a tension between modernity and the past, while looking forward to the conventions of modern horror. Set in contemporary Paris, Fredo and Bava's film is highly reminiscent of the investigative vampire films of the early 1930s, *The Vampire Bat* and *Mark of the Vampire*, where a series of murders in which the bodies were drained of blood are investigated. In contrast to these earlier films, it is eventually revealed that these women are, in fact, the victims of a vampire, stalking the streets of Paris, but this time it is a vampire with a modern twist. A reworking of the Countess Elisabeth Bathory myth – in which the countess reputedly bathed in the blood of virgins – the vampire in *I vampiri* is the elderly Countess Du Grand, a woman who uses scientific experiments in blood transfusions to restore her youthful vitality. In this film, Gothic spaces such as the Countess's castle become modernised through the iconography of science, such as test tubes, gurneys, electrical equipment and flashing lights. Furthermore, the film's emphasis upon location shooting also prefigures the tendency within modern horror to situate horror narratives within recognisably modern locations so as to blur the lines between the fictional and the real world, prefiguring such landmark horror films as George Franju's *Eyes Without a Face* (France, 1959), Michael Powell's *Peeping Tom* (UK, 1960) and Roman Polanski's *Rosemary's Baby* (USA, 1968).

Unlike *I vampiri*, Hammer's vampire films are generally set in a rather abstract Victorian or early Edwardian period. While they do include repeated references to Stoker's preoccupation with modern technology, such as Van Helsing's use of a gramophone diary in *Horror of Dracula* and General Gerald Harcourt's possession of a modern automobile in *Kiss of the Vampire* (Don Sharp, UK, 1963), these technologies are presented from the perspective of 1950s and 1960s Britain, making them seem quaint and old-fashioned rather than 'up-to-date with a vengeance'. In contrast, however, Hammer's visual style does provide the films with a modern edge, choosing to shoot in Technicolor and widescreen, which immediately distanced the films from the black and white expressionism of Hollywood Gothic. Additionally, the casting choices of Christopher Lee and Peter Cushing, as Dracula and Van Helsing respectively, emphasise youth and vigour. Van Helsing in particular is a young, action-oriented vampire hunter, and not an ageing scientist and a scholar. This is best demonstrated in his final confrontation with Dracula in *Horror of Dracula* (1958) when he chases the vampire through his mansion, sprints across the room to pull down the curtains, letting the fatal light cascade into the room to trap Dracula in its rays, and then leaps on to the desk while grabbing two candlestick holders together in the shape of a crucifix in order to force Dracula into the light. This image of Van Helsing foreshadows the transition of the vampire *hunter* into a vampire *slayer*, in which physical power to fight the vampire is prioritised over knowledge in vampire films such as *Blade*, *Underworld*, *Van Helsing* and even the television series *Buffy the Vampire Slayer*.[33]

The casting of Lee as Dracula is also significant because he was not presented as racially or culturally Other in the manner of Max Schrek as

Orlok or Bela Lugosi as Dracula, but rather as equally 'English' as Cushing's Van Helsing. While Lee's Dracula is presented as monstrous, particularly as the series continued and Lee's performance became reduced to a set of bloodthirsty mannerisms, the lines between vampire and vampire hunter were beginning to be blurred. The distinction between vampire and humans that enabled the audience to safely project their anxieties on to the vampire as 'other' was gradually being eroded. In this manner, Hammer prefigures the shift to the more humanised, and eventually sympathetic, vampire that emerged through the television series *Dark Shadows* (1966–1972); novels such as Saberhagen's *The Dracula Tape* (1975), Rice's *Interview with the Vampire* (1976) and Yarbro's *Hôtel Transylvania* (1978); and George Romero's film *Martin* (1978). Margaret L. Carter argues that this shift from the Victorian to the modern representation of the vampire reflects a changing 'attitude toward the outsider, the alien other' in which readers and audiences identify with rather then fear the 'other'.[34] This 'shift of emphasis from the threat of the other to the lure of the other' has, since the 1970s, become one of the prevailing characteristics of the contemporary vampire genre, as evidenced in *Bram Stoker's Dracula* (1992), *Buffy the Vampire Slayer*, *Vampire Diaries* and *Twilight*.

What becomes apparent as one tracks the rise of the vampire in film is that this new cinematic genre was in constant dialogue with its nineteenth-century precursors, reworking and reinventing a diverse range of traditions as filmmakers worked to establish a formula that was suitable for this new medium. The formation of this formula into the tradition of Hollywood Gothic was by no means simple and, while Browning's *Dracula* maintains a significant place within the evolution of the genre, it was one of many reimaginings of the vampire genre in a period of experimentation. Once a guiding formula was established through a series of successful sequels to Browning's film, however, the vampire film entered into a dialogue with itself, repeatedly reinventing the genre for new audiences and to reflect changing attitudes toward both the past and the present. The vampire has always been a creature that evolves to suit the media that represent it, from folklore to literature to stage to cinema to television, and in this ever continuing process of transformation the vampire shows itself as embodying the essence of modernity: neither fixed nor stuck in the past but forever evolving and stretching out to the future.

Notes

1   Neale, *Cinema and Technology*, p. 8.
2   Gorky, newspaper review of Lumière programme at the Nizhni-Novgorod fair, p. 5.

3 Tom Gunning, interview by Adam Simon in the documentary *The American Nightmare*.

4 In Chapter 4 above, Sam George notes that it was Stoker's intention that Dracula would cast neither a reflection nor a shadow. The inclusion of the shadow in *Nosferatu*, as well as a reflection although less notably, seems designed to equate the vampire with the properties of the cinema – itself a medium designed to capture and preserve reflections.

5 Gelder, *Reading the Vampire*, p. 87.

6 Skal, *Hollywood Gothic*; Tudor, 'Unruly Bodies, Unquiet Minds', p. 35.

7 For a more detailed discussion of the Universal Studios approach to the vampire film, with detailed discussion of Browning's *Dracula* and its sequels, see Abbott, *Celluloid Vampires*, pp. 61–72.

8 *Ibid.*, p. 8.

9 Stoker, *Dracula*, ed. Ellman, p. 36.

10 Please note that *Drakula halála* is a lost film and as a result I can only mention it in passing. For further information, see Rhodes, '*Drakula halála*'.

11 Callahan, *Zones of Anxiety*, p. 85

12 Staiger, *Bad Women*, p. 147.

13 Auerbach, *Our Vampires*, p. 197.

14 Basinger, *Silent Stars*, p. 204. Kipling's *The Vampire* is purportedly based upon Philip Burne-Jones's painting *The Vampire* (1897) (in *A Choice of Kipling's Verse*, p. 109).

15 Dijkstra, *Idols of Perversity*, p. 351.

16 Staiger, *Bad Women*, pp. 147–8.

17 Basinger, *Silent Stars*, p. 203.

18 Botting, *Gothic*, pp. 1–2; Punter, *The Literature of Terror*, I, p. 1.

19 Anon., 'Luna Park First Night'.

20 Abbott, *Celluloid Vampires* pp. 141–62.

21 Karl Marx, cited in Gelder, *Reading the Vampire*, p. 20.

22 Sam George above describes a similar ambivalence in Stoker's novel, in which the modern technologies utilized by Mina and the Crew of Light are presented as possessing vampiric qualities through their emphasis upon the mechanics of reproduction, not capturing the essence of life but a hollow, or shadowy, reproduction much like cinema itself.

23 Todorov, *The Fantastic*.

24 Frayling, *Vampyres*, pp. 19–36.

25 Stoker, *Dracula*, ed. Ellman, p. 5

26 It is worth noting that *Mark of the Vampire* is a remake of *London after Midnight*. Both films were directed by Tod Browning for MGM who, in between these two films, directed the Universal Studios adaptation of *Dracula*. *London after Midnight* is a lost film but, thanks to Rick Schmidlin's photo reconstruction of the film, in which he uses production stills and intertitles, taken from the film script, we have an indication of what the film would have been like. This reconstruction is available on the *Lon Chaney Collection* (Turner Entertainment, 2000).

27 See Freud, 'The Uncanny'.

28 For a detailed discussion of the vampire as an embodiment of modernity in *Dracula* and *Nosferatu*, see Abbott, *Celluloid Vampires*, pp. 15–60.

29 Rudkin, *Vampyr*, p. 53

30 This does have some connection with *Dracula* in which science is, at times, presented as oblivious to what is right before them. While Van Helsing, Doctor Seward and the others search for Dracula, they are blind to the symptoms that show that Harker's wife Mina is falling under the hypnotic sway of the vampire.

31 In this, Dreyer's film has much in common with Mary E. Braddon's 'The Good Lady Ducayne' (1896) in which an older female vampire uses a doctor to assist her in draining the life blood of her young female victims.

32 Auerbach, *Our Vampires*, p. 116

33 While the figure of the Slayer in *Buffy* does come to emphasise physical power, endowed as she is with super-human strength, the series does not necessarily prioritise the physical over knowledge, but rather splits body and mind between the figure of the slayer and the watcher.

34 Carter, 'The Vampire as Alien', p. 27.

7

Crossing oceans of time: Stoker, Coppola and the 'new vampire' film

Lindsey Scott

Fᴙᴏᴍ ᴛʜᴇ ᴅᴀʀᴋ ᴛᴀʟᴇs of popular novels to the resurrections of contemporary cinema, the vampire continues to adapt itself to suit the ever-changing climate of our culture. While the zombie of Romero-remakes waits for us in the shadows, a stagnant, lurking reminder of what we still fear and the horrors that are yet to come, the twenty-first-century vampire moves closer to our homes to become a more complex insider, a sympathetic, humane or romanticised figure who ultimately succeeds in becoming 'one of us'. Edward Cullen of the Twilight Saga is no blood-sucking monster or coffin-keeper: instead he is a 'vegetarian' vampire who loves Bella, lives a 'normal' family life with his other human-loving vampires and still attends high school in the dreary Washington town of Forks. As Catherine Spooner deftly illustrates in Chapter 9 below on representations of Goth subculture, a quick perusal of *Gothic Charm School*, it seems, can do wondrous things for a vampire's social life. Given the huge commercial success of Meyer's Twilight novels and their adaptations on film, not to mention popular series for television like *True Blood* and *The Vampire Diaries*, our critical interest in the vampire has no doubt been reignited by this latest capacity for radical evolution. And yet, as fans and critics alike become enthralled by the idea of vampires taking biology lessons and bodies that sparkle in sunlight rather than spontaneously combust, we might ask ourselves: is Stephenie Meyer's approach to the vampire in fact nothing new?

A brief review of novels and films from the last thirty-five years would seem to suggest just that. Literary sagas such as Fred Saberhagen's Dracula novels (1975–2002), Anne Rice's Vampire Chronicles (1976–2002) and Chelsea Quinn Yarbro's ongoing Saint-Germain Cycle (beginning 1978), and films including John Badham's *Dracula* (1979), Joel Schumacher's *The Lost Boys* (1987), Francis Ford Coppola's *Bram Stoker's Dracula* (1992), Neil Jordan's *Interview with the Vampire* (1994), Stephen Norrington's *Blade* (1998) and the *Underworld* films (2003–2012) allow us to trace a visible shift in the vampire's representation that spans several decades, positing a more gradual metamorphosis from inhuman outsider to humane insider than Meyer fans may have initially considered. Literary trends in vampire culture in the 1970s and 1980s played a major part in transforming vampires from objects of anxiety into objects of desire, and, in the 1990s, two major film productions drew on such innovations directly: Francis Ford Coppola's *Bram Stoker's Dracula* (1992) and Neil Jordan's *Interview with the Vampire* (1994).

As Rick Worland observes, Coppola's *Bram Stoker's Dracula* 'typifies the ambivalent or even sympathetic portrayal of the vampire' that has been 'common in the past 20 years', a character motif that 'permits audience indulgence in his supernatural powers, particularly the seeming sexual irresistibility of the undead'.[1] Thus Gary Oldman's tormented Romanian knight is ultimately a liminal recreation of Stoker's vampire: remorseless, blood-thirsty killer and earnest courter of his long-lost love, this vampire manages to evoke our sympathy despite his late-night escapades. As Deborah Knight and George McKnight point out, while 'the standard configuration of characters in a horror film depends upon the clear tension between those who represent "good" and those – most notably the horror villain – who represent "evil"', in the case of *Bram Stoker's Dracula* the villain is 'far more seductive and compelling than the plodding but virtuous heroes'.[2] Similarly, Anne Rice's Louis de Pointe du Lac is played by none other than Brad Pitt in Neil Jordan's film adaptation of Rice's novel *Interview with the Vampire*. Attractive, compassionate and ultimately a victim of his own kind, Pitt's Louis is a vampire who incites our pity and excites our pulses. Such deep-rooted dualities in Jordan's titillating outcast and Coppola's 'demon lover'[3] suggest that these films also exemplify a key turning point for representations of the vampire in mainstream cinema, one that has led many 1990s viewers and film-goers since to welcome its transformation from monster to martyr with open arms. If the teenage girls who flocked to cinemas to see Meyer's Twilight Saga made up the largest portion of the franchise target audience, then women in their thirties and forties who made up its second-largest portion were no doubt the same viewers that Coppola had shamelessly targeted in the 1990s with movie taglines like 'Love Never Dies'.

But if we agree that the vampire has changed significantly in the last forty years, which textual anchor, exactly, are we using as the basis from which to form such opinions? The Hammer films, Murnau's *Nosferatu* or Stoker's novel, perhaps? If the 'remorseless predators incarnated by Max Schreck, Bela Lugosi and Christopher Lee' have indeed 'given way to more thoughtful portrayals', then when and where exactly did we cross the line?[4] Why did we turn from vampire stakers to vampire stalkers, and what can we gain from tracing the relationships that exist between the latest incarnations and earlier prototypes? As Paul O'Flinn observes of *Dracula* and the process of adaptation, 'these images and the story that contains them do not persist in an archetypal, unchanging way'; rather, each new telling 'is a remaking, as the old terms are smashed up and reassembled to enable them to address new fears and new desires'.[5] In a discussion that foregrounds our cultural rewriting of the vampire, the same principle, of course, must be applied to Stoker's novel, a Victorian telling that is also a 'remaking' of existing cultural mythologies that seeks to address 'new fears and new desires' for readers at the close of the nineteenth century. For critics such as Stephen D. Arata, Stoker's *Dracula* clearly represents 'a break from the Gothic tradition of vampires', transforming elements of the vampire myth and 'making them bear the weight of the culture's fears over its declining status'.[6] For Conrad Aquilina, the Romantic, Byronic legacy that has informed the literary vampire is periodically interrupted through writers such as Stoker reintroducing the monstrous (see his Chapter 2 above).

This chapter aims to shed further light on the 'remaking' process of vampire texts by exploring the intertextual relationships that exist between Stoker's novel, Coppola's *Bram Stoker's Dracula* and the 'new vampire' film Catherine Hardwicke's *Twilight* (2008), based on Stephenie Meyer's novel. By forming a critical dialogue between these influential vampire narratives (Stoker, Coppola, Meyer), I will consider how all vampire texts function primarily as intertexts and explore how audience responses of anxiety have been replaced ultimately by those of desire in the *Twilight* texts. Although frequently derided by vampire scholars, *Bram Stoker's Dracula* operates as a significant milestone text here, for the film not only borrows from a range of sympathetic vampire narratives in order to rewrite the content of Stoker's novel; it also functions as a template for Hardwicke's own cinematic rewriting of Meyer's *Twilight*. A brief exploration of Hardwicke's film reveals a conscious or unconscious imitation of Coppola's romantic subplot – and an ironical, although perhaps not entirely unexpected, return to the ideological landscape of Stoker's novel. In this context, Coppola's *Dracula* helps us to recognise the similarities that exist between Stoker's approach to the vampire and Meyer's, and, in both cases, the outcome is at once compelling and conservative; all-encompassing, yet stifling. The twenty-first-century vampire may indeed have crossed oceans of time, but, despite the opportunities presented by this latest popular reworking to explore its transgressive potential, it oddly seems to have much in common with Stoker's original position.

Learning from beasts

For some readers and critics, discussing Stephenie Meyer's *Twilight* alongside Bram Stoker's *Dracula* may seem an ahistorical or obsolete approach. The idea of comparing a twenty-first-century saga of popular Gothic-romance novels written primarily for the crucial teenage demographic to a Gothic epistolary novel written for 'a wide cross-section of the 1890s reading public' does seem to suggest little scope for fertile comparison.[7] Stoker's novel bears no immediate resemblance to Meyer's story beyond a common interest in the vampire, and comparisons become even more diluted once we consider the endless line of Dracula adaptations that have boosted the status of the vampire film as horror's 'most popular sub-genre'.[8] Meyer herself also seems to go out of her way to avoid making direct comparisons with Stoker, asking her readers instead to commit to a sort of blissful unawareness of *Dracula*'s unavoidable influence in modern popular culture. In the first of the Twilight novels, when Bella decides to conduct a little online research concerning the unfathomable behaviour of the mysterious Edward Cullen, she visits her 'favourite search engine' and types in one word: 'Vampire'.[9] But the search results noted are vague and over-generalised to say the least: 'everything from movies and TV shows to role-playing games, underground metal, and gothic cosmetic companies' (115). Meyer never intends for us to doubt the intelligence of her young protagonist, but any internet user researching the word 'vampire' need only click on the first hit of the search engine Google to find a mention of Bram Stoker's *Dracula*.[10]

While Meyer unashamedly draws on such well-known romances from canonical literature as Jane Austen's *Pride and Prejudice*, Emily Brontë's *Wuthering Heights* and Shakespeare's *Romeo and Juliet* to form the backdrop of her novel, the very absence of Stoker in this intertextual web of literary references only draws the reader's attention to where it is perhaps least wanted. In fact, many young fans and readers have felt compelled to draw comparisons between the popular vampire teen-read that revolves around high school and the more 'traditional' vampire novel that still crops up on the teaching curriculum and has its own array of screen adaptations to choose from. To give an example from countless online social platforms, recent YouTube posts from viewers of the Bela Lugosi *Dracula* (1931) included anything from 'Why the hell are you comparing Robert Pattinson with Bela Lugosi?' to more judgmental comments like 'Count Dracula is THE real vampire of film,

Edward should burn up under the sun like he's supposed to'.[11] All healthy competition aside, the decades of critical responses and textual revisions that Stoker's novel has generated still creep in at the margins of Meyer's popular (or, in some cases, unpopular) vampire narrative.

As critics of the vampire narrative, we encounter a similar dilemma when faced with categorising our responses to the latest vampire text. Stoker's novel has been adapted, reinvented and revisioned so many times since it first went to print in 1897 that it has become our own shorthand for what we believe the vampire to be in the popular imagination. Its influence has shaped our conceptions to such an extent that it is now regarded as a type of urtext for all vampire narratives, one that has infiltrated the realms of Marxist, Freudian, feminist and psychoanalytic criticism and provided us with a basis for the majority of twentieth- and twenty-first-century readings. As Milly Williamson explains, '*Dracula* (both Bram Stoker's novel and the many screen adaptations) has dominated critical interpretations of the vampire, eclipsing earlier incarnations … and their many progeny'.[12] While many of Stoker's earliest reviewers were able to observe upon the novel's release that the 'vampire idea' is, in fact, 'very ancient indeed', our own acute awareness of Stoker's influence has prompted us to regard his novel as something of a starting point for critical debate, one that has also taken much of the credit for the vampire's iconic status in popular culture.[13] The 'critical concentration on *Dracula*' that has been so 'tremendously influential in staking out the symbolic and metaphoric territory that the vampire is considered to occupy' encourages us to read the latest vampire texts through the extensive critical material written in relation to Stoker's text, an expedition that can be as confusing and misleading as it can be beneficial.[14]

To pose a further problem as situated from within the realm of adaptation studies, a critical comparison of *Dracula* and *Twilight* also runs the risk of identifying Stoker's novel as the superior text and embarking on a list of drawn-out comparisons that position Meyer's novel(s) as the inferior work. Although current adaptation discourse suggests that it is now 'common practice' for scholars to 'start from the assumption that all adaptations have more than a single source', many still favour rigid hypotext/hypertext comparisons over broader explorations of intertextuality so that even those with the best of intentions seem doomed to 'return to the question of fidelity' either through a probing of a so-called 'original' text or the confinements of an inherently moralistic language so frequently adopted in the field.[15] However, in forming a critical dialogue between these two 'unrelated' vampire texts via a reading of Coppola's *Bram Stoker's Dracula* (a film that paves the way for Meyer as much as it recalls Stoker), I am seeking to embrace what Robert Stam describes as 'the infinite and open-ended possibilities generated by all the discursive practices of a culture'.[16] Like the vampire myth itself, the process of adaptation demonstrates 'the ongoing whirl of intertextual reference' through stories that we re-create and continue to tell, with 'texts generating other texts in an endless process of recycling, transformation and transmutation'.[17] All vampire texts are recycled texts, consciously or unconsciously borrowing from earlier plotlines and prototypes.

'Yes, I too can love': *Bram Stoker's Dracula*

When the Count intrudes upon Jonathan Harker's 'encounter' with the three vampire women in Bram Stoker's *Dracula*, he hurls the fair woman away and, on declaring 'in a storm of fury' that Jonathan belongs to him, is met by a strange accusation from her: 'You yourself never loved; you never love!' After looking at Jonathan's face 'attentively', the Count replies: 'Yes, I too can love. You yourselves can tell it from the past. Is it not so?'[18] The response hangs in the air, an unanswered, open-ended question – and it remains so for the duration of Stoker's novel. The claim that Dracula 'can love' is not evidenced by any further information concerning the Count's past or any display of affection or humanity. In the mutually reinforcing dialogues of Jonathan Harker, Mina Murray, Lucy Westenra and Dr John Seward that make up the major content of Stoker's novel, Count Dracula is, quite simply, 'a monster' (57).

Instead, then, the declaration that a vampire too 'can love' serves less as a rebuke from the Count to his audience and more as a question that Stoker poses to his readers, readers who are, more than likely, familiar with the stories of other literary vampires: 'You yourselves can tell it from the past. Is it not so?' In posing this question, Stoker indirectly prompts his readers to recall earlier instances of the vampire in nineteenth-century culture, like the infamous Varney of the 'penny dreadful' serial *Varney the Vampyre* (1840s), a tortured, sympathetic vampire whose strong sense of guilt elicits responses of empathy; or the mysterious and sensuous Carmilla, a female vampire who forms a close and amorous bond with the young Laura in J. Sheridan Le Fanu's 'Carmilla' (1872). While the story of 'Carmilla' casts one woman as a vampire and the other as her human 'victim', Le Fanu's novella has been credited with forming 'the basis for a very modern context' and representing its two female characters as 'reflections of each other in their loneliness and repressed desire'.[19] In this sense, Stoker does, as Nina Auerbach observes, turn Dracula into 'the most solitary vampire we have met', a creature who can 'anticipate no companionship, for Stoker's rules allow only humans to unite'.[20] Ironically, then, by declaring that his vampire 'can love', Stoker banishes his readers from the pages of his own novel, asking them instead to recall the 'more playful and sinuous' vampires of earlier texts and dividing them irrevocably from the representations that *Dracula* was set to inspire for many decades to come.[21] In searching for the vampire that displays any signs of affection or humanity, Stoker's contemporary readers can only look back.

Of all the various screen incarnations of *Dracula* that have surfaced over the decades, Francis Ford Coppola's *Bram Stoker's Dracula* certainly has received its fair share of criticism. This is hardly surprising, given that the film makes some hefty claims to fidelity that are accompanied by an unashamed violation of Stoker's novel and endless encounters with other vampire texts. Lamenting the end of the Gothic, Fred Botting berates the film for its 'artificial claims to authenticity' and the 'uncertainties, accidents, and excesses of forms whose multiplicity and mobility seem imponderable and meaningless'.[22] Indeed, postmodern 'excess' seems to be of central concern here: as Ivan Phillips summarises in Chapter 14, the film has been seen as 'so saturated in awareness of its sources, its predecessors, its points of historical, folkloric, literary, technological and cinematic reference, that it becomes a spectacular paradigm of empty and self-parodying excess'.[23]

Coppola's 'prestige horror' Gothic-romance is certainly more 1990s than nineteenth-century, more in tune with its scriptwriter James Hart's romantic backstory and a society's accumulating fears over AIDS than with Stoker's novel.[24] Viewed through the kaleidoscope of intertextual reference and allusion, the film borrows from Jean Cocteau's *La Belle et la Bête* (1946) as much as it borrows from Stoker, with the earnest and beautiful Mina Murray (Winona Ryder) falling in love with the 'hated and feared' Prince Dracula, a 'beast' and a 'monster' whose redemption depends ultimately on a reunion with his beloved. Gary Oldman remarked in an interview that 'Francis always wanted to make a version of *Beauty and the Beast*, and he's sort of done it with this'.[25] But like any other vampire text, Coppola's *Dracula* takes influence from a variety of earlier prototypes, and, while its postmodern spectacle alludes self-consciously to 'classic' screen predecessors like Murnau's *Nosferatu* (1922) and Tod Browning's *Dracula* (1931), the film also, as a product of its time, builds upon the sympathetic or romantic representations of the vampire that were already thriving in the later twentieth century.

With the infamous predators of the 'Hammer horror' films officially dying out in the late 1960s and early 1970s after attempts to resurrect Dracula revealed that directors were 'not entirely sure what to do with him', a new type of vampire that addressed the concerns of the time was required if the subgenre was to survive another decade.[26] James V. Hart, who began writing the screenplay for *Bram Stoker's Dracula* in 1977, was openly 'affected' by two productions that sought to portray the vampire less as an outside threat and more as a victim: the '1977 Broadway revival starring Frank Langella' and 'John Badham's revisionist 1979 screen version'.[27] The Langella *Dracula*, while still dependent on its star's erotic appeal to women, was notably a step away from the sexual predators of the Hammer films and the image they perpetrated of a remorseless, destructive killer with exhausted taglines such as 'The world's most evil vampire lives again!' (*Dracula, Prince of Darkness* tagline, 1966). Another 1970s production often credited with influencing Hart's screenplay is the 1974 televised adaptation *Dracula*, directed by Dan Curtis.[28] Badham and Curtis both portray Lucy as Dracula's love interest, with Curtis's version also casting Lucy as the reincarnation of Dracula's dead wife and making a connection between the Count and the historical figure, Vlad Tepes (an association that is only loosely implied by Stoker but dramatically emphasised in the Hart/Coppola script).

However, while Hart evidently takes many cues from the Badham and Curtis productions, his script echoes other screen and literary innovations in vampire culture from the period. Curtis's Gothic soap opera *Dark Shadows* – originally aired in 1966–1971 and remade the year before Coppola's film was released – had already familiarised its audiences with the idea of a vampire seeking a lost love. Similarly, Hart's introduction of the love story between Dracula and Mina – as set up by the 1462 prologue in which Dracula lives as the Romanian knight Vlad Tepes with his wife, Elisabeta – also recalls Chelsea Quinn Yarbro's historical, romantic Saint-Germain novels, which, despite achieving ongoing widespread appeal since the cycle began in 1978, have never been adapted for the screen.

Coppola's *Dracula* also maintains a close relationship with Rice's *Interview with the Vampire* (1976). While Rice presents the vampire as a type of social outcast who elicits pity rather than hatred, Coppola's reconfiguration is less concerned with 'containing and destroying the vampire' and more committed to addressing 'the pressing question of his cure'.[29] Both narratives communicate themes of loss and 'failed desire' through their eternally suffering vampires.[30] Louis de Pointe du Lac, although an object of desire for Lestat and Armand, searches across the centuries for a 'truth' or meaning to his existence that persistently eludes him. Prince Vlad, after losing his wife and renouncing God, becomes a vampire 'out of his uncontrollable sense of loss and desolation', doomed to cross 'oceans of time' before he is finally reunited with her.[31] In both cases, the film project was not to be realised until the early 1990s. The adaptation of Rice's novel suffered much financial stalling before it finally appeared as Jordan's *Interview with the Vampire* in 1994, ironically coming to fruition only after the commercial success of Coppola's film, a 'solid hit that won three Academy Awards'.[32] The sympathetic vampire, born out of an earlier time of social and cultural permissiveness, evidently had to wait for the dust to settle.

Although Hart/Coppola's romantic subplot has been perceived by many as an act of textual violation that situates 'almost everything that happens' in Stoker's novel 'under the umbrella of the Hollywood romance genre', its inclusion evidences the film's engagement with pre-existing vampire narratives that had already tapped into a broader female market.[33] Coppola's film was organised as a highly dispersible text, intended to appeal to women as much as men by shifting in part to 'concerns of the woman's picture' through a complex hybridisation of generic conventions.[34] The film's ability to attract female viewers was an essential part of the film's overall success: as Austin explains, 'the commercial opportunity presented by the female audience can be seen as a crucial reason why Hart's script was picked up and developed by Coppola's company American Zoetrope and by Columbia'.[35] Although Stoker purists and avid horror fans were appalled by the changes that Hart and Coppola made to Stoker's 'classic' novel, for those who embraced its hybridisation of horror and romance (and there were plenty), *Bram Stoker's Dracula* opened up a broader space for the sympathetic vampire in the cinematic mainstream, paving the way for the likes of Meyer and Summit to migrate him with ease and fluidity from the typically marginal avenues of horror to the broader, more marketable territory of teen-romance.

In its attempt to 'do it all' and present a diverse blend of generic conventions and textual allusions that would draw in Stoker fans, horror aficionados, epic romance lovers and Gothic thrill-seekers alike, Coppola's film ironically achieves something greater by endeavouring to attract multiple audiences. More than any other vampire film, Coppola's *Dracula* challenges its audiences to feel horror and compassion in equal measure: to be repulsed by a monster that we must also empathise with; to desire its destruction as much as we desire its redemption; to find something beautiful in the 'waste of desolation' that Stoker's novel presents.[36]

When we first encounter Gary Oldman's Dracula in the fifteenth-century prologue, he is at once 'Draculea', Romanian knight 'of the Sacred Order of the Dragon', and Prince Vlad, newly married husband of his bride, Elisabeta, whom he prizes 'above all things on earth'. The action aptly begins in the middle of things, 'on the eve of the battle', and Draculea, dressed in a red suit of armour that denotes the fragile veins and arteries beneath the armour of his flesh, is both powerful and vulnerable, protected yet exposed. The scene includes a passionate farewell between Draculea and his bride before Coppola's camera cuts to a dramatic scene of battle where Draculea, shot in bleak silhouette, stalks the ground of the battlefield, the terrifying outline of his beastlike helmet towering menacingly above the ground. We then see him raise his spear and impale one of his enemies before a consuming, blood-red sky, and, after committing his heinous deeds on the battlefield, Draculea kisses his crucifix and praises God for blessing his victory. From the beginning, then, Coppola's *Dracula* conflates desire and anxiety, sexuality and violence, as the expected union and consummation of Draculea's and Elisabeta's marriage is replaced by the bloody acts of impalement that occur in battle between Christian and Turk.

In the impending rage that follows Draculea's discovery of his wife's suicide, love turns to hate, life to death, blood to life, and Draculea becomes the Undead, renouncing God and vowing to avenge his wife's death 'with all the powers of darkness'. The sequence is as visually beautiful as it is grotesque, as grand in its implied geographical scope as it is reductive in its scaling of table maps, matte-painted backdrops and miniature model settings. Thus the opening of Coppola's film informs its audiences that, in this retelling, we will always be caught 'in the midst' of things: between love and hate, life and death, light and dark, fear and desire, horror and romance, author and auteur, novel and film, reality and illusion. It is a liminal landscape that works in harmony with the vampire's nature rather than against it. As Creed observes in her psychoanalytic reading of the film, in 'representing Dracula as a creature rent by unfulfilled passion, Coppola brings out and illuminates – for the first time – the strangely beautiful aspects of the uncanny that are present in the vampire myth'.[37] This notion of 'beauty in horror' has also been located in Wojciech Kilar's score, with its achingly beautiful 'rising and falling minor third' that contributes to 'the overarching project of humanising Dracula'.[38] The film moves its protagonist from villain to hero and back again with an absorbing fluidity – however, this is an accomplishment that is often overlooked, essentially because a lovelorn vampire should have no place in a film that pledges fidelity to Stoker's novel. Although Coppola's *Dracula* was by no means the first vampire–human love story, the film has been openly criticised for confirming or 'normalising' the vampire's heterosexuality through its romantic storyline and essentially conservative framework. Rick Worland points out that while the vampire typically 'defies conventional codes of sexual propriety', in Coppola's film the additional love story between Dracula and Mina 'will work foremost to reunite the traditional heterosexual couple'.[39] Correspondingly, David Glover notes that in providing Dracula with 'a traumatic personal history, Coppola not only romanticises the vampire, he also sentimentalises him and, as a corollary to this, effectively removes him from the realm of sexual polymorphousness'.[40]

But endless doublings occur in Coppola's film. Just as viewer's are permitted to associate Mina's and Prince Vlad's heterosexual relationship with its 'monstrous' doubling in the seduction/rape of Lucy by Dracula as a wolf-beast, so too are they permitted to associate the overtly homoerotic overtones of the relationship between the aged, androgynous, sexually ambiguous Count and the young and virile Jonathan Harker with its darker doubling in the Count's relationship with Renfield, a sexually ambiguous 'madman' who becomes a devoted, imprisoned slave to his former 'lover'. Both homoerotic relationships are relinquished for the film's heterosexual union, as Dracula abandons his male guest when he spies Mina's picture and disposes of Renfield before making his way to Mina's bedchamber. But, in its endless juxtapositions, Coppola's film never entirely overthrows the sexual ambiguity of the vampire. After the 'consummation' scene where Dracula plays 'the feminised, passive, bleeding lover' and Mina becomes 'the active, assertive sexual predator', we see Dracula's traditionally heterosexual image as the young Prince Vlad dissolve to reveal not a wolf-beast (Lucy's mate) but a sinewy, bat-like creature who mocks the 'Crew of Light': 'You think you can destroy me with your idols?'[41] As the Count makes his escape across the ocean to his homeland, he shape-shifts again to become the aged, androgynous creature that seduced Jonathan Harker across the threshold.

While the ending of Stoker's novel implies a restoration of social order, mortal bonds and the sanctity of marriage and family, the ending originally selected for Coppola's *Dracula* where Mina returns to husband Jonathan was rejected by the film's preview audiences. After Mina's soul-wrenching affair with a vampire, audiences 'did not want to see her return to the earnest but dull Jonathan, Stoker's image of the "normal" restored'.[42] In this sense, spectators played their own part in bolstering the liminalities of Coppola's film, for who could imagine a 'normal' ending for Mina now? If the close of Stoker's novel celebrates the triumph of the virtuous, we might ask, what does the ending of Coppola's film celebrate, besides the redemption of a vampire? Two victorious battle sequences frame the opening and close of this film, but neither one is presented as a triumph. In breaking down the barriers between good and evil, human and vampire, *Bram Stoker's Dracula* openly declares that any triumph against this enemy will inevitably be a hollow one. As Anthony Hopkins's maniacal Van Helsing announces, 'we've all become God's madmen, all of us', Coppola's camera invites us once again to cross the threshold, leaving us within the confines of Dracula's castle. In the closing shot of Coppola's film we are with Mina, looking up at the mosaic ceiling beside Dracula's corpse, ready to take his place. By upholding and violating the content of Stoker's novel, Coppola's *Dracula* becomes a site where audiences may look back across the vampire's history as succinctly as they can look forward to its future evolution. When Gary Oldman's Dracula announces with steely conviction, 'Yes, I too can love', the remainder of Stoker's passage is replaced by the words: 'and I shall love again'. Spectators are probably aware at this point in the film that Dracula intends to travel to England in search of Mina, but in the broader context of the myth's metamorphosis, this additional sentiment instinctively pre-empts the next phase of the vampire's evolution: *'And I shall love again'*.

Love song (for a vampire): *Twilight*

Stephenie Meyer's infamous claim that she has 'never read *Dracula*' might well be true.[43] But as a teenager growing up in the North American state of Arizona in the early 1990s, it is unlikely that she could have so easily avoided the media circus that surrounded Coppola's film, or the 'vampire fever' that was set to sweep across the nation as financial investors tried to reel in the film's target audiences. Huge commercial projects such as Coppola's, whether they are actually consumed or not, seep far into the popular psyche. The film's ability to communicate its vampire–human love story on such a phenomenally grand scale no doubt paved the way for writers like Meyer to pluck out its romantic heart and leave the horrors of Stoker's novel behind. But in picking up its romantic threads, Meyer's Twilight novels ironically close the door on more transgressive revisions of the vampire myth in the same way that Stoker closed the door on his literary predecessors. I shall conclude by drawing some brief parallels between *Bram Stoker's Dracula* and Catherine Hardwicke's *Twilight* (2008) with the intention of revealing Coppola's film as a significant template for this adaptation and highlighting some striking similarities between the ideological landscapes of Stoker's novel and Meyer's.

In many ways, the doomed love affair between Dracula and Mina in *Bram Stoker's Dracula* provides an ideal model for Edward and Bella's fraught teenage romance, evidencing how fluently the ideas of literary texts can consciously or unconsciously seep into film, and films into literature, with the 'inherent intertextuality of literature' evoking 'the ongoing, evolving production of meaning, and an ever-expanding network of textual relations'.[44] Edward (Robert Pattinson), like Oldman's Dracula, is caught between his 'human' feelings for Bella (Kristen Stewart) and his 'inhuman' desire to drink her blood. In both cases, the conflict between danger and attraction is made evident from their first meeting, with Dracula almost biting Mina during his initial courting of her at the Cinematograph and Edward gagging uncontrollably when he must sit beside Bella in a biology lesson (interestingly, both meetings have a scientific context that underlines the 'unnaturalness' of the vampire, its status as neither living nor dead and defiance of the laws of nature).

While Coppola's film relies on its fifteenth-century prologue to inform us that Dracula and Mina are destined to be together ('Do you believe in destiny?'), *Twilight* reaffirms this notion by making Bella 'unique' to Edward's senses: 'you're like my own personal brand of heroin'; 'I can read every mind in this room, except yours'. Certain lines from Hardwicke's film seem to echo or recall Coppola directly: 'You don't know how long I've waited for you', says Edward, while Dracula says to Mina: 'I have crossed oceans of time to find you'. In the film's final scene at the prom, Bella asks Edward to turn her into a vampire: he replies, 'You don't know what you're saying' (Dracula: 'You cannot know what you are saying'); however, Bella persists: 'I want you, always' (Mina: 'I want to be with you, always'). When Edward tries to make her see the importance of living, Bella says 'I'm dying already' (Mina: 'Take me away from all this death').

How should we interpret these instances of textual allusion? Do they imply the work of sustained appropriation, or unconscious imitation?[45] More importantly, what do they reveal about the complex intertextual networks that exist between vampire texts and their audiences? The connections between Coppola's film and *Twilight* are of course dependent on audience recognition; furthermore, intertextual purpose becomes difficult to pinpoint when these conscious or unconscious borrowings from Coppola's film could have found their way into Hardwicke's script in any number of ways. In the DVD voiceover commentary between Hardwicke, Pattinson and Stewart, all parties reveal that they had to improvise lines on set owing to tight scheduling and the film's relatively modest budget. Lines that recall Coppola directly could have come either from the director (who does mention Coppola once during the commentary) or from the actors themselves, as they do not appear in Meyer's novel. Either way, the fact that Coppola's *Dracula* is selected wittingly or unwittingly as a suitable resource for Hardwicke's adaptation testifies to how deeply its regurgitation of the vampire–human love story had become embedded in the popular imagination.

In terms of its sexual politics, the *Twilight* novels seem to echo Stoker as much as they do the romantic subtexts of the late twentieth century, concerned as they are with re-establishing the barriers regarding sexuality that Stoker's novel imposes on the vampire myth. It is not simply the central heterosexual vampire–human relationship that is of concern here: rather, it is *every* social grouping that Hardwicke's film puts under the magnifying glass. Heterosexual couples are the object of her camera's gaze: Rosalie and Emmett,

Alice and Jasper and of course their 'parents', Esme and Carlisle. These
couplings are also mirrored in Bella's group of human friends – Mike and
Jessica, Eric and Angela – so that the incessant framing of heterosexual couples
becomes the film's most stifling visual motif. In a brief flashback sequence
that shows Carlisle biting Edward (the only instance of a same-sex bite), the
handheld camera shoots unsteadily from above, positioning Edward as victim
and focusing on his expression of pain in a second close-up. In the mirror
flashback that follows, we see Carlisle biting Esme, only here the act of biting
suggests sexual gratification as Carlisle approaches Esme as a tender lover
and her response exudes only pleasure (during the DVD audio commentary,
Pattinson jokes 'Hey, that was much sexier than my one!') The transgressive
possibilities left open for the vampire by other vampire texts since the 1960s
are thus stabilised here, as heterosexual relationships are also adopted as a
means of distinguishing between 'good' and 'evil' vampires. Even though a
coupling exists between James and Victoria in Meyer's 'bad' vampire camp,
this relationship is marginalised in Hardwicke's film. Here, James and Victoria
move independently from one another in a repeated 'triangle' formation with
the third vampire, Laurent, a visual indication of the evil vampire's prescribed
isolation that is set to be repeated in later films. Interestingly, then, while
'Stoker's rules allow only humans to unite', Hardwicke's film reaffirms that
only 'good' vampires should have a heterosexual mate.[46]

Although *Twilight* appears to re-establish 'the bond between vampire
and mortal' that 'Stoker did his best to break',[47] this sensitive repairing as
evidenced through Bella and Edward's relationship is muted by the film's
(and indeed the novel's) evident preference for romance conventions over
the excesses of Gothic fiction. For the majority of the film, vampires are
simply *humans*. While they may still be considered 'different', they are
certainly not represented as monsters. In fact, the only thing that separates
these vampires from us is that they are more powerful, more skilled and
more beautiful as immortals. With all this in mind, who wouldn't want to
become one? In other words, there is nothing dark or threatening about the
vampire's alterity: we have simply fallen in love with an idealised version of
ourselves. In the Twilight texts, the vampire's 'Otherness' itself becomes a
kind of allusion: implied but never realised; glamorised or fetishised but never
effectively explored. This is conveyed most disturbingly when Pattinson's
Edward exposes his 'Otherness' to Bella, stepping into the sunlight to reveal
his sparkling flesh, 'like diamonds'. Bella exclaims, 'you're beautiful', while
Edward seems repulsed by his own difference: 'this is the skin of a killer,
Bella'. But there is nothing unsettling or frightening about Edward's alterity;
therefore Bella has to reconcile nothing within herself in order to accept

it. While we may judge Bella's character for falling in love with a vampire so easily (when Edward informs her that he is a killer, she barely shrugs: 'I don't care'), her decision is obviously an easy one to make, given that this vampire is all hero and no villain. Meyer's/Hardwicke's vampires therefore assume the alterity that audiences commonly associate with the vampire not to explore the painful realities of social exclusion but to revel in its attractive or dangerous implications.

Similarly, while Meyer's novel frequently implies that Bella feels accepted by her new vampire family because she too is estranged from her father and her more conventional peers, Bella's 'difference' never provokes social prejudice or intolerance – quite the opposite, in fact. Loved and adored by Mike, Eric, Jacob, Jessica and Angela, Bella's implied difference instead fulfils the adolescent fantasy of social integration and acceptance. Her character has a double appeal for teenage readers or viewers who can identify with her feelings of isolation and exclusion and simultaneously feel reassured by her popularity and ability to secure the affection of the most attractive boy in school. In the *Twilight* film, 'difference' becomes highly desirable, its appeal magnified by Stewart's performance as the awkward yet beautiful Bella Swan and Pattinson's immaculate portrayal of the devastatingly handsome Edward Cullen. Pattinson's representation of the role also seems to contribute to the film's allusions of alterity, as his Edward speaks, acts and responds to Stewart's Bella with all the hesitancy, acute self-consciousness and juvenile moodiness of a typical teenager. *This* vampire could never be as old as Meyer imagines him to be, and, as a result, Bella's claim that Edward speaks as if he's 'from a different time' falls like a bad joke by the wayside. To add a further unavoidable subtext to Pattinson's all-too-human vampire, the real-life dramas that parallel the film's plot (such as the off-camera relationship between Pattinson and Stewart) saturate *Twilight*'s press coverage and its paratexts to conflate Pattinson's star image with his onscreen persona as Edward Cullen. In Hardwicke's film, Edward plays a song for Bella on the piano, an addition to Meyer's source text that came about only because Pattinson revealed a talent for playing during filming: as Hardwicke explains in the DVD audio commentary, 'we wanted to see the *real* hands of the vampire!'[48] Ironically, such conflations of star image and character serve only to undermine the film's already meagre implications of vampiric difference.

In its uncompromising hybridisation of horror and romance and its mutual recalling of remorseless bloodsuckers and sympathetic vampires of twentieth-century texts, *Bram Stoker's Dracula* illuminates the liminal aspects of the vampire that underline its status as a powerful, enduring cultural signifier. In doing so, the film actually breaks down many of the hierarchies that Stoker's novel erected; barriers that were, as Auerbach notes, 'hitherto foreign to vampire literature' such as 'the gulf between male and female, antiquity and newness, class and class, England and non-England, vampire and mortal, homoerotic and heterosexual love'.[49] Coppola's film therefore 'sets out to replace Stoker's meanings, not to copy them', and its usurpation of the novel is the film's ironical achievement.[50] Meyer certainly doesn't set out to copy the meanings of Stoker's novel; however, in presenting us with vampires that are, ironically, too close to our own image, the *Twilight* novels and films succeed in erecting their own barriers, reinscribing the premise that any creature that is *truly* a monster should not be pitied, or indeed, desired. With Meyer turning the vampire into a human as successfully as Stoker turned it into a monster, it may be some time before the tide turns again.

Notes

1 Worland, *The Horror Film*, pp. 254–5.
2 Knight and McKnight, *'American Psycho'*, p. 218.
3 Worland's term in *The Horror Film*, p. 253. The term also recalls Coleridge's 'Kubla Khan', with its woman 'beneath a waning moon … wailing for her demon-lover!' (lines 15–16) (*The Complete Poems*, pp. 249–52).
4 Silver and Ursini, *The Vampire Film*, p. 129.
5 O'Flinn, '"Leaving the West"', p. 68.
6 Arata, 'The Occidental Tourist', p. 629.
7 Leatherdale, *Dracula*, p. 68.
8 Silver and Ursini, *The Vampire Film*, p. 9.
9 Meyer, *Twilight*, p. 115.
10 In the Wikipedia article, 'Vampire' (the first search result using Google UK), a reference to Stoker's *Dracula* appears at the beginning of the third paragraph. As if to prevent viewers coming to this same awkward conclusion, Catherine Hardwicke has Bella research some more 'specialist' terms when she logs on to Google in the first of the *Twilight* films (2008): 'Quileute Legends' and 'Cold One'. The only example from popular culture that the film draws our attention to is an image from Murnau's *Nosferatu*.
11 Comments by 'Rastajay93' and 'Bladepaw18', dated October 2010, 'Dracula, 1931 (part 1/8)', *YouTube*.
12 Williamson, *The Lure of the Vampire*, p. 5.
13 'Review of *Dracula*'; p. 59.
14 Williamson, *The Lure of the Vampire*, p. 5.
15 Cartmell and Whelehan, *Impure Cinema*, p. 7 and p. 82. The hypotext/hypertext distinction is from Gérard Genette (*Palimpsests*, p. 7).
16 Stam, Introduction, in Stam and Raengo (eds), *Literature and Film*, p. 27.
17 *Ibid.*, p. 31.

18 Stoker, *Dracula*, ed. Luckhurst, p. 40.

19 Silver and Ursini, *The Vampire Film*, p. 173.

20 Auerbach, *Our Vampires*, p. 81.

21 *Ibid.*, p. 66.

22 Botting, *Gothic*, pp. 177–80.

23 Chapter 14, pp. 232–3.

24 Worland, *The Horror Film*, p. 253.

25 Oldman in an interview with Melvyn Bragg on *The South Bank Show*, 24 January 1993. Thomas Austin also makes this comparison in *Hollywood, Hype and Audiences* (p. 125), as does Barbara Creed in her psychoanalytic reading of the film: 'Coppola's tale is similar to Cocteau's *Beauty and the Beast*, except that Dracula, who has committed terrible deeds, is far from an innocent beast' (*Phallic Panic*, p. 90).

26 Hutchings, *Terence Fisher*, p. 141.

27 Worland, *The Horror Film*, p. 255.

28 See Silver and Ursini, *The Vampire Film*, p. 146.

29 Glover, *Vampires*, p. 149.

30 Creed, *Phallic Panic*, p. 88.

31 *Ibid.*, p. 87. Silver and Ursini forge another important connection between Coppola's *Dracula* and Rice's *Interview*: 'Because it derives as much from grand opera and the Romantic literary tradition as from Stoker, Coppola's film, as forcefully as Rice's books, represents neo-Romanticism in the genre' (*The Vampire Film*, p. 146).

32 Worland, *The Horror Film*, p. 253.

33 Gelder, *Reading the Vampire*, p. 90.

34 Worland, *The Horror Film*, p. 256. For an excellent analysis of Coppola's film as dispersible text, see Austin's chapter 'Bram Stoker's *Dracula*', in *Hollywood, Hype and Audiences*, pp. 114–51.

35 Austin, *Hollywood*, p. 120.

36 Stoker, *Dracula*, ed. Luckhurst, p. 421.

37 Creed, *Phallic Panic*, p. 87.

38 Deaville, 'The Beauty of Horror', pp. 189–95.

39 Worland, *The Horror Film*, p. 260.

40 Glover, *Vampires*, p. 141.

41 Creed, *Phallic Panic*, p. 91.

42 Here Worland is referring to remarks made by the scriptwriter James Hart at the Deep Ellum Film Festival, Dallas, Texas, 19 November, 2005. See Worland, *The Horror Film*, p. 265 and p. 303.

43 McElroy and McElroy, 'Eco-Gothics', p. 81.

44 Sanders, *Adaptation*, p. 3.

45 According to Sanders, textual appropriation, occurring in a variety of art forms, 'frequently affects a more decisive journey away from the informing source into a wholly new cultural product and domain. This may or may not involve a generic shift, and it may still require the intellectual juxtaposition of (at least) one text against another' (*Adaptation*, p. 26).

46 Auerbach, *Our Vampires*, p. 81.

47 *Ibid.*, p. 77.

48 DVD Audio Commentary, *Twilight*.

49 Auerbach, *Our Vampires*, p. 66.

50 O'Flinn, '"Leaving the West"', p. 77.

8

'I feel strong. I feel different': transformations, vampires and language in *Buffy the Vampire Slayer*

Malgorzata Drewniok

THE TV SERIES *Buffy the Vampire Slayer* was created by Joss Whedon and aired from 1997 till 2003, spanning over seven seasons. The series's protagonist, a young girl, Buffy Summers, is the chosen one, the Slayer, the only one strong enough to fight and defeat vampires.[1] *Buffy* is still hugely popular and often rerun. Although the focus of the show is Buffy and her helpers, owing to Buffy's calling as the Slayer vampires are present in the series too. What is unusual about *Buffy* is that the long-running nature of the series means that the writers were able to develop an extremely wide variety of vampire types. There are background vampires, whom Buffy stakes without a blink, and there are more prominent ones, who stick around longer and significantly influence the plot. There are conventional vampires, reminiscent of Bram Stoker's Count Dracula, such as the Master in Season One or Dracula himself in Season Five; more contemporary vampires, like Darla (Season One) or Spike and Drusilla (from Season Two onwards); as well as 'good' vampires, who have a soul and do not kill, like Angel (from Season One) and Spike (as he has become by the final season). It is clear then that to construct a vampire in *Buffy* one needs more than just a black Bela Lugosi cape. The vampires in the show are constructed through acting, costume and props, but also through language.

Transformations are a significant part of *Buffy*; humans are turned into vampires; humans fighting vampires die and rise again; vampires are reformed; vampires become insane; humans are magically transformed into someone or something else. In a way, the whole series is about transformation and change: not only Buffy's coming of age as a young woman and Slayer, but also redefining what it means to be human and monster. Transformations demonstrate an extremely broad and inclusive picture of what it means to be human. *Buffy* is also about being an outcast, while at the same time about being part of a highly inclusive group: humans, reformed vampires, demons, witches, and werewolves all working together. In this chapter I will explore three different types of transformations which contribute to the construction of vampires in the show. These are: being revived from the dead, being turned into a vampire and having one's soul restored as a vampire. At the end I will also mention briefly the situation when a human becomes a vampire in an alternative reality. I will examine how those transformations are expressed in language. As a linguist, I focus on the language accompanying transformations, rather than speculate about what this may signify, leaving this open for literary analysis.

Stephen Prince has said of the horror text:

> The anxiety at the heart of the genre is, indeed, the nature of the human being. Within the terrain of horror, the state of being human is fundamentally uncertain. It is far from clear, far from being strongly and enduringly defined. People in the genre are forever shading over into nonhuman categories. They become animals, things, ghosts and other kinds of undead. Having assumed such forms, they return to threaten ordinary characters and upset our sense of how life is to be properly categorized and of where the boundaries that define existence are to be reliably located. The experience of horror resides in this confrontation with uncertainty, with the 'unnatural,' with the violation of the ontological categories on which being and culture reside.[2]

I will apply this idea to *Buffy* where, as in horror films, being human is uncertain and unclear. People are turned into vampires, vampires are transformed, and both return to threaten others. The boundaries between human and vampire, and between soulless and ensouled vampire become blurred. At the start of the series, the binary oppositions – human/non-human and good/evil – are clear-cut; as the series progresses, they are deconstructed, forcing the audience to reconsider how they see some characters. Through this deconstruction, Whedon moves from the exclusivity of fixed categories to the inclusivity of a group of outcasts, each blurring the boundaries in their own way. This boundary blurring is visible in various aspects of the characters involved, including the language they use.

'If the apocalypse comes, beep me'

When a person is turned into a vampire, they die and return to life in a changed form. Although they look the same, they are different. In *Buffy*, when someone is revived from the dead, they have a similar status. They are not vampires, but they are still transformed. Buffy herself is a good example of such revival. She is a very strong character. One of her characteristics is her language: she often quips; she always has a sharp retort. Both the audience and other characters are aware of Buffy's particular way with words. This is verbalised by Xander, one of Buffy's friends and helpers, at the beginning of Season Three. Buffy disappears at the end of Season Two and the following season begins, surprisingly, without her. The Scoobies try to continue the Slayer's work, but find it hard without Buffy.[3] Xander then comments: 'I've always been amazed with how Buffy fought, but in a way I feel like we took her punning for granted.'[4] Xander recognises Buffy's use of language as one of her weapons against vampires.

Fighting vampires on a daily basis is dangerous; therefore it comes as no surprise that Buffy herself dies twice: first at the end of Season One (drowned by the Master), and later at the end of Season Five (when she sacrifices herself to save the world). In the first instance she faces the Master, an ancient vampire, although she knows she might get killed.[5] The Master drinks from her and leaves her to die by drowning. Luckily, she is resuscitated by Xander, declaring on her recovery, 'I feel strong. I feel different.' She then gets up and goes on to fight and kill the Master. She is changed – she strides more confidently, she says less, she acts without hesitation.

When Buffy dies for the second time, her experience is more complex. At the end of Season Five she sacrifices herself to save her sister and the world. She is magically resurrected, but feels lost and confused. The Scoobies believe Buffy has been in hell. Buffy returns as Season Six opens but only at the very end of the second episode does she speak.[6] And her words are, 'Is … this hell?' The risen Slayer is presented as animalistic; she is bestial; her body might have come back to life, but her brain is only catching up; she has to relearn language. When Buffy returns to the place where she died, she says: 'It was so … clear … on this spot. I remember … how … shiny … and clear everything was … But … now … now …'. It has been noted that language has been one of her weapons; now, she is inarticulate and hesitant, struggling in pain with every word she utters.[7]

At the beginning of Season Six Buffy avoids speaking about her experience. When she realises the others expect her to share her feelings, she quickly leaves the house to patrol. However, she eventually feels obliged to say:

> You brought me back. I was in a … I was in hell. I, um … I can't think too much about what it was like. But it felt like the world abandoned me there. And then suddenly … you guys did what you did.[8]

Buffy says what she thinks she ought to; but her true feelings are different. Later she tells Spike:

> Wherever I ... was ... I was happy. At peace. I knew that everyone I cared about was all right. I knew it. Time ... didn't mean anything ... nothing had form ... but I was still me, you know? And I was warm ... and I was loved ... and I was finished. Complete. I don't understand about theology or dimensions, or ... any of it, really ... but I think I was in heaven. And now I'm not. I was torn out of there. Pulled out ... by my friends. Everything here is ... hard, and bright, and violent. Everything I feel, everything I touch ... this is Hell. Just getting through the next moment, and the one after that ... knowing what I've lost.[9]

In both her utterances Buffy's lack of fluency shows how difficult it is for her to say those words. Although non-fluency is typical of everyday speech, we hardly ever notice it in real life and it is not usually used on screen unless for a specific purpose; here, to show how difficult the situation is for Buffy.[10] She lies to her friends in order not to hurt their feelings; she tells the truth to Spike, which makes her realise she is more like him than her friends now. That is why she leaves him with: 'They can never know. Never.'

And yet, she does reveal the truth in a later episode.[11] In this episode a demon makes everyone in Sunnydale (where the series is set) sing and dance and thus express their true, often hidden, emotions. At the end of the episode Buffy faces the demon but cannot help singing about her pain. She bursts into a song ('Life'), but, in the third verse, the melody changes and she sings:

> There was no pain
> No fear, no doubt
> Till they pulled me out
> Of Heaven.
> So that's my refrain
> I live in Hell
> 'Cause I've been expelled
> From Heaven
> I think I was in Heaven

On hearing this the Scoobies are horrified. Buffy first uses 'pulled me out', pointing to the fact that she would still be in Heaven if Willow had not magically brought her back. However, later she chooses 'expelled from' which has a different meaning to 'pull out'. 'Pull out' might suggest birth imagery (Buffy being born again); 'expel' might allude to the fall of man and the

Christian doctrine of original sin. Those two notions seem to be describing the same event but from different perspectives. Being reborn suggests a new beginning; being cast out marks the end of a period, a negative change. Being pulled out implies the action is performed from outside (here: Willow's spell); whereas being expelled points to a decision from inside of Heaven. One would expect those two verbs to be used in the opposite order: being cast out might sometimes be crafted into being reborn. This might also reflect Buffy's own interpretation of events: she has been told she was revived owing to Willow's spell ('pulled out'); she herself thinks she was in Heaven and thus feels expelled.

Overall, after being revived Buffy does not fit in the human category so easily. She returns changed and unnatural. She has now more in common with the monsters she fights than with her human friends. Her transformation not only threatens other characters but also upsets her self-identity: she realises the experience has changed her. It might also be part of the exploration of her Slayer heritage; the series gradually reveals that the origins of Slayer powers are much darker than everyone anticipated.

'I can hear the worms in the earth!'

Although the series features many vampires, it is rarely shown in full what happens to a person when they are turned into one. At the beginning of Season One Xander's friend, Jesse, is kidnapped by the vampires (the Master's minions). First they plan to feed off him, but eventually they turn him into a vampire and use him as a bait to lure the Slayer. Xander and Buffy try to rescue him and discover he is undead now. Xander is sorry for his friend, but Jesse responds: 'Sorry? I feel good, Xander! I feel strong! I'm connected, man, to everything! I ... I can hear the worms in the earth!'[12] And later Jesse shares his views on his transformation: 'Okay ... Let's deal with this. Jesse was an excruciating loser who couldn't get a date with anyone in the sighted community! Look at me. I'm a new man!'[13] For Jesse, the initial feeling is liberation and power. Jesse is no longer human but is not a fully fledged vampire yet. Yet, as Wilcox says, 'what really damns Jesse is his rejection of "loser" status'.[14] He has become so sure of himself that he is staked by accident. Later in the series there are 'new' vampires, emerging from the graves, encountering the Slayer in the cemetery, as well as more prominent ones, like Angel, Spike or Drusilla. Yet, the exact moment of the transformation into a vampire is never fully and explicitly shown. Angel's backstory is cut off when Darla sinks her teeth in his neck; Spike (William) is only shown pre- and post-transformation; Drusilla's story is scattered among flashbacks

in *Buffy* and *Angel*, the spin-off from *Buffy*. This absence (that is, the transformation happening off-stage) draws our attention, as well as opening the door
to further explorations of the vampire state. This absence might also serve the
dramatic function of preserving the mystery of the change.

Even the protagonist herself is turned into a vampire for a brief time.
This confirms that contemporary horror 'tells us that our belief in security
is a delusion, that the monsters are all around us', and that in fact everyone
can become one.[15] In an episode where Buffy and her friends' nightmares
become reality, Buffy is buried alive by the Master and then emerges from
her coffin as a vampire (sporting a 'vamp face').[16] Willow, Xander and Giles
(Buffy's Watcher) witness Buffy's shame at her transformation, but then she
surprises both the Scoobies and the audience by saying matter-of-factly: 'This
isn't a dream' and 'Well, we better hurry … 'cause I'm getting hungry'.[17] It
is arguable whether Buffy is a real vampire here since this is her nightmare
coming to life rather than reality; yet again, she transgresses categories. She
looks like a vampire, she *is* – physically – a vampire, and yet she still acts
like the Slayer. Only her words ('I'm getting hungry') reveal that she makes
a conscious effort to suppress her new vampire urges.

One of the most prominent vampires in the series is Spike, who was sired
by Drusilla. His transformation is shown in flashbacks through the encounter
with his mother.[18] In his former, human life as William he is presented as an
unpopular, sentimental poet. As a vampire, he seems more confident as he
tells Drusilla his plans for the future: 'We'll ravage this city together, my pet.
Lay waste to all of Europe.'[19] This episode is crucial to revealing more about
Spike's transformation, shown through a series of flashbacks. First Spike is
presented as the mortal William, in the company of his mother, in London
in the year 1880. Then, soon after his transformation, William comes home
with his sire and new companion, Drusilla. The mother notices her son is
behaving differently when he tells her: 'I am no longer bound to this mortal
coil. I have become a creature of the night. A vampire.' Her only reaction is
'Are you drunk?' But at the end of this scene William turns his mother into a
vampire to save her from consumption. As the episode progresses, yet another
flashback takes the viewers back to London in 1880, this time showing both
William and his mother as vampires.

But the mother is not grateful at all. As with her son, the woman is not
shown at the moment of her transformation, only pre- and post-factum.
Already undead, she says:

> I feel extraordinary. It's as though I've been given new eyes. I see everything.
> Understand … everything … I hate to be cruel – No, I don't. I used to hate to

be cruel in life. Now, I find it rather freeing. Nothing less will pry your greedy little fingers off my apron strings, will it? … ever since you first slithered from me like a parasite … Had I known better, I could have spared myself a lifetime of tedium and just … dashed your brains out when I first saw you.[20]

William defends himself ('Whatever I was, that's not who I am anymore'), but she tells him emphatically: 'Darling, it's who you'll always be. A limp … a sentimental fool.' Newly turned, William hoped for an eternity with his mother; yet after hearing her words he gives in to rage and stakes her. William and his mother might remind the viewers of Anne Rice's Lestat and his mother, Gabrielle.[21] William's mother's verbal cruelty echoes the mockery he had suffered as a human. He had aspired to be a poet, but people dismissed his work with comments such as: 'I'd rather have a railroad spike through my head than listen to that awful stuff'. Both these experiences contribute to his transformation – from William the Bloody Awful (Poet) through William the Bloody to Spike. His transformation is visible when William the vampire stands up to Angelus, the leader of the vampire pack William has joined:

> Angelus: Perhaps it's my advancing years that make me so forgetful, William. Remind me, why don't we kill you? [grabs William by the throat]
> William [choking]: …ike.
> Angelus: What's that? [releases him]
> William: It's Spike now. You'd do well to remember it, mate.[22]

Both William's personality and language change – from sentimental to cruel. And, unlike Angelus (discussed in the next section), Spike never loses his British accent (although it changes class connotation – from upper class to working class), which distinguishes him from other vampires and positions him as a 'bad guy' (as in so many US films whose 'baddies' speak with a British or at least European accent, in contrast to the US protagonists). It also puts him in a strange pairing with Giles. Giles's Britishness sets him in contrast with the young characters (Buffy and the Scoobies) and underlines the generation gap – his accent being that of the older generation.[23] Spike's accent also points to the generation gap among the vampires; however, this time he is of a younger generation than Angel(us) or Darla. Matthew Pateman suggests that Giles represents cultured Englishness; Spike, English counterculture:

> Giles is an image of Englishness that owes its status to cultural represen- tations from the Victorian period through Second World War films up to icons such as James Bond. He is intelligent, well-mannered, courageous but not unduly violent, thoughtful and witty. Spike owes his Englishness to

violent counterculture, to anti-heroes, anti-establishment values and a certain brutality.[24]

Giles had been a rebel in his youth, nicknamed Ripper, but later he assumes the poise of a stereotypical British man clad in tweed and stands for education and parenthood. In contrast, Spike began his life as a sentimental, Victorian gentleman and, upon becoming a vampire, opted for a more violent image, representing counterculture and youth. *Buffy* writers exploit the Britishness and by proposing various types of it (Giles, Spike, but also Drusilla and Wesley) they avoid superficiality.[25]

Spike transgresses human/vampire boundaries. As a newly turned vampire he returns as a threat to his mother. As a punk vampire (his first appearance on the show) he upsets the status quo in Sunnydale, threatening both the Scoobies and the Order of Aurelius.[26] And later, as an ensouled vampire and one of the Scoobies, he threatens the established image of a vampire. And these threats are both physical and linguistic.

'Oh, my god, "a vampire with a soul"? How lame is that?!'

In the series the notion of a vampire with a soul has a prominent place. The vampires in the Buffyverse are not human, but soulless, demonic creatures.[27] There are two exceptions to this rule – Angel and Spike. Angel becomes a vampire in the eighteenth century and at the end of the following century is cursed by the Gypsies: his soul is returned and, with it, his conscience. From then on he is forever tormented by the memories of the killings he has done, hence he decides to reform. His transformation from a cruel killer into a creature with a soul is shown briefly in the series. Moreover, his transformation back – when he loses his soul again – is also presented. Flashbacks scattered across *Buffy* and *Angel* show Angel as human, before being turned into a vampire. Thus, the audience can see Angel (vampire with a soul), as well as evil Angelus and human Liam.

When the show starts, Angel is a 'good' vampire with a soul, but because of the curse he reverts to his evil self, Angelus, when he experiences a moment of true happiness (that is, sex with Buffy).[28] Angelus's use of language becomes uncaring and aims to hurt. Justifying why he had been working with the Slayer, he says, 'What can I say, hmm? I was going through a phase.' When he faces Buffy again, he hurts her deeply with his words. After having had sex and his subsequent disappearance, she wants reassurance; he gives her: 'Like I really wanted to stick around after that'.[29] Buffy does not grasp what he is implying, asking, 'Was I not good?' But he replies mercilessly, 'You were great. Really. I thought you were a pro.' Evil Angelus not only enjoys using the language to hurt, he also chooses ellipses, such as 'Been around' (when asked where he has been) and clichés, such as 'Love you too. I'll call you' when Buffy calls after him, 'Angel, I love you'. Through ellipses and clichés Angelus intentionally depreciates the emotional bond between Buffy and Angel.

When Angel is shown in flashbacks when still the human Liam, he speaks with an Irish accent, whereas both Angel and Angelus lose it later on.[30] And it seems there is another linguistic difference between Angel and Angelus: Angel uses language seriously most of the time, whereas Angelus is playful. For example, when Angel appears for the very first time in the first episode of the series, Buffy asks him who he is, and he replies 'Let's just say ... I'm a friend'.[31] Angel takes time to reply and pauses in the middle of his utterance; hence it is clear he chooses what he says carefully. In contrast, when Angel reverts to Angelus and rejoins Spike and Drusilla, he speaks differently: the others wonder aloud what happened to Angelus when he interrupts: 'Well, he moves to New York and tries to fulfil that Broadway dream. It's tough sledding, but one day he's working in the chorus when the big star twists her ankle.'[32] Here he is being playful. By this performance, together with different clothes (leather trousers) and a cigarette, Angelus is making a statement: he is cutting himself off from reluctant, ensouled Angel and coming back to the fold. His performance is significant in two ways: he is clearly represented as the threat of a soulless, evil vampire; it also serves to persuade himself, as well as Spike and Drusilla, that Angelus is truly back.

At the end of Season Two, Angel's soul is magically returned through Willow's spell.[33] However, by that time he is doomed – as Angelus he sets free a powerful demon and Buffy has to kill him to stop the demon. Just before she delivers the final strike, Angelus turns into Angel. His style of speaking and his voice quality immediately change and what he says is expressed through that change. He suddenly says softly, 'Buffy?', as if he has woken up from a dream. Angel is a very good example of a character constantly transgressing categories: throughout the series he changes back and forth several times. He upsets the state of things as a vampire and as an ensouled one, and his transformations are evident in his language.

In contrast to Angel, Spike first appears in the show as a soulless vampire, a former companion to Angelus. He is cruel and ruthless, nicknamed after his favourite torture tool. The audience do not learn much about him for a long time; it is stated only that Angelus, Darla, Drusilla and Spike used to be a pack. Spike's backstory is gradually revealed through flashbacks.[34] He is a dynamic character and changes gradually from a cruel killer and the Slayer's enemy to a fighter on the good side and the Slayer's champion. Unlike

Angelus, who had been cursed by the return of his soul, Spike *decides* to get his soul back. At the end of Season Six he travels to Africa and undergoes many painful tests, but he maintains his sarcastic way of speaking: 'Got any more ruddy tests for me, you ponce? I'll take anything you can throw at me if it'll get me what I need to take care of the Slayer. Give her what's coming to her.'[35]

At this point in the series's narrative it is not clear whether and why Spike wants to regain his soul. It is possible he needs his soul to impress Buffy, to be worthy of her love. However, it might also be a means to kill her. His choice of words here contributes to this ambiguity – he says 'I'll take anything you can throw at me if it'll get me what I need to *take care of* the Slayer'. This sounds as if he is motivated to revenge or hatred. Having passed all the ordeals, he says: 'Make me what I was. So Buffy can get what *she deserves*.' Again, his statement sounds full of hate. Although Spike might have changed his attitude towards the Slayer, he has maintained his linguistic mannerisms: his British accent and the façade of sarcasm and cruel language.

When Spike regains his soul, he becomes insane and in his vulnerable state he is tormented by The First, the source of evil. He hides in a basement and, when Buffy runs into him, he seems distracted and speaks in a disordered way: '[Yelling] Don't you think I'm trying? I'm not fast. I'm not a quick study. [Suddenly crying] I dropped my board in the water and the chalk all ran. Sure to be caned. [Laughs] Should've seen that coming.'[36] When Buffy tries to communicate with him, he replies: 'No visitors today. Terribly busy' and 'Nobody comes here. It's just the three of us.' It remains unclear what he means by 'the three'. It is likely he is having constant conversations with The First, but only he can see the demon. He explains the scars on his chest with: 'I tried … I … I tried to cut it out.' Again, it is not clear whether he means his heart or his newly regained soul, or something else. He also says to himself: 'The thing is … I had a speech. I learnt it all. Oh, God. She won't understand, she won't understand.' His words reveal his mind is preoccupied with something. In the final scene of the episode several characters from the past episodes appear next to him to torment him, each transforming into one another (it is The First toying with Spike's mind; all the characters are evil ones that Buffy fought in the series, culminating in Buffy herself). Although each persona retains their style of speaking, it is in fact one long utterance. This is an externalisation of Spike's state of mind. One might ask if a mentally unstable Spike still fits in the vampire category. If vampires in Buffyverse have nothing in common with humans in terms of personality, if they are demons, one might presume they also do not have mental problems (doubts, regrets, guilt). Hence Spike is an outcast both to humans (being a vampire) and to other vampires (having had his soul restored and being mentally unstable).

'Bored now'

There is one more vampire in the series worth mentioning here: vampire Willow. I will discuss her separately as she exists in an alternative reality. Although it is only a temporary transformation, I believe it is significant to the overall narrative of the series. In Season Three, Cordelia, one of the Scoobies, is trying to recover from her break-up with Xander.[37] It is particularly painful for her since she used to be the most popular girl in the school. When Buffy arrived in Sunnydale and Cordelia accidentally became involved in some of Buffy's 'adventures', she eventually became one of the Scoobies and thus lost her social position (Willow and Xander are considered unpopular 'losers'; therefore, being friends with them damages Cordelia's reputation). In a moment of anger Cordelia wishes that Buffy had never come to Sunnydale; she blames the Slayer for her social failure. And thanks to a revenge demon, Anyanka, who just happens to be around, Cordelia's wish is granted.

Suddenly Cordelia finds herself in a different reality, where everyone is wearing dark clothes, there is a curfew for students and no one goes out after it gets dark. In this reality Buffy had never come to Sunnydale and, as a result, vampires have taken over the town. Willow and Xander, Buffy's closest friends in the world before the wish, are now vampires.

As with other vampire characters, Willow's and Xander's transformation into vampires is not shown. However, the contrast between human Willow and Xander (shown at the beginning of the episode) and vamp Willow and vamp Xander (later in the episode) is quite striking. Both characters turn from shy and naive teenagers into aggressive and very sexual vampires. Xander seems to be more confident than his human self, but the change is particularly shocking in Willow: she is a girl known for wearing colourful girly clothes which do not emphasise her figure much, and for often being nervous and inarticulate. Vamp Willow, on the other hand, is clad in black tight leather. She also speaks differently. In the first episode of the series, Willow speaks about her experience with boys: 'Well, when I'm with a boy I like, it's hard for me to say anything cool, or, or witty, or at all. I … I can usually make a few vowel sounds, and then I have to go away.'[38] When she is a vampire in the alternative reality, she does not have such problems. She kisses Xander very sensuously.

Although at the end of the episode everything goes back to 'normal' (that is, to the previous reality) and the audience never sees vamp Xander again, vamp Willow makes another appearance, crossing over from the alternative reality to the 'main' one.[39] Owing to a backfired magic spell vamp Willow finds herself in the world where Buffy keeps vampires at bay. Thus for a period of time there are two Willows in Sunnydale. They are distinguishable because of their outfits, their behaviour and their language. Even if vamp Willow were not clad in leather, it would be clear it is her when she utters her signature phrase, 'Bored now'.[40]

Language plays an important role in 'Doppelgangland' (when vamp Willow crosses over). In the course of the episode human Willow and vamp Willow switch places and pretend to be each other. Human Willow tries to seem evil and confident. When she pretends to be vamp Willow and announces that she has killed her human counterpart, Anya does not believe her, but she announces bravely: 'I don't like that you dare to question me'. And she continues (still pretending to be vamp Willow): 'She bothered me. She's so weak and accommodating. She's always letting people walk over her.' The vampires seem to believe she is vamp Willow; however, later on she becomes hesitant as they decide to go on a killing spree: 'I don't know if I feel like killing anymore'. Then she adds: 'I'm so bored'. This is striking because this inaccurate use of the characteristic feature of vamp Willow reveals the deceit: evil Willow would say 'bored now'.

Just when human Willow is impersonating vamp Willow, the reverse is happening somewhere else (vamp Willow is locked in a cage in the school library). Vamp Willow pretending to be human Willow tries to persuade Cordelia to release her. She says: 'Let me out … 'Cause I'm so helpless.' When Cordelia wants to know how Willow locked herself in the library cage, she answers: 'I was looking at books. I like … books … 'Cause I'm shy.' Neither evil Willow nor human Willow succeeds in impersonating the other one; their language use gives them away.

The simple elliptic phrase 'bored now' points to something much more complex: it is a sign of Willow's transformation. This character undergoes many changes as the series progresses – becoming a more confident person, honing her magical abilities and discovering her sexuality. 'Bored now' at an early stage of the process foreshadows what is to come. Towards the end of Season Six Willow goes over the edge because of the death of her partner, Tara, who had been accidentally shot dead by one of the villains of the season, Warren. At this point in the series's narrative Willow has already become a very powerful witch. She is so shattered by Tara's death that she succumbs to dark magic. She hunts Warren down, tortures him and then flays him alive. But before she kills him, she says 'Bored now', echoing her evil self from the alternative reality.[41]

Willow's change is complex and the series succeeds in showing that transformations from good to evil (and back) are not simple: 'Bored now' not only foreshadows Willow's succumbing to dark magic, becoming an evil witch, but also suggests that they are the same person, that every person has an inner potential to be good or evil and that everyone has to constantly make the choice between the two. This coexistence of both good and evil in every creature is touched upon in *Buffy* and more developed in *Angel*. *Buffy* explores the idea in the stories of Buffy herself; of Faith, the rogue slayer; of Angel and Spike, as well as evil Willow and Anya, the vengeance demon turned human. At the beginning of the *Buffy* series, vampires are presented as soulless demons that have nothing in common – in terms of personality – with the humans whose body they have taken over. As the series progresses, this becomes a more and more complicated issue, with Angel reverting to Angelus and Spike switching from being foe to friend. In *Angel*, it becomes harder and harder to see the distinction between good Angel and evil Angelus. The creators of the show explored the notion that Angel and Angelus are the same person and that Angel has to put a lot of effort to keep his evil counterpart, buried deep inside of him, at bay. For Stacey Abbott, 'he is a vampire who must live with the dark side that is an integral part of himself and from which he gains much of his strength'.[42] Willow's transformations mentioned above as well as her signature 'bored now' prepare the way for a more complex representation of vampires in the show. Such preparation is needed because accepting the potential for good and evil in human characters is easier and paves the way to doing the same with evil characters such as vampires and demons. The latter is morally more complex; it requires more effort to see good in characters very often too easily marked as monsters.

Conclusion

Transformations in *Buffy the Vampire Slayer* are never simple. When a character is revived from the dead, the experience is bound to be traumatic, temporarily destroying the ability to use language. On being turned into a vampire, one might feel liberated (like Jesse or William/Spike), traumatised (Buffy) or excited (Angel), but the new vampire also craves blood whether they like it or not (Buffy) and becomes cruel (Spike's mother). Even becoming a vampire in an alternative reality (Willow) might influence the reality one lives in. And it becomes even more complicated when a vampire regains the soul – the remorse and memories of past killings might drive them insane (Spike) or force them to work for the good (Angel). A vampire with a soul might change the way they speak (Angel) or maintain their old ways (Spike). Whatever the transformation, it is hard to speak of it: Buffy avoids the subject and lies; Angelus dismisses any further questions with 'You wouldn't believe me if I told you'.[43]

In the horror genre, according to Prince, the state of being human is uncertain and every transgression or transformation returns to threaten others and upset the status quo. I have shown here how this applies to *Buffy*, where transformations provide a way of redefining characters' identity, and that the 'shading over to non-human categories' in *Buffy* can also be seen in language. This series puts its characters – both human and vampire – through many transformations; humans and monsters escape easy labelling; these transformations dramatise an immensely inclusive world. If you thought being turned into a vampire was simple and straightforward, *Buffy* will prove you wrong.

Notes

1 The series's premise is that in every generation there is a slayer. When one slayer dies, another one is called. This is first revealed in the very first episode, 'Welcome to the Hellmouth', 1.1.
2 Prince, Introduction, *The Horror Film*, p. 2.
3 The Scoobies: Buffy's friends and helpers, Willow and Xander, later on joined by other characters (Cordelia, Oz, Spike, Tara and Dawn). The name of the group is coined by the characters themselves, alluding to the *Scooby-Doo* TV series.
4 'Anne', 3.1.
5 In Season One's finale, 'Prophecy Girl', 1.12.
6 'Bargaining Part 1', 6.1 and 'Bargaining Part 2', 6.2.
7 Overbey and Preston-Matto, 'Staking in Tongues', pp. 73–84.
8 'Afterlife', 6.3. All ellipses in this chapter indicate hesitations in transcribed speech rather than editorial deletions.
9 *Ibid.*
10 See Leech and Short, *Style in Fiction*, pp. 132–3.
11 'Once More, with Feeling', 6.7.
12 'The Harvest', 1.2.
13 *Ibid.*
14 See Wilcox, 'There Will Never Be a "Very Special" Buffy', p. 18.
15 Prince, Introduction, *The Horror Film*, p. 4.
16 'Nightmares', 1.10. Vampires in *Buffy* look like humans most of the time. When they attack or are aroused, their faces change into monstrous ones, with visible fangs and deformed, furrowed foreheads. This is called a 'vamp face' or a 'game face'. Interestingly, 'game face' is a colloquial American term popular before *Buffy* aired and only appropriated by the series's creators. According to the *OED*, a game face is 'a look or manner characterised by single-minded dedication, determination and seriousness'.
17 Watcher: a guardian and trainer for the Slayer, with expertise in ancient texts and vampire lore.

18 To sire: to turn someone into a vampire.

19 'Lies My Parents Told Me', 7.17.

20 *Ibid.*

21 Lestat is one of the vampire characters in Anne Rice's Vampire Chronicles. He makes his first appearance in the first novel of the series, *Interview with the Vampire* (1976), but his backstory and his relationship with his mother is revealed in the second book, *The Vampire Lestat* (1985). Like William, Lestat had been very close to his mother; when he returns home, already a vampire, and discovers his mother is dying, he sires her. They roam the world together for some time, but at some point they part, one of the reasons being Gabrielle's new-found independence.

22 'Fool for Love', 5.07.

23 See Wilcox and Lavery, Introduction, *Fighting the Forces*.

24 '"You Say Tomato"', p. 109.

25 Drusilla is Spike's companion and sire. She was born in the nineteenth century in England and was turned into a vampire by Angelus; Wesley Wyndham Price is another Watcher, appearing in Season Three of *Buffy*.

26 The Order of Aurelius: an old-fashioned group of vampires in Sunnydale, led by the Master.

27 Buffyverse: the fictional universe of *Buffy the Vampire Slayer* and its spin-off, *Angel*. The fact that vampires in the Buffyverse are soulless demons is made explicit by Giles in 1.07 'Angel' when Angel's identity (that is, his being a vampire) is revealed.

28 At the end of 'Surprise', 2.13.

29 'Innocence', 2.14.

30 'Becoming Part 1', 2.21.

31 'Welcome to the Hellmouth', 1.1.

32 'Innocence', 2.14.

33 'Becoming Part 2', 2.22.

34 'Fool for Love', 5.07, and 'Lies My Parents Told Me', 7.17.

35 'Grave', 6.22.

36 'Lessons', 7.1.

37 'The Wish', 3.9.

38 'Welcome to the Hellmouth', 1.1.

39 'Doppelgangland', 3.16.

40 The phrase 'Bored now' is first uttered by Willow in 'The Wish', and repeated in 'Doppelgangland', 3.16, as well as in 'Villains', 6.20.

41 'Villains', 6.20.

42 Abbott, *Angel*, p.7.

43 'Innocence', 2.14.

9

Gothic Charm School;
or, how vampires learned to sparkle

Catherine Spooner

Sparkle

'Real Vampires Don't Sparkle' announced a web campaign *circa* 2010, protesting at the pervasiveness of Stephenie Meyer's *Twilight* novels (2005–2008) and their film adaptations (2008–2012), in which vampires do not avoid the sun for fear of any physical damage it might do them, but because it will expose the scintillating quality of their skin and reveal their carefully concealed difference to humans. The sparkly vampire has come to be regarded as representative of a 'de-fanged' vampire, a vampire more likely to be regarded as a desirable romantic partner than a bloodthirsty killer. These vampires have supernatural abilities and tortured souls but avoid drinking human blood, instead sating themselves on wild animals, as in *Twilight* and *The Vampire Diaries* (2009–);[1] on artificial blood substitutes, as in Charlaine Harris's Southern Vampire Mysteries (2001–) and their televisual adaptation *True Blood* (2009–); or simply by going 'cold turkey' and not drinking at all, as in the BBC TV series *Being Human* (2009–). While scintillating skin may be unique to Meyer's vampires – her lawyers have reportedly been aggressive in attacking the appearance of sparkly vampires appearing anywhere outside the official *Twilight* franchise – the Cullen family's sparkliness has become symbolic of critics' disillusionment with the insipid properties of these vampires. Indeed several of the series mentioned above, as they have progressed, have attempted to shed sparkly associations by allowing their lead vampires to revert to a nastier, more bloodthirsty image, with *The Vampire Diaries'* Stefan returning to human blood-drinking, *True Blood*'s Bill betraying Sookie and *Being Human*'s Mitchell wreaking havoc in a crowded train carriage. Despite these subsequent negotiations, however, the appearance of so many vampires seeking to live amicably alongside humans during the first decade of the twenty-first century remains a striking cultural phenomenon.

The sparkly vampire has also come to represent the seemingly relentless *Twilight* teen-marketing machine. The sparkle effect has become a marketing tool in its own right: it is even possible to reproduce that special vampire radiance with a bit of 'First Light Face Glow' from the Luna Twilight make-up range. Vampirism has always provided an apt metaphor for consumer culture: as Rob Latham points out, 'The vampire is literally an insatiable consumer driven by a hunger for perpetual youth'.[2] The sparkly vampire represents the apex of that process. The *Twilight* novels and films are not only phenomenally successful products in their own right but also part of an immensely profitable franchise – something that *True Blood* ironically acknowledges in its fake promotional campaign for TruBlood, the beverage. The sparkly vampire is one that has been made palatable for a mass market and readily convertible into a range of consumer products, from make-up and jewellery to cars and even sex-toys.

Sparkly vampires are divisive: they incite adoration from fans and loathing from their detractors. They are easy to deride, but this does not make them any the less popular or pervasive. As Hannah Priest argues,

> the reason so many of us hate sparkly vampires is because, put simply, they are not written for us … When we rail against sparkly vampires, we are railing against another generation's Gothic. We embody *Northanger Abbey*'s description of commentators who 'abuse such effusions of fancy at their leisure, and over every new novel to talk in thread-bare strains of the trash with which the press now groans' … What is significant is that the 'trash' to which Austen refers is now the 'correct' Gothic against which sparkly vampire fiction is now measured.[3]

Rather than simply dismissing a new generation's Gothic, it is more interesting to ask why sparkly vampires have appeared in the twenty-first century, and what this tells us about shifting tastes in Gothic narrative. Over a period of about two hundred years vampires have changed from the grotty living corpses of folklore to witty, sexy super-achievers: vampires to whose condition we may aspire. Why did these changes come about? How did vampires learn to sparkle?

This chapter attempts to demonstrate that the sparkly vampire is just one element of a wider shift in mood in Gothic fictions; one that is linked to the changing fortunes of Goth subculture and its representation in the mainstream media. Fictional vampires, and real Goths, no longer appear so comfortable in the position of outsider as they once did. Making peace with the mainstream is a strategy that is becoming increasingly visible in some sections of alternative culture, and this uneasy desire for assimilation is acted out in vampire narratives. Much has been written about the rise of the sympathetic monster in the second half of the twentieth century, the monster who is given a voice and an interiority and with whom the reader or viewer is invited to identify. As other chapters in this volume attest, the twenty-first century has seen the rise of the assimilative monster, the monster who is no longer a sympathetic outsider but who is, or at least attempts to be, one of us.

Rules

The seeds of today's aspirational vampires were first sown in John Polidori's *The Vampyre* (1819). Polidori's Lord Ruthven is transparently based on his employer and mentor, Lord Byron, and possesses all of Byron's mythic charisma – as Conrad Aquilina describes in Chapter 2 above. Byron, widely described as the first celebrity in the modern sense of the word, provides a model that informs the development of the vampire myth in the succeeding two centuries: witty, aristocratic, intelligent, tormented and wildly sexually attractive to both sexes.[4] Lord Ruthven, nevertheless, while possessing a kind of irresistible charm and a titillating novelty to the jaded aristocrats about him, never seeks to integrate himself with society or play by its rules: he stands apart, 'entirely absorbed in himself'.[5] In fact his apparently social acts, such as his generous distribution of charity, appear to generate disruption rather than cohesion: 'all those upon whom it was bestowed, inevitably found that there was a curse upon it, for they all were either led to the scaffold, or sunk to the lowest and the most abject misery'.[6] Vampires from Ruthven onwards possess a thrilling mixture of rebellion and charm; of social polish and deliberate defiance of socially approved morality and convention. Nineteenth-century vampires from Varney to Carmilla fascinate because they are apparently sophisticated, cultured beings while simultaneously constituting a destructive force that challenges their culture's cohesion, order and ethical premises. While in the nineteenth century this doubleness was intended to horrify, in the later part of the twentieth century the charismatic rebel became an increasingly lionised figure and the vampire began to be presented as sympathetic. In Anne Rice's influential *Interview with the Vampire* (1976), the interviewee, Louis de Pointe du Lac, is emotionally articulate and struggles with the loss of his humanity. From this lineage the sparkly vampire springs: as Priest points out, Rice's anti-hero Lestat even pre-empts the Cullens' luminosity with his 'extremely white and highly reflective skin that has to be powdered for cameras of any kind'.[7]

It is Edward Cullen's radiance in particular, of course, that is of central importance to Meyer's text: he is the focal point of vampire spectacle for the heroine Bella and by extension the reader. Edward first reveals his sparkliness to Bella once their relationship has begun to develop in *Twilight*, and Meyer describes it as follows:

> His skin, white despite the faint flush from yesterday's hunting trip, literally sparkled, like thousands of tiny diamonds were embedded in the surface. He lay perfectly still in the grass, his shirt open over his sculpted, incandescent chest, his scintillating arms bare. His glistening, pale lavender lids were shut, although of course he didn't sleep. A perfect statue, carved in some unknown stone, smooth like marble, glittering like crystal.[8]

In this passage, Edward is presented as exotic, marvellous, eminently consumable – a rare and precious object, a work of art rather than a man. He is, however, oddly asexual. The vampire body normally emphasises the mouth as orifice and the exchange of bodily fluids; it is transformative and aligned with the bestial, and as such meets Bakhtin's descriptions of the grotesque body in *Rabelais and His World*.[9] Edward's body, on the other hand, is a 'perfect statue', permanent and unchanging; it is 'smooth', closed off, and thus more resembles Bakhtin's criteria for the classical body – not the monstrous, grotesque body of the vampire we might more conventionally expect. Edward as spectacle draws the female gaze, but also repels it. He reflects rather than absorbs light. His glittering skin is a focus for female desire while also simultaneously denying its satisfaction. The ultimate commodity, Edward's scintillating, sculptural body leaves only the desire for more.

Apollonian rather than Dionysian, Edward is in one sense anti-Gothic – he and his supernaturally enlightened family represent order, control and civilisation rather than the barbaric forces that threaten to overturn it. Historically, of course, Gothic has been about the play of barbarism versus civilisation and usually functions to restore order; as Fred Botting argues, 'The terrors and horrors of transgression in Gothic writing become a powerful means to reassert the values of society, virtue and propriety: transgression, by crossing the social and aesthetic limits, serves to reinforce or underline their value or necessity, restoring or defining limits'.[10] The vampire, however, has almost always been on the side of barbarity: conventional critical readings tend to present the vampire as a force disrupting social decorum, from Dracula destabilising Victorian values to the Lost Boys posing a threat to Reagan's youth in the 1980s. To have the monster representing the limit, rather than the transgressive impulse, is a development stemming from the merging of the vampire narrative with a popular romance tradition in the later 1970s, most vividly illustrated by Chelsea Quinn Yarbro's *Hôtel Transylvania* (1978) and its sequels. This tradition has been overlooked by critics who have emphasised Gothic over romance, but shapes the sparkly vampires of the twenty-first century in important ways.

The idea that there are 'rules' of vampirism that must be learnt and followed derives from Anne Rice: in *Interview with the Vampire* Louis discovers too late and to his cost that the Parisian *Théâtre des Vampires* possess a series of binding laws or social codes that govern their interactions. Rice's Vampire Chronicles nevertheless favour vampire iconoclasts who overturn the moribund conventions of their predecessors. Claudia attempts to murder her vampire sire; Louis burns down the theatre and incinerates its inhabitants in revenge for her death; Lestat flouts the injunction to secrecy by proclaiming his vampire identity as rock star. In twenty-first-century vampire narratives, the 'rules' are not just limited to the vampire community or dedicated to maintaining its continuation but go above and beyond. They appeal to a moral imperative and a sense of decorum that are not just about preserving the social contract but also a kind of self-fashioning – even, perhaps, soul-making.

Through the character of Edward Cullen, Stephenie Meyer constructs the vampire as representative of order rather than chaos. One of the defining features of Edward's personality is his self-control. Previously, this has been largely considered in the context of sexuality: Edward and eventually also the werewolf Jacob must restrain their sexual desire for Bella, out of the risk of hurting her. The concept of self-control, however, is much more far-reaching than this in the Twilight quartet. The Cullens' identity is produced through a discourse of self-control: their existence within human society is enabled by the daily restraint they exercise over their vampiric impulses. In *Eclipse* (2007), the third novel in the series, it is revealed that this very quality is what enables them to exist as a family. Jasper's tale of the vampire wars of the south describes the western vampire community as an uneasy balance between wild, lawless vampire gangs that kill humans indiscriminately and engage in bloody wars and vendettas against one another, and the civilised Volturi who periodically descend from Europe to assert punitive control and re-establish order. The Cullens, it transpires, are the largest group of vampires to have thus far avoided the Volturi's intervention, because they have internalised this process of control – good Foucauldian subjects, they are docile bodies who have internalised the operations of power and operate a form of self-surveillance[11] – of keeping check on their own impulses through a self-imposed ethic of 'vegetarianism'.

Moreover, Jasper's account of the vampire wars reveals that this internali-sation of control is specifically a learned process. He explains, 'Very young vampires are volatile, wild, and almost impossible to control. One newborn can be reasoned with, taught to restrain himself, but ten, fifteen together are a nightmare'.[12] Newly made vampires constitute an inchoate force that either can be corralled and used as a weapon, or can be schooled, guided, to become a self-controlling being. The latter is privileged: through learning self-control, a quasi-human identity is produced. Bella, it transpires, constitutes the epitome of this process: in the fourth novel, *Breaking Dawn* (2008), her own initiation into vampirism is remarkably smooth as her special ability proves to be the power to control her bodily needs and impulses to a supernatural degree. Bella does not need to learn to be human as she never relinquishes her humanity, and in this manner becomes the most powerful vampire of them all.

Similar patterns can be found in other contemporary vampire narratives. In the first season of *True Blood*, vampire protagonist Bill sires a teenage vampire and must take responsibility for her; his failure to 'parent' her effectively leaves her dangerously out of control. Jessica's initiation into the 'adult' world of vampirism presents a microcosm of *True Blood*'s vampire community, who are enabled to control their blood-lust through an artificial blood substitute, and as a result coexist with humans. *Being Human* repeatedly emphasises abstention from blood-drinking through the character of Mitchell, who views his desire for blood as an addiction with which he is engaged in a perpetual struggle. In the second series, Mitchell founds a kind of 'blood-drinkers anonymous' group for his fellow vampires. As the series title suggests, 'being human' is not a pre-existent condition but a process, in which the continual effort of self-control enables a human or quasi-human subject to be produced.

In the Twilight quartet, the Cullens's self-control is so perfected that they not only manage to live undetected alongside humans but exhibit an almost supernatural politeness. Although the younger members of the family do have occasional lapses, in general the family's manners are so immaculate that they are unsettling. They do not eat, but they provide Bella with appetising food when she visits. They offer lavish and beautifully wrapped gifts on her birthday. They easily charm any human who comes into their orbit – aided by vampiric skills of fascination, of course, but also by a more worldly appreciation of how to avoid causing offence, or to placate when it is already taken. Their existence within the human world is eased by a respect for social customs and niceties that extends to Edward's insistence on marriage before sex – a position to which the initially sceptical Bella eventually comes round with the realisation that she wants to 'do this right … Responsibly. Everything in the right order.'[13]

This is articulated in a slightly different way in The Southern Vampire Mysteries and *True Blood*. As Bill informs Sookie, vampires are dependent on 'Courtesy and custom' in order to cement a kind of vampiric social contract reminiscent of Rice. '"We're all observant of custom"', he informs her. '"We have to live together for centuries."'[14] Yet Bill's charm offensive is also a vital part of his attempt to 'mainstream', as he operates strategic politeness in order to win over the occupants of Bon Temps. Bill's manners, it is suggested, may partly be a legacy of his nineteenth-century upbringing, but are also put to good use easing his acceptance into the present-day community. In *Dead Until Dark* (2001), Sookie notes that 'Bill proved as adept at social tactics as my grandmother'.[15] Similarly when in *True Blood* Bill speaks to the Descendants of the Glorious Dead about his part in the Civil War, he removes the American flag from the altar where it has been concealing the crucifix, hoists it on its pole and returns it to its designated spot, declaring, 'As a patriot of this great nation, I wouldn't dream of putting myself before Old Glory'.[16] His formal display of patriotism wrong-foots his more conservative opponents and underscores his argument for assimilation. Adele refers to him as a 'perfect gentleman' rather than a vampire: his manners confer on him humanity. Indeed, his behaviour in this scene is shown to be rather better than that of his distrustful and in some cases disrespectful audience. While not all vampires in *True Blood* or The Southern Vampire Mysteries display similar manners, Bill's politeness is, like Edward's, privileged by his positioning as principal romantic lead.

Goth

How, and when, did vampires learn to be so polite? In order to answer this, I want to look at twenty-first-century vampire narratives alongside Goth subculture. Goth, which emerged from the UK's post-punk underground in the late 1970s, has now become a massive global phenomenon. Thanks to digital communications media, its music, fashions and images can be instantaneously accessed by millions of fans around the world. Goth is periodically picked up and exploited by mainstream commodity culture, turned into the theme of the latest fashion season or broadsheet commentary. Nevertheless it has not, in the way of the majority of other subcultures, become thoroughly incorporated by the mainstream. It is still regarded as oppositional, threatening or just plain weird by a sizeable portion of the mainstream population. This results in some very tangible effects, such as the media blame for the Columbine shootings in the USA on 20 April 1999, and, in Britain, the murder of self-defined Goth Sophie Lancaster on 11 August

2007. Like most subcultures, Goth has been forced to renegotiate its identity in the twenty-first century, and the shifts it has undergone cast an interesting light on the concurrent surge in vampire narratives.

Vampire imagery has been a prominent feature of Goth culture since its inception: the release of Bauhaus's iconic single *Bela Lugosi's Dead* in 1979, is sometimes credited as being the originating moment of the subculture.[17] When the 1983 film *The Hunger* opened with Bauhaus performing this track as vampires played by David Bowie and Catherine Deneuve seduce a couple in a nightclub, the link between vampires and Goths was cemented in the Hollywood imagination. Although Goths themselves frequently reject associations with vampires as reductive and point to the existence of a separate, if sometimes overlapping, subculture more focused on role-playing and conventional fandom, the association has proved difficult to shake. Arguably, the most significant reason for this is dress: both subcultures subscribe to similar dress-codes, and are often difficult to distinguish visually, especially to outsiders. Moreover, in current cinema convention, costuming choices usually acknowledge Goth just as Goth style appropriates vampire looks from fiction and cinema. To cite only a brief selection of examples, Selene from the *Underworld* films (2003–12), Spike from *Buffy the Vampire Slayer* (1997–2003), the Volturi from *Twilight: New Moon* (2009) and the patrons of the vampire bar Fangtasia in *True Blood* all recognisably draw on a Goth sartorial idiom. As Maria Mellins demonstrates, vampire fans often painstakingly replicate these costumes in the fashioning of their own vampire identities, thereby completing the circle.[18]

Goth is so visible in terms of the costuming and aesthetics of contemporary vampire narrative that in interpretative terms, it becomes invisible. In other words, it seems so obvious – even clichéd – that there is nothing to say about it. But this elides the interpretative judgments audiences make about Goth, the cultural work to which the subculture is put in these narratives; it also excludes Goths themselves, reducing them to a set of visual stereotypes rather than living individuals. The convention of costuming vampires as Goths is a relatively new one. Although it is evoked in 1980s films such as *The Hunger* and, to a certain extent, *The Lost Boys* (with the exception of Kiefer Sutherland's David, the vampires sport a classic American rock/biker look), it crystallised some time in the 1990s, echoing the increasing visibility of Goth aesthetics in pre-millennial culture. There are nuances in the use of Goth style as vampire costume – Goth style is not appropriated wholesale by Hollywood but consciously put to work. In *Twilight: New Moon*, for example, it is the aristocratic, hierarchical, European Volturi who are clad in black robes and red contact lenses, while the democratic, all-American Cullens dress in a

Figure 9.1.   Pam and Eric wearing Goth style at Fangtasia

preppy style. This costuming decision, of course, stems from Meyer's novels in which the Volturi are ancient and backward-looking while the Cullens represent modernity and the New World. Goth style communicates the weight of history – and identifies the 'bad' vampires from the 'good' ones. More subtly, in *True Blood*, Pam and Eric wear Goth style within their vampire bar, Fangtasia – literally putting their vampire identities to work (Figure 9.1) – while opting for more mainstream styles when off duty. *True Blood* comments ironically on the expectations that customers bring to vampire bars and viewers to vampire drama: that vampires should dress Goth. The pre-credit sequence for the debut episode of the show has the camera pan slowly up the body of the pale, black-haired and tattooed clerk in the twenty-four-hour store, lingering on apparently threatening details such as his biker boots, skull rings and piercings. The drunken young couple who enter the store in search of 'V' or vampire blood (which has hallucinogenic properties for humans) are easily taken in, along with the viewer, by his pretence of vampirism – while in fact the genuine vampire is the unassuming redneck in the corner. In the show's internal universe, vampires have as diverse taste as the humans they once were. Stereotyping according to dress is a form of prejudice suffered by vampires, but it is also a stereotype they use to their economic advantage.[19]

I do not want to suggest a reductive pattern whereby vampires embody contemporary Goth culture and vice versa. Clearly, one of the joys of the vampire narrative, and one celebrated by this book, is that vampires provide rich and multilayered symbols that can be interpreted in all sorts of ways,

and as Judith Halberstam has stated in *Skin Shows*, like all Gothic monsters
'transform the fragments of otherness into one body'.[20] Charlaine Harris has
explicitly declared that vampires are 'a metaphor for alienated minorities'
and that she was 'thinking specifically of the gay community' in the Southern
Vampire Mysteries.[21] The Louisiana setting and references to the history of
slavery and segregation also invite comparisons with the black civil rights
movement, as Michelle Smith suggests in Chapter 12 below. These allusions
are clearly visible within the texts and have been widely commented on
by critics, readers and viewers. Goth narratives, however, are taken for
granted in mainstream culture; where we may be alive to the nuances of
race or sexuality, how subcultures signify is often left unexamined. Goth,
however, is no less a significant shaping context on these narratives than
any other. Moreover, as the remainder of this chapter will demonstrate, it
is an increasingly politicised context, as twenty-first-century subcultures
have become mobilised around a series of campaigns to defend the right to
alternative lifestyles.

A passage from the first of the Southern Vampire Mysteries, *Dead Until
Dark*, illustrates the cultural imbrication of Goths and vampires particularly
effectively. Sookie's first visit to the vampire bar Fangtasia reveals the detailed
striations of vampire culture:

> The bar was full. The humans were divided amongst vampire groupies and
> tourists. The groupies (fang-bangers, they were called) were dressed in their
> best finery. It ranged from the traditional capes and tuxes for the men to many
> Morticia Adams [*sic*] ripoffs [*sic*] among the females. The clothes ranged from
> reproductions of those worn by Brad Pitt and Tom Cruise in *Interview With the
> Vampire* to some modern outfits that I thought were influenced by *The Hunger*.
> Some of the fang-bangers were wearing false fangs, some had painted trickles
> of blood from the corners of their mouths or puncture marks on their necks.
> They were extraordinary, and extraordinarily pathetic.
>
> The tourists looked like tourists anywhere, maybe more adventurous than
> most. But to enter into the spirit of the bar, they were nearly all dressed in
> black like the fang-bangers … Strewn among this human assortment, like real
> jewels in a bin of rhinestones, were the vampires, perhaps fifteen of them.
> They mostly favored dark clothes too.[22]

The vampire groupies' dress is mediated through popular cultural and film
images of vampires, and suggestively recalls contemporary Goth style.
The vampires, on the other hand, while also mainly wearing dark clothes,
sparkle: 'real jewels in a bin of rhinestones'. On one level, Goth appears
to be being repudiated in this passage. The groupies' attempt to mimic

vampires is presented as 'pathetic', and lacks the sophistication of the real vampires. On another, however, the passage also replays strategies deployed within subcultures in general and Goth in particular with which to shore up what Sarah Thornton, adapting Bourdieu, has called 'subcultural capital'.[23] The groupies are presented as lacking the authenticity of the 'real' vampires, a common manoeuvre in subcultural narratives seeking to distance the 'weekenders' or 'wannabes' from those with greater subcultural commitment. In fact, groupies, tourists and vampires are all dressed in dark clothes and it is through Sookie's discerning gaze that we can distinguish the nuances between them. Moreover Sookie's sympathies in this passage are clearly aligned with the vampires – they are the closest thing to the dominant social norm in the bar. The qualities valued here are restraint, decorum and good taste – qualities possessed by the real vampires, but not the groupies. Real vampires do not seek to stand out, even if they can't help doing so by virtue of their innate superiority. Real vampires have manners – they have learned to sparkle.

Charm

And so we come to *Gothic Charm School*: a book, and blog, by self-styled 'Lady of the Manners' Jillian Venters, a kind of Goth agony aunt. Since 1998, Jillian has advised her readers on essential problems of Goth etiquette, from 'Do you have to be spooky every day?' to 'Why friends don't let friends dress like the Crow'.[24] At the heart of the *Gothic Charm School* ethos is the notion that it is even more important for Goths to be polite than for other people, as there is more at stake when they create a bad impression. Outsiders tend to assume one Goth stands for them all, and a bad attitude can confirm negative preconceptions that lead to prejudice. Prejudice, Venters argues, has real social effects, from bullying of teenagers and difficulties in finding employment to media blame for social ills. As Venters explains,

> if everyone associated with the subculture takes up the Lady of the Manners's cause of politeness, maybe (just maybe) Goths will quit getting labelled as 'baby-eating Satanic murderers' and merely be labelled as 'those people who wear black and dye their hair funny colours.' Mass awareness can lead to more understanding and less stereotyping – we just have to work at it.[25]

And again:

> Yes, it's a bit strange to think that what started out as a shadowy refuge has become well known enough to be regarded as a profitable target demographic,

but as the Lady of the Manners had said before, the more 'mainstream' awareness of what Goth really is, the fewer young babybats [*sic*] will have to go through the bullying and harassment that many ElderGoths [*sic*] suffered. The more people who have even a vague understanding about Goth, the smaller the chance that Goths will be regarded with suspicion, fear, and hostility.[26]

The mainstreaming of Goth may be annoying to a subculture committed to difference, but, as Venters points out, it has its benefits. These range from increased tolerance in the workplace to being able to snap up Gothy fashion bargains in the seasonal chain-store sales. Moreover, Venters argues, being polite is the most subversive thing you can do as a Goth, as it messes with preconceptions more effectively than sulkiness and surliness.

Venters's book draws, semi-ironically, on the Victorian etiquette book and its eighteenth-century predecessor, the conduct manual. The Gothic novel has a complex and vexed historical relationship with the conduct book, which has frequently been read as an important context for eighteenth-century fiction in general, and Gothic in particular, the height of its popularity coinciding with that of the Gothic between 1760 and 1820. Eighteenth-century fiction had a presumed didactic purpose, fulfilling a similar role to the conduct book in educating its young readers into properly moral behaviour. Eighteenth-century objections to the Gothic novel frequently centred on the fact that 'terrorist novel writing', as it was infamously labelled, did not fulfil this didactic purpose: an anonymous commentator of 1797 argued that,

> A novel, if at all useful, ought to be a representation of human life and manners, with a view to direct the conduct in the most important duties of life, and to correct its follies … Can a young lady be taught nothing more necessary in life, than to sleep in a dungeon with venomous reptiles, walk through a ward [wood] with assassins, and carry bloody daggers in their pockets, instead of pin-cushions and needle-books?[27]

Indeed, when it came to Matthew Lewis's controversial bestseller *The Monk* (1796), Samuel Taylor Coleridge in the *Critical Review* considered that the presentation of sensational and salacious incident was likely to corrupt rather than educate youth.[28] On the other hand, many Gothic novelists, most prominently Ann Radcliffe, did present their heroines undergoing an educative process parallel to that found in conduct literature of the period. This tension is often played out within individual novels: Stephanie Burley, for example, writes of how Charlotte Dacre's *Zofloya, or the Moor* (1806) combines a salacious, sensational tale with a didactic narrator, 'a good woman with a bad story to tell'.[29] The 'double-consciousness' of the narrator nevertheless appears not to have convinced contemporary reviewers, one of whom deplored 'a romance so void of merit, so destitute of delicacy, displaying such disgusting depravity of morals'.[30] The Gothic novel plays out the binary of civility and barbarity, the latter continually threatening to destabilise the former even as, for the most part, civility remains the privileged term.

Venters's blog plays out this dynamic in a rather different way. For a start, her emphasis is on etiquette rather than conduct – a subtle distinction, but one that shifts the emphasis from generally morally correct behaviour to appropriate behaviour in specific social circumstances. The etiquette book came to the fore in the mid-nineteenth century as a guide for the *parvenu* in an age of unprecedented social mobility. It performed a socially conservative role, preserving the mores and conventions of the upper classes against the threat of encroaching vulgarity. Venters's blog participates in a semi-ironic nostalgia for Victoriana that has become increasingly prominent in some sections of Goth subculture, embodied in loving recreations of nineteenth-century costume or, latterly, in Steampunk. On one level, Venters's text does appear to be socially conservative, affirming the values and mores of mainstream culture as it suggests, for example, that a corset might not be the most appropriate garment for school after all. This is the very opposite of Goth's roots in the punk subculture of the late 1970s, with its cultivated call to anarchy and mission to cause offence. On another level, however, *Gothic Charm School* recognises the now clichéd nature of punk resistance and its lack of purchase in the world of globalised media. By imagining resistance through politeness, Venters inverts the expectations not only of the so-called mainstream but also of subcultural discourse itself, long dependent on a punk-derived model. The light vein of self-parody that runs through the book, and the knowing incongruity of the concepts of Gothic and etiquette, subtly disarm critical accusations. The biggest Goth crime, it seems, is taking oneself too seriously.

Assimilation

In its *Northanger Abbey*-like promotion of good sense and good manners as the most effective way of dealing with prejudiced social tyrants, *Gothic Charm School* is one of the more clearly defined examples of how Goth has renegotiated its identity in the last decade in relation to a series of media-generated moral panics associated with the subculture. These tend to fall into two categories. Most commonly, they identify Goth as a source of violence against others, including the Columbine Massacre in April 1999, Kimveer Gill's attack on students at Dawson College in Quebec, Canada, in September

2006, and the German case of the so-called 'Vampire Killers' Daniel and Manuela Ruda in 2002. Alternatively, Goth is depicted as a cult of depression that encourages children to self-harm, as in the British newspaper *The Daily Mail*'s campaign against Emo in 2008, which collapsed the two subcultures.[31] Columbine was perhaps the first and most far-reaching of these news stories, as well as the most spurious in its association of the killers with Goth. The night after the massacre, ABC's *20/20* news show linked the killings to 'the Gothic Movement', describing it as a violent cult.[32] Although this sensationalist reporting relied on only one flimsy source, it was almost immediately taken up by the global media, who seized on details of the killers' lives including a purported liking for industrial music and a peripheral association with a school clique calling themselves 'The Trenchcoat Mafia', identifying these as markers of a Goth identity. Goths themselves were quick to point out the specious nature of these claims, insistently distancing the subculture from violent action and pointing out that Goths tend to be the victims of violence and persecution rather than its perpetrators. According to the Goths who rose to their community's defence, Goth was not miserable and certainly not violent: its values cohered around creativity, self-expression, communality, the embrace of difference and the perception of beauty in the darker side of life. Eloni Feliciano is typical when she states, 'I have never considered the scene to be a gateway to violence against my peers. In fact, quite the opposite – I always felt that the scene was a cohesive community that gave me support during tough times ... The Goth community itself is more like Jack Skellington from *A Nightmare Before Christmas* [sic] – gentle, inquisitive, and a little odd.'[33] As the reiteration of the Columbine narrative cemented the relationship between Goth and high-school shootings in the American public imagination, the media finding evidence in each new case that superficially confirmed the connection, an increasing number of Goths were drawn into the attempt to build positive public relations. The process of repositioning Goth as peaceful, creative and essentially performative in its embrace of darkness culminated in the response to Sophie Lancaster's murder in 2007, which was remarkable in that it reversed the conventional mainstream media reaction to the association between Goth and crime.

Lancaster's case was a major news story in the UK but did not receive the same international coverage as Columbine, despite its spread through alternative channels on the World Wide Web. Lancaster and her boyfriend Robert Maltby, both of whom self-identified as Goths, were attacked by a group of teenagers while walking home through the small town of Bacup, Lancashire, late at night. Both were severely injured and Lancaster later died in hospital from the injuries she sustained. After a trial which whipped up media concern with a supposedly 'feral' youth roaming Britain's streets, two of the assailants were convicted of murder and sentenced to life imprisonment; three others were convicted of grievous bodily harm with intent and given shorter sentences.

As I have suggested in an earlier essay, Lancaster's murder was the reverse situation to Columbine in that individuals labelled as Goths were the victims of crime rather than the perpetrators.[34] Historically, the British media have had a greater tendency to incorporate spectacular style through comedy or domestication than their American equivalents. Following Sophie Lancaster's death, the British press characteristically recuperated Goths as possibly eccentric but creative and ultimately harmless individuals, while displacing moral panic onto other social problems, in particular the contemporary debates over 'bad' parenting, binge-drinking and 'hoodie' culture. As I have previously demonstrated, Britain's biggest-selling tabloid *The Sun* repeatedly centred stories on Sophie's Mum and the killers' parents, while the second-biggest-selling newspaper, the conservative *Daily Mail*, positioned Sophie and her killers as representatives of two sides in a class war, between well-educated, aspirational, middle-class kids and unruly, criminal, binge-drinking lower-class teenagers.[35] The characteristically Gothic opposition between civilisation and barbarity is played out again in these accounts, and Goths – like Meyer's vampires – are firmly positioned on the civilised side of the binary.

In Dick Hebdige's classic account of the ideological incorporation of youth subcultures by mainstream culture, he emphasises how, over time, the media inevitably attempt to minimise their Otherness by returning them to the family, or by emphasising the Otherness of other kinds of unruly youth.[36] It is not that surprising, therefore, that the press responses to Goth subsequent to Sophie Lancaster's death follow this pattern with unnerving accuracy, particularly as it gave the right-wing media a platform to pontificate on what would eventually become known, in future prime minister David Cameron's phrase, as 'broken Britain'. What is more unexpected is the reaction to the murder from within the subculture itself. In the weeks and months following Sophie's death, Goths both within the UK and further afield mounted a series of campaigns to promote awareness and tolerance of alternative lifestyle choices. Indirectly, these campaigns also sought to minimise the otherness of Goth, by demanding its recognition and protection by mainstream society.

These campaigns were controversial amongst Goths and it should be stressed that they were not universally adopted or admired by the subcultural community. Nevertheless, there was sufficient support for a petition to the British government calling for the legal definition of hate crime to be changed to include crimes against subcultures for it to attract seven thousand signatures. Although the petition was unsuccessful, its aims remain central to the Sophie Lancaster Foundation, a charity set up by Sylvia Lancaster in her daughter's memory, which 'work[s] in conjunction with politicians and police forces to ensure individuals who are part of subcultures are protected by the law.'[37] At the time of going to press, the campaign had begun to bear fruit: in April 2013, Greater Manchester Police announced that they will record attacks on members of alternative subcultures as hate crimes. Although this decision has not been recognised nationally under British law and therefore will have no effect on sentencing, it will enable police to provide greater support to victims. The story was reported widely in the national press and therefore also had symbolic significance. Other UK police authorities have yet to follow suit.[38]

This is an entirely new phenomenon: when subcultures have previously mobilised *en masse* it has always been to resist the imposition of legislature perceived to inhibit alternative lifestyles: for example the widespread and vocal campaigning against the UK's Criminal Justice Act of 1994, which effectively outlawed raves and free parties by legislating against unauthorised public gatherings, collective trespass and amplified music with repetitive beats. In contrast, to seek to 'authorise' subculture by legislating to protect lifestyle choice is a radical repositioning of what subculture means. The 'sub' in subculture implies something hidden, underground, beneath the radar of mainstream culture. To 'protect' subculture by bringing it within the disciplinary networks of the legal system is to remove that subterranean element, bring it into the light.

To reprise my argument from my earlier essay, subcultures thrive on the concept of resistance, whether real or imagined; to become entirely tolerated by mainstream culture would also be to be fully assimilated by mainstream culture, youthful rebellion reduced to a style option. At the same time, the 'resistant' element of subculture that Clarke, Hall, Jefferson and Roberts identified as symbolic in the landmark text *Resistance Through Rituals* has become more than an inarticulate expression of dissatisfaction with the parent culture, but a literalised, self-conscious and articulate demand for the right to individual lifestyle choice.[39] Goth in the twenty-first century is thus in a highly ambivalent position where it hovers on the brink of assimilation even as it has achieved a more coherent, unified and self-aware identity than ever before.

It is no accident that over the same period of time as Goth underwent this repositioning, a new generation of vampire narratives emerged, in which vampires attempted, in different ways, to insert themselves within mainstream society. Meyer's vampires are wholesome all-American beings who are 'vegetarian', play baseball, and refuse sex before marriage. Harris's grittier novels, and their TV adaptation, explore an American South where vampires seek their civil rights in an effort to live amicably alongside humans. *Being Human*'s flat-sharing ghost, vampire and werewolf attempt to come to terms with their otherness while 'passing' as human. There are nuances between these narratives: Meyer's 'good' vampires seek surreptitious assimilation, for example, being unable to reveal their difference to the community at large, while Harris's novels explicitly play with the imagery of the civil rights movement and gay liberation. None of these texts can be reduced to a metaphor for Goth subculture; rather, through the long-standing cultural association between Goths and vampires, they play into a general atmosphere or share a pervasive mood that evokes Goth liberation.

As such, these narratives offer a new kind of 'conduct book' for the twenty-first century. Like *Gothic Charm School*, they teach us that we can preserve our difference, our specialness, our Otherness and enjoy the benefits of living in globalised consumer culture at the same time – but, in order to do so, we must be unfailingly polite. Resistance to the norm can be achieved only by working *with* the dominant culture rather than aggressively against it. Inevitably, different narratives offer differently nuanced versions of this message, sometimes even presenting that 'double-consciousness' Burley identifies in *Zofloya*, where the didactic voice scarcely contains the more sensational material of the narrative. Stephenie Meyer's covert sanctioning of social convention tends to play into conservative politics, while Charlaine Harris's and Alan Ball's more self-consciously political narratives espouse a more liberal worldview. Harris and Ball, too, allow more room for dissent from the assimilative position, while in Meyer the 'bad', that is, undisciplined, vampires are scarcely given a voice – and scarcely ever given the chance to sparkle.

To conclude, sparkly vampires provide a fantasy space in which the risks and rewards of subcultural assimilation can be played out. In the dilemmas they face in their respective narratives they enact the uneasy status of subcultures, and specifically Goth subculture, in the twenty-first century. Sparkly vampires have manners; they suppress their desire to snarl in order to enjoy the benefits of integrating with mainstream society. At the same time their sparkliness indicates their difference, their otherness, their specialness. As such they offer an important representation of subcultural politics, and specifically Goth politics, as they undergo a series of unprecedented changes. In doing so, vampire narratives can show us new ways to negotiate identity politics and alternative lifestyle choices in an increasingly commodified twenty-first century.

Notes

1 The TV series developed by Alex Lloyd, Kevin Williamson and Julie Plec and broadcast on the CW Television Network is based on a series of novels by L. J. Smith, which nevertheless differ substantially from their adaptation and were written somewhat earlier than the other texts considered in this chapter (the original trilogy was published in 1991, although a second trilogy coincided loosely with the TV series, 2009–).

2 Latham, *Consuming Youth*, p. 1.

3 Priest, 'What's Wrong With Sparkly Vampires?'

4 'Byromania' was a widely discussed phenomenon from the publication of *Childe Harold's Pilgrimage* in 1812. Ghislaine McDayter is typical of critics who use the language of modern celebrity to describe this phenomenon, commenting, for example, that, 'What London was witnessing in the frenzy of Byromania was ... a symptom of the birth of the larger phenomenon now known as celebrity culture' (Introduction, McDayter (ed.), *Byromania*, p. 4).

5 Polidori, *The Vampyre*, ed. Baldick, p. 5.

6 *Ibid.*, p. 6.

7 Priest, 'What's Wrong With Sparkly Vampires?'; see Rice, *The Vampire Lestat*, p. 9.

8 Meyer, *Twilight*, p. 228.

9 Bakhtin, *Rabelais and His World*.

10 Botting, *Gothic*, p. 7.

11 See Foucault, *Discipline and Punish*, p. 201.

12 Meyer, *Eclipse*, p. 257.

13 *Ibid.*, pp. 548–9.

14 Harris, *Dead Until Dark*, p. 251.

15 Harris, *Dead Until Dark*, p. 51.

16 'Sparks Fly Out', *True Blood*, 1.5.

17 See Jennifer Park, 'Melancholy and the Macabre', in Steele and Park, *Gothic*.

18 Mellins, 'Fashioning the Vampire'.

19 Films and TV series that do not costume vampires as Goths are also deliberately working against this set of conventions. Usually, as in *Being Human*, they are implying that they are seeking to freshen up the genre, connoting that they are edgy, hip and realist.

20 Halberstam, *Skin Shows*, p. 92.

21 Charlaine Harris, quoted in Wright, 'Southern Lady', p. 74.

22 Harris, *Dead Until Dark*, p. 115.

23 Thornton, *Club Cultures*.

24 Venters, *Gothic Charm School*, pp. ix, x.

25 *Ibid.*, p. 201.

26 *Ibid.*, p. 229.

27 Anonymous, 'Terrorist Novel Writing', p. 184.

28 Coleridge, 'Review of *The Monk*', pp. 185–9.

29 Burley, 'The Death of Zofloya', p. 207.

30 Cited in Burley, 'The Death of Zofloya', p. 207.

31 Sarah Sands, 'EMO Cult Warning for Parents'.

32 'The Goth Phenomenon'.

33 Cited in Sweeney, 'Dark Days for Goths'.

34 For a fuller discussion of these issues, see Catherine Spooner, '"Forget Nu Rave"'.

35 *Ibid.*

36 Hebdige, *Subculture*.

37 *The Sophie Lancaster Foundation*.

38 'Manchester Police to Record Attacks on Goths, Emos and Punks as Hate Crimes', *Guardian*, 4 April 2013, online.

39 Clarke *et al.*, 'Subcultures, Cultures and Class', pp. 9–74.

10

A vampire heaven:
the economics of salvation
in *Dracula* and the Twilight Saga

Jennifer H. Williams

THE PROBLEM OF VAMPIRES has always been a peculiarly religious one. When Professor Van Helsing explains to his 'Crew of Light' what is at stake in their quest to destroy the vampire, Dracula, he casts it in religious terms:

> My friends ... it is a terrible task that we undertake, and there may be consequence to make the brave shudder. For if we fail in this our fight he must surely win; and then where end we? ... To us for ever are the gates of heaven shut; for who shall open them to us again? We go on for all time abhorred by all; a blot on the face of God's sunshine; an arrow in the side of Him who died for man.[1]

Christ's death is no longer sufficient to open the gates of heaven for the poor vampire convert because such a creature has achieved eternal life by drinking the wrong blood. Van Helsing's fear is realised only two days later when Dracula forces Mina to drink his blood in a perversely eucharistic act, thus rendering her unclean. Significantly, Mina bears the mark of her future damnation even in her mortal life – her flesh is burned by the Host, she becomes increasingly lethargic, she sleeps without the others being able to wake her, her teeth sharpen, her eyes become harder, and, as Van Helsing puts it, 'I can see the characteristics of the vampire coming in her face' (280). To save Mina, the men must reopen the gates of heaven for her by killing Dracula once and for all.

Although the power of religion may no longer hold the sway that it did for Van Helsing, the sweep of secularisation since the time of Bram Stoker's writing has not done away with the vampire. Rather, the impulses of religion have been turned into something like the vampire itself, undead remainders with a disturbing and still vital presence in modern culture. According to Paul Barber, the popular belief that it is bad luck to break a mirror stems from the superstition that the mirror can contain one's soul in the form of a reflection.[2] It is no wonder, then, that vampires are thought to have no reflection in mirrors – they have no souls to reflect. However, this does not free them from the optics of reflection and refraction. Instead, the vampire is the captured soul that mirrors the human. That is, hold the mirror up to modern humans and captured inside is the vampire as mimetic copy of their souls. Shine light on them, and their image is refracted back in a sparkling haze that seduces instead of horrifies. Thus, vampires have become the displaced religious impulses of their human counterparts.

When comparing Stoker's *Dracula* to Stephenie Meyer's Twilight Saga, this shift from the vampire as threat to the Christian mechanics of sin and redemption to the vampire as revenant of such a system becomes interestingly prominent. In the Twilight Saga, Edward, the vampire boyfriend, refuses to transform his human girlfriend, Bella, because he believes vampires are 'the eternal damned', and thus to change her would be to forever shut the gates of heaven. He argues that she does not understand that she is 'bartering [her] soul'.[3] Bella herself espouses no religious views and reports that her own life 'was fairly devoid of belief' (36). Although she is shocked by the antique cross over the door to Carlisle's office[4] and she admits that talking with Carlisle about religious faith was 'the last thing I expected, all things considered' (36), she says that the 'the only kind of heaven *I* could appreciate would have to include Edward' (37). That is, it does not strike her as contradictory to imagine a heaven that includes vampires. In Bella's estimation, if there are such places as heaven and hell, these will be places of retributive justice and good works; thus the Cullens, the vampire family to which Edward belongs, will surely not go to hell since they are the best 'people' Bella has ever met. However, Bella's system implies that it is the fact that the Cullens *are* vampires that ensures their place in heaven. For example, Carlisle, the vampire patriarch, is a doctor and boasts a record of saving more lives than any human doctor can because of his longevity and because his finely tuned vampire senses make him a better surgeon than any human. When Carlisle explains to Bella why he works so hard to do good, she thinks, 'I couldn't imagine anyone, deity included, who wouldn't be impressed by Carlisle' (37). According to this logic, Edward would be ensuring Bella's place in heaven, not stealing her soul, if he were to convert her, because a vampire has the potential to amass an infinite number of infinitely good works.

Nevertheless, the vampires in the world of *Twilight*, like Dracula, are still the kind of disruptive presence that must be removed from human society. Dracula and his vampire consorts must be destroyed in order to ensure that human beings remain accountable for their actions and can enjoy the rewards of immortality offered only through the differentiating wisdom of God and the Anglican Church as his solicitor. In the Twilight Saga, the threat that must be contained over four volumes is the anxiety that vampires will set the bar too high and that humans will be shut out of heaven and relegated to hell; for their actions and choices are inconsequential in the face of the hyperbolic justice and accomplishment that vampires, both good and bad, represent. In what follows, I explore the economics of heaven and hell represented in *Dracula* and *Twilight*. As it is beyond the scope of this chapter to engage with the particular theologies of both the Christian and Mormon faiths, I will consider religious thematics more broadly in order to make a larger claim about the kind of work that these stories seem to be doing now in relation to the post-secular texture of our culture. I argue that vampires offer a mechanism through which humans can achieve the utopian promises traditionally reserved for the faithful in heaven without leaving Earth and without having to grapple with the larger questions that religion raises. Or, as Bella says near the end of *Twilight*, 'through the heavy water, I heard the sound of an angel calling my name, calling me to the only heaven I wanted'.[5]

A queer sting on the tongue

Whereas religion is conspicuously absent in the Twilight Saga, *Dracula* is a landscape of crosses. When Jonathan arrives in Bistriz, he finds that crucifixes not only are sprinkled liberally along the roadside on the way to the Borgo Pass but also adorn the necks of the locals and are pressed on him at every opportunity. When his first dinner in Bistriz includes Golden Mediasch, he explains that it is a wine 'which produces a queer sting on the tongue, which is, however, not disagreeable' (13). Similarly, although Jonathan clearly associates the preponderance of crosses as evidence of the superstitious nature of the peasants who live in Transylvania, or even as proof of idolatry, the crosses are also what make the people and landscape 'picturesque' in his estimation.[6] Jonathan comes to associate both the sign of the cross and the crucifixes with the warmth and sincerity of the people who try to offer him warnings and protection before he goes to Castle Dracula. The crosses are, to him, a queer sting that is not disagreeable.

This analogy captures nicely the complicated attitude that Jonathan and his companions, excluding Van Helsing, have towards religious faith. On the one hand, as a good 'English Churchman', Jonathan aligns himself with

Victorian Anglicanism and appears uncomfortable with anything that smacks of Roman Catholicism. On the other hand, as one who is 'nineteenth century up-to-date with a vengeance' (40), he is also a proponent of nineteenth-century secularism. This secularism is represented by Jonathan and the rest of the Crew of Light's use of modern gadgets. Jonathan's commitment to Anglicanism seems weak at best as he quickly throws away his repugnance of idolatrous crucifixes and takes solace in them when the Count reveals himself to be something more, or perhaps less, than human. The morning after he witnesses the Count slithering out of a window and down the wall head first, Jonathan writes most poignantly in his journal, 'the old centuries had, and have, powers of their own which mere "modernity" cannot kill' (41). These old centuries are the centuries of crosses and crucifixes that previously struck the modern Jonathan as mere superstition. But the English vampire hunters must gain absolute faith in the 'essence' of the crucifix by the novel's end if they are to survive with their souls intact.[7]

For the most part, it is precisely Abraham Van Helsing's job to help Jonathan, Mina, Seward, Quincy and Arthur achieve this absolute faith in the essence of the thing itself. Van Helsing says to Seward, 'I want you to believe … [t]o believe in things that you cannot. Let me illustrate. I heard once of an American who so defined faith: 'that which enables us to believe things which we know to be untrue'. … He meant that we shall have an open mind, and not let a little bit of truth check the rush of a big truth' (172). Van Helsing refers not only to Mark Twain here, but also to Hebrews 11:1, 'faith is the substance of things hoped for, the evidence of things not seen', although he will subsequently emphasise that Seward and the other men must believe what they *see*, even if what they see defies belief. For Van Helsing, an open mind means believing in what one sees. Put another way, an open mind means believing in the invisible worldview that enables what one sees to be true; that is to say, it means not allowing the 'modern' worldview, of which Jonathan and the others are so proud, to make the existence of such things as vampires to be rendered irrational or impossible. For example, when Van Helsing takes Seward to Lucy's tomb, he continually emphasises what can be seen. Seward reports in his journal,

> 'Are you convinced now?' said the Professor … and as he spoke he … pulled back the dead lips and showed the white teeth. 'See', he went on, 'see, they are even sharper than before. With this and this', – and he touched one of the canine teeth and that below it – 'the little children can be bitten. Are you of belief now, friend John?' (178)

Elsewhere, Van Helsing explains that 'the beliefs are justified by what we have seen in our own so unhappy experience' (211), and '[w]e have seen it with our eyes' (212). Van Helsing emphasises that one must first see and then believe as opposed to letting what one already believes to be true determine or discount what one sees.

The reliance on visual evidences that Jonathan, Mina and the other men exhibit in the novel should be no surprise. For the most part, the specular economy of *Dracula* is of a simple one-to-one correspondence: if someone looks evil, then he or she is evil; if someone looks good, then he or she is good. For example, Jonathan writes that, when he first meets Count Dracula, 'the light and warmth of the Count's courteous welcome … dissipated all my doubts and fears' (22–3). That is, the Count's behaviour represents him as a good and safe host. However, once Jonathan gets a good look at Dracula's appearance, he realises that he has a very 'marked physiognomy' with a 'cruel-looking' mouth, 'peculiarly sharp white teeth', and strange pale ears and face (23–4). Jonathan remarks that, when the Count comes close to him, he 'could not repress a shudder' and immediately tries to rationalise his response by logically reasoning that '[i]t may have been that his breath was rank, but a horrible feeling of nausea came over me' (24). But Jonathan's ability to reason away what his eyes see doesn't last once he encounters the three women in Dracula's castle and sees Dracula's response to their attempt to claim him for themselves. Jonathan writes, '[a]s my eyes opened involuntarily I saw his strong hand grasp the slender neck of the fair woman and with giant's power draw it back, the blue eyes transformed with fury … But the Count! Never did I imagine such wrath and fury, even to the demons of the pit. His eyes were positively blazing. The red light in them was lurid, as if the flames of hell-fire blazed behind them' (43). Jonathan's eyes are opened literally and figuratively, and the truth of what both the Count and the women are is reflected in their eyes – there is hell-fire blazing within them. Now Jonathan sees the terrible truth. Had Jonathan not spent so much time trying to rationalise his emotional and instinctual responses to the Count, attributing them to Dracula's breath or some other reasonable explanation, he might have been able to prevent his entrapment. In short, Dracula is ugly, marked by hell, and has an ugly soul, if he has any soul at all.

As mentioned above, Van Helsing sets the consequence of not seeing and believing, and therefore becoming vulnerable to the vampire, in the context of heaven and hell as opposed to mere life and death. His description of the vampire indicates that vampirism is more of an ontological problem than one of behaviour. That is to say, it is not what Dracula does that makes him a monster. Rather, he is a monster simply because he is a vampire. Van Helsing tells the group:

> There are such beings as vampires, some of us have evidence that they exist.
> Even had we not the proof of our own unhappy experience, the teachings
> and the records of the past give proof enough for sane peoples. I admit that
> at the first I was sceptic. Were it not that through long years I have trained
> myself to keep an open mind, I could not have believed until such time as
> that fact thunder on my ear. 'See! See! I prove, I prove.' ... he is brute, and
> more than brute: he is devil in callous, and the heart of him is not; ... Life is
> nothing; I heed him not. But to fail here, is not mere life or death. It is that
> we become as him; that we henceforward become foul things of the night like
> him – without heart or conscience, preying on the bodies and the souls of
> those we love best. To us for ever are the gates of heaven shut; for who shall
> open them to us again? We go on for all time abhorred by all; a blot on the
> face of God's sunshine; an arrow in the side of Him who died for man. (209)

Val Helsing claims that the vampire *is* devil, *is* brute, *is* callous, *is* heartless –
he underscores what the vampire is as opposed to what the vampire does. If
the Crew of Light fail, they will 'become as him ... foul things of the night
like him'. And because the sin of vampirism is an ontological sin, it cannot
be forgiven through the sacrifice of Christ, who died for the sins committed
by humans alone. Were their fight simply a matter of life and death, failing
would not prevent them from going to heaven. But in this case, to fail is to
lose heaven.

The distinction between the cost of life and the cost of heaven is what
allows Van Helsing to persuade Lucy's fiancé and former suitors that they
must kill the vampire she has become – such an act of mercy, though
gruesome and not without great emotional cost to the men, is what will free
her human soul for heaven. Seward records in his journal that 'the Professor
looked pityingly at [Art]. "If I could spare you one pang, my poor friend", he
said, "God knows I would. But this night our feet must tread in thorny paths,
or later, and for ever, the feet you love must walk in paths of flame!"' (183).
Later, Van Helsing explains that

> if [Lucy] die in truth, then all cease; the tiny wounds of the throats disappear,
> and [the bitten children] go back to their play unknowing ever of what has
> been. But of the most blessed of all, when this now Un-Dead be made to rest
> as true dead, then the soul of the poor lady whom we love shall again be free.
> Instead of working wickedness by night and growing more debased in the
> assimilating of it by day, she shall take her place with the other Angels. (191)

Unmaking Lucy in death will unmake her as vampire and thus open the gates
of heaven for her entrance. And, indeed, once she has been destroyed, Seward
reports that

> [t]here, in the coffin lay no longer the foul Thing that we had so dreaded …
> but Lucy as we had seen her in life, with her face of unequalled sweetness and
> purity. True that there were there, as we had seen them in life, the traces of
> care and pain and waste; but these were all dear to us, for they marked her
> truth to what we knew. One and all we felt that the holy calm that lay like
> sunshine over the wasted face and form was only an earthly token and symbol
> of the calm that was to reign for ever (192).

Seward has evidently learned his lesson from Van Helsing well, for he sees
the evidences that she is no longer undead. She bears the marks on her face
that she is human and is now in heaven.

The marks and traces of one's salvation or damnation are a common trope
through the novel, and the marks work both ways. For example, Seward
writes that, after Dracula attacks Mina, and after Van Helsing burns her
with the communion wafer, it becomes painful to see her because the scar
constantly reminds them that her goodness and her efforts to thwart Dracula
on behalf of humanity will not save her from damnation. 'Oh that I could give
any idea of the scene', he writes,

> of that sweet, sweet, good, good woman in all the radiant beauty of her youth
> and animation, with the red scar on her forehead of which she was conscious
> … her loving kindness against our grim hate; her tender faith against all our
> fears and doubting; and we, knowing that so far as symbols went, she with all
> her goodness and purity and faith, was outcast from God. (268)

Despite the fact that Mina is superlatively sweet and good, the mark on her
forehead indicates that she is damned. The red scar is the symbol that nothing
that she has done or will do can save her. Indeed, the end of the novel is not
signalled so much by the destruction of Dracula as it is by the recognition that
Mina's forehead has been freed from the red scar, a sight that causes Quincy,
with his dying breath, to exclaim, '"[i]t was worth this to die! Look! Look!"'
(326). And, as if to confirm Mina's restored purity, all the men kneel around
her and say 'Amen' in a scene that evokes worship of the pure Virgin Mary.
She who was once the mediator between the four men by listening to their
tears and correlating their journals is now figured as the ultimate mediatrix
between Christ and men, a trace of the purity of heaven on earth.

Finally, that the vampire's damnation is connected to his or her status
as vampire as opposed to works is also what causes Mina to argue that
Jonathan and the other men must have pity on Dracula and to not regard
their destruction of him as a 'work of hate' because '[t]hat poor soul who has
wrought all this misery is the saddest case of all. Just think what will be his

joy when he too is destroyed in his worser part that his better part may have spiritual immortality. You must be pitiful to him too' (269). And indeed, although she is perhaps the only one who can see it, Mina reports that, when Dracula is stabbed in the heart with the bowie knife, 'there was in the face a look of peace, such as I never could have imagined might have rested there' (325). The look of peace on the faces of both Dracula and Lucy, and Mina's restored white brow, all serve for the vampire hunters as symbols of salvation restored, heaven's gates open wide.

Impressing God

Unlike the vampires in *Dracula*, the Cullen vampires are not represented as evil.[8] Edward and his family are always described as angelic, perfect; Bella says that they are 'devastatingly, inhumanly beautiful'.[9] Their appearance is godlike, and their talents are remarkable even compared to other vampires. Apart from Edward's self-loathing, a trait he shares with Bella, there is no question that the noble Carlisle, compassionate Esme, the loyal Rosalie, strong Emmett, charismatic Jasper and the psychic Alice all belong in heaven. They look beautiful, and they have beautiful souls, perfectly accomplished and impressive in every way.[10] When asked by her curious friend Jessica why Edward is more than just 'unbelievably gorgeous', Bella responds, "'I can't explain it right … but he's even more unbelievable *behind* the face." The vampire who wanted to be good – who ran around saving people's lives so he wouldn't be a monster' (179). Bella's remark is telling. First, that Edward doesn't want to be a monster seems to suggest the same kind of ontological language used in *Dracula* regarding the vampire – to be a vampire is to be a monster. This in turn suggests that perhaps the Cullens' beauty is more along the lines of the coquettish wives of Dracula and their seductive beauty. Indeed, Alice remarks that 'like a carnivorous flower, [vampires] are physically attractive to our prey' (361). This carnivorous beauty is one that is actually false because it is meant only to entice and deceive, a perversion of what the vampire hunters in *Dracula* would consider to be beauty's true purpose.

But to say that vampires are like carnivorous flowers, attractive to their prey, for Bella to say Edward is even more beautiful behind his face, is to introduce a split into the simple speculative economy of vampires and salvation of *Dracula*. In the Twilight Saga, there is a contiguous space between the physical appearance of the Cullens and their moral position in the universe. In fact, their physical beauty is a mark that functions more like the Derridean supplement – it is both the sign of their goodness and their status as monsters.[11] That is to say, for Edward, his beautiful appearance belies his damned soul. It is also a mark of his damned soul *because* he uses beauty to entice human prey.[12] And, his beautiful appearance is a mark of the beauty of his soul as Bella considers him a creature that strives to be good even when such goodness and self-restraint would not be expected of him, a vampire. Thus, Edward's beauty is both the sign that he is good and the sign that he is a monster. The instability of the status of the vampire's beauty is made possible because in the world of *Twilight*, a monster is not what one is, but rather what one does.[13]

Just as the Golden Mediasch wine, with its queer sting on the tongue, serves as an image of the attitude of the Crew of Light toward religious faith in *Dracula*, we might call the infamous sparkling skin of Meyer's vampires a figure for the paradoxical mark of their beauty. Meyer's vampires have skin that sparkles, a phenomenon that presumably occurs when light hits the crystalline structure of their skin and is refracted multiple times until it is bounced back to the viewer. 'Edward in the sunlight was shocking', reports Bella when she sees him in the sun for the first time. 'His skin, white despite the faint flush from yesterday's hunting trip, literally sparkled, like thousands of tiny diamonds were embedded in the surface ... [He was a] perfect statue, carved in some unknown stone, smooth like marble, glittering like crystal' (228). The bouncing and bending of the light produce the variable glittering that distorts a clear image of the vampire's skin. This trope suggests that one cannot get a clear picture of the vampire's physical appearance because of the refracted light from his or her skin, and thus the meaning of what the vampire's appearance remains similarly variable, glittering, shifting.

The slippage engendered by the unclear status of the Cullens' appearance manifests itself in several ways throughout the saga. For example, although both Edward and Carlisle talk about being a vampire as something that makes them monsters and therefore damned, they are both able to make fine ethical distinctions that mark them as capable of differentiating what they are from what they do. This, of course, is the basis for their entire project of being 'vegetarians', hunting animals and not humans. Carlisle's own conversion story best exemplifies these acts of differentiation at work. Carlisle explains to Bella that his father was an intolerant man with 'a rather harsh view of the world'[14] who, as Edward says, 'believed very strongly in the reality of evil ... [and] hunted for witches, werewolves ... and vampires' (289). When the human Carlisle goes on a hunting expedition with a group of humans and is attacked and poisoned by a vampire, he realises that because his father has a simplistic view of the world – things are either good or evil – the bodies of the victims in the hunting party, including his own, 'would be burned

– anything infected by the monsters must be destroyed' (290). However, unlike his father, Carlisle is able to differentiate between what he has become and his own actions. Or, as Edward puts it, '[Carlisle] realized there was an alternative to being the vile monster he feared. ... Over the next months his new philosophy was born. He could exist without being a demon. He found himself again' (295). Carlisle's ability to separate what he is from what he does is what allows him to find his lost humanity.[15]

Edward's rebellion from Carlisle's philosophy of good works also manifests the instability of the mark of his physical beauty and also demonstrates that salvation and ethics are a matter of actions. Edward explains to Bella that, when he was a young vampire, he left Carlisle and Esme, his vampire mother, for a time and hunted humans instead of animals. Edward explains,

> [i]t took me only a few years to return to Carlisle and recommit to his vision. I thought I would be exempt from the ... depression ... that accompanies a conscience. Because I knew the thoughts of my prey, I could pass over the innocent and pursue only the evil. If I followed a murderer down a dark alley where he stalked a young girl – if I saved her, then surely I wasn't so terrible ... as time went on, I began to see the monster in my eyes. I couldn't escape the debt of so much human life taken, no matter how justified. (299)

Although Edward claims this story proves he is a monster, he speaks of being a monster in terms of debt and justification. Debt implies actions rendered and transactions made, persons under obligation to one another, and his decision to return home can be described only as a response to the demands of his conscience. Moreover, Edward explains, 'I went back to Carlisle and Esme. They welcomed me back like the prodigal. It was more than I deserved' (299). The story of the prodigal son is the story of return and forgiveness, one that does not leave the wayward son out in the world to wallow in his sin and misery, forever damned for his irresolute nature.

Bella's response to Edward's story seems to associate these matters of conscience with the decisions of divine justice. She reports, 'I shivered, imagining only too clearly what he described – the alley at night, the frightened girl, the dark man behind her. And Edward, Edward as he hunted, terrible and glorious as a young god, unstoppable. Would she have been grateful, that girl, or more frightened than before?' (299). Bella rightly shivers in recognition that Edward acts as an agent of Justice in saving the girl by killing the man – a Justice that is monstrous in the sense that it is inhuman. Edward's human conscience is rightly troubled, too, when what he sees reflected in his eyes is not at all human. Although we might imagine that Edward's ability to read the minds of his prey would ensure his estimations to be accurate, by leaving off hunting those he believes deserve death, Edward avoids both a demonic existence and a terrifyingly inhuman and divine one. He returns to the very human place of leaving such judgments to God or fate.

The goodness of one's soul in the Twilight Saga, then, cannot be rightly judged by the glittering, unstable mark of appearance. After all, in Meyer's world even predatory vampires such as Laurent are beautiful.[16] Rather, goodness is a matter of what one does, and it becomes quite clear that the efforts of some are worth more than the efforts of others. Edward is right to say he saw the monster reflected in his eyes when he hunted those whom he believed deserved death, because, as mentioned above, such acts of retributive justice are monstrous in that humans are not capable of making such determinations. His actions may make him monstrous, but not in the way that he supposes. Furthermore, Carlisle sees something different reflected back when he looks at Edward. Carlisle tells Bella,

> I didn't agree with my father's particular brand of faith. But never, in the nearly four hundred years now since I was born, have I ever seen anything to make me doubt whether God exists in some form or the other. Not even the reflection in the mirror ... I look at my ... *son*. His strength, his goodness, the brightness that shines out of him – and it only fuels that hope, that faith, more than ever. How could there not be [a heaven] for one such as Edward?[17]

Not only does Carlisle's own reflection not give him reason to doubt God's existence, but what he sees shining out of Edward confirms that God exists all the more, for how could Edward not be the reflection of heaven and God's perfection on Earth? And this is a reflection that is the result of Edward's actions, accomplishments, self-restraint, love for his family – the things he can only do because he is, in fact, a vampire, and not because the vampire is the dialectical opposite of God as Dracula was.

A vampire heaven

Although Meyer's vampires do not close the gates of heaven for humans by damning them, and are not the same demonic and wicked threats that Stoker's vampires are, their goodness and brightness nevertheless continue to trouble the possibility of earning salvation for humanity. They do not close heaven to humans by making humans into monsters. Instead, they take heaven for themselves. Bella says she would not *want* to be part of a heaven that excluded Edward. 'If you stay, I don't need heaven', she tells him.[18] Immortality on Earth with him will suffice. But the problem is that she could never enter the place that allowed him entrance. Her simple human beauty, even humanity and bravery, cannot earn her a place in such a heaven. The bar has been set too high.

As opposed to the Cullen clan who do everything in their considerable power to save Bella and her mother and father when the non-vegetarian vampire James decides to hunt her, Bella's great gesture as a human is always annihilation, the self-sacrificial death that never works because she has nothing of real value to sacrifice. Indeed, Bella's 'breakability' and the litany of injuries she endures over the course of the saga have caused critics to wonder just why *Twilight* is so popular with young, female fans in the first place, as discussed by Sara Wasson and Sarah Artt in Chapter 11 below. *Twilight* itself starts with her rumination on death. Bella says, 'I'd never given much thought to how I would die … Surely it was a good way to die, in place of someone else, someone I loved. Noble, even. That ought to count for something' (1). Similarly, when, in *Eclipse*, Jacob takes Bella to a gathering of his tribe, she hears the story of Taha Aki, one of the first Quileute ancestors; the Cold Woman, the first vampire; and Taha Aki's human wife, called only the 'third wife'. As Bella listens to the story of sacrifice and bravery in which the third wife stabs herself in the heart so her flowing blood will distract the Cold Woman from slaughtering her family, Bella finds herself strangely empathetic with the third wife's choice. After all, the third wife is the human wife who cannot change into a wolf. She has nothing to offer other than her humanity and her life's blood, which she freely gives. 'I was thinking of someone outside the magic altogether', Bella tells us.

> I was trying to imagine the face of the unnamed woman who had saved the entire tribe, the third wife.
> Just a human woman, with no special gifts or powers. Physically weaker and slower than any of the monsters in the story. But she had been the key, the solution. She'd saved her husband, her young sons, her tribe.[19]

Bella repeats the sacrificial gesture of the third wife when Victoria attacks Edward, and Bella fears that he will be defeated. At the moment of crisis she says, 'If I had to bleed to save them, I would do it. I would die to do it, like the third wife' (578). Bella finds a sharp stone and cuts through the veins in the crook of her arm.

However, all of Bella's seemingly grand sacrifices are in vain. Bella's mother is not really held captive by James, and Seth, a member of the wolf pack who is fighting with Edward against Victoria, feigns being hurt only in order to draw Victoria in – Bella had not needed to cut herself at all. Thus, Bella's two attempts at self-sacrifice are empty gestures with no value. Ultimately, to save her vampire family, Bella must sacrifice her mortality, not her life. This is a sacrifice that she can make quite easily – one, in fact, that she was eager to do from almost the beginnings of her relationship with Edward. And what does she have to live for? Her broken home? The low income of her parents compared to that of the Cullens? Her virginity? Bella cannot shed these things quickly enough, and, by sacrificing them, she earns passage into vampire heaven – a heaven that includes wealth, beauty, grace, self-control, self-determination, super powers, a whole family, sex and children – by becoming a vampire herself.

Bella quickly recoups whatever she loses, and she becomes better than she ever was as a human. After she wakes up transformed in *Breaking Dawn*, she sees Edward for the first time and realises that the great, sacrificial love she thought she had for him is nothing compared to what her new vampire heart can allow. She says, '[f]or the first time, with the dimming shadows and limiting weakness of humanity taken off my eyes, I saw his face. I gasped and then struggled with my vocabulary, unable to find the right words. I needed better words'.[20] Later she adds, 'I hadn't imagined that I could love him more than I had. My old mind hadn't been capable of holding this much love. My old heart had not been strong enough to bear it' (394). Her meagre efforts to love are far outstripped by what her vampire heart is capable of doing.

The vampire Bella also reflects the same god-like perfection that terrified Edward and inspired Carlisle. Soon after she wakes up, Bella is instructed to look at her transformed body in the mirror by Alice, and her first response is 'unthinking pleasure' (371). She says that

> [t]he alien creature in the glass was indisputably beautiful, every bit as beautiful as Alice or Esme.
> [...]
> My second reaction was horror.
> Who *was* she? At first glance, I couldn't find my face anywhere in the smooth, perfect planes of her features.
> And her eyes! Though I'd known to expect them, her eyes still sent a thrill of terror through me. (371–2)

Much like Edward's horror at discovering something inhuman reflecting back out of his eyes at him, Bella's first response to her perfected body is terror. Ostensibly, she is terrorised because her eyes are blood red, but she finds herself so changed that she has, in fact, become alien to herself. And just as the monster that Edward sees gazing back at himself is more the inhuman terror of facing a god, so, too, has Bella been transformed into something godlike.

Finally, her status as the mother of the half-vampire, half-human Renesmee seems to even restore the purity lost along with her virginity. The fact that Bella has given birth to Renesmee allows her to occupy the position of the mother of God, the Virgin Mary. Bella quickly notes that whenever Carlisle or any of the other Cullens speaks about Renesmee, they are almost worshipful. Bella says that there was 'a gleam I'd never seen before in [Carlisle's] eyes. He said her name with an understated fervor. A reverence. The way devout people talked about their gods' (365–6). Even Edward, whose initial impulses had been to abort Renesmee, comes to speak of her with 'an almost religious devotion' (396). As the mother of the object of such fervor and devotion, Bella is positioned as the Virgin Mary, thus restoring her lost purity as well. In sum, Bella has lost nothing and gained everything in becoming a vampire.

What then is to be done? If life as a vampire offers incomparably more than human life can, and if works of righteousness are able to gain one access into heaven, then heaven becomes not only a moot point for humans but inaccessible as well. Meyer attempts to mitigate this problem somewhat by having Carlisle insist that it is self-restraint that allows him to recapture his humanity and that his work as a surgeon is a form of penance for the supernatural and beautiful creature he has become. From those who have been given much, much will be required. Edward, during his rebellious stage, is like a wrathful god, inhuman, trying without success to achieve goodness by only killing evil humans. But he soon discovers that doing good above the law does not make him worthy. Instead, the vampires reclaim their humanity by acting human – living with humans, working with humans, going to school and assimilating as best they can.

Although Edward ultimately chooses to change Bella into a vampire when her life is in danger, this transformation means that she will never need to consider questions of religious faith or ponder what the cost of heaven is. Instead, his transformation of her is a gift that keeps her forever grounded on the earth, even at it raises her well above it. She, too, will possess the beauty that results from the daily sacrifices required for the godlike vampire to live as a human. In other words, by finally achieving the means to open the gates to heaven, she no longer needs to do so. At the end of *Twilight*, Edward asks Bella, 'Is that what you dream about? Being a monster?' She responds, '[n]ot exactly … Mostly I dream about being with you forever' (433). Thus, rather than provide a stabilising resistance that serves only to ensure the role of religion in culture, as they do in *Dracula*, vampires today offer the possibility of religion without religion.

Notes

1 Stoker, *Dracula*, ed. Auerbach and Skal, p. 209. All further references are to this edition and in parentheses in the text. Note that Stoker himself does not use the phrase 'Crew of Light'; this was coined by Christopher Craft but has fallen into common usage (see Craft, '"Kiss Me"', note 7, p. 130).

2 Barber, *Vampires*, p. 180.

3 Meyer, *New Moon*, p. 541. All further references in parentheses.

4 Meyer, *Twilight*, p. 288.

5 *Ibid.*, p. 394.

6 See, for example, pp. 14–15. Mina shares Jonathan's interpretation of the people and landscape of Transylvania as picturesque (pp. 311–12). However, she does remark with some distaste that, when the woman at the house in Bistritz where she and Van Helsing stop to eat saw the scar on her forehead, the woman began to cross herself and put extra garlic in her food.

7 See Auerbach and Skal, Introduction, *Dracula*, p. 33, n. 3.

8 To address questions of religion in the Twilight series seems to invite questions about Meyer's own Mormonism. In fact, to discuss it at all appears to invite such questions. Caitlin Flanagan remarks, in her oddly enthusiastic review of the series: '[t]hat the author is a practicing Mormon is a fact every review has mentioned, although none knows what to do with it, and certainly none can relate it to the novel' (Flanagan, 'What Girls Want', p. 7). Perhaps interest in Meyer's beliefs attracts such attention because of the particular position Mormonism occupies in the religious spectrum of American culture. Viewed as similar to Protestantism and yet unorthodox by Protestant standards, Mormonism occupies a place of mystery for many Americans. Indeed, Clarke and Osborn remark that Meyer's self-identification with Mormonism would be 'unlikely to attract as much attention if she said she was Catholic or Jewish' (p. 7). Meyer's responses to questions about the relationship between her Mormonism and her writing have not always been helpful either. When asked in *Time* magazine if her 'views on religion affect[ed her] way of writing in the Twilight series?', Meyer responded 'Really, not so much. Not consciously at all … I do think that because I'm a very religious person, it does tend to come out somewhat in the books, although always unconsciously' ('10 Questions for Stephenie Meyer'). Meyer's double answer seems to both affirm and disavow a connection between the series and Mormon faith.

9 *Twilight*, p. 17. Further references in parentheses.

10 The shift of the vampire from demonic to virtuous is the topic of several studies on vampires in media – as of many chapters in this book. Carol Senf claims that a decline in religious authority and a change in orthodox views of death and dying are among the causes (*The Vampire in Nineteenth-Century English Literature*, p. 163). See also Gordon and Hollinger, *Blood Read*, p. 1; Clements, *The Vampire Defanged*, p. 2; Branch, 'Carlisle's Cross', p. 61.

11 In *Of Grammatology*, Derrida writes that the supplement is a paradoxical element

that, in being both something that can be added on to something that is already complete in itself and something that can be added on to something incomplete in order to complete it, simultaneously signifies presence and absence. Therefore, the supplement is that which in its presence always already guarantees a lack. To say, then, that the beauty of the Cullens functions like the supplement is to say that their beauty simultaneously signifies their goodness as well as their seductive monstrosity.

12 Dracula's brides and Lucy use beauty to entice the men in *Dracula*. However, Stoker is always careful to leave indications that their beauty is off, not quite right in some regard, in order to distinguish it from Mina's pure beauty. Meyer does not give the Cullens those differentiating marks. They are simply, and without qualification, beautiful.

13 This distinction is also what allows the Quileute tribe, who can change into wolves, to avoid being labelled 'monsters' as well. Their job as shapeshifters is to protect.

14 Meyer, *New Moon*, p. 36.

15 Lori Branch writes that '[w]ith the Cullens we are not far from the form of religion that Max Weber so famously describes in *The Protestant Ethic and the Spirit of Capitalism*: a faith that would regard Carlisle's good deeds in the world as indirect evidence of an otherworldly election' (pp. 74–5). For a contrasting account of vampires and the Protestant work ethic, see Franco Moretti's 'A Capital *Dracula*', pp. 90–104.

16 Meyer, *Twilight*, p. 329

17 Meyer, *New Moon*, pp. 36, 37.

18 *Ibid.*, p. 547.

19 Meyer, *Eclipse*, p. 231.

20 Meyer, *Breaking Dawn*, p. 360. Further references in parentheses.

11

The Twilight Saga
and the pleasures of spectatorship:
the broken body and the shining body[1]

Sara Wasson and Sarah Artt

E VER SINCE Laura Mulvey identified the visual pleasures of narrative cinema, the objectification of the female body on screen has been a staple of film criticism.[2] Our chapter argues that Stephenie Meyer's Twilight Saga complicates that story of spectatorship by positioning the female hetero-sexual viewer as ambivalent agent, not just victim. The Twilight Saga, both books and films, poses two invitations to spectatorship studies. First, we will examine why the books and films may have generated such a vast popular appetite among women for the sight of another woman being progressively mutilated. Second, we will examine the films' recurring fascination with looking at the body of a man, the female spectator's gaze simultaneously tempted and defensively obscured by the glitter of vampire skin. Together, we suggest that these two elements partially explain the saga's tremendous popularity.

The reactionary politics of the Twilight Saga have been catalogued by many.[3] What has not been examined in much detail is why these texts elicit such pleasure in fans.[4] This chapter offers a partial answer to that question. In the post-feminist landscape, feminist critics have admittedly had to grow more comfortable with paradox; as Stéphanie Genz notes, 'the paradoxes of contemporary femininity' simultaneously invoke 'traditional narratives of feminine passivity *and* more progressive scripts of feminine agency'.[5] Yet this chapter strives to go further than merely identifying paradox. Instead, we identify what animates that paradox: exactly what pleasures complicate a simple political reading.

Bella's broken body

In the Twilight Saga, the role for female bodies is to break: Bella's injuries throughout the saga are extensive. In book one, *Twilight*, she scrapes her palms, incurs minor injuries from nearly being crushed by a car, has her head smashed against glass, multiple ribs broken, hand and leg broken, concussion and extensive glass wounds across her head and body. In book two, *New Moon*, she crashes her motorbike repeatedly and nearly drowns after jumping off a cliff. In book three, *Eclipse*, she deliberately cuts herself twice to distract vampire attention from her beloved. In book four, *Breaking Dawn*, she is bruised across her whole body every time she has sex with Edward as a mortal, and when she becomes pregnant the foetus breaks multiple ribs and ultimately snaps her spine. Her beloved then gives her an emergency caesarean with his teeth. Bella's physical fragility even dominates the sections not directly featuring physical injury: indeed, *Midnight Sun*, Edward's first-person narration of the events in *Twilight*, is essentially a litany to Bella's fragility, in which he repeatedly contemplates how easily he could snap her body. 'Her delicate fingers, her fragile wrist – they were so breakable, looking for all the world like just my breath could snap them'.[6]

This emphasis on the broken female body arguably fulfils three purposes. First, it is tempting to see it as symbolic of Stephenie Meyer's ideological ambivalence towards the female body, as a devout Mormon. A second explanation could be that these fascinating wounds are a displacement symbol for sexual penetration, a kind of hymeneal rupture. Both readings would be persuasive, but both arguably fail to capture the tremendous *pleasure* that *Twilight* elicits in its vast spectatorship, overwhelmingly young and female. Why would so many women take pleasure in identifying with another woman being mangled on page and screen?

As it happens, the novels themselves suggest a clear explanation for their appeal. It is striking how often Bella's injuries result in her *being looked at* in fascination by her male friends, then cared for and physically cherished. Although Bella repeatedly declares that she hates attention, there is a particular kind of beholding to which she is not at all averse: a rapt, transfixed gaze at her many wounds. When, for example, Edward notices the scrapes on her hand from falling at the beach, they both spend many pages gazing at the scars. The interaction is typically structured so: '"Your hands", he reminded me. I looked down at my palms, at the almost-healed scrapes across the heels of my hands. His eyes missed nothing.'[7] This pattern of being injured and watched intensifies throughout the tetralogy, and, by book four, a whole family of vampires and werewolves sit around Bella, and watch transfixed for hours on end as she suffers, leaping to help her with every flicker of pain that crosses her face. Bella's extraordinary catalogue of wounds is thus not only a symbol of deferred sexual penetration – rather, the wound is an intensity that gives the female character substantial power over the male protagonists, particularly since the men are often those who inflicted the wounds, albeit sometimes inadvertently. As such, these films and novels can give their audience profound pleasure in identifying with not so much being wounded but with being watched and cherished as a result of those wounds.

Throughout the Twilight Saga, Bella's wounds are invariably accompanied by a rapt mutual gaze. This particular pleasure can be described as masochistic spectatorship, as developed by film theorists Gaylyn Studlar and Michele Aaron from the theory of Gilles Deleuze. Traditional film theory sees the suffering female body as an object for sadistic male scopophilia (Mulvey, Doane), giving the female spectator the grim options of either identifying with a sadistic male gaze or identifying with a suffering female body. These theories are predicated on Freud's formulation of sadism and masochism as closely related structures, either inversions of each other or linked developmentally. Freud suggested in 1905 that masochism and sadism essentially share the same root, the sadistic desire to control or destroy another person; his confidence that the two postures are closely allied can be seen in the way he even spoke of 'sado-masochism'.[8] Deleuze challenges that assumption, arguing that sadism and masochism have fundamentally different aesthetics and textual forms. Aesthetics have been core to an understanding of sadism and masochism ever since the terms were coined: the very terms are derived from the authors of literary texts, sadism from the Marquis de Sade and masochism from Leopold von Sacher Masoch, author of *Venus in Furs*, who took sexual delight in being beaten by a woman.[9] Deleuze contends, however, that the aesthetics of masochism and sadism differ: that masochism involves stage managing a scene in which the victim seems helpless and vulnerable but in fact directs the unique, dedicated attention of a supremely powerful figure. In this theory, masochistic spectators are by no means passive victims. On the contrary, they are entirely in control, staging tableaux in which their suffering can be watched and in which they can feel treasured for their (deceptive) fragility.

Deleuze's theories of masochism enable Studlar and Aaron to propose an alternative model of masochistic spectatorship that film audiences might experience. Aaron asks,

> Who ... is this dramatization of masochistic pleasure for? ... Who looks on in rapt attention, seated, silenced, watching the overtly dramatic strategies

play out? … [T]hrough the masochistic pleasure of our sacrificial heroine we
can better see the masochistic pleasure of the film spectator, as each submits,
willingly, to the unfolding but not unexpected story.[10]

Yet saying *Twilight* invites masochistic spectatorship is not the same as saying
Twilight appeals to a self-destructive urge in a character or even in the
audience; film criticism is at its weakest when it degenerates into psycho-
analysing fictional characters or audiences. Indeed, whether masochistic
spectatorship is actually even pathological is actually debatable – Studlar,
for example, contends that it is, while Aaron defends it.[11] Either way, the
debate gains intense political urgency when put into the context of the
existing controversies over *Twilight*'s retrograde gender politics. We do not
intend to psychoanalyse the fictional construct of Bella, nor do we wish to
assume that a masochistic posture, in the Deleuzian sense, is inherently
self-destructive or immature. Rather, we want to explore the pleasures the
text offers when viewed through this frame. We argue that the textual forms
of the books and films are structured by a masochistic economy discernible
in the narrative logic, in the sensuous focus of the narrator's experience,
and in deconstructive moments where the staging of the masochistic scene
is unmasked. This reading uncovers a covert and startling form of agency
to tempt the fans who identify with Bella – not necessarily a particularly
liberating or positive agency, but an agency nonetheless.

Deleuze argues that masochism is fundamentally an aesthetic, a fantasy
tableau of two frozen figures, straining towards each other with consummation relentlessly deferred. Prolonged suspense is a defining textual element:
'it is the moments of suspense that are the climactic moments … Waiting
and suspense are essential characteristics of the masochistic experience …
Formally speaking, masochism is a state of waiting'.[12] The Twilight Saga
– like much other vampire fiction – echoes that suspense, in the delayed
bite or sexual wound. A second hallmark of the masochistic aesthetic is
a cold disavowal of the fleshly weight of the body: indeed, Leopold von
Sacher-Masoch, the author whose masochistic fantasies gave masochism its
name, repeatedly mistakes his lover for a marble statue, a disorientation
that Bella Swan shares.[13] She tells us repeatedly that Edward's skin is like
marble, his lips like stone, so cold to the touch, so pale. Deleuze explains
the icy metaphors of masochism as 'not the negation of feeling but rather
the disavowal of sensuality', again a structure that chimes with *Twilight*'s
ideological ambivalence about sexual pleasure and the body.[14]

Freud's model explains masochism through an Oedipal drama, driven by
fear of, and fascination with, the father.[15] Deleuze, by contrast, contends that

the rapt masochistic tableau is fundamentally pre-Oedipal in its fixations, a victim submitting to the gaze of a cold, powerful beloved. For Deleuze the masochist craves to be clasped and wounded by a superpowerful maternal figure, massively beyond them in strength, exalted and idealised, cold and 'perfect'. This maternal dimension may help explain why so many fans astonish critics by reading the books as describing a healthy, nurturing relationship. Our research among *Twilight* fans has revealed surprising cognitive schemata underpinning interpretations of the franchise. Fans we surveyed tended to depict Edward's controlling behaviour in terms reminiscent of a benevolent, even maternal posture. When we asked self-identified *Twilight* fans to describe Edward the terms that cropped up most were 'caring', 'loving' and 'unconditional love'.[16] When asked why they feel Edward controls Bella by taking her car keys and trying to control her actions, for example, the majority argued that he does this because, since he is so much stronger than her, he feels responsible for her. With Deleuze's maternal model in mind, the power differential between Bella and Edward smacks in many ways of that between mother and child early in a child's life. Any mother–child relationship is initially a profoundly unequal one, in which the mother's physical presence, strength and control can seem overwhelming to the infant.[17] This reading also makes sense of Bella's relentless insistence that Edward is godlike, a radically more powerful being. Even Edward's spooky watching of Bella while she sleeps takes on a different cast through that maternal schema. We would hesitate to imply that a maternal posture is invariably benevolent: feminisms (plural) have long recognised the mother–daughter relationship as a fraught one, and not necessarily one of mutual respect; even second-wave feminism's relationship to post/feminism, after all, has typically been cast in the metaphorical terms of an ungrateful daughter disregarding a wise mother's advice.[18] Nonetheless, a partially maternal scheme makes sense of much fan response, and is a possible explanation for how a fan can 'read' this text against feminist consensus.

Highly evocative of Deleuze's vision, the Twilight books and films abound in the staged tableaux of surrender to the gaze of a cold, perfect, physically powerful figure. In *Twilight*, Bella fantasises about seeing herself recline on velvet while Edward bites her. Such a scene is paradigmatic of the aristocratic, Byronic vampirism of eighteenth- and nineteenth-century literature, as discussed by Conrad Aquilina: Bella scripts that scene by drawing on those literary legacies.[19] Further, in yet another staged tableau of surrender, the denouement of *Twilight* happens in a ballet studio – a site for performance, seen from multiple angles thanks to the mirrors. Bella herself uses the language of scripted performance to describe the event: 'I had no choices now but one: to go to the mirrored room and die … I had just one script and I'd never manage improvisation now.'[20] In addition, this showdown is filmed, and described by the villain as a form of visual art: when he smashes her into the mirrors, he says, '"That's a very nice effect … I thought this room would be visually dramatic for my little film"'.[21] In *New Moon*, Bella's masochistic staging involves her literally wounding herself in an attempt to hear Edward's voice again – and, in the film adaptation, to force a semblance of Edward to appear and to respond to her injuries. In terms reminiscent of the masochistic contract between 'victim' and persecutor, Bella deliberately seeks out danger because she can hear his voice at key moments of peril, and she repeatedly describes her actions as breaking a contract: 'I might feel better if I weren't holding fast, all alone, to a broken pact. If I was an oath-breaker too … I wanted to be stupid and reckless, and I wanted to break promises'.[22] In *Eclipse*, Bella fantasises – and eventually fulfils – a dream of re-enacting the story of the Third Wife in Native American Quileute legends, a woman who stabs herself in the heart to distract a vampire and thus enable her beloved to defeat him.

Being subjected to a perilous gaze is not unique to Bella: the gender dynamics of *Twilight* are more complex. Edward, too, is vulnerable to the gaze, particularly in his attempted suicide in *New Moon*: what will kill him is essentially the massed gaze of hundreds of human spectators, for if his vampiric nature is revealed to so many humans he will be executed by the Volturi vampire aristocrats. As a whole, the Cullens are all wary of the human gaze, for fear that their mortal observers may recognise their inhumanity, but for Edward becoming the object of a knowing human gaze is repeatedly linked to fantasies of suicide and self-destruction. Edward's sacrificial mode can also be read as part of a masochistic contract, but since the novels and films are told so emphatically from Bella's point of view, there are fewer invitations for the reader to identify with Edward's own fragility, his own (unfinished) story *Midnight Sun* being the exception.

Studlar says of masochistic spectatorship in general that 'the apparent victim speaks a deceptive discourse masking the true hierarchy of desire'.[23] *Twilight*'s litany of marble metaphors, its relentless sensual deferrals, its staged tableaux and its suspended narrative structure all exemplify masochistic textual form. Next, we will discuss an additional way in which *Twilight* defensively handles female agency: the film's ambivalent engagement with the woman's transgressive desire to look.

From here on the discussion will examine how the films construct the female gaze. While the books do this too, given space constraints it makes sense to focus on the film representations of the longing look, particularly with a view to putting this research in dialogue with the wealth of existing scholarship on the female spectator. In addition, since Deleuzian masochism is so fundamentally about a *visual* aesthetic, film is a particularly rich medium for examining how it is enacted in cinematic tableaux.

The shining body and the female gaze

Laura Mulvey, in 'Visual Pleasure and Narrative Cinema', argues that one of the pleasures of the cinema is 'scopophilia (pleasure in looking) … [Freud] associated scopophilia with taking other people as objects, subjecting them to a controlling and curious gaze'.[24] This is the kind of gaze we see in operation in *Twilight*. Both Bella and Edward subject one another to the kind of prolonged, curious gazes that seek to categorise and control the other. Bella wants to know why Edward is looking and she interprets his gaze as hostile in the first instance. Edward initially refuses to meet her gaze and, when he does, it is still a hostile gaze because of the threat he poses to her.

There is a prolonged silence surrounding this cinematic couple's clear sexual desire for one another in *Twilight*. Because the desire cannot be consummated it must therefore be confined to a series of gazes or looks. Edward can watch Bella uninterrupted, as he does consistently throughout the narrative. This occurs most memorably (and disturbingly) when Bella glimpses him in the corner of her bedroom and also just prior to Edward's revelation of his Otherness in the forest, where he forces Bella to utter the word 'vampire' and to describe his cold, pale and distant figure. Bella, on the other hand, must be invited to gaze at Edward in the sequence where he insists that she must see what he looks like in the sunlight, revealing his otherworldly glittering torso. So, even though (for a brief moment!) the woman is given permission to look and the man here positions himself deliberately as the object of the woman's gaze, Bella is not granted the power of the fan audience who may gaze uninterrupted and signal their gazing quite vocally.[25] Mulvey also argues that the woman on screen functions on two levels 'as erotic object for the characters within the screen story, and as erotic object for the spectator within the auditorium'.[26] It can be argued that *Twilight* the film illustrates this from a slightly different perspective, foiling notions of the passive woman as object of the look. Instead, it is Edward/ Robert Pattinson who functions as the erotic object of Bella's gaze and those of the auditorium spectators.

Pattinson-as-Edward is there to be gazed at and, when he first enters the narrative in the sequence where he is pointed out to Bella in the cafeteria, his gaze does not seem to be directed anywhere in particular, until it alights on

Bella. The series of shots as he enters the cafeteria depicts him as the object
of the girls' discussion, but also leave him open to the gaze of the audience.
Ken Gelder argues in a psychoanalytic reading of Bram Stoker's novel *Dracula*
that the text 'overcodes sexuality at the level of performance, but undercodes
it at the level of utterance. Critical analysis intervenes at this point, enabling
these deafening silences to "speak".'[27] We would like to argue that the same
may be said for *Twilight*.

So, when Edward declares that he cannot be seen in direct sunlight because
'"people would know we're different. This is what I am"', the vampire figure
can be seen to once more represent sexual difference, underscored by the
film's display of the male body as an erotic object without the confines of
the action film. Steve Neale argues that 'there is no cultural or cinematic
convention which would allow the male body to be presented [as an erotic
object] ... we see male bodies stylised and fragmented by close-ups, but
our look is not direct, it is heavily mediated by the looks of the characters
involved. And those looks are marked not by desire, but rather by fear, or
hatred, or aggression.'[28] In the sequence where Edward reveals his sparkling
skin to Bella in the forest, crucially, he does not move; he stands and invites
(even orders) Bella to look at him, as he unbuttons his shirt.

Bella's now well-known reaction, where she gasps in a mixture of
trepidation and delight – 'it's like diamonds' – can be read as a troubling
conflation of masculinity and the supposedly sought-after diamond solitaire
of an engagement ring, and yet she is not entirely 'blinded by sparkle'. The
shimmer is a tissue-thin veil through which the passive male body may be
viewed, and yet the context of the look combines desire, fear, awe, and
aggression. Kirsten Stewart as Bella conveys this in her shifting expression as
she is confronted by Edward's aggressive revelation of his desirable difference,
which is nonetheless 'the skin of a killer', as he puts it in the film. Elsewhere
in this book, Lindsay Scott and Catherine Spooner (Chapters 7 and 9) both
explore the transgressive symbolisation of Edward further. Jennifer Williams
also explores the textual representation of the beautiful *Twilight* vampire as
both good and monstrous in Chapter 10.

But what is also interesting here is that Edward as embodiment of the
vampire figure becomes the symbol on to which the woman maps her
desires. Yet there is still the threat that something bad will happen to her if
she *continues to look*. Linda Williams, in her widely reproduced essay 'When
the Woman Looks', also comments on this threat to the woman's gaze as it
occurs in both the woman's film and the horror film: 'more instructive are
those moments when the good girl heroines are granted the power of the
look, whether in the woman's film ... or the horror film ... In both cases

as [Mary Ann] Doane suggests, the woman's exercise of an active, investigating gaze can only be simultaneous with her own victimization.'[29] Brigid Cherry also discusses Williams and the assertion that 'women's possession or ownership of the gaze is thus problematical [within horror cinema] and it may be that women are thus "taught" that they should refuse to look'.[30] This brings us back to the problem of *Twilight* and whether Bella Swan is indeed 'blinded by sparkle'. What if *Twilight* advises us that all we are supposed to do is look – but that there can never be anything more? *Twilight* fandom is driven by the tension between the permission to look at the body of the star (specifically Robert Pattinson as Edward but, with the release of *New Moon*, *Eclipse* and *Breaking Dawn* Part 1 and 2, we now also have the spectacle of Taylor Lautner as Jacob to add to the classic Gothic triangle of two male suitors vying for a single woman) and the desire to establish contact with that body. The appeal of *Twilight* may also lie in this fantasy of overwhelming desire that is constantly delayed but may potentially find consummation and in its transgressive, teasing pleasure of looking when we think we should not.

Overall, then, we suggest that the Twilight franchise offers satisfactions to female viewers and readers that cannot be explained through traditional film or literary theory. The 'deceptive fragility' of Bella's victimhood is part of a sustained aesthetic of staged submission, and the fantasy of permission to look at and desire the male as still ultimately transgressive and there is pleasure in that sense that she is 'not supposed to look'. Studlar says that, in masochistic spectatorship, 'A performance of dramatised powerlessness allows the female masochistic subject to use suffering and, in particular, suffering attached to "sacred" aspects of femininity like sexual purity as the deceptive cover for the exercise of forbidden powers – and pleasures'.[31] Our readings could build towards making sense of the passionate controversy around *Twilight*, in which the work is understandably excoriated for antiquated notions of womanhood and yet defended by fans as healthy and positive. *Twilight* finds unexpected pleasures in both the broken body and the shining body.[32]

Notes

1 [Editors' note: This chapter was to have been accompanied by illustrations but, unfortunately, Summit Entertainment refused permission to reproduce screen shots from *Twilight*.]

2 Mulvey, 'Visual Pleasure and Narrative Cinema'; Williams, 'When the Woman Looks'; Doane, *The Desire to Desire*.

3 See, for example, Barreca, 'Five Reasons a Smart Middle Aged Woman Loathes TWILIGHT'; Czech, 'Bella Swan – A Feminist's Nightmare'; McCulloch, 'Twilight

Sara Wasson and Sarah Artt

Relationship Unhealthy'; Jen Nedeau, 'Twilight: A Feminist Nightmare'; Nikkigassley, 'Feminism Doesn't Sparkle'; Rebelliouspixels, 'Buffy vs Edward: *Twilight* Remixed'; Selzter, 'A Feminist's Guide to Curing Yourself of Twilight-Mania'; UWMKatie, 'A Significant Step Down from Buffy'.

4 A caveat: we want to acknowledge that one cannot talk of 'the' fans, for, like all fans, these enthusiasts are highly diverse. Fans unironically wearing Team Edward T-shirts may not be doing the same work as fans writing Edward/Jasper slash fan fiction, for example.

5 Genz, *Postfemininities in Popular Culture*.

6 Meyer, *Midnight Sun: Partial Draft*, p. 98.

7 Meyer, *Twilight*, p. 165.

8 Freud, 'Three Essays on the Theory of Sexuality'; Laplanche and Pontalis, *The Language of Psycho-Analysis*, pp. 245, 401.

9 Laplanche and Pontalis, *The Language of Psycho-Analysis*, p. 244.

10 Aaron, *Spectatorship*, pp. 61–2.

11 *Ibid.*, p. 62.

12 'Coldness and Cruelty', in *Masochism*, pp. 33, 71).

13 *Ibid.*, p. 69.

14 *Ibid.*, p. 52.

15 Freud, 'A Child Is Being Beaten', in *On Psychopathology*, pp. 163–93.

16 We conducted qualitative analysis of 51 self-identified *Twilight* fans in online survey and interview from December 2009 to January 2010.

17 Julia Kristeva, *Powers of Horror*, p. 13.

18 Creet, 'Daughter of the Movement'.

19 See Chapter 2 above.

20 Meyer, *Twilight*, pp. 375–6.

21 *Ibid.*, p. 392.

22 Meyer, *New Moon*, pp. 125, 127.

23 Studlar, 'Masochistic Performance and Female Subjectivity', p. 41.

24 Mulvey, 'Visual Pleasure and Narrative Cinema', p. 60.

25 Click, 'Rabid, Obsessed and Frenzied'.

26 Mulvey, 'Visual Pleasure', p. 63.

27 Gelder, *Reading the Vampire*, p. 67.

28 Neale, 'Masculinity as Spectacle', p. 18.

29 Williams, 'When the Woman Looks', p. 61. Considered alongside other classic, Gothic women's films of the 1940s such as *Gaslight*, *Dragonwyck*, *Suspicion* and *Rebecca*, Hardwicke's film makes a convincing contemporary addition to the subgenre of the woman's film. For a full discussion of the Gothic woman's film, see Hanson, *Hollywood Heroines*.

30 Cherry, *Horror*, p. 142.

31 Studlar, 'Masochistic Performance', p. 44.

32 The implications of further readings in this area could also shed light on the current popularity of E. L. James's Fifty Shades of Gray series, which began life as *Twilight*

fan fiction. More work needs to be done in terms of analysing the current vogue for sadomasochistic erotic fiction marketed to women. The similarities between the cover artwork alone for *Twilight*, *Fifty Shades* and the recent rebranding of Pauline Reage's *The Story of O* by Random House all warrant extended commentary and analysis.

12

The postmodern vampire in 'post-race' America: HBO's *True Blood*

Michelle J. Smith

In an expression of the figure's mutability, Nina Auerbach writes that 'every age embraces the vampire it needs'.[1] The twenty-first-century vampire is a substantially different creature from the grotesque monsters who lurk in the shadows of narratives from the mid-nineteenth century to the middle of the twentieth century. The HBO television series *True Blood* (prod. Alan Ball, 2008–) is an example of the postmodern Gothic in which the opposition between good and evil is collapsed.[2] A lack of faith in metanarratives manifests in the most marginal of voices, that of the vampire, becoming valid, and in the upending of traditional structures of authority, such as religion. The line between the vampire and the human, emblematic of racial and sexual difference, is blurred in the series. Moreover, *True Blood* does not evoke anxiety about the dissolution of boundaries, as in canonical Gothic fictions. Instead, the series acknowledges that the flaws and evils of humans are an equal match for those evidenced by vampires. A postmodern age has embraced a vampire that displays some of the most valuable human traits such as loyalty, love and compassion, and also exposes humans as capable of being as equally murderous as vampires.

Franco Moretti's essay 'The dialectic of fear' has proved influential in the critique of Gothic fiction, opening the way for analysis of the monster, especially the vampire, as metaphor. From Moretti's own equation of Bram Stoker's Dracula with capitalism, the vampire has been read as symbolic of a range of anxieties from those concerning racial difference to non-normative sexuality and AIDS.[3] While scholars have recognised that the contemporary vampire is usually less monstrous than its earlier counterparts,[4] the vampire in *True Blood*, rather than emphasising the transgression of racial

Figure 12.1. Promotional image of Sookie Stackhouse (Anna Paquin)

and sexual boundaries between 'us' and 'them', injects uncertainty into the foundation of the binary oppositions that make such metaphors surrounding their transgression possible. What may be interpreted as a range of racial identities is exposed among the inhabitants of the small Southern town of Bon Temps, Louisiana – the vampire, werewolf, werepanther, fairy, witch and shapeshifter – obliterating the very concept of normality against which to define deviance or monstrosity.[5] In place of fears of a diversity of races coming together, anxieties of 'conversion', and 'post-race' erasures of difference, *True Blood* champions a multiplicity of 'racial types' and critiques those who are intolerant of difference, whether of race or of sexual orientation.

The series's human heroine, waitress Sookie Stackhouse (Anna Paquin), has a unique capacity to perceive the feelings of others in a way that further reinforces the breakdown of the dichotomy of humans as good and vampires as evil (Figure 12.1). Though Sookie displays none of the physical prowess of Buffy Summers from the popular television series *Buffy the Vampire Slayer*, she does have supernatural abilities as a telepath, which derive from her status as a fairy. Sookie's telepathic ability gives her the ultimate capacity to demonstrate quickness of perception and sensation, and her insight into other people's thoughts gives her ample opportunity to show concern for the suffering of others and to do good deeds.

Furthermore, Sookie's telepathy exposes the tarnished reality of human nature lurking beneath acceptable exteriors. She feels and perceives too much and is unable to conduct a regular relationship with another human as a result. For instance, she is able to hear the lewd thoughts of potential suitors, which makes relationships impossible. Bill Compton's (Stephen Moyer) status as a vampire means that Sookie cannot access his mind, a decided relief from the feelings of hatred she perceives in most people. In a postmodern Gothic text like *True Blood*, the heroine's unique capacity to experience the thoughts of others further reveals that there is no way to fix good and evil into neat categorisations. This is made particularly evident by characters who cling to superficial markers of 'good' like religion yet display bloodlust that rivals the most murderous vampire. While Sookie is a conventional white, blonde-haired heroine who helps to protect small-town America, the racial, supernatural and sexual diversity of the world of *True Blood*, this chapter suggests, complicates any sense of a fixed ideal of 'Americanness' in need of defence.

Problematising good versus evil

From its debut episode 'Strange Love', the series sets itself up in playful opposition to the coherence of Gothic conventions, as Eve Kosofsky Sedgwick terms the ubiquitous coexistence of the genre's 'characteristic preoccupations' and 'obligatory scenes'.[6] It begins with a young woman and her boyfriend travelling in a car at night. As the woman sexually stimulates her boyfriend, the viewer familiar with horror film tropes anticipates imminent danger. The couple stop at a convenience store after observing a sign advertising the sale of 'Tru Blood' (a bottled substitute for human blood developed in Japan that has recently enabled vampires across the world to emerge from centuries in hiding).[7] The store clerk, who is dressed in black, wears a neck chain containing the figure of Baphomet and an inverted cross and speaks with an affected European accent. Contrary to the expectations of the couple, and the viewer, the old-world European cliché of the distinctly Other and anti-religious vampire is a sham. An actual vampire browsing the store's fridge, who is dressed in a camouflage shirt, blue jeans and a trucker's hat emblazoned with the Confederate flag, is offended by the clerk's theatrical pretence at being a vampire, especially when the girl asks for 'V', or vampire blood, which produces a high surpassing that of illicit drugs in humans (Figures 12.2 and 12.3). The vampire aggressively bares his fangs and threatens the human imposter.

From the outset, stereotypical images of vampires are mocked and real vampires are depicted as virtually indistinguishable from the prosaic human

Figures 12.2 and 12.3.   The cliché meets a real vampire

residents of the American South. Necessarily, it is no longer entirely obvious of whom audiences should be afraid, if anyone. As Lindsey Scott observes in relation to 'new vampire' film in Chapter 5, this reflects a broader generic movement from the obvious grotesqueness of Dracula and F. W. Murnau's iconic bald and talon-fingered Nosferatu to sexually desirable and comparatively normalised vampires such as Edward Cullen from Stephenie Meyer's *Twilight* novels and Bill in *True Blood*. Joan Gordon and Veronica Hollinger note that the contemporary vampire has undergone a process of 'domestication', by which it has, in some ways, been rendered ordinary.[8] He or she is not an external threat posed to ordinary America, but is interwoven in the fabric of that America. Visually, the vampire looks little different to humans, albeit with a slight pallor, except when sexually aroused or intending to feed. Vampire Bill's ordinariness is a frequent object of humour, such as when he shops under harsh fluorescent lighting for women's clothing for his vampire progeny, offers drinks to human house guests or informs Sookie of his mundane name (which she assumes would be something exotic like 'Antoine'). Indeed, the vampire of historical Gothic fiction would never be found shopping at Walmart.

There is a communal identity to contemporary vampirism that marks the Undead as a segment of society, rather than as isolated outcasts. Following Anne Rice's family vampire groups in The Vampire Chronicles (1976–2003), in *True Blood* vampires live together in 'nests', a term that implies a sense of community and nurturing. Moreover, The American Vampire League organisation lobbies for equal rights for vampires in a concerted effort to become accepted among humans. In contrast with the vampire as 'citizen of the world', as Ken Gelder describes the vampires of the past to whom national boundaries were unimportant, these vampires are firmly located within America.[9] Vampires have devised local hierarchical governmental structures in the form of sheriffs (such as Eric Northman (Alexander Skarsgård), sheriff of Area 5 in Louisiana), kings and queens of states (like Russell Edgington (Denis O'Hare), the King of Mississippi) and, ruling above all, The Magister.

As a by-product of the infiltration of the Undead into suburbia, the contemporary vampire does not necessarily embody evil or serve as an allegory for the battle between God and the Devil. Both vampires and humans have the potential to be good or bad. Therefore, vampires such as Russell, who kills a news reporter mercilessly on national television, setting back the cause of vampire rights in the process, coexist with 'good' vampires such as Eddie Gauthier (Stephen Root), an overweight homebody who is used by multiple characters for his blood, culminating in his being chained up in his basement like a bear being milked for its bile and his eventual unprovoked staking. The typical relationship between vampire and human is between predator and prey, yet *True Blood* problematises the once clear dividing line between monster and human. Vampires, at the same time as being preternaturally strong, are potential victims of 'drainers', who mimic heroin addicts in their insatiable quest for 'V'.

When Bill is forced to become a 'maker' by converting a human into a vampire, the process of transformation alludes to the tragedy and sorrow inherent in each vampire's loss of their human life and family. Jessica Hamby (Deborah Ann Woll) is a God-fearing innocent virgin from a home-schooled environment before she is forcibly made vampire, eliciting the viewer's sympathy. Hollinger proposes that the vampire is a deconstructive figure because it dissolves boundaries and problematises distinctions between binary oppositions: '[I]t is the monster that used to be human; it is the undead that used to be alive; it is the monster that *looks like us*'.[10] A postmodern Gothic text like *True Blood* does not present a vampire's acts of violence and murder as issuing from innate evil (an essentialist fixed identity), but as the product of life experience and environment. Jessica's earlier innocence and struggles to control her new vampire impulses, Bill's violent creation by Lorena Krasiki (Mariana Klaveno) during the Civil War, and Eric's battlefield choice to survive as a vampire rather than die of his injuries make it harder to fix identities as pure evil.

Certain folkloric aspects that we associate with vampire fictions have disappeared alongside the diminution in the use of the vampire as symbolic of evil. Jules Zanger points out that most contemporary vampires 'can no longer transform themselves into bats or mist or wolves or puffs of smoke; in addition, they need no longer wait to be invited over a threshold, and mirrors and crucifixes appear to have relatively little effect on them'.[11] Vampire texts tend to modify established generic tropes to determine which aspects of superstition remain effective in combating the vampire.[12] In *True Blood* religious symbols, such as crucifixes, holy water, the host, priests and churches hold no power over vampires, while non-religious folklore remains effective: vampires must be invited into a human home, silver will pin a vampire down and cause excruciating pain, exposure to sunlight will gradually kill, and a stake through the heart will instantly reduce a vampire to a mess of sticky ooze. The total loss of religion's power against the vampire dispenses with a need for faith in a God to ensure protection and reflects a diminishing belief in Christianity that has its roots in an increasing secularism, fostered originally by the Enlightenment; it is symptomatic, too, of the postmodern condition's 'incredulity toward metanarratives', as Lyotard explains it.[13]

David Punter and Glennis Byron observe that '[i]n nineteenth-century vampire fiction, the representation of the vampire as monstrous, evil and other serves to guarantee the existence of good, reinforcing the formally dichotomized structures of belief which ... still constituted the dominant world view'.[14] A monster such as Dracula ensures that there is also good: the Crew of Light. When a pure, unadulterated source of evil is destroyed in a canonical Gothic novel, the closure gives the reader a sense that good has triumphed and that the right way of life, usually middle-class morality, has

Figure 12.4. Promotional image of Reverend Steve Newlin (Michael McMillian)

prevailed. In the postmodern Gothic, evil is not a straightforward concept and cannot be vanquished through the destruction of one character or another. Not only are symbols of faith powerless in *True Blood*, but the mutually exclusive relationship of good and evil is dismantled by showing the endearing side of the vampire and the scurrilousness and hypocrisy of purveyors of Christianity. A key plot development in Season Two is the conspiracy of the Fellowship of the Sun church to kill vampires. While vampires are active only at night, in the darkness, this Christian church claims dominion of what is good and right and all that is the preserve of the light, or the 'sun', which also has the potential to destroy vampires. The Reverend Steve Newlin (Michael McMillian) and his wife, Sarah (Anna Camp), oppose the burgeoning movement for vampire rights, both blaming family tragedies on vampires. Reverend Newlin is waging war on vampires in the media and by attempting to destroy them one by one by staking or forcing them to 'meet the sun' (Figure 12.4).

Both Reverend Newlin and the intellectual lightweight Jason Stackhouse (Ryan Kwanten) use polarising language to describe the perceived threat of vampires – 'You're either with us or against us' – recalling President George Bush's similar phrasing after the 11 September attacks in 2001: 'Either you are with us, or you are with the terrorists'.[15] The political parallel between an imagined battle between the side of good and the side of evil is so antithetical to the postmodern condition that an 'us' and 'them' construction of the situation is impossible to maintain. The side of 'good' is exposed as having as much hypocrisy and badness to it as the side of 'evil': Reverend Newlin is ostensibly a murderer and kidnapper, and his superficially pious wife, Sarah, engages in an extra-marital affair with Jason. As good is dismantled, however, so too is the monolithic construction of evil. The vampire that Reverend Newlin holds hostage is Godric (Allan Hyde), a two-thousand-year-old being in the body of a teenager, who has grown to hate himself and seek peace from his existence. As an ancient vampire with exceptionally strong powers, Godric could easily have laid waste to the church and its armed zealots, but he does not wish to further inflame strained relations between humans and vampires, showing that he is far removed from the purportedly murderous bloodsucker that Newlin targets.

Godric demonstrates that a vampire, through extended 'life' experience, may develop a higher degree of humanity than most humans. In the episode 'Timebomb', at the moment of greatest conflict in which the vampires hold the upper hand, Godric proposes a truce, but Newlin is blindly adherent to his cause of hatred and refuses to place the safety of his parishioners first.[16] When Godric asks who of the people is willing to die for Newlin's cause, none steps forward and he defuses the situation without a drop of blood being spilled. The enigmatic Godric is older than Jesus and, while he represents evil to the Fellowship of the Sun Church, he is more Christian in his attitudes and approach than the Newlins. Godric acknowledges that vampires are frightening and argues that they have not evolved morally over time but have become more predatory. He remarks, 'no wonder they hate us' and picks out Lorena, Bill's maker, as an exemplar of what is wrong with vampire society. He can perceive that she is an old vampire, but chastises her for not having 'bettered herself' in her hundreds of years of existence to aid in vampire–human relations. The monologue is especially timely in that the Fellowship of the Sun's mission to destroy vampires has not been quashed and the celibate devotee, Luke McDonald (Wes Brown), has appeared at the vampire nest with a bomb strapped to him. The resulting explosion kills both vampires and humans: the side of supposed good has no neat victory over evil, with deaths on both sides.

The series exposes the motivations of vampires, furthering dismantling the good and evil binary, through its revision of the traditional point of view of Gothic fictions that situate the human as victim at their centre. Most famously, Stoker's *Dracula* (1897) unfolds through the narrative perspectives of the diaries, letters and journals of Jonathan Harker, Mina Murray, Dr Seward and Lucy Westenra. A shift toward narration and focalisation through the marginal voices of vampire protagonists originates in vampire literature of the 1970s, including Anne Rice's *Interview with the Vampire* (1976),[17] which was preoccupied with relationships between vampires, relegating humans to the narrative margins. Chelsea Quinn Yarbro's Saint-Germain Cycle, commencing with *Hôtel Transylvania* (1978), also marked a generic transformation that ascribed a degree of heroism to the vampire and minimised the threat to humans posed by the vampire's requirement for human blood. The inclusion of vampire and human points of view has a different outcome in the postmodern Gothic in that greater understanding of, and sympathy for, the vampire's perspective make long-term loving relationships between humans and vampires possible. The on-again, off-again vampire–human relationship between Bill and Sookie forms the core of *True Blood* and, combined with the relationships between Jessica and Hoyt Fortenberry and Isabel and Hugo, dissolves the concept of monster and sexual prey. Those who are the victims of vampires, however, are almost exclusively dispensable, with little attention devoted to their perception of events. There is a notable exception, however, when central character Tara Thornton (Rutina Wesley) falls victim to the insane vampire, Franklin Mott, and the good versus evil dichotomy is more familiarly rendered.

Biting back against a 'post-race' era

With the election of Barack Obama as the first African-American President of the United States in 2008, the existence of a post-racial era in which racism and intolerance had been extinguished was, for some, confirmed. Rona Tamiko Halualani defines the 'post-race' era as 'the period from the late 1990s to the present during which US society invoked a neoliberal stance through which race, in all social and political matters, was to be avoided, shunned, and discarded'.[18] In her analysis of regional Californian newspapers in this period, Halualani concludes that the ideological representation of diversity has come to signify 'an abstract, idealized and/or raceless representation and reality, in which cultural communities are collocated, while simultaneously emptied of any particular histories, social structures, or structural inequalities'. Conceptions of a 'post-race' era not only show difference as universal (we are all equally different), but as non-threatening and 'raceless'.

True Blood actively works against any 'post-race' notion of diversity divested of race; instead, it foregrounds differences and dramatises conflicts between a plethora of what might be interpreted as racial identities, from the vampire, werewolf, werepanther, fairies and witches, to shape-shifters such as the bar-owner Sam Merlotte (Sam Trammell). Gothic fictions once expressed a fear of the possibility of a diversity of races coming together. As Gelder writes of the racial threat posed by vampires, 'Diversity means instability: it invites contestation: identities become confused: one can no longer tell "who is who"'.[19] In contrast, *True Blood* gradually exposes so many metaphoric racial identities that the privileging of non-supernatural human identity becomes impossible, unsettling the self/Other dichotomy on which vampire fictions once relied.

While 'the great revelation' saw vampires emerge across the globe,[20] the series is set in the Southern USA, a place where, as Teresa Goddu argues, the Gothic and race are most visible in the United States:

> Indeed, the South's 'peculiar' identity has not only been defined by its particular racial history, but has also been depicted in gothic terms: the South is a benighted landscape, heavy with history and haunted by the ghosts of slavery. The South's oppositional image – its gothic excesses and social transgressions – has served as the nation's safety valve: as the repository for everything the nation is *not*, the South purges contrary impulses. More perceived idea than social reality, the imaginary South functions as the nation's 'dark' other.[21]

Goddu proposes that the Gothic criticises any notion of innocence in the new world by revealing the contradictions that undermine its claims to purity and equality, most notably through the haunting effects of slavery.[22] The South, then, can function as a repository for the Other; its housing of the Gothic contains any threat to broader American identity. In a supposedly 'post-racial' USA, *True Blood's* Louisiana dramatises metaphorical racial conflicts and power imbalances that are imagined as non-existent elsewhere. Nevertheless, while it is a distinctive trope in contemporary vampire fictions, it is important to note that regionalism is not mobilised consistently across these texts. As Kimberley McMahon-Coleman demonstrates with *The Vampire Diaries*, the Southern setting can also heighten the sense of belonging and 'home' for former vampire 'citizens of the world' (see Chapter 13 below).

Gothic fictions have typically evoked fear about the collapse of boundaries between self and other, human and animal, and life and death. The vampire, in particular, has been read as trading on an anxiety of conversion by suggesting that race is fluid, not fixed.[23] This threat of racial contami-nation is posed to white people since, as Richard Dyer's central work on the representation of whiteness in Western culture exposes, whiteness disappears and is constructed as 'non-raced', or a state of normality from which other races are variations.[24] *True Blood* minimises the racial threat traditionally encoded in human/supernatural opposition, by redistributing and recoding such racial identifications as white, African-American, Hispanic or Asian to multi-racial supernatural identities. This postmodern Gothic text abolishes conversion anxiety by broadening conceptions of race beyond the safe absence of race evoked by whiteness.[25] Tensions are most commonly generated across the metaphorical racial lines of supernatural status. The working-class werewolves, who dress in the style of bikers with leather clothing and beards, are engaged in a tense relationship with the wealthy vampires who despise them, and are sometimes employed to perform their dirty work. The underclass inbred werepanthers, who live in squalor in the isolated town of Hotshot, are hostile to humans, even those who attempt to help them, because of their total preoccupation with the survival of their own 'bloodline' or race. *True Blood*, then, minimises the threat of the Other conventionally evoked by the vampire by inserting a diversity of racial types into small-town America. Yet, importantly, it does not subscribe to a vision of a 'post-race' America in which equality has erased the importance of race, as the inequalities entrenched between vampires, werewolves, werepanthers and humans, and the resultant conflicts inspired by them, suggest.

The series also negates the concept of 'post-race' America through its representation of the 'racial' discrimination prompted by the public emergence of vampires. In the contemporary world of the South, racial intolerance cannot be openly practised, but anti-vampire sentiment is largely acceptable and enshrined in legislation. *True Blood* reasserts that race is still problematic and that the notion of no ruling racial majority is a fiction. Nan Flanagan of the American Vampire League markets vampires to the human population in the media, advocating for vampire rights and seeking to minimise opposition to their integration into society.[26] She argues that the invention of Tru Blood means that there is no reason to fear vampires as they 'want to be part of mainstream society'.[27] Nan's lobbying for equal rights presents vampires as an oppressed race. In one of her frequent television appearances, she says, 'We're citizens. We pay taxes. We deserve basic civil rights just like everyone else.' When debating the violence of vampires, Nan argues with her human adversary: 'Doesn't your race have a history of exploitation? We never owned slaves, Bill, or detonated nuclear weapons.'[28] A postmodern lack of faith in grand narratives is again made manifest, for while the series presents shocking abuses by vampires, such as humans being kidnapped and tortured in the basement of the vampire bar Fangtasia, it also illuminates the human history of crimes against humanity, such as slavery and warfare, that are far greater in scale. Bill was a soldier in the Civil War, an active fighter in the Confederate army of Southern States that sought to secede from the rest of the nation, in part motivated by a desire to continue the practice of slavery. Bill agrees to conduct a first-hand talk about the war for Sookie's grandmother and her historical group, the Descendants of the Glorious Dead, but he remarks that there is nothing glorious about dying in war so the rich can stay rich, furthering the idea of human conflict as a real, but unacknowledged evil.

Vampire marriage is initially illegal in the series (becoming legal in Vermont in Series Two), which mirrors current vacillations over same-sex marriage in the United States. This type of discrimination also mirrors historical conditions in which marriage between people of colour has been prohibited, as well as marriage between whites and non-whites for fear of miscegenation. While a vampire cannot inseminate a human to produce offspring, what are effectively interracial relationships between humans and vampires do face discrimination and judgment from both the vampire and human communities. Hoyt Fortenberry's (Jim Parrack) intolerant mother, Maxine (Dale Raoul), for example, is aghast when he begins to date Jessica, refusing to accept the relationship, cancelling his mobile phone to curtail his ability to contact her, and actively encouraging a relationship with a human girl to take her place. Maxine's intolerance of vampires is linked with her broader dislike of particular consumer goods such as checked curtains and women who wear red shoes, but also to her dislike of African-Americans, a fact which is not supposed to be public knowledge: she chides Hoyt, 'Hush! That's supposed to be a secret.'[29] A Southern bigot like Maxine can be seen as a repository for the beliefs that a 'post-race' America does not wish to acknowledge; any racial tolerance she may seem to possess goes only so far as what she is allowed to publicly express (hatred of vampires) and that which is no longer acceptable (hatred of African-Americans) is simply concealed.

'God hates fangs': *True Blood* and sexuality

The vampire has been read not only as a metaphor for race but also of threatening, uncontained sexuality. The roadside sign 'God Hates Fangs' (Figure 12.5) that appears in *True Blood's* rich title sequence knowingly invokes the homophobia of the real-world Westboro Baptist Church, whose members are notorious for picketing the funerals of gay people and their placard slogan 'God Hates Fags'.[30] The vampire in Gothic fiction is able to simultaneously evoke anxieties about both racial and sexual transgression. H. L. Malchow

Figure 12.5.   Still of a roadside sign from the *True Blood* title sequence

yokes together the visceral effects of 'devouring unnaturals' who symbolise deviant races and sexualities:

> The hungry gaze of the cannibal terrifies his objects; that of the vampire mesmerizes and entices. That of the Jew, another species of bloodsucker, is veiled and calculating, perhaps hypnotic, and a sign of pathological difference. That of the aggressive homosexual, another devouring unnatural, with, like the vampire, a double life, invites one to share a different (forbidden but alluring) communion.[31]

The series continues to entangle race and sexuality in the figure of the vampire through its explanation of vampires' emergence from enforced hiding as 'coming out of the coffin', an overt parallel with the ideological transformations in the West that enabled gays and lesbians to openly acknowledge their sexuality. The discussion of vampire rights also draws on the rhetoric of contemporary debates about same-sex marriage. In the first episode of the series, Jason declares that vampires do not deserve 'special rights', parroting a common argument against extending equal rights to gays and lesbians that upholds heterosexuality as the norm.

Yet despite progress in the acceptance of, and granting of rights to, gays and lesbians, the series is still distinctive in its representation of non-normative sexualities. The Gay and Lesbian Alliance Against Defamation

(GLAAD) 'Where We Are on TV Report 2010–2011' determined that *True Blood* represents the greatest number of lesbian, bisexual and transgendered characters of any series, with six recurring LGBT characters constituting a substantial 15 per cent of gay and lesbian characters on American television at the time.[32] This is perhaps unsurprising considering Dyer's contention that there is a connection between vampirism and gay and lesbian sexualities in the construction of a 'private sexuality': 'homosexual desire, like other forbidden sexual desires, may well find expression, as a matter of necessity rather than exquisite choice, in privacy and voyeurism'.[33] He extends the comparison to the invisibility of sexual orientation in that it is not initially obvious on the body in the same way that recognition of who is and who is not a vampire is not always superficially apparent.

The series presents a diversity of gay and lesbian humans as well as vampires. Lafayette Reynolds (Nelsan Ellis), a short-order cook at Merlotte's bar, road crew worker and sex worker with a propensity for wearing make-up and effeminate headwear, embodies the tensions of both race and sexuality in the series as a gay, black man. Against the backdrop of the American South, as I have suggested, attention is now focused toward hatred and suspicion of the vampire, rather than open discrimination against African-Americans. Lafayette is, therefore, subject to homophobia rather than racism, such as when redneck customers at the bar reject a burger he has cooked because it 'might have AIDS'.[34] Lafayette comments to the waitresses at Merlotte's that they would be 'surprised' by who desires him,[35] alluding to the fact that vampires may be 'out of the coffin', but many homosexuals are still 'in the closet' because of societal attitudes, particularly within the South where Christianity holds sway among a significant proportion of the population. A minor plotline shows Lafayette's sexual involvement as a prostitute with a white Senator, David Finch, who publicly campaigns against homosexual rights, further evidencing a lack of faith in metanarratives, as those in political power, in addition to those who promote religion, are revealed as equally hypocritical.

While Lafayette is a stereotype of camp homosexuality and runs an online male porn site, he is complicated by his physical strength and relentless survival instinct, which saves his life when he is chained in the basement of Fangtasia for dealing vampire blood. The vulnerable gay vampire Eddie, whom Lafayette uses as a living supply of 'V', represents domesticated and non-threatening homosexuality, painting a nuanced portrait of gay men as much as it does of vampires. Eddie's quotidian habits contrast with the high camp of Russell and the elaborate dinner parties he hosts with his lover Talbot, which feature a menu of blood sorbet and warm blood bisque infused with rose petals. The lesbian vampire Queen of Louisiana, Sophie-Anne Leclerq's (Evan Rachel Wood) involvement with women is coded through the feeding relationship of vampire and human, rather than as an explicitly sexual one. Nevertheless, Fangtasia's Pam Swynford De Beaufort (Kristin Bauer) is bisexual and is shown performing oral sex upon an eager female recipient, and Tara enjoys a same-sex relationship in Season Four, ensuring that sex between women is actually depicted rather than merely alluded to.

Alongside the series's progressive representation of a range of gay and lesbian characters, normative sexuality is also transformed. Marriage once contained sexuality, especially for women, and excluded homosexuals from legitimate sexuality.[36] Contemporary vampire fictions are culturally located in a moment in which marriage does not contain sex – even Sookie's traditional grandmother does not oppose pre-marital sex. Sookie is able to be highly sexual – proclaiming that sex with Bill is near transcendental – without compromising any of her small-town goodness and likeability. The institution of marriage itself, as part of the postmodern collapse of metanarratives, is no longer sacred. The waitress Arlene Fowler (Carrie Preston), for instance, has been divorced multiple times, and becomes involved with two more men in the first three series of the show. In the postmodern Gothic, the breakdown of marriage as a container of sex and sexuality opens up the potential for vampires to interact with humans either through feeding alone, or combined with sex, in a way that is no longer marked with a degree of revulsion. There is no equivalent of *Dracula*'s Mina bearing a sign of shame and rejection by God, in the form of red mark seared into her forehead by the Host after she feeds from an open wound on Dracula's chest.[37] Though a heterosexual love triangle occupies *True Blood*'s core, it celebrates sexualities of all kinds, including same-sex attracted relationships and sexual relationships with and between vampires. The series does not invite repulsion in the viewer over non-normative sexualities. Rather, it trades on the thrill of sex between humans and vampires in ways that deny any binary opposition between normative and non-normative sexuality.

True Blood dissolves boundaries between the supernatural and the human without evoking fear and anxiety, as was typical of vampire narratives from the mid-nineteenth century onward. The series acknowledges that the flaws and evils of humans are an equal match for those evidenced by vampires, especially through the exposure of humans' innermost thoughts by its telepathic heroine, Sookie. Furthermore, it recasts race across supernatural lines to dismantle any notion of a 'post-race' era at the same time as diminishing the metaphor of vampire as racial threat. The series embraces a vampire who resides in the midst of small-town America, alongside an assortment of other supernatural beings, long considered imaginary, all of whom are largely indistinguishable from humans. This vampire narrative encourages us to desire difference, not because of the thrill of transgression, but because, in postmodern fashion, racial and sexual binaries demarcating 'self' and 'other' are no longer meaningfully upheld.

Notes

1 Auerbach, *Our Vampires*, p. 145.
2 *True Blood* also evidences postmodern tropes such as the interplay of genres (melding detective fiction, horror, romance and comedy) and parody (mocking our expectations of vampires and generating humour at their expense, such as the brutal vampire King Russell Edgington carrying the remnant ooze of his exterminated life partner with him in a crystal urn). These postmodern elements are not as prominent in Charlaine Harris's The Southern Vampire Mysteries novels (2001–2013), on which the television series is based. The novels are narrated in the first person by Sookie Stackhouse, returning the focalising perspective to the non-vampire, as in earlier vampire fiction. Moreover, many of the metaphors of race and sexuality in relation to vampirism are not as overt in *True Blood*'s novelistic sources.
3 Moretti, 'The Dialectic of Fear', p. 73. On the vampire and anxieties about race, see Malchow, *Gothic Images of Race in Nineteenth-Century Britain* and Arata, 'The Occidental Tourist'. On vampirism and homosexuality, see Dyer, 'Children of the Night'. For consideration of the vampire as a manifestation of both racial and sexual anxieties, see Gelder, *Reading the Vampire*. For anxieties about AIDS in vampire films, see Taubin, 'Bloody Tales'.
4 For example, William Patrick Day observes: 'today we have good vampires, bad vampires, ambiguous vampires, lonely vampires, vampires who only drink cow blood; we also have reluctant vampire killers and vampires who kill other vampires' (*Vampire Legends*, p. 2). More recently, J. M. Tyree has argued that contemporary vampire incarnations, such as *True Blood*'s Bill and *Twilight*'s Edward, are not 'false friends', but genuinely wish to end 'their interminable loneliness' through authentic relationships with humans ('Warm-Blooded', p. 37).
5 Other contemporary Undead and paranormal fictions share these concerns with destabilising normality through representations of difference; see, for example, the transformations undergone in *Buffy the Vampire Slayer* as delineated by Malgorzata Drewniok in Chapter 8, or the zombie-like teens in Bill Hughes's Chapter 15 below.
6 Sedgwick, *The Coherence of Gothic Conventions*, pp. 9, 10.
7 Vampires who do not wish to harm humans can also obtain blood from blood banks and by 'glamouring' victims so that they do not recall being fed upon.
8 Gordon and Hollinger, Introduction, p. 2.
9 Gelder, *Reading the Vampire*, p. 111.
10 Hollinger, 'Fantasies of Absence', p. 201.

11 Zanger, 'Metaphor into Metonymy', p. 19.

12 Marcus Sedgwick enumerates these in the final chapter of this volume, discussing their provenance and his rejection of them in transforming the genre for his own fiction.

13 Lyotard, *The Postmodern Condition*, p. xxiv.

14 Punter and Byron, *The Gothic*, p. 270.

15 'Timebomb', *True Blood*, 2.8; George Bush, 'Transcript of President Bush's Address'.

16 'Timebomb'.

17 Zanger, 'Metaphor into Metonymy', p. 21.

18 Halualani, 'Abstracting and De-racializing Diversity', p. 248.

19 Gelder, *Reading the Vampire*, p. 11.

20 The Series One DVD includes a bonus mock documentary, 'Shedding Light on Vampires in America', which shows rioting on the streets of Latin America, the Middle East and Europe upon the emergence of vampires. The US is constructed as a tolerant place in which many foreign vampires, who are described as 'refugees', seek protection. This reignites debates about 'immigration'.

21 Goddu, *Gothic America*, p. 76.

22 *Ibid.*, p. 10.

23 See Malchow, *Gothic Images*, pp. 5, 162–4. In his analysis of *Dracula*, Stephen Arata points out vampires destroy real selves and, in their place, create versions of their own 'race' ('The Occidental Tourist', p. 630).

24 Dyer, *White*, p. 2.

25 Other contemporary vampire fictions are not necessarily as progressive. Kent A. Ono argues that *Buffy the Vampire Slayer* 'privileges an antiseptic white culture and takes part in TV's overall habit of marginalizing people of color and other marginalized groups' (p. 164). This is achieved, he suggests, through the pervasive 'villainization' and elimination of characters who are people of colour ('To Be a Vampire', pp. 163–86. Two chapters in this collection present a different perspective on the 'Buffyverse', however. In Chapter 8, Malgorzata Drewniok suggests that the transformations present in *Buffy* embody inclusivity while, in Chapter 15, Bill Hughes maintains that *Angel* sympathetically embraces diversity in the context of 'groups' of others.

26 This marketing was translated across media by HBO with the creation of an internet site for the American Vampire League that included campaign posters with slogans such as 'Vampire Pride'.

27 'Strange Love', 1.1.

28 *Ibid.*

29 'I Will Rise Up', 2.9.

30 The URL of the hatefully named website for the Westboro Baptist Church is www.godhatesfags.com.

31 Malchow, *Gothic Images*, p. 125.

32 Gay and Lesbian Alliance against Defamation, p. 11.

33 Dyer, 'Children of the Night', p. 57.

34 'Sparks Fly Out', 1.5. Lafayette's cousin Tara continually tries to reassert the impact of racism on her life, which is repeatedly dismissed as paranoid overreaction in a 'post-race' era. This is effectively shown by Arlene's response to Tara after the death of her African-American boyfriend in 'Bad Blood', 3.1: 'Why do they always have to make it about race?'

35 'Strange Love', 1.1.

36 Dyer, 'Children of the Night', p. 64.

37 Stoker, *Dracula*, ed. Auerbach and Skal, p. 259.

13

Myriad mirrors: *doppelgängers* and doubling in *The Vampire Diaries*

Kimberley McMahon-Coleman

> Elena: Crucifixes?
> Stefan: Decorative.
> Elena: Holy water?
> Stefan: Drinkable.
> Elena: Mirrors?
> Stefan: Myth.[1]

As Sam George notes in Chapter 4 above, mirroring is of fundamental importance in Gothic literature and film. It is also a prevalent trope in the CW network teen drama *The Vampire Diaries*. The television series is itself a 'doubling' in that it is an adaptation of a series of novels by L. J. Smith, creating a situation wherein the same central characters inhabit the parallel townships of the novels' Fells Church and television's Mystic Falls, and consequently have histories which are, at times, contradictory.[2] The television version also explicitly explores the concept of the *doppelgänger*, and thus the idea of reflection, even as it manipulates the historical and cultural contexts of the characters. Nuclear families are noticeably absent in the television series, yet significant emphasis is placed on the twin themes of brothers as foils to each other, and an ongoing focus on matrilineal power. The series focuses on the new, humanised vampire (as examined elsewhere in this book), but also explicitly attempts to reflect 'real' contemporary teenage society and adolescent relationships, albeit it through the lens of the supernatural.[3]

The narrative centres on a love triangle involving two vampire brothers and their mortal love interest, Elena Gilbert. The brothers, Stefan and

Damon Salvatore, are themselves configured as foils to each other. Stefan is constructed as a 'good' vampire, who seeks to retain his humanity and make choices that are moral and compassionate. He hunts animals rather than humans to satisfy his blood cravings, and his desire for human blood is configured as an addiction; he insists that he is not a monster when he is 'clean'. He establishes and maintains a monogamous and loving relationship with Elena. Stefan's older brother, Damon, however, is constructed as the shade to Stefan's light; usually dressed entirely in black, he is impetuous, promiscuous, self-serving and pragmatic. In short, he embraces the darkness and its associated powers. Indeed, it has been argued that of all the contemporary iterations of the vampire, Damon is – at least initially – the most like Lord Ruthven, a 'celebration of self-absorbed, self-mocking, arrogant, charming, cruel, noble romanticism'.[4] Even their names denote the good/ evil binary, with Damon, whose name evokes the demonic, making sarcastic comments about 'Saint Stefan', the martyr, in the books.[5] Melissa Ames even goes so far as to compare the brothers to Cain and Abel.[6]

In the TV series, the rivalry between the brothers dates back to 1864, when they were concurrently romantically involved with the vampire Katherine Pierce. Their enmity only increased when she began to turn them both into vampires but was captured and apparently entombed by the Founding Families of Mystic Falls before the process was completed. As in the seminal 1980s young adult vampire text *The Lost Boys*, the world of *The Vampire Diaries* utilises the concept of the half-vampire, so that an act of will is required in order to effect the transition. According to the narrative of the television show (which differs markedly from L. J. Smith's novels, in terms of both characterisation and the need for such a conscious decision), Damon had no intention of completing the transition if he could not spend eternity with Katherine, but was lured into completing the transformation by the machinations of his younger brother.[7]

The demon next door: regionalism and the modern vampire

Zach: I know that you can't change what you are. But you don't belong here anymore.
Stefan: Where do I belong?[8]

Like Anne Rice's *Vampire Chronicles*, HBO's *True Blood* and Charlaine Harris's Sookie Stackhouse novels (on which *True Blood* was based), *The Vampire Diaries* seeks to embed itself in a recognisably Southern US setting. It has been argued that the South is 'Othered' and represented as fearsome, monstrous and desirable in Southern Gothic narratives, evoking memories of the South's bloody history.[9] Damon, like *True Blood*'s Bill Compton, had been a Confederate soldier, making explicit textual links to the area's Civil War history. In a self-reflexive moment, Elena's brother Jeremy earnestly explains away his ancestor's journal account of the rise of vampires in Mystic Falls during the Civil War as being 'a metaphor for the demons of the day ... The Union soldiers. I read the stories myself, they talk about the demons that attack at night ... Allegorical vampires, which is what it is: creative expression during a very volatile time. A country at war doesn't want realism, they want fantasy, thus: vampire fiction.'[10]

It has been argued elsewhere that the regionalism expressed in these texts can be read as a contemporary domestification of the monster, but, equally, it suggests an engagement with a blood-soaked regional history of Othering particular social groups, and the ongoing tension between this problematic history and the apparent normality of contemporary small town life.[11] Rituals of small town normalcy like high-school dances and football matches are given significant airtime, suggesting that, despite the supernatural focus, the events depicted reflect aspects of contemporary society to which its primarily teenage audience can relate.

As Kindinger argues, drawing heavily on the work of David Jordan, stories with a strong focus on a particular region are effectively a counter-narrative to rootlessness, because they are imbued with the sense of belonging and identity that is created by the shared history of a region's inhabitants.[12] When adapting *The Vampire Diaries* for the screen, Kevin Williamson and Julie Plec eschewed the characters' European provenance in the novels, instead making them founding members of the antebellum township, thus creating a remarkably long relationship between the brothers and the region. *The Vampire Diaries* also argues strongly about the pull of 'home' to an uprooted individual, privileging the idea of the Salvatore brothers belonging in Mystic Falls from the opening voiceover in the Pilot episode, when Stefan declares: 'I shouldn't have come home. I know the risk. But I have to know her.'[13]

Stefan is inexorably drawn 'home' to Mystic Falls and to one of its inhabitants, Elena Gilbert. His need to be 'at home,' articulated in the Pilot episode, is mirrored by Damon's comments in the second episode: 'It's good to be home. Think I'm gonna stay a while.' This is immediately undercut, however, with the more ominous remark, 'This town could use a bit of a wakeup call, I think'.[14] In these early episodes, Damon is constructed as the binary opposite of 'new vampire' Stefan. Yet these initial depictions are simplistic and, as the series progresses, viewers are shown more nuanced representations of the characters which strongly imply that the brothers are each capable of behaving like the other. Sarah Rees Brennan explains the allure of the Salvatore brothers thus: 'it is always a question of Damon, as well as Stefan ... Stefan is the good vampire boyfriend, and Damon is the bad one. By separating out the two sides we can see even more clearly how very alluring, but also how very disturbing, a vampire boyfriend can be.'[15]

The brothers are often depicted throughout the series almost as two halves of one whole; the 'traditional', monstrous bloodthirsty vampire and the domesticated loving vampire who is passing as human, with their subject-positions at times shifting from one to the other as the programme's narrative arc develops.[16] The traditional vampire, as exemplified by Damon in the early episodes, is a 'deterritorialised, even transnational character that is not subject to borders, but rather constantly on the move looking for prey'.[17] Stefan, on the other hand, is the monster who has been 'domesticated and transformed into an American citizen'.[18] Like his counterpart Bill Compton in *True Blood*, Stefan has returned to a place which held meaning for himself and his family during his mortal life. The programme explores the dangers inherent in returning home – namely that the vampire's true nature will be discovered, and that locals will be injured or killed. Indeed, it is after a chance meeting with an old man who notes that Stefan 'hasn't aged a day' since 1953 that Elena learns of Stefan's status as vampire.[19] Stefan and Damon, like their literary and filmic predecessors, have been forced into lonely and nomadic lives because of their monstrous natures, yet the lure of home is as strong for many of the vampires in *The Vampire Diaries* as it is for any diasporan. In Season One, twenty-six entombed vampires are released thanks to Damon's stubborn desire to free Katherine (who he incorrectly believes was interred along with the others), and the imperfect magic of a novice witch, Bonnie Bennett. When Damon asks Pearl, the leader of the tomb vampires, what she hopes to achieve by remaining in town, her motives are shown to be all-too-human: 'Mystic Falls is our home, Damon. They took that away from us. Our land, our home. It's time we rebuild.'[20]

Mid-way through the first season, however, we start to see another side of Damon; that there is potentially more to him than his previous configurations as 'dangerous' and 'the bad guy'.[21] Rather unexpectedly, it is Damon who rescues Elena from her smoking wreck of a car after an accident, and he then takes her with him on a road trip to Atlanta, Georgia, telling her that his motivations for doing so were no more complex than her 'not being the worst company in the world' and knowing that it would annoy Stefan.[22] Elena, for her part, is uncharacteristically relaxed during this sojourn. Damon later confesses that he refrained from compelling her because 'we were having fun. I wanted it to be real', demonstrating a level of vulnerability not

previously seen.[23] Stefan also demonstrates an unexpected vulnerability when
he is tempted into drinking human blood late in Season One, and again at
the end of Season Two.

It is noteworthy that Stefan's own episodes of 'monstrosity' and bloodlust
are configured as an addiction and therefore beyond the realms of free choice
or personal control, given that a number of *The Vampire Diaries*' storylines focus
on the notion of choice. Indeed, Stefan tells his brother that, despite their
closeness when they were mortal, 'all I can remember is hating you. Your
choices have erased anything good about you.'[24] The mythology of the series
suggests that vampires have even more choice than mortals, in that that they
can 'switch off' their human emotions. When Elena's brother Jeremy asks
Damon whether life – or more accurately, undeath – is better as a vampire,
the ever-pragmatic Damon tells him: 'Life sucks either way, Jeremy. At least
if you're a vampire you don't have to feel bad about it if you don't want to.'[25]
In this, the final episode of Season One, Damon admits to Jeremy that he
did 'switch off' his emotions for a long time, and it was easier; but these
admissions are noticeably and adamantly in the past tense, reflecting the
changes in Damon's behaviour over the season as he begins to transform from
the alluring but dangerous Byronic vampire towards a yet more sympathetic
model.

Landers argues that current incarnations of the vampire are notable for
making conscious choices rather than being driven by innate and inhuman
bloodlust, and thus

> [m]odern vampire representations dissolve the boundary between humans and
> monsters, demonstrating that monsters have a level of 'humanity' somewhere
> inside of them and have the capacity to act on that humanity and live in a
> morally acceptable manner. As a result of the blurring between monsters
> and humans, modern vampires also imply that humans might have a level of
> 'monstrosity' inside them.[26]

When Stefan's bloodlust is out of control on 'the human stuff' and he
becomes unreliable, it is Damon who steps in to take his place, escorting
Elena to the Miss Mystic Falls pageant, dancing with her, and offering advice
about Stefan's condition.[27] During this part of the story's development,
the viewer learns that Stefan's bloodlust is greater than Damon's, and that
Damon not only was once averse to drinking human blood but also played the
role of self-sacrificing romantic hero. The complete reversal of their roles,
demonstrated through the televisual technique of the flashback, shows that
they are each 'truly half of one whole and a divided self that is capable of
oscillation between two extremes'.[28] The notion of the brothers as a divided

Figure 13.1. Brothers in arms: Similarities between Damon (left) and Stefan (right) Salvatore are represented visually through their shared stance in this image of Ian Somerhalder and Paul Wesley from Season Two episode 'Brave New World'

self is sometimes depicted visually through closely aligned costuming and body language (Figure 13.1).

As Andrew Bennett and Nicholas Royle point out, the uncanny as understood by Freud and others is more than just a sense of mystery or eeriness: '[m]ore particularly, it concerns a sense of unfamiliarity which appears at the very heart of the familiar, or else a sense of familiarity which appears at the very heart of the unfamiliar'.[29] This is certainly true of the Salvatore brothers, who live in a town which was once very familiar; who were once close, then rivals and mortal enemies, and now have forged an uneasy alliance against both the descendants of the Founding Families (who would once again force them out of Mystic Falls), and the supernatural forces which threaten Elena. Much is made of the motif of brotherhood, and it is suggested that brothers' bonds cannot be severed; indeed, Stefan at one point admits to his fellow vampire, Elijah: 'I've wanted to kill my brother a million times but could never do it'.[30]

Elijah and Klaus are also once-close, warring brothers who are pivotal to the plot in Season Two. Klaus is depicted as the traditionally monstrous vampire. He is nomadic, bloodthirsty, and demonstrates no familial loyalty. Elijah works with Elena and the Salvatore brothers to bring about Klaus's downfall but wavers when Klaus offers to reveal where their staked siblings are kept. Elijah allows Klaus to escape, only to be double-crossed and staked.

The pair operate as foils or mirrors to the Salvatore brothers, demonstrating just how badly a rivalry between two vampire brothers can end, particularly if one brother eschews domestication and continues to operate out of self-interest.

The notion of brotherhood is thus examined in multiple ways throughout the series. Although Damon's drawled 'brother' is almost always used sarcastically and pejoratively when addressing Stefan, the notion of family ties surviving above all else is regularly implied through the actions of the sympathetic, regionalised characters.[31] Indeed, in the Season Two finale Stefan sacrifices everything, including his freedom and his relationship with Elena, to procure a cure for the fatally ill Damon.[32] A sense of strong family allegiance is also implied in the adoption of Elena by her biological father's older brother, and by the ways in which Elena and Jeremy continue to refer to each other as brother and sister even after the revelation that they are actually cousins.

As Jennifer Lynn Barnes summarises,

> *The Vampire Diaries* is a show in which family matters: the entire premise revolves around Damon and Stefan being brothers; Elena's connection first to Katherine and later to Isobel propelled season one's dominant story arcs; Bonnie's character went through a witchy (and sometimes bitchy) metamorphosis almost entirely because of her grandmother's death; and even minor characters, like Tyler and Matt, struggled with abusive and absent parents, respectively.[33]

Other postmodern Gothic narratives (such as Poppy Z. Brite's novel *Lost Souls* or the Canadian *Ginger Snaps* werewolf movies) replicate nuclear family units located within their 'normal, contemporary … setting[s] … to expose the dysfunction beneath this veneer of stability'. In contrast, *The Vampire Diaries* rejects the nuclear family as a social unit completely, while still focusing on the importance of constructed brotherly and maternal relationships.[34] Mystic Falls may be a 'normal, contemporary' southern US setting, but the nuclear family unit of 'two heterosexual parents and a few children' as the 'fundamental unit for transference of ideology' is remarkable by its absence.[35] Rather, *The Vampire Diaries* constructs a plethora of family types and structures, including orphaned children and sole parent families; absent, irresponsible or workaholic parents; and even a gay parent. Some characters even demonstrate or declare sibling-like relationships with characters to whom they are not related; Bonnie declares in Season One that Elena is like a sister and she would therefore die for her; and the initial antipathy between vampire Damon and slayer Alaric is attenuated into a sibling-like relationship by the end of Season Two.[36] All of the adolescents – and some of the adults – within the narrative identify with or articulate isolation and dislocation even before they enter into the complexities of supernatural politics. The allegiances they consciously create in lieu of biological families, however, ultimately afford some protection from the supernatural risks inherent in the bloodlines of many of the characters.

Any discussion of family must inevitably turn back to the figures of Katherine and Elena, two characters for whose romantic attention the Salvatore brothers vie. The brotherly vampiric relationship is itself reflected in complex ideas about identity and matrilineal heritage.

The *doppelgänger* next door: mitochondrial DNA and the modern vampire

The antagonism between the brothers, as viewers soon learn, is a direct result of a previous love triangle in which they were involved, with a vampire named Katherine Pierce. Elena Gilbert is Katherine's *doppelgänger*, and – at least in the world of the television series – her descendant. Both roles are played by the same actress, visually suggesting that the good girl and *femme fatale* roles are mirror images of each other that may exist in the one individual, just as the calculating and monstrous side of the vampire is twinned with the capacity for love and compassion.

The suggestion that the Other and the Self are interchangeable is an uncanny one, as is the idea of the nomadic and monstrous vampire being 'at home' in the small community from which he or she was previously ostracised. The majority of dualities in Mystic Falls involve the supernatural. As Thurber points out,

> Elena appears to be a human at first, but the series eventually reveals that ... she is also Katherine's ancestor and her mythical *doppelgänger* – making her part of an ancient *doppelgänger* curse involving Katherine's (and therefore, Elena's) family. Bonnie (Katerina Graham) is a witch and shares a double (although not a lookalike) in the form of her ancestor who was a witch working for Katherine during the Civil War. Tyler ... is both a wolf and a teenage boy – the new werewolf representing a similar fantasy and gender crisis to the new vampire.[37]

Arguably the Salvatores are blood brothers twice over; their status as biological siblings is mirrored in their lives as vampires, because they share the same 'Maker' or vampire parent in Katherine.

As the close relationships between Elena and her friends, among others, demonstrate, the series implies that family is not something which is easily quantified using the metaphor of blood. As with a number of vampire narratives, however (including *Twilight* and *True Blood*), the sharing of blood by vampires in a more literal sense comes with obligations. Damon is shown to be negligent in his mentoring duties with Vicki Donovan during her brief life as a vampire; in contrast, he is more supportive of Stefan's efforts to nurture Caroline Forbes following her transition. Despite his strong mistrust of them, Damon remains apparently incapable of ignoring either Katherine, who turned him, or Isobel, whom he turned, throughout the first two seasons.

The complex rivalry between the brothers seems to be the key to understanding the worst excesses of Damon's behaviour: their rivalry over Katherine's affections and transformation into vampires because of her were the impetuses for his vow to make Stefan's life an eternal misery. When Katherine returns to Mystic Falls, her actions again maximise the friction between the two brothers. In an inversion of usual gender stereotypes regarding love and lust, a seductive Katherine refuses to tell Damon what he wants to hear: that she loves him. The usually confident elder brother debases himself before her, declaring that he will forgive a century and a half of neglect and thoughtlessness if they can begin an eternity together. Katherine is dismissive and needlessly cruel, telling him, 'It was always Stefan'.[38] As Melissa Ames notes, the depiction of women as more sexually aggressive is a trend within the vampire subgenre, citing the Twilight Saga, *Buffy the Vampire Slayer* and *The Vampire Diaries* as examples.[39] Arguably, the long history of love triangles in teen narratives is also at play here, harkening back to the John Hughes films of the 1980s, and even making an appearance in the 1985 supernatural comedy *Teen Wolf*.[40]

Just as Katherine incites rivalry between the Salvatore brothers, so too does she cause significant friction within Elena Gilbert's family. In flashback, viewers see the 1864 version of Katherine, coquettishly playing matchmaker between Elena's ancestor Johnathan Gilbert and the soon-to-be-entombed Pearl. Johnathan Gilbert (an ancestor after whom John Gilbert is named) was a vampire hater and, along with Giuseppe Salvatore (the brothers' father), had been integral in rounding up the vampires who had taken up residence in Mystic Falls. Johnathan's journals and artefacts are used to again round up the same vampires in 2010, and the unusual spelling of his name[41] links him explicitly to Elena's 'Uncle John', hailed as the town's prodigal son and saviour in the face of a renewed vampire threat.

Late in Season One it is revealed that Elena had been adopted, and Damon's suspicions about her parentage are later confirmed through investigations conducted by Aunt Jenna and Elena herself which reveal that John Gilbert is not Elena's paternal uncle, but her biological father. Her mother was Isobel Fleming Saltzman, a descendant of Katherine and student of the paranormal who asked to be made vampire. This raises questions for Elena about her identity, and which of her mothers was 'real'. The influence of Miranda Gilbert on Elena is clearly significant; it was she, viewers are told, who gave Elena her first journal, from which *The Vampire Diaries* takes its name.⁴² Elena's first conversation with Stefan takes place when she is journalling at her adoptive parents' grave.⁴³ It was also Miranda who suggested that Elena enter the Miss Mystic Falls pageant, so that they could share the campaign experience; Elena's lack of interest in completing the competition without her mother is palpable, and provides the opportunity for Aunt Jenna to note once again that she is failing in her role as *ersatz* mother.⁴⁴

When John Gilbert gives Elena a bracelet which he tells her belonged to her mother, he answers for her the question of who is her 'real' mother. Elena assumes that John – who has had an ongoing allegiance with Isobel even after her mortal death – means that it belonged to her birth mother. John corrects her, saying, 'It belonged to your mother. Miranda.'⁴⁵ John affirms that Miranda and Grayson were the ones who undertook the parenting roles with Elena, with their love for her even extending to giving up their lives for her. Stefan reveals to Elena that he had previously met her on the night of her parents' fatal car accident, but that Grayson had insisted that he help Elena first, meaning that ultimately she was the sole survivor. John Gilbert later echoes this act of self-sacrifice, forgoing his own life in order to save Elena's by binding their life forces through a magical spell cast by Bonnie.⁴⁶

Elena is also biologically linked to Katherine. Like her descendant, Isobel, Katherine has the ignominy of an unwanted teen pregnancy as part of her backstory. Originally known as Katerina Petrova, Katherine is a Petrova *doppelgänger*, with the supernatural ability to break a curse which allegedly affects both vampires and werewolves. Elena, as the next Petrova *doppelgänger*, holds similar power and is therefore the target of the vampires and werewolves who wish to access it. Thus Elena's circumstances are very much linked to her maternal heritage, as her biological links to Katherine and Isobel have effectively driven the narrative arc to date. Katherine is more than a matriarch, however; she is the undead mirror to Elena. They are not just lookalikes (as in Smith's novels) but are identical. Indeed, in the Season One episode 'Masquerade', injuries intended to punish Katherine also appear on Elena's body.⁴⁷

The complex *doppelgänger* storyline is brought to the screen through having lead actress Nina Dobrev play both roles. Visual cues such as jewellery are used to alert keen viewers as to whether Katherine or Elena is involved in any given interaction. Elena's trademark is her *über*-straight hair, whereas Katherine prefers to wear hers curled. In another visual mirroring, when the Salvatore brothers are shown in their pre-vampire lives, the main cue that this is the Civil War era, other than costuming and rosy cheeks, is that they both have wavy hair. This signifies their closer allegiance to Katherine at that time. A photo double is also used in some scenes, creating a layered doubling. As Ann Thurber points out in her recent thesis, the photo double is effectively doubling for the *doppelgänger*, herself a double.[48] Dobrev has acknowledged that at some point she may be required to play a third character, since Katherine's status as Petrova *doppelgänger* implies that she is herself a copy of an earlier incarnation.[49] Katherine is, at the time of writing, a copy without an original;[50] Elena, in turn, is a copy of the copy, but has become more meaningful or 'real' to the Salvatore brothers, both of whom have ultimately transferred their affections to her, rather than Katherine.

In deciding how best to play Katherine, however, Dobrev has consciously enacted another form of mirroring, noting that 'Damon gets a lot of who he is from Katherine, because he's basically learned everything that he knows about being a vampire from her. So I actually adopted Ian's performance … so that the transition would make sense.'[51] When playing Katherine, Dobrev uses what she calls 'quirks' of Ian Somerhalder's portrayal of the character, including swaggering, his use of his eyes to convey meaning, and a drawled delivery. Of course, Stefan had also learned how to be a vampire under the influence of Katherine, but viewers learn that his early bloodlust and 'ripper' status were mediated under the maternal influence of his friend and vampire mentor, Lexi.[52]

Given the prevalence of 'good' maternal and quasi-maternal influences, including Aunt Jenna, Miranda Gilbert, Lexi and even Elena herself (in the way that she 'mothers' and protects Jeremy and Stefan in the face of their addictions, for example), it is difficult to see the Katherine/Elena doubling as anything other than a Madonna/whore dichotomy. As Landers argues, the programme suggests that a woman who is both Madonna and whore is effectively a divided self and must kill one half or the other.[53] Indeed, the first two seasons centre on Elena's role in breaking The Curse of the Sun and the Moon. Elena comes to see her death as inevitable, and her attempts to have agency over when and where it happens becomes as much a part of the story as the brothers' efforts to live up to their surname and protect her from that fate.

What do the myriad mirrors reflect?

A number of critics have noted that vampire fiction enjoys popularity at times of economic or social change. Vampire narratives reflect both the positive and negative aspects of contemporary realities. Nina Auerbach, for example, notes that the popularity of vampires in the 1950s 'personified the fears within the supposed national bliss of those years – fears of communism, of McCarthyism, of nuclear war, and not being certified sexually normal by paternalistic Freudian authorities – fears that field the ghostly compulsion to be liked'.[54] More recently, the Twilight Saga has been viewed through feminist and post-feminist lenses, with critics questioning its conservative return to heteronormative morals and its rejection of the vampire's traditionally queer role (although such readings are, of course, problematised by other critics, such as Sara Wasson and Sarah Artt in Chapter 11 above).[55] Elsewhere I have argued that this conservative trend is particularly noticeable in Young Adult, as opposed to mainstream adult, iterations of contemporary Gothic narratives, although of course this observation may depend upon the texts selected.[56] What is clear is that the vampire narrative is becoming more nuanced and sophisticated than merely fearing the monstrous Other. Televisual vampires post-*Buffy* are often reflected in mirrors and can be photographed (see Sam George, Chapter 4 above). This suggests an increased closeness between the monstrous and the human in that they are no longer easily identified by visual markers, reflecting the trends of domestication and normalisation of the vampire.

Punter and Byron have argued that the 'Gothic always remains the symbolic site of a culture's discursive struggle to define and claim possession of the civilised, and to abject, or throw off, what is seen as other to the civilised self'; or, as actor Ian Somerhalder argues: 'Vampires used to be ugly, … now they're more aesthetically appealing, but they're still there to answer one question: What's it like to be an outsider?' The Gothic is at its core about the role of the outsider.[57] The figure of the revenant is intrinsically an outsider because of his or her undead status. Those vampires who choose to engage with their human emotions are further Othered by eschewing their monstrous sides and choosing to establish a (semi)permanent home within a region or community; they are uncannily situated as outsiders who also belong within the local community. In the case of the Salvatore brothers, who operate in a world where most of the population do not know of the existence of vampires and other supernatural creatures, this brings with it inherent risks: the risk that someone will recognise them and query why they haven't aged; as well as the risk that a slip in control could mean harming or killing community members with whom they have bonded. Like *True Blood*'s Bill Compton, they illustrate a further uncanniness in that there is the potential for them to have had unusually long connections with the local community and unique insights into the town's history, as witnesses to it.

Even though the nomadic traditional vampire remains a figure to be feared, the queer or Othered position of the regionalised and domesticated vampires within society is seen as acceptable and – particularly in Young Adult vampire narratives such as *The Vampire Diaries* – even desirable.[58] It is perhaps this reflection of the uncanny – that which is slightly unfamiliar – which is appealing to an adolescent audience, caught in the interstices between childhood and adulthood, where the familiar typically becomes less so. The evil and good *doppelgängers* and the two fluid representations of the vampire simultaneously draw on the popular fascination with supernatural romances, while reflecting that adolescence is fundamentally a period of change and personality development.

Notes

1 'There Goes the Neighbourhood', *The Vampire Diaries*, 1.16.
2 L. J. Smith, *The Awakening* (1991); *The Struggle* (1991); *The Fury & Dark Reunion* (1991); *Nightfall* (2009).
3 For the development of sympathetic vampires in film and literature, see Lindsey Scott's Chapter 7 above.
4 Skovron, 'Ladies of the Night, Unite!', p. 59.
5 L. J. Smith has Stefan explain that he was named after St Stephen, the first Christian martyr, and that 'Salvatore' means 'salvation' in Italian, in her first book, *The Awakening* (p. 229).
6 Ames, 'Twilight Follows Tradition', p. 47.
7 'Blood Brothers', 1.20.
8 'The Pilot', 1.1.
9 Kindinger, 'Reading Supernatural Fiction', p. 17.
10 'Bloodlines', 1.11. This scene is also ironic, in that his girlfriend, to whom he is making this argument, is (unbeknownst to him) herself a vampire and had seen the recounted events first-hand.
11 See Kindinger, 'Reading Supernatural Fiction', p. 12. Many have commented on the links between the history of how both people of colour and LGBT people have been treated in the conservative Southern states, and the contemporary Southern vampire narratives. See, for example, Hudders, 'The Southern Vampire in American Popular Fiction' among others; and a number of *True Blood* panels at the 2011 ACA/PCA.
12 Kindinger, 'Reading Supernatural Fiction', p. 13; Jordan, *Regionalism Reconsidered*.

13 'The Pilot', 1.1.

14 'The Night of the Comet', 1.2.

15 Brennan, 'Women Who Love', p. 6.

16 'Traditional' here should be qualified; Damon is not the bestial vampire of East European folklore but is far closer to the ambivalent, amoral, bloodthirsty but often seductive vampire that may be characterised as 'Byronic'; see Conrad Aquilina in Chapter 2 above. For further analysis of other representations of vampires which can vacillate between valued human traits and monstrous behaviours, see Michele Smith on *True Blood* in Chapter 12 above; the Southern US context is important here, too, of course.

17 Kindinger, 'Reading Supernatural Fiction', p. 2.

18 *Ibid.*, p. 12.

19 'You're Undead to Me', 1.5.

20 'There Goes the Neighborhood'.

21 'You're Undead to Me', 1.5.

22 'Bloodlines', 1.11.

23 'Fool Me Once', 1.14.

24 *Ibid.*

25 'Founder's Day', 1.22.

26 Landers, 'The Modern Vampire', p. 36.

27 'Miss Mystic Falls', 1.19.

28 Thurber, 'Bite Me', p. 66

29 Bennett and Royle, *Introduction*, p. 35.

30 'The Sun Also Rises', 2.21.

31 This trait of Damon's is also present in the books (see, for example, Smith, *The Awakening*, p. 137).

32 'As I Lay Dying', 2.22.

33 Barnes, 'Sweet Caroline', pp. 150–1

34 Greenburg, 'Sins of the Blood', p. 166.

35 *Ibid.*, p. 166.

36 'Unpleasantville', 1.12; 'As I Lay Dying', 2.22.

37 Thurber, 'Bite Me', p. 74.

38 'The Return', 2.1.

39 Ames, 'Twilight Follows Tradition', p. 50.

40 For a more detailed discussion of this trend in 1980s YA film, see Shary, 'Buying Me Love'.

41 As shown in the credits and on the journals themselves.

42 'The Pilot', 1.1.

43 *Ibid.*

44 'Miss Mystic Falls', 1.19.

45 'Daddy Issues', 2.13.

46 'The Sun Also Rises', 2.21.

47 'Masquerade', 2.7.

48 Thurber, 'Bite me', p. 67.

49 Quoted in MacKenzie, *'Vampire Diaries' star*.

50 See Baudrillard, 'The Precession of Simulacra', in *Selected Writings*, p. 12.

51 Nina Dobrev, quoted in MacKenzie, *'Vampire Diaries' star*.

52 'The Dinner Party', 2.15.

53 Landers, 'The Modern Vampire', p. 66.

54 Auerbach, *Our Vampires*, p. 4.

55 See Kane, 'A Very Queer Refusal', pp. 103–18, among others.

56 McMahon-Coleman and Weaver, *Werewolves*, pp. 20–1; 91. See also Platt, 'Cullen Family Values', pp. 71–86, among others.

57 Punter and Byron, *The Gothic*, p. 15.

58 See the vampires Liam and Dianne in *True Blood*; Victoria and Laurent in *Twilight*; and Klaus, Ben and Logan in *The Vampire Diaries*.

14

The vampire in the machine: exploring the undead interface

Ivan Phillips

THE EXPLORATION BEGINS, appropriately, at night. It is 1980, a static caravan in Widemouth Bay, Cornwall. A ten-year-old boy, on holiday with his family, is watching television. His younger brother is asleep nearby and his parents have gone to the caravan park's bar. Widemouth Bay is well named: it is a bay, and it is wide, a gaping mouth open to the best and the worst of the weather coming off the southern Irish Sea. On this particular summer evening there is lashing wind and hard, fine rain. The caravan creaks like the rigging of an old ship. The curtains are open. The windows frame a wet dense blackness. The boy is watching a TV movie and it has him transfixed, terrified, unable to move. The scene shows a floating, smiling vampire child clawing at a casement window in modern day, suburban America to gain access to his still-human, still-mourning brother. Grief, relief and fatal mesmerism, nails scratching unbearably on glass, a hellish mist that drifts into the intimate, familiar, domestic space with the solid, brutal, gentle embrace of undead brotherhood ...

The TV movie is Tobe Hooper's *Salem's Lot* (1979), starring David Soul and based on Stephen King's 1975 novel.[1] The young boy is me. And it will be a long, long time before I'm able to sleep in a room with the curtains open at night.

Windows are interfaces. So are mirrors. The tradition of seeing them as such goes back at least as far as Brunelleschi and Alberti, and is a commonplace within discussions of new media.[2] This chapter is an attempt to investigate the peculiar and striking relationship that the mythical figure of the vampire has always had with such interfacial objects, in particular the most popular and important media adjuncts of the mirror and the window in modern times, the printed page and the moving image screen. Languages – verbal, visual, computational – are interfaces, too, and these are inevitably implicated in any discussion of media. The vampire has drifted and shifted through the pages of newspapers, travel journals, novels, poems, comics and plays for three hundred years, it has haunted cinema and television for almost a hundred, its shadow is creeping into the social, narrative and ludic networks of the digital. A creature of ambivalence, a haunter of thresholds and dweller on the margins, the vampire is uniquely well adapted to the conditions of media convergence. It is impatient of windows and doors, invisible to mirrors, but it will be found wherever – to attempt a definition of the interface – one thing meets another.[3]

An interface is much more than the place where one thing meets another, of course; or, at least, the nature of that meeting is more complex than such a shorthand will allow. It would be restrictive to adhere closely to computer science contexts and definitions, or to become distracted by discriminations between hardware interfaces (wires, plugs, sockets) and software interfaces (codes, languages). A soft definition offers richer hermeneutic possibilities, allowing for the subtleties and ambiguities of the *'semantic'* dimension identified by Steven Johnson in his consideration of interfacial relationships 'characterized by meaning and expression'.[4]

An interface is fundamentally a place of translation and feedback, where *x* is able to feel the presence of *y* and, more importantly, enjoy the illusion of contact with *y* or even of becoming *y*. The contact and the becoming are illusory, because the two sides of the interface never actually merge: instead, they become mutually implicated, more or less intimate. Touch-screen technologies, widescreen, surround-sound, the elsewheres and the somehows of virtual reality: these are all cultural fantasies of the erased interface or, in N. Katherine Hayles's term, 'material metaphors' of full translation.[5] The interface imagines a condition of achieved union, where *x* and *y* become indivisible, but it can only enact an approximate condition of divided commonality. The illusions of interfacial transcendence are closely associated with related illusions of aliveness, responsiveness, *animation*: the moment when the engine ignites, the laptop awakens, the avatar moves or the corpse rises from the grave. The vampire is a product of this liminal ontology.

The concept of the medium – from *medias*: the middle, the junction, the in-between – is fundamentally connected to that of the interface. I have sketched a general arc of the vampire through mass media forms, from print to pixel, but it might be useful to think of media in more expansive terms. For Marshall McLuhan, media are not objects – a television, a newspaper, a telephone – but environmental and social processes. In his well known but often misunderstood axiom 'the medium is the message', the medium is anything that *extends* the human, and its message is its social *impact* or *effect* rather than its informational content.[6] In this respect, a car, a house, a woolly hat or the pockets in a pair of trousers are all forms of media, variously extending the legs or the hands or the hair on the head, effectively shrinking space or overcoming physical limitations. Adapting McLuhan's ideas, it is possible to see the relationship of the vampire and the interface in a more historically and culturally alert way: offering to 'extend' its victims in tantalising but grim ways, the vampire doesn't simply follow the evolution of representational media forms but it also embodies the social changes, anxieties and periods of unsettlement that are the correlatives of this evolution. This is recognised by Stacey Abbott when she examines the rise of 'vampire cyborgs' in film and by Allucquère Rosanne Stone when she adopts and adapts Anne Rice's Lestat de Lioncourt as a prototypical boundary figure for the dawn of the digital era: 'a vampire for our seasons, struggling with the swiftly changing meanings of what it is to be human or, for that matter, inhuman'.[7] It is also evident in Freidrich Kittler's seminal essay 'Dracula's Legacy', in Jennifer Wicke's exploration of 'the technologies that underpin vampirism' and, more recently, in Van Leavenworth's reading of Bram Stoker's *Dracula* as the source text for Star Foster and Daniel Ravipinto's *Slouching Towards Bedlam* (2003).[8] In this interactive fiction, set in the Bethlem Royal Hospital in nineteenth-century London, a vampiric word virus threatens to disintegrate the communication networks of incipient modernity.

Unsettlement is a key idea here, and it can be related closely to the changing nature of the media interface. In particular, it can be observed that all media, when new, seem to undergo a period of unsettlement or radical instability, which is characterised by formal self-consciousness and experimentation. The early years of the printing press, of the novel, of photography, of cinema, of the computer, all provide evidence of this. An initial period of creative openness and cultural uncertainty is followed by absorption into a 'mythic' (in the Barthesian sense of the word) worldview, characterised by more settled and comfortable processes of narration, representation, reception.[9] Once a medium has been culturally assimilated, the restless energies of its inception are diverted into marginal practices which nevertheless inform and, at times of major political or cultural change, challenge the mainstream. One of the persistent myths of modernity is that the media of the past (unlike those of the present) were always stable, settled, known, welcomed, understood. The vampire, constantly embodying resistance at the interface, conveys an awareness that this state of settled grace was never the case.

The vampire is, after all, a profoundly unsettled creature. It drifts *between*. Neither alive nor dead – definitively *un*-dead – it dramatises humanity's troubled sense of being vulnerably, temporarily, uniquely alive while the rest of the universe is either differently (unselfconsciously) alive, inanimate, or dead. It is caught in the eternally collapsing architecture of oppositions, an inhabitant of the anomalous zone. As a myth, the vampire embodies erotic allure and necrotic repulsion, the dead flesh made sexy, the kiss that kills but at the same time embalms. It is both *vagina dentata* and 'a penis with teeth', sexually restless and disoriented, veering between the asexual, the homosexual, the heterosexual and the pansexual, between a pitiful impotence and the most compulsive potency. The vampire represents impossible antiquity and an infinite present, both the ultimate old age and the promise of eternal youth. Typically depicted on or beyond the edges of society, it attains the classlessness of the outsider even as it oscillates wildly between the extreme co-ordinates set by the peasant Peter Plogojowitz and the aristocratic Lord Ruthven. The vampire is at once the most desolate remnant of the human and the most inhuman manifestation of the monstrous. It can be ferociously atavistic, transported in the soil of a melancholy nationalism, but it is also stateless, nationless, dispossessed. It belongs nowhere but is found everywhere.

Something of the mythic power of the vampire's paradoxical nature is captured in another piece of television viewed by my ten-year-old self. *State of Decay* (1980), a story from the classic series of the BBC's *Doctor Who* features the eponymous hero in an encounter with Zargo, Camilla and Aukon, the three vampire rulers of an exploited, drained, medieval culture.[10] The power behind this triumvirate is revealed to be the Great Vampire, the last of an ancient scourge that was supposedly eradicated by the Doctor's own people, the Time Lords. Examining the chronicle of 'the last great battle', he reads that the king of these gigantic cosmic parasites apparently escaped the field, 'vanished, even to his shadow, from Time and Space'.[11] The Great Vampire has, it now transpires, been recovering for millennia beneath the Tower of the three vampire rulers, feeding on peasants, and is now beginning to stir. More significantly, from a mythical perspective, it has been recovering on a remote, insignificant planet in E-Space, or Exo-Space, a space beyond known space, a kind of nowhere between universes, a celestial interface. Luring a ship full of Earth colonists from the twenty-second century into its bleak, marginal refuge, the Great Vampire has transformed the crew into his vampiric servants and fixed the descendants of the original passengers into a state of unchanging, premodern, superstitious abjection. Outside everything, poised among the lost, waiting on eternity for its terrible return, this

Figure 14.1. The Great Vampire glimpsed briefly on a salvaged scanner from the lost Earth spaceship *Hydrax* in *Doctor Who – The State of Decay* (1980)

monstrous creature is a figure of the vampire as unsettled interfacial shadow. Significantly, it is represented only as a spectral trace on various troubled interfaces: present in the ritualised, high-camp language spoken by both the peasantry and the rulers, which draws on the lexicon of vampiric horror clichés (The Great One, The Three Who Rule, The Wasting, The Selection, The Arising), it is also glimpsed briefly as a blurred image on a forbidden and antiquatedly hi-tech scanner screen (see Figure 14.1), and finally as a gigantic clawed hand breaking through the membrane of its underground resting place as it attempts resurrection.

Examples of vampiric unsettlement at the interface are innumerable, varied and ramifying. When *The Vampyre* was published in 1819 – in an unsettled period for the novel itself, as it transformed rapidly from an elite artefact into a popular medium – the issue can be traced both in the fabric of the narrative and in the briefly disputed question of authorship. Worked up by Polidori from a prose fragment abandoned by Byron, it was initially attributed *to* Byron, has a main character partly based *on* Byron, and became the focus of an irritable display of pique *from* Byron, who simultaneously laid claim to the tale (by publishing his original fragment as an appendix to his contemporaneous poem *Mazeppa*) and distanced himself from it: 'Damn "*The Vampire*," – what do I know of Vampires? it must be some bookselling imposture.'[12] Issues of parasitism, influence and infection – not to mention society, politics and literary fashion – haunt the authorial interface of this founding fiction of modern vampire mythology just as much as they haunt the tale itself.

When F. W. Murnau came into conflict with Florence Stoker over questions of authorial rights for his film *Nosferatu: A Symphony of Horror* (1922) a hundred years later – at a time when cinema was arguably emerging from a quarter-century of unsettlement into a state of cultural self-assurance – the shadow of *The Vampyre* might have been seen to fall across them. Intriguingly, the exaggerated shadows which are one of the most powerful visual tropes of Murnau's film have been recognised by Abbott as spectral links between the myth and the medium, specifically in the scenes where the Count attacks Hutter and Ellen: 'In these sequences, Orlock's "shadow" is projected onto the bright, white surfaces – Hutter's bed and Ellen's nightgown, respectively – like film itself is projected onto a screen'.[13]

In the early years of sound cinema, the vampire again appeared to mark a troubling of the interface. Bela Lugosi's selection for the title role in Tod Browning's *Dracula* (1931) was remarkable for its counterintuitive brilliance, his limited English meaning that his lines were delivered with such slow, relished determination that he would forever seem to be straining against the newly sonic medium as much as against the language itself. Within a year, Carl Dreyer's *Vampyr: The Strange Adventure of Allan Gray* (1932) – a talkie that almost entirely abstains from talk – would exploit a comparable unease to gloriously poetic effect, affecting an apparent nostalgia for the recently deceased silent film. As Jean and Dale Drum have written, with wonderful understatement: 'Dreyer's first sound film was a radical departure from other sound films of the time, for the dialogue of *Vampyr* is very sparse'.[14] In fact, as the Drums reveal, *Vampyr* was actually shot as a silent film, with sound being added in post-production. Even more strikingly, it was shot as a silent film in three different versions, with English, German and French mouthings respectively. The polyphonic complexity of a world of mass communication, symbolised by the rise of global sound cinema, is indulged through Dreyer's perfectionist multiplication of effort and expense at the same time as it is parodied by his presentation of a talkie that feels like a silent.

A consonant case study is *Bram Stoker's Dracula* (1992) which, at the beginning of the digital screen era, saw Francis Ford Coppola and his son Roman determinedly, even obsessively, exploiting the possibilities of primitive cinema technologies. The effects of this go beyond the 'affectionate recuperation of early cinematic styles' identified by Ken Gelder.[15] Appearing between James Cameron's visual effects milestones *The Abyss* (1989) and *Terminator 2: Judgement Day* (1991), and John Lasseter's game-changing computer animation *Toy Story* (1995), the film – disliked and dismissed by many vampire scholars – is remarkable for the opulence of its 'in camera' effects.[16] Spatial juxtapositions and distortions, appearances and disappearances, inversions of physical laws and other elements of baroque spectacle, are achieved using methods which frequently date back to the origins of cinema itself, to the founding experiments of the Lumière Brothers, Georges Méliès, R. W. Paul and Cecil Hepworth. Physical projections, multiple exposures and combined takes, forced perspective shots using scaled model work, matte paintings and glass shots, hand-cranked footage filmed with an antique camera, jittery first-person viewpoints achieved with an intervalometer: such regressive techniques achieve a quality of visual force, noise and fluidity which is comparable to that of the 'hybrid aesthetics' associated by Lev Manovich with the innovations of the digital age.[17]

When Dracula's eyes burn in the sky, or his shadow takes on a life of its own, or a train rattles along the top of Jonathan Harker's open journal, spilling steam across the pages, these effects are accomplished with an immediacy equivalent to that of many digital sequences. This immediacy – to adopt the 'twin logic' of Jay David Bolter and Richard Grusin's influential book *Remediation* – is also a form of *hyper*mediacy.[18] In other words, its very transparency draws attention to itself, the active presence of the medium being visible at the moment of its illusionistic erasure.

Just as many critics have indicated a law of diminishing returns for Coppola's 'postmodern' adaptation, the insistence on pre-digital effects might be seen as a gratuitous and hollow nostalgia at odds with the blockbuster context. This would be, however, to miss the sophisticated ironies that Coppola's film implies and, in its physical realisation of a digital age spectacle, masks.[19] These are typified by the elaborate simplicity and primitivism of Coppola's technique in realising the shaving scene, in which Jonathan is surprised by the Count's sudden appearance at his shoulder, the mirror having shown no reflection. A mirror-shaped hole is cut into the wall and the actor, Keanu Reeves, stands behind it, his face visible in opposition to a stand-in actor who has his back to the camera. The mirror is a glassless window: the assumed interface is absent, the reflective surface perceived but never present. Reeves, in other words, performs as his own reflection, and Gary Oldman's Dracula is seen to lack one altogether. A live and naive trick stands in place of – in a sense, simulates – a post-produced digital illusion. Brilliantly, the mechanics of the scene embody several of the thematic oppositions of vampire mythology – presence/absence, self/Other – at the same time as literally merging two of its recurrent interfacial tropes, the transparent glass and the reflective one.[20]

Just as Dreyer's *Vampyr* performs a redaction of silent era cinematics within the new contexts of the 'talking' interface, so Coppola's version of *Dracula* enacts a critique of the emergent digital spectacle through retrospective celebration of the physical. From a metacritical point of view, it embodies an extreme form of Fredric Jameson's notion of *le mode rétro*, one taken beyond the surface details of intertextual referencing and into the mechanical interior of the production.[21] Dreyer's near-silent talkie might, in a similar sense, be seen as expressing something of the spirit of Rudolf Arnheim's *Film as Art*, which dates in its original form from 1932, the year of *Vampyr*'s release, and which famously probes the impact of speech on cinema.[22]

The formalisation in these films of distinct critical sensibilities – sensibilities alert to unsettlement in media – is evidence of the particular responsiveness of the vampire myth to deep cultural change. In the case of *Bram Stoker's Dracula* this is manifested to such an extent, and with such an overflow of excited self-awareness, that the entire film effectively becomes – to borrow from William Empson – a 'self-inwoven simile'.[23] Empson coined the phrase in order to characterise a form of figurative poetic language in which, 'not being able to think of a comparison fast enough [the author] compares the thing to a vaguer or more abstract notion of itself, or points out that it is its own nature, or that it sustains itself by supporting itself'.[24] Empson's exemplar for this is Percy Shelley ('So came a chariot in the silent storm / Of its own rushing splendour'), but in relation to Coppola's version of *Dracula* it is possible to see a tendency towards extreme symbolic self-referentiality, a kind of intertextual implosion of the mythic representation.[25] This seems to be what many of the commentators who have denigrated the film have targeted, Fred Botting's analysis being representative: 'Coppola's film mourns an object that is too diffuse and uncertain to be recuperated: it remains, reluctantly, within a play of narratives, between past and present, one and other'.[26] Botting uses the adaptation to close his survey of the Gothic mode in culture: 'with Coppola's *Dracula*, then, Gothic dies'.[27] Nina Auerbach prefers to confine the film almost entirely to the endnotes of her study, where she argues that it 'turned the quest for authenticity into a sad joke', her judgment chiming with Botting's: 'it may be that Coppola has killed Dracula at last'.[28] Gelder, in a bracketed aside, simply accuses the director and co-producer of 'self-monumentalisation'.[29] In the interfaces of academic practice – notes, parentheses, conclusions – the critics lament what they see as the decadence of vampiric apotheosis. Then again, Tomasz Warchol (in unusually approving tones) makes the point titular and core to his 2003 paper 'How Coppola Killed Dracula'.[30]

In blunt terms, Coppola's film is so saturated in awareness of its sources, its predecessors, its points of historical, folkloric, literary, technological and cinematic reference, that it becomes – in some readings – a spectacular paradigm of empty and self-parodying excess. The more it strives towards definitiveness, authenticity and a rich distillation of meaning, the more it lapses into circularity and hectic imitation, the 'short-circuited comparison' that Empson bemoans in Shelley. It is unsurprising, perhaps, that criticisms of Coppola's adaptation should so consistently sound like the criticisms traditionally levelled at both Romanticism and postmodernism within cultural discourse. 'The *Form* is its own justification', Empson writes, 'it sustains itself, like God, by the fact that it exists'.[31]

A self-inwoven simile is vampiric, *auto*-vampiric, feeding off itself. The same might be said about the vampire genre in fiction. Coppola's film, named explicitly after the book that is its primary source text, is also thick with the cinematic tradition of adaptations that it can never escape but that it consciously seeks to transcend. The distorted shadows that attend Oldman's Count are projections from Max Schreck's Count seventy years earlier. In the same way, Coppola's foregrounding of the technologically mediated nature of the story environment is predicated on Stoker's novel, with its newspapers, typewriters and phonographs; its mindfulness of the medical and psychological trends of the late nineteenth century. Conscious that *Dracula* was written at the interface of the Victorian and modernist eras, Coppola creates a version of the myth that aims to be definitive not only in its putative closeness to the novel but also in its depiction of cultural paradigm shift. The shift (to the mass media age) that textures the world of the film is in balance with that (to the digital era) which negatively informs its production. A strict adherence to pre-digital methods of spectacle becomes, in this respect, far more than a wilful eccentricity on Coppola's part. It enacts a formal irony that is fundamental to the film's complex and vital representation of Stoker's novel.

An irony that has not gone unnoticed is the emphatic presence at the heart of the film of the one major mass media technology that is pointedly *not* referenced by Stoker: the cinema. In a conspicuous deviation from fidelity to the original book, *Bram Stoker's Dracula* extends the Count beyond the bitter, brittle ancientness of his literary original – closely approximated in the initial scenes between Dracula and Jonathan – and introduces a rejuvenated Byronic anti-hero, bursting naked from the crated earth of Transylvania and into a distinctly modern England. The Count transforms from a withered, alienated, ethnic grotesque into a youthful, attractive *flâneur*, a cosmopolitan European who reads the newspapers and – when he first encounters Mina (or re-encounters Elisabeta) – is eager to experience the wonders of the cinematograph. This transformation has irritated many,[32] but it is consistent with Coppola's tendency to see suppleness as the abiding characteristic of both the Dracula myth and the idea of authenticity. The true copy – the accurate translation – is as elusive and illusory as the vampire. It is, like the idea of settled, stable, discrete traditions, a figment of the interface.[33]

Oldman's Dracula, sauntering through London as love-struck tourist rather than pestilent invader, has inevitably proved controversial. Even so, those who have held up his blue-tinted sunglasses as evidence of Coppola's travesty might consider that, far from being incongruously 'cool' anachronisms, they are both historically accurate and mythically cogent. After all, one of the accursed undead, walking in daylight, would be well advised to sport a pair of such interfacial screening devices, designed by the English optician James Ayscough in the mid-1700s.[34]

The fundamental interfaces are the door and the window. These quiet translators of experience – from one to other, here to there – are the symbolic and actual locations of boundary rituals ranging from the baby's first arrival home to the deceased's final exit from it. They are built into the customs of intimacy (the bride carried over the threshold) and those of state (the arrival of Black Rod); they are culturally ingrained as sites of rapture (Romeo: 'what light from yonder window breaks'), trauma (Catherine's ghost in *Wuthering Heights*), voyeurism (Hitchcock's *Rear Window*), trepidation (Philip Larkin's 'Sad Steps' or 'Aubade') and daily domestic routine (Mrs Ogmore-Prichard: 'before you let the sun in, mind it wipes its shoes').[35] A door that creaks or slams, that is locked, knocked at or bricked up; a window that is jammed, boarded over or broken: these are resonant, evocative signs.

Within the mythos of the vampire, of course, the door and the window have a potent place, making the site of encounter a key feature of any narrative representation. The entrance of Sir Francis Varney into the gigantic tale which bears his name is relevant here: 'A tall figure is standing on the ledge immediately outside the long window. It is its finger-nails upon the glass that produces the sound so like the hail, now that the hail has ceased.'[36] Dracula's first appearance in Stoker's novel is similarly emblematic. Following a nightmare journey, Jonathan is confronted by 'a great door, old and studded with large iron nails, and set in a projecting doorway of massive stone'.[37] He is immediately menaced by a sense that the apertures of this 'vast ruined castle, from whose tall black windows came no ray of light' (17) are barriers rather points of transit: 'Of bell or knocker there was no sign; through these frowning walls and dark window openings it was not likely that my voice could penetrate' (17). Revealingly, it is thoughts of familiar windows which comfort him at this point – 'I expected that I should suddenly awake, and find myself at home, with the dawn struggling in through the windows' (18)

– and light and sound through the castle door which fixes him in the terrible present:

> I heard a heavy step approaching beyond the great door and saw through the chinks the gleam of a coming light. Then there was the sound of rattling chains and the clanking of massive bolts drawn back. A key was turned with the loud grating noise of long disuse, and the great door swung back. (18)

This is noise at the interface, what a communication theorist would identify as entropic information, a perplexing overload of stimulus. Dracula has arrived to greet his guest but can make no initiating move towards him, must wait on the frozen moment until approached:

> He made no motion of stepping to meet me, but stood like a statue, as though his gesture of welcome had fixed him into stone. The instant, however, that I had stepped over the threshold, he moved impulsively forward, and holding out his hand grasped mine with a strength which made me wince. (18)

The vampire, in one tradition at least, requires invitation: the predator must be welcomed, permitted to cross the interface.[38] (Ruthven, we might remember, is 'invited to every house' in London society.)[39] This aspect of the folklore provides the titular, narrative and emotional core of John Ajvide Lindqvist's novel *Let the Right One In* (2004) and its cinematic adaptations by Tomas Alfredson (2008) and Matt Reeves (*Let Me In*, 2010).

Drawing its title from a song by Morrissey, that quintessential inside-outsider, the story reinvents the vampire as Eli, a misfit living among misfits in the anonymous 1950s-built Blackeberg suburb of Stockholm. An eternal and subtly androgynous twelve-year-old, Eli forms a desperate and touching bond with her bullied next door neighbour, Oskar Eriksson. Psychologically aligned with her, Oscar is both sexually drawn to her and physically disgusted by her, even before the many secrets of her existence are revealed. From the title of the tale onwards, it is fundamentally concerned with margins, boundaries, thresholds and moments of crossing. Most obviously, Eli must receive an invitation before entering a dwelling, as in her first visit to Oskar at night:

> 'Oskar ...'
> It was coming from the window. He opened his eyes, looked over. He saw the contours of a little head on the other side of the glass. He pulled off the covers, but before he managed to get out of bed Eli whispered, 'Wait there. Stay in bed. Can I come in?'
> Oskar whispered, 'Ye-es ...'

Figure 14.2.   Eli and Oskar touch through the interface in *Let the Right One In* (2007).
Tomas Alfredson (Sandrew Metronome, 2008)

> 'Say that I can come in.'
> 'You can come in.'
> 'Close your eyes.'
> Oskar shut his eyes tightly. The window opened and a cold draught blew
> into the room. The window was carefully closed.[40]

Powerfully, in Alfredson's film adaptation, the scene in which Oskar confronts
Eli about his suspicions of her vampirism presents the children talking through
the glass pane of a door in the girl's bare flat, their outspread hands touching –
or *seeming* to touch – through the interface (see Figure 14.2). This can be seen
as a crystalline refinement of the solid wall through which the two, who have
adjacent rooms, have previously communicated using Morse Code. Common
to the novel and both films, this 'Pyramus and Thisbe' tableau embodies the
theme of connection-and-division and is given added richness by the contrast
between Oskar's *trompe l'oeil* picture wall – depicting 'a forest meadow' – and
Eli's blank partition:

> Oskar lay there with his hand pressed against the green surface and tried to
> imagine what the other side looked like. Was the room on the other side her
> bedroom? Was she also lying in bed right now? He transformed the wall into
> Eli's cheek, stroked the green leaves, her soft skin. (83)

Even before it is 'opened' by a shared code, the wall becomes a screen for
Oskar to play out his fantasies of otherness and association.

Dominated by an architecture of connections – not just windows and
doorways but also bridges, paths, subways, underpasses, staircases – *Let the
Right One In* might almost have been written as a model of the vampire tale as

interface fable. The novel begins with a metaphorically freighted description of the first inhabitants crossing the Traneberg Bridge in 1952 'with sunshine and the future in their eyes' (7), and much of the action, notably the killing of Jocke Bengtsson, takes place in the Björnsongatan underpass and on the nearby pathways (77–83). This is made explicit when Lacke follows Virginia after their row in Gösta's flat and sees her being attacked ahead of the point 'where "Jocke's path" – as he had started to call it – met "Virginia's path"' (243–4).

The symbolic importance of these physical interstices is emphasised in both film adaptations, Alfredson's especially. Here, as well as recurrent shots of bridges, underpasses and so on, the poetics of transparency are employed not only in the previously mentioned scene between Eli and Oskar but also in the episode in which Jocke's body is recovered from the river. Cut from the ice, the corpse is raised high by a crane, embedded in a glassy slab, caught in the interface between water and air. In Reeves's version – in which the main characters are renamed Owen and Abby – the voyeurism of the former is accentuated through his habit of spying on his neighbours using a telescope. This is, indeed, how the audience first encounters him. Oskar, in the Alfredson film, is first seen staring into his own reflection in his bedroom window.

With its liminal concerns articulated through topography as well as character and event, *Let the Right One In* demonstrates a continuation of the classic thematic structuring of vampiric mythology through opposition: life/death, youth/age, human/non-human, desire/repulsion, male/female. It also indicates how intricately and forcefully these are bound into the fabric of the imaginative interface, not least in the tension between morality and immorality. Håkan Bengtsson, the paedophile who 'cares for' Eli, is able to justify his feelings for the child – and the crimes he is prepared to carry out for her – by reflecting on her anomalous condition:

> It was the best of all possible worlds. The young, lithe body that brought beauty to his life, and at the same lifted him from responsibility. He was not the one in charge. And he did not have to feel guilt for his desire; his beloved was older than he. No longer a child (119).

When he is discovered in the act of child murder, acquiring more blood for Eli, his response – to protect her, since his face is now known in Blackeberg – is to destroy his own first interface, his face, his skin, ultimately his identity, using acid. Significantly, when he returns as a mutilated, brain-dead, priapic vampire following his eventual death (an element of the plot removed from both films), it is on the Traneberg bridge that he is first seen (323–6).

A prominent facet of Eli's boundary nature in the novel is her androgyny, movingly poised alongside her uncertain humanness in a question to Oskar: 'Would you still like me even if I wasn't a girl?' (137).[41] The theme of gender ambiguity is understated in the films, particularly in the US adaptation, but one of the most haunting qualities of Alfredson's production is the design of Eli's voice. Deciding that the voice of teenage actress Lina Leandersson was too childlike and girlish, he had her lines overdubbed throughout the film by the adult voiceover artist Elif Ceylan. In a fascinating replication of the dubbing of Dreyer's 'silent talkie' in the 1930s, Anderson modulates the sonic interface to convey the alienated, indeterminate existence of his vampire. Eli's voice, sultry, uncanny, not-quite-right, effectively 'speaks' the anomalies of her being, neither alive nor dead, neither adult nor child, neither male nor female, neither human nor monster.

The melancholy paradox of Eli's condition – of the vampire in general – is communicated with terrible beauty in the moment when she is goaded by Oskar into entering his flat without invitation:

> He stopped when he saw a tear in the corner of one of Eli's eyes, no, one in each eye. But it wasn't a tear since it was dark. The skin in Eli's face started to flush, became pink, red, wine-red and her hands tightened into fists as the pores in her face opened and tiny pearls of blood started to appear in dots all over her face. Her throat, same thing. (380–1)

A spectacular gift for the filmmakers, this scene – Eli 'bleeding out of all the pores in her body' – represents a collapse of boundaries, spatial, physical, ethical, mythical. Eli, having reluctantly breached Oskar's dwelling, suffers perforation of her own physical limits. The existential liminality of the vampire has never been so vividly, painfully, tragically represented. Lindqvist's in many ways highly traditional vampire tale nevertheless constitutes a radical restatement of the essential features of the mythology.

Claiming cinema as 'the rightful place of occupation for the vampire', Gelder describes it as 'a suitably nomadic home' for the creature, one which 'eventually goes everywhere' as 'an internationalised medium'.[42] Abbott's *Celluloid Vampires*, which begins by referencing Méliès's *Le manoir du diable* (1896), is written from a similar conviction. The exploration within this chapter does nothing to contradict (and much to confirm) the centrality of the cinematic depiction, but hopefully suggests a slight adjustment to our sense of how the mythology has been mediated since the early twentieth century. As we move further into the 2000s, it is clear that the structures of the media world are becoming increasingly complex and involved, bringing a profound transformation in the nature of knowledge and information, of creativity and audiences, of the possibilities of storytelling, the relationship between media forms, the meanings and significance of the interface. This would seem to endorse Milly Williamson's portrayal of an alternative, non-mainstream tradition within recent vampire culture, one in which 'creativity takes numerous shapes; sartorial self-expression, fan fiction, role-playing, the creation of clubs, journals, websites, and more'.[43] Williamson's socio-political reading – reminding us of Marx's invocation of the 'vampire' of capitalism[44] – accepts that the mythology can never escape the 'hierarchical cultural field' of the market, but the most cursory internet search will indicate the extent of the vampire's Web-based nomadism. Similarly, a brief sampling of computer game history illustrates the occupation of this bright young medium by the forces of the undead, from *The Count* in 1981 to *Vampire Rush* in 2011. If nothing else, the migration of the vampire across the new media environment might suggest that counterculture and culture have never been harder to disentangle.

Perhaps what the vampire manifests most powerfully is the cultural narrative of change, specifically the tension between imposed change and desired change, between the attack and the seduction. This, I have argued, is why the notion of the interface – the point and process of translation, transition, transfer, transformation – is such a useful one when considering the mythic endurance and adaptability of the vampire. It offers a means of seeing anew those representations of the undead which have ghosted modern media since before 1819, especially those moments when the creature stands at a threshold. In Browning's *Dracula*, for instance, there is the iconic scene in which Renfield arrives at Dracula's castle. The Count bids the solicitor to follow him up the vast, curved staircase, and in doing so passes through the colossal screen of a spider's web without breaking or even troubling it (see Figure 14.3). Renfield, understandably disturbed by this event, is forced to tear at the silk with his cane to gain entrance. We are reminded, at this moment, of one of the key features of the vampire, its ability to transcend the continuities of physical space, in a vital sense manifesting the fantasies of virtual reality. To pass through a giant web without breaking it is to pass through the interface as if it wasn't there. The dream of the erased material interface that seems to drive so much of twenty-first-century technological design is a dream that the vampire (excepting the barrier of an invitation) takes for granted. This is a point given detailed and persuasive attention by Abbott, when she traces the technologically determined shifts between the material and the spectral vampire in modernity.[45]

Of course, a vampire doesn't just walk through cobwebs, float through

Figure 14.3. The Count emerges from the unbroken cobweb in *Dracula* (1931)

windows, seep under doors: one way or another, it punctures skin, the
locus of our primal and most fundamental interface. It bleeds one self into
another self and, in doing so, radically disrupts the idea of boundaries. This
is the significance of the solid undead flesh becoming immaterial mist, or the
human(oid) figure transforming into bat or wolf or rat-swarm. In its physical
metamorphoses and its predatory *modus operandi* the vampire destabilises the
line between transformation and permanence, the line where all our dreams
and nightmares of technology begin.

   As I suggested earlier, the interfaced machines of the digital age fascinate
us, in part at least, because they affect the appearance of life. Just as the
steam engines of the early Victorian Age must have astounded and unnerved
with their animal warmth, their growling motion, their steam-farts and
bellows, and the disembodied voices of the phonograph, the telephone and the
wireless must have haunted the late Victorians, so the winking lights on our
own sleeping technologies, the vibrations of our mobile phones, the actions
of our on-screen avatars, the voices of our sat navs, seem to either seduce or
threaten us with their apparent aliveness.[46] It is an aliveness conjured from the
interplay of memory, calculation, responsiveness, and dialogue. In the early
days of cinema, Maxim Gorky reacted with unease to the travesty of life he

Figure 14.4. A coffin with a view in Carl Dreyer's *Vampyr* (1932)

saw projected before him at a Lumière Brothers screening. For Gorky, Lisa Bode has written,

> [t]he screen becomes a window onto a disturbing terrain between life and death, between flesh and shadow, and between the animate and the inanimate, where apparently living figures appear 'condemned' and 'bewitched' by the actions of this, then new, image technology.[47]

This recalls to me the horrific poetry of the episode in Dreyer's *Vampyr*, where Allan Gray – disembodied, apparently dreaming – witnesses himself staring up out of a windowed coffin, alive but dead (see Figure 14.4). Briefly glimpsing the withered vampire, Marguerite Chopin, peering down at him, he is presented with a view of a burning candle dripping wax, then massing clouds in a sky beneath which he is being carried, presumably to be buried. This scene communicates, perhaps better than any other, the ideas that this chapter has been presenting; it captures perfectly, disturbingly, the presence of the vampire where x meets y in the mediation of experience. It also, in its conjuring of sheer frozen terror, takes me back to that ten-year-old boy watching *Salem's Lot* in a Cornish caravan park in the days of Margaret Thatcher.

Notes

1 The visits of the undead Ralphie Glick to his older brother Danny is not detailed in the novel (King, *Salem's Lot*, pp. 68–71, pp. 74–6, p. 104) but Danny's subsequent attack on his friend Mark Petrie is clearly an influence on Hooper's screen adaption (pp. 239–41).

2 See, for instance, Bolter and Gromola, *Windows and Mirrors*, and Friedberg, *The Virtual Window*.

3 See Sam George's Chapter 4, above, exploring the mirror motif within vampire mythologies. Attempting to trace the elusive origins of the non-reflection motif, George highlights the reference in Stoker's *Dracula* notebooks to contemporary technology ('Could not codak him') and makes a compelling case for seeing this conceit as fundamental to the vampire's enigmatic potency as 'a pervasive reflection of modern culture' (p. 56).

4 Johnson, *Interface Culture*, p. 14.

5 *Writing Machines*, pp. 21–4.

6 Hayles, *Understanding Media*, p. 7 and *passim*.

7 Abbott, *Celluloid Vampires*, pp. 197–214; Stone, *The War of Desire and Technology*, p. 178.

8 Kittler, 'Dracula's Legacy'; Wicke, 'Vampiric Typewriting'; Van Leavenworth, *The Gothic in Contemporary Interactive Fictions*, pp. 144–79. The study can be downloaded in full via the SwePub website.

9 Barthes, *Mythologies*. According to Barthes 'the very principle of myth' is that 'it transforms history into nature': 'it abolishes the complexity of human acts, it gives them the simplicity of essences' (p. 140, p. 150).

10 *Doctor Who – State of Decay*. The story was originally transmitted on BBC1 between 22 November and 13 December 1980 and was subsequently novelised by Terrance Dicks as *Doctor Who and the State of Decay*. It is currently available as part of the DVD box set, *Doctor Who: The E-Space Trilogy*.

11 Dicks, *Doctor Who and the State of Decay*, pp. 90–1.

12 Letter to John Murray, 15 May 1819, in *Selected Letters*, ed. Marchand, p. 194. Byron's antipathy to the vampire had, of course, not prevented him from utilising the myth to dramatic effect in his earlier poem *The Giaour* (1813). See Conrad Aquilina's Chapter 2 above.

13 Abbott, *Celluloid Vampires*, pp. 52–3. Abbott extends her reading of the emblematic connection between vampires and cinematic technologies in her Chapter 6 above: 'Cinema is undeath and therefore it is an ideal place to find vampires' (p. 96).

14 Jean and Dale Drum, 'Film-Production Carl Dreyer', p. 34, in the book accompanying *Vampyr*, dir. Carl Dreyer. The text is extracted from Jean and Dale Drum, *My Only Great Passion: The Life and Films of Carl Th. Dreyer*.

15 Gelder, *Reading the Vampire*, p. 88.

16 Reviewing the film for *The New York Times*, Vincent Canby wrote: 'This movie was

imagined, written and directed, then somehow engineered into being as if it were one long, uninterrupted special effect' ('Coppola's Dizzying Vision of Dracula').

17 Manovich, 'Image Future', p. 26, p. 32; p. 43, n. 8, and *passim*. See also 'After Effects, or Velvet Revolution' (2006) and *The Language of New Media*. Each of these – and much besides – is available to download at http://manovich.net/.

18 Bolter and Grusin, *Remediation*.

19 Lindsey Scott's Chapter 7, above, argues persuasively for the sophistication and distinctive renewals of Coppola's film, making vivid reference to its mixing of the 'visually beautiful' and the 'grotesque' to create 'a liminal landscape' (p. 122).

20 This transposition recalls that of Sheridan Le Fanu's *In a Glass Darkly*, the title of the volume which culminates in 'Carmilla', effectively converting St Paul's shadowy spiritual window into a Gothic mirror: 'For now we see through a glass, darkly' (1 Corinthians 13:12).

21 Jameson, 'Postmodernism and Consumer Society', p. 116. See also Jameson, *Postmodernism*.

22 'Not only does speech limit the motion picture to an art of dramatic portraiture, it also interferes with the expression of the image' (Arnheim, *Film as Art*, p. 228).

23 Empson, *Seven Types of Ambiguity*, pp. 160–1.

24 *Ibid.*, pp. 160–1.

25 *Ibid.*, p. 161. The quoted lines are from Shelley's last, unfinished poem *The Triumph of Life* (1822).

26 Botting, *Gothic*, pp. 177–80.

27 *Ibid.*, p. 180.

28 Auerbach, *Our Vampires*, p. 213, n. 50; pp. 208–9, n. 16.

29 Gelder, *Reading the Vampire*, p. 89.

30 In Kungl (ed.), *Vampires*, pp. 7–10. Warchol concludes: 'While the vampires he helped breed are alive and well, Dracula himself, for those of us who have seen and known him for the past century, has been dead since 1992. It was Francis Ford Coppola who killed him' (p. 9).

31 Empson, *Seven Types of Ambiguity*, p. 161. Empson goes on: 'Poetry which idolises its object naturally gives it the attributes of deity, but to do it in this way is to destroy the simile, or make it incapable of its more serious functions.' Coppola, it can be argued, has been led into a state of Shelleyan creative overexcitement by his idolisation of Stoker's novel and the traditions of adaptation that have stemmed from it.

32 Auerbach, for instance, derides 'Gary Oldman's whimpering costume-changes' (*Our Vampires*, p. 112).

33 Although I have tended to take Coppola's apparent attempt at adaptational fidelity at face value, there is nevertheless considerable contiguity between my reading of the film's deceptively subtle incorporation of prior versions (including Stoker's original novel) and Lindsey Scott's argument above.

34 Drewry, 'What Man Devised That He Might See' and Dain, 'Sunglasses and Sunglass Standards'. Ayscough's tinted glasses – available in green as well as blue – were in

fact developed to correct vision, not to protect the eyes from sunlight. Nevertheless, they are widely taken to be precursors of the filter spectacles which became popular in the early 1900s.

35 Dylan Thomas, *Under Milk Wood*, p. 15.

36 Rymer, *Varney, the Vampyre*, p. 7.

37 Stoker, *Dracula*, ed. Luckhurst, p. 17. Further references are to this edition in parentheses.

38 Here, interestingly, the classical formula is inverted: the implication is that Jonathan Harker must *accept* the Count's invitation.

39 Polidori, 'The Vampyre', in Frayling (ed.), *Vampyres*, p. 108.

40 Lindqvist, *Let the Right One In*, p. 184. All further references in parentheses in the text.

41 In Lindqvist's novel, Eli is revealed to have been born male, but had been castrated during the ordeal which led to him becoming a vampire (383–91).

42 Gelder, *Reading the Vampire*, p. 87.

43 Williamson, *The Lure of the Vampire*, p. 184.

44 *Ibid.*, p. 183.

45 Abbott does this in both *Celluloid Vampires* and in her chapter, above, in which she traces the intricate ways in which 'the supernatural is made manifest through technology' (p. 104) in both Murnau's *Nosferatu* and Dreyer's *Vampyr.*

46 I am grateful to my colleague Alan Peacock not only for the phrase 'steam-farts' but also for a number of long, enjoyable conversations in which many of the ideas for this chapter took shape.

47 Bode, 'From Shadow Citizens to Teflon Stars', p. 174.

15

'Legally recognised undead': essence, difference and assimilation in Daniel Waters's *Generation Dead*

Bill Hughes

VAMPIRE LITERATURE, at least since Le Fanu's 'Carmilla' (1872), has been conspicuously about 'Otherness', that crucial term of identity politics, and has thus rendered itself most obligingly to interpretation in terms of those politics. In a concise survey of the history and problems of identity politics, Cressida Heyes says,

> While doctrines of equality press the notion that each human being is capable of deploying his or her practical reason or moral sense to live an authentic life qua individual, the politics of difference has appropriated the language of authenticity to describe ways of living that are true to the identities of marginalized social groups.[1]

This tension between the Enlightenment notion of universal equality and the concentration on the 'authentic life' of marginalised others has been explored, wittingly or unwittingly, in many contemporary fictions of the Undead. Appearing deceptively human, animated, yet (despite the etymology of 'animated') without a soul, vampires have conveniently represented alterity, whether foreignness or deviant sexuality, or both. Vampire fiction is currently enormously popular; in part, I will argue, because of how easily it dramatises contemporary concerns with this politics of difference, in a new demonstration of the adaptability of the Undead as political metaphor.[2] Lately, zombies have been spotted lurching alongside their fellow Undead in greater numbers, embodying otherness in a different, perhaps less exotic manner.[3]

The Undead tend to quicken in Western literature (as opposed, I mean, to folklore) at moments when the certainties of Enlightenment come under suspicion somewhat. In the eighteenth century there had been the earnest

rational investigations into vampirism of Calmet, but that which escapes
rationality in the Gothic reaction coalesced in the Romantic literary vampire
as exemplified by Polidori. With Stoker, the scope of Enlightenment universalism had narrowed and others of its tenets regarded with suspicion in some
quarters; the Undead became very visibly what lies outside Enlightenment,
registering unease with foreigners, sexuality, modernity and women. And in
the twenty-first century, amidst the postmodern antiuniversalism of identity
politics, the undead Other may be examined in a way that dramatises,
critically or otherwise, that fragmentation.

The shift towards the depiction of the sympathetic vampire has been
delineated elsewhere in this volume.[4] Typically, when the monstrous Other
gains our sympathies, he (as it is most usually) is cast as a Miltonic or
Byronic hero-villain.[5] Here are the origins of the rapidly proliferating genre(s)
variously labelled 'paranormal romance', 'dark romance, 'dark fantasy',
which explores, sometimes transgressively, sometimes conservatively, love
between humans and supernatural beings, most famously between Bella Swan
and Edward Cullen in Stephanie Meyer's *Twilight*.[6]

Identity politics, however, is concerned with subcultures, individuals in
social groups, and their integration into, or rejection from, wider society. It
was probably Joss Whedon's TV series, *Angel* (1999–2004) that first showed
undead *subcultures* as somewhat sympathetic *groups* of others, existing alongside
mainstream society. Two films, Joel Schumacher's *The Lost Boys* (1987)
and Kathryn Bigelow's *Near Dark* (1987), which Whedon cites as seminal
inspirations for *Buffy the Vampire Slayer* (from which *Angel* emerged), conspicuously show a vampire subculture which is unassimilated to mainstream
culture; the protagonists have to be rehabilitated to the latter.[7] Rice's Théâtre
des Vampires and the Undead of Poppy Z. Brite's *Lost Souls* (1992) are similarly
estranged subcultures, but receive much more sympathy. But we first see
monsters interacting in groups within a larger culture in the Buffyverse
(at a time, the late 1990s, when identity politics in the US and Western
world generally became somewhat absorbed into the establishment). Here,
cultures of the undead are either tolerated, if not granted legal status, or
are persecuted for their difference, and these issues are very self-consciously
raised with regard to carefully specified demon identities. Terry Eagleton
recounts how a politics of culture became normalised during this period:

> What had survived of the politically turbulent 1960s was life-style and
> identity politics, which as the class struggle froze over in the mid-1970s
> surged increasingly to the fore. [...] Culture [...] had severely challenged a
> philistine, patriarchal, ethnically blinded left. But as national liberation passed

into post-coloniality, and the politicized culture of the 1960s and early 1970s gave way to the postmodern 1980s, culture was the supplement which came gradually to oust what it had amplified.[8]

We see this mirrored in various demon joints in *Buffy*, and particularly in *Angel*, where groups of demons, each highly differentiated from other groups, interact on the neutral ground of the Caritas nightclub.[9] Thus in this later phase of the fiction of the Undead, we discern the possibility of an imagining of an undead identity politics – and, from human characters, kinds of responses that reveal the common stances towards contemporary identity politics, ranging between radical, liberal and conservative attitudes. Charlaine Harris's Sookie Stackhouse, who – herself alienated by her telepathy – loves a vampire, sets out my theme early on: 'We had all the other minorities in our little town – why not the newest, the legally recognised undead?'[10] In addition, in these fictions we often see the dramatisation of the state's responses to calls for recognition from different groups and the legal apparatuses erected in response.

Harris creates a United States where vampires, having emerged from darkness to claim their rights, have been granted legal status (though this is precarious and they are still subject to intolerance). In the Anita Blake series by Laurell K. Hamilton, vampires have semi-legal status where their rights are slackly defended and full of loopholes.[11] Hamilton's vampires are still powerful, still killers: Anita talks of 'a bleeding heart liberal who thought vampires were just people with fangs'.[12] She is no integrationist, and initially there are few counter-tendencies to show that Hamilton's fiction is anything other than a reaction against the politics of cultural diversity. Anita is curiously tempted to this otherness nevertheless, and by the later, raunchier books in the series, she is sleeping with various combinations of werewolves, wereleopards and vampires with abandon; these others have, through the sequence of novels, also been granted sympathy as human-like subjects.

Vampires are cool; they have long been seen as sexy and glamorous.[13] Zombies, by convention, are not so. The publishing world is well aware of the limits of sexually encountering otherness in a vein that tolerates vampires, werewolves and, lately, faeries[14] and angels:

> 'Zombies are not sexy. Romances don't feature zombies,' [...] 'Zombies are rotting dead flesh who eat brains. When you say vampire, you think David Boreanaz. Until David Boreanaz becomes a zombie – no way.'[15]

And yet zombies do seem to be very popular at the moment for other reasons. For Christie and Lauro, there have been three phases of the fictional zombie:

'the classic mindless corpse, the relentless instinct-driven newly dead, and the millennial voracious and fast-moving predator'.[16] There is no slot here, it seems, for the sympathetic zombie, and certainly none for the zombie as lover. However, alongside the apocalyptic horrors of *28 Days Later* and *Walking Dead*, there are glimpses of a more humanised incarnation.

The current fascination with the zombie may well be due to the need to fill a monstrous gap left by the assimilation of the vampire into human society.[17] But the non-vampiric Undead is also employed – particularly in Young Adult fiction – to dramatise coping with death. This is spelt out unmistakably by the bereaved heroine of one revenant novel for young adults: 'I was lost and looking for answers to big questions about love, loss, and the meaning of life.'[18] Narratives of the returning dead enable these big questions to be posed, and 'closure' (a favourite word) to be achieved.

Thus the Undead may appear in zombie fictions as alien and monstrous but there are also narratives featuring returning loved ones (though here the zombification is usually sanitised, even prettified) where a new, sympathetic zombie has been constructed. Sympathy for the zombie may be elicited through the depiction of pitiable, but non-human and barely sentient creatures, or simply through respect for the human beings they once were and for their families.[19] More rarely, though, the zombie is granted autonomy and a voice. This may be revealed through autodiegesis, revealing the interiority of a trapped subjectivity; the self-narration reveals one who is conscious but denied corporeal autonomy, usually because they have been enslaved; or, alternatively, through the same narrative voice and perspective, pity is aroused through the narrator's dawning awareness of their approaching loss of subjectivity as they become a zombie.[20]

The father of the modern filmic zombie, George Romero, in one of the most recent of the series which began with *Night of the Living Dead* (1968), portrays the beleaguered human community surrounded by zombies who appear to be regaining their subjectivity, acting out parodic scenes of their dimly remembered lives of normality, invoking sympathy (*Land of the Dead* (2005)). In Eden Maguire's Young Adult *Beautiful Dead* series, the revenants are paradoxically corporeal phantoms rather than resurrected corpses; they bear signs of their death, but not grotesquely. The Undead in Yvonne Woon's *Dead Beautiful* (2010) are closer to the zombie, as they are in Rachel Caine's adult urban fantasy, the ingenious *Working Stiff* (2011), with its heroine reanimated, not supernaturally but through nanotechnology. But none of these revenants is characterised by the abjection of the 'true' zombie.[21] These are still exceptions, however; effective because of that exceptional nature, feeding upon the image of the classic, abject zombie. However, despite these isolated models of sympathetic zombies, none of them is perceived as a social being. None of them aspire to be citizens.[22]

Yet one of the most dialectically subtle of recent presentations of legally undead would-be citizens is to be found in Daniel Waters's *Generation Dead* (2008) novel for young adults, and its sequels, *Kiss of Life* (2009) and *Passing Strange* (2010). Waters's significant gesture is to choose zombies as the subject of a teen romance and thriller rather than the over-fashionable vampires. All over the US, teenagers, and only teenagers, are mysteriously coming back from the dead, but with their movements and, perhaps, thought processes impaired, and sometimes bearing the wounds of their death. The choice of zombie over the more glamorous vampire is crucial, I think, for Waters's eliciting sympathy and exploration of agency. *Generation Dead* and its sequels tackle identity politics more subtly and acutely than others in this genre, highlighting through satire and the paranoid thriller subplot the limitations and indeed ideological force of that politics – yet recognising the need to affirm particular identity within some sort of more collective affiliation.[23]

What *Generation Dead* does is to portray minorities sympathetically in terms of both discrimination and powerlessness (a powerlessness which may, indeed, be a biological disability). It also explores with great sensitivity questions of identity, particularly as experienced by young adults; yet it also satirises the language and uncritical assumptions of varieties of identity politics. Over the three novels in the series, a sinister narrative accumulates which exposes the latent threat of the state and allied sectors. Waters delineates how easily identity politics can be appropriated by these forces as ideological cover for oppression. Thus, the satire is not a cheap, or indeed illiberal, gibe, but works as part of this unmasking.

There are various levels and strategies of reading that can be applied to this text, which mediate the problems of identity politics in different ways. On one level, difference here is rooted in biology; here, scientists investigate the cause of this phenomenon that has hit America's young; the kinds of causes speculatively invoked are themselves revealing about contemporary cultural anxieties. Thus Waters oscillates between a literal representation of an imaginary physical difference (though akin to disability) and a metaphor for cultural exclusion – a very productive ambiguity that calls into question assumptions concerning naturalness, essence and immutability that so often surround notions of difference (from radical as well as from conservative or oppressive perspectives).

The empathy that the text creates is one with people who are struggling with very real barriers to their mobility and self-expression; the cultural politics is that of disabled people. The search to establish a convincing and materialist origin helps to satisfy the demands of verisimilitude. But there is more to this; a very important strand emerges out of this concern with causality. In Waters there is an almost existentialist concern with becoming and with self-fashioning, which is thus very much to do with the origins of identity itself. On another level of reading, difference is akin to 'race' or, more nebulously, 'ethnicity'; on yet another, it represents lifestyle. At this latter level, the zombies mirror Waters's (living) heroine, Phoebe, who is herself culturally apart: she is a Goth, interested in literature and non-mainstream music, estranged from the more conventional teenagers around her.

Waters is very good at dissecting the vicissitudes of the language of prejudice: we encounter first the raw and unthinking language of the school canteen: 'zombies, dead heads, corpsicles' (2).[24] Then, refracted through the bigoted coach's voice, we hear the first phase of condescendingly PC language imposed from above: 'We are required to refer to them as the *living impaired*, okay? Not dead kid. Not *zombie*, or *worm buffet*, or [in the first of many allusions to horror movies and their clichés] *accursed hellspawn*, either' (23). Then, the neutral term, 'differently biotic' is introduced, with its hint of celebration of the fact of difference; previously, says the high-school principal, 'the term diversity had been most typically used to describe a diversity of culture, religion, ethnicity, or sexual orientation'. Now, 'the term may also be applied to diverse states of being' (100). Finally, from the most angered and alienated dead teens themselves, the 'Z' word is actively reclaimed as a symbol of positivity and revolt, and of difference as separatism. I shall often use the word 'zombie' myself in this chapter, asking forgiveness for any offence this may cause.

Zombies, in Afro-Caribbean mythology, are created slaves. By contrast, vampires are always empowered, if not legally so. The 'vegetarian' vampires of Stephanie Meyer may have willed away their viciousness but the temptation to succumb to blood lust is always there. They are not 'out', however, and do not publicly claim rights. Charlaine Harris's vampires are a bit more complex and, because of the invention of synthetic blood, can be portrayed more sympathetically, as aliens who can make claims to be integrated. In Laurell K. Hamilton there is a suggestion that the rights have been claimed illegitimately. But Waters's undead are threatless, and significantly powerless, and have *no* rights. Here, then, questions of identity intersect with the state.

In Waters's novel, a proposed 'Undead Citizens Act' explicitly compares 'differently biotic people to illegal immigrants' (276).[25] Immigration presents significant concerns to Western establishments, and here the Undead represent those without citizenship – Hispanic migrant workers, or black people in earlier struggles. The Undead are stateless, yet unsupervised; there are loopholes in the state apparatus, since 'your social security card expires when you do, right? So no one is really keeping records on dead kids, are they?' (277). And the spectre of the state is explicitly raised by Karen, the enigmatic dead girl. The presence of sinister Men in Black at various points in the narrative has alerted the reader to hints of a conspiracy thriller plot. Here, it begins to take a more definite form: '"I'm not sure the government wants to wait around for their shadow organization to take us out," Karen said. "I guess it would … be quicker to have us all registered and shipped to the Middle East"' (277).[26] Thus Waters gives us the context of an ongoing, unnamed war – one much like current ones where excluded working-class youth are specifically targeted for drafting; in this world, 'There's legislation that calls for the mandatory conscription of all differently biotic persons within three weeks of their traditional death' (277).

The legal void leaves the Undead curiously free: 'The laws … do not always protect … the dead. And sometimes they do. A parent is no longer legally … responsible … to take care of their … deceased children. Colette was abandoned. As were many of us' (204). To this Phoebe responds, somewhat wistfully, 'if I tried to go and live in an abandoned house somewhere they would come and get me and put me in a reform school or something' (204). They can escape parental supervision and that of the state, but also eschew their love or protection. Thus, the Undead are abandoned, but their future is indeterminate – a state that young people are often intensely aware of and made existentially anxious by – and thus a theme of determination, determination by self or by culture or biology, of essences and personality emerges. This lawlessness, arising out of the enforced denial of rights, mirrors the indeterminacy subtly argued for in Waters's rejection of mechanical materialism; paradoxically, then, the expulsion of the dead from society spurs their sense of agency. Thus death grants freedom to the dead Karen: 'She's crazy. It's like dying has given her a license to act how she pleases, to do whatever she wants. Death seems to have frightened some of the kids, but I think it's freed her in some way' (300).

With *Generation Dead*, we are back on the same high school terrain that *Buffy*, and, more recently, L. J. Smith's The Vampire Diaries and Meyer's Twilight series explore. The setting allows the usual (here, very effective) exploration of the issues of becoming a young adult: love and sexuality (thus sharing concerns with the adult 'paranormal romance' genre); looming adult responsibility; and developing a sense of who one is, where one belongs – identity, in other words.

Phoebe and her best friends – Margi; and Colette, now dead and risen – are

Goths, mocked by jocks and cheerleaders but defiant and able to articulate what defines their specificity.[27] Phoebe's Goth identity is both defensive and assertive:

> Phoebe was used to being stared at. Her all-black wardrobe, an even mix of vintage and trendy clothing, practically guaranteed she would get odd looks from her classmates [...] She didn't mind. She found that her look repelled people she didn't want to talk to and attracted those she did. The goth look wasn't nearly as popular as it once was, probably due to the appearance of the living impaired, but to Phoebe that just gave the style a subtle hint of irony, a private joke to be shared by a special few. (45–46)

But Phoebe is fascinated by and attracted to 'the living impaired' because of their otherness, 'their bravery' (32) – and the specific otherness of the mystery of death, thus invoking the perennial angst of young adults making sense of the big questions. Phoebe is an introspective, poetic, and slightly morbid girl, whose favourite song titles always contain the words 'sorrowful, rain, or death' (26), whose thoughts often drift to 'the topic of death' and 'What is it like to be dead? What is it like to be living impaired?' (6). At this point, the Undead are not standing in for any kind of ethnicity or disability; for Phoebe, they, the 'certain bravery' they display in adjusting to life once more, and the whole process of returning (and implicitly, death itself) are stimuli for her own moral and intellectual development: 'There's so many questions, so much mystery about the whole thing' (32).

Phoebe's childhood friend, Adam, who loves her and then dies and is reborn for her, is developing a sensibility that sets him apart from his more uncritical footballer friends, and this, very perceptively, is bound up with class – the arena usually most effaced in identity politics. Adam is trapped by his class position, his future rigidly constrained: 'Without football he wouldn't be going anywhere: he'd end up staying in Oakville all his life, working at his stepfather's garage, lifting tires and handing wrenches to his stepbrothers' (58). Yet he reshapes himself in a way that Pete, the bigoted jock and Adam's former friend, refuses to do. Adam chooses not to be bound by the identities which threaten to entrap him, either working-class or jock, but he will encounter the far more ineluctable ones of death, then living death.

Unlike Phoebe's, Pete's strategy towards the mystery of death is to direct the fear into hatred and resentment for his dead love Julie, who has abandoned him and turned monstrous (by *not* returning):

> He wanted all the dead kids in their graves, where they belonged.
> Like Julie.

　　Maybe if Julie had come back, he thought. Maybe if she'd come back he'd feel differently, and he'd learn to stand them despite their blank staring eyes and their slow, croaking voices. But she didn't come back anywhere except in his dreams. And now, ever since the dead began to rise, when she returned even to that secret place, she came back changed. She wasn't the girl he'd held hands with at the lake, she wasn't the first girl he'd kissed on the edge of the pine woods. She wasn't his first and only love.

　　She was a monster. (23–4)

The weight of the metaphor shifts. The Undead begin here as aliens, who need to be repatriated to the state of death back where they belong. For Pete, femaleness and death are parallel; he directs his anger at both; each motivates the other, and so Waters here is using the Undead to stand in for women.

　　Pete and his mates bond through that male dialect which treats everything female as sexual object – even if dead: 'I think I could bring her back to life, if you catch my meaning?' (19), unconsciously himself blurring the boundaries; or Goth: 'She ought to get some colour in her cheeks and start wearing normal chick clothes. She looks like a freakin' worm burger, you know?' (16). So the Otherness of the Undead at moments like this represents the otherness of the feminine, inspiring attraction and rage simultaneously. Thus the Undead once more have a metaphoric fluidity about them in that they can represent any of gender, sexuality, race and illness at different moments.

　　In Pete's consciousness, the unknown sexuality of women slides threat-eningly from the relatively unthreatening nymphomania attributed to all women to the deplorable coupling with the radically Other: 'I might get pretty damn upset', he tells her, 'that the girl I had pegged for a closet nymphomaniac is really a closet necrophiliac' (80). It then careers into the perhaps less unacceptable perversion of zoophilia: 'A living, breathing blossoming sixteen-year-old girl having a thing for a dead kid? It was just plain unnatural. Why not go and lie down with a farm animal? At least an animal is *alive*' (80). That 'closet' suggests the possibility of lesbianism too – although, and characteristically, Pete confusedly claims Phoebe is also a virgin whom he is certain he will be able to 'convert' (16).[28]

　　Pete senses the immanent power of revolt among the oppressed, and voices the familiar fears of economic and sexual replacement through invoking the clichés of Hollywood:

　　'I don't think they're human, and they're certainly not alive. I'm just waiting for the day when they throw down and start shuffling around trying to eat our brains [...] what next? Worm burgers making your milk shakes down at the Honeybee? Taking up scholarship money that should be going to kids with a life ahead of them? Just wait until a zombie wants to date your sister, Harris.' (149–50)

There are class anxieties being expressed here; those of white working-class people made vulnerable by economic instability and sensing their disposability.

Thus the Undead may be ethnically, culturally, sexually Other, and Waters self-consciously invokes the politics of diversity as a background. Waters often depicts the sudden crisis that has struck US youth in terms of 1960s politics, the era of the Civil Rights movement and birth of what would later be identity politics. The Undead are 'bussed over' (18), echoing 1960s programmes for racial integration. The significantly named Dallas Jones, the first dead person to rise, is caught on CCTV in what is referred to as 'the Zapruder film' (6; 117–21); Colette even dances like a hippy girl from Woodstock (368). The final decision of the persecuted and radicalised zombies of 'going underground' in the second book, *Kiss of Life*, has strong echoes of 1960s radical groups like the Weathermen, but has a distinctly twenty-first-century resonance with one of the framed Undead, Tak, being labelled as a 'terrorist'.[29]

Waters engages in some very sharp mimicry of the different voices of identity politics as it later became absorbed into mainstream US society; often satirically, sometimes with sympathy. The language of assimilation is captured perfectly in all its utopianism. The philanthropic, zombie-supporting Hunter Foundation claims: 'Our goal is the complete integration of differently biotic persons into society. We dream of a world where a differently biotic person can walk down a crowded city street without fear' (103). This recalls the 1960s yearnings of Luther King; yet this is parody, too, and the Foundation will turn out to be not all it seems.

Liberal integrationism can be tragically ineffectual. In this fiction, the legal status of the differently biotic is horrifically void – like Blacks at one time in the Deep South, like Jews in the Third Reich, they can be burnt alive; Phoebe and Margi watch a horrific piece of news footage:

> Two men with jerricans were pouring gasoline on a sluggish living impaired girl whose arms were bound behind her to a metal basketball pole set into concrete, like you'd see in a schoolyard. The girl went up in a sudden rush of yellow flame, and her twitching seemed to grow more animated, but that might have been a trick of the flames dancing around her. (121)

Note the grim irony of the parodic resurrection invoked by Waters's wordplay on 'animation' (something he does with cognate terms throughout the book). As Waters hints, talk about integration is cruelly ridiculous here, where 'talking about how parents should raise their differently biotic youth and help them integrate into a society that still does not have any legislation that prevents burning them at the stake' exposes the impotence of mere tolerance (121). There is a telling moment when Phoebe questions the shallowness of some versions of tolerance, or of a bland universalism, wondering 'why everyone thought that commonality was the lynchpin to the whole "why can't we all just get along" deal' (134). But, immediately, she faces the sheer crassness and banality of the bigotry of the protesters at the football match where the undead Tommy is about to play; they are bearing slogans like 'DEAD = DAMNED' and linking intolerance, in an all too familiar way, with US national identity, perverting the Enlightenment goals of 'LIFE, LIBERTY AND THE PURSUIT OF HAPPYNESS [sic]' (135). The opening speech by the state representative invokes a contrasting, liberal narrative of nationhood, which has incorporated the 1960s struggles of 'American athletes' like Jesse Owens and Billie Jean King against the 'obstacles of injustice and hate' of those who would 'shame our country' (137–8). Yet already, ominously, Phoebe's conspiracy-loving father has identified the dark underside of national identity and the state's coercive power – the Men in Black who first appear here among the crowd and who later appear to be linked to covert state activity.

One manifestation of how US society has absorbed identity politics is represented in the book by Skip Slydell Enterprises, who are what are currently, voguishly, called 'social entrepreneurs'. The ideology under examination here is that capitalism can be benevolent; profit can be accumulated through serving nobly philanthropic, even radical, ends. Waters accurately captures the glib slickness of business speak, of self-help and motivation talk, and the 'culture' word gets tossed around: 'How can we make that acclimation happen?' asks Slydell; 'Change the culture' (190). 'Culture' here is *not* essentialised, however; on the contrary, as with much postmodern theory, it is as endlessly mobile as capital itself.

In this ideology, the transformation of culture is achieved through a simple linguistic redefinition (one thinks of Richard Rorty here):

> 'That's the second necessary ingredient of culture change, people. The second key to transformation. Conflict. Radical action coupled with radical response [...] There was a reason that I used strong words with you, impolite words like 'zombie' and 'undead' and 'bloodbags' [that is, the living], and the reason was not because I wanted to be offensive. I used those words because *right now* they are radical words, and I wanted to provoke a radical reaction in you [...] The first step toward transforming a culture is to give names and definitions to the transformative aspects of that culture. You are *zombies*, kids. And you need to use that term with pride.' (195)

All the materiality of culture (underpinned, in this particular case, by the brute biology here of being dead) has vanished. Eagleton observes how:

> [i]n the dogmatic culturalism of our day […] the suffering, mortal, needy, desiring body which links us fundamentally with our historical ancestors, as well as with our fellow beings from other cultures, has been converted into a principle of cultural difference and division.[30]

Not only is this culturalism divisive, it has been, all too easily, co-opted by entrepreneurs such as Slydell, whose 'conflict' and 'radical action' is, of course, mere sales talk. This is a brasher version of the careful politeness of the PC talk elsewhere. Waters has fun with the slogans on Slydell's range of T-shirts: 'Dead … And Loving It', 'Zombie Power!', and (inspiring this book and its parallel project) 'Open Graves, Open Minds' (196). Ultimately this is about shifting commodities. It is a picture of how capitalism voraciously, vampirically, seizes on both youth culture and that of minorities:

> 'I need a street team […] to help me get this message out. Many of these products are going to be carried in Wild Things! stores and at select music outlets. […] I want you to think on […] what other products – be they fashion, entertainment, whatever – you think we could put out that would help us get our message out there, and really start changing the world.' (197)

Tommy, the articulate undead boy to whom Phoebe is attracted, becomes a celebrated spokesperson for the zombies, and an advocate of pacifist reformism. He takes advantage of the Internet's potential to host a twenty-first-century public sphere, where unconstrained discourse can take place and rights argued for, by setting up a blog.[31] His blog acutely penetrates what the corporate 'necrohumanitarian experiment' (207) is about and his critique of it has much validity:

> Skip's main thesis seems to be that the zombie community can achieve legitimacy through consumerism and sloganeering […] You can't help but question his motives, which almost certainly are profit driven, but at the same time you can't help but be drawn into his circle of 'positive transformation.' If there is cheesy packaging around a universal truth, does that make the universal truth any less valid?[32] (208)

Tommy here has identified what Marx saw as the contradictory energies of capitalism which (if only in its early phases) is both motivated by private interest and yet has a transformative energy towards universalism.

In contrast to social transformation through consumption and liberal tolerance, or by pacifist reformism, Waters also presents the position of urgent and angry action. Tak (an undead boy who advocates separatism and forceful resistance) is dramatised in dialogue with Tommy as the background of bigoted 'bioist' terror escalates, with Men in Black and mysterious white vans being closely associated with the murders of zombies (308–12).[33] Waters is not afraid to show that Tak's violence might be perfectly rational when confronted by a state that is indifferent or even complicit in the murderous suppression of difference, where 'The police will do nothing. Words … will do nothing' (310).

The boundaries between the dead and the living are continually blurred, particularly with the pale, enigmatic and disturbingly quick Karen, who doesn't 'move like a dead girl' and has 'a slight, barely perceptible smile', whereas 'Most of the other zombies [Adam had] seen wore blank expressions' (38). This blurring is reinforced by language play throughout, as an ostinato theme with the existential subject of changing life, of the borders between life and death, between identities, shifting as Angela Hunter's smile which, 'like her legs, could bring the dead back to life' (128). Thus Alish Hunter declares that the work at the Foundation to 'change lives' (129). Pete, watching the zombie, Evan, whom he is about to murder, observes 'his jerky undead limbs trying to coax the machine to life' (286). As a TV narrator says, 'The presence of the living impaired has irrevocably altered the American way of life – no pun intended', revealing the instability of the very idea of an America encountering difference (118).

Waters performs brilliant verbal plays on life and death throughout the novel. Here, he weaves this wordplay into flirtatiousness:

> Karen laughed […] 'You're sweet. I'm just trying to bring my date, Kevin here back to life.' Her hand left Phoebe's skin, which tingled where the dead girl had touched her.
> [...]
> 'And the rest of these boys,' she said. 'I'm trying to knock dead.'
> 'Well,' Tommy said, 'you are drop dead … gorgeous.' (355)

Karen's sexual attractiveness is frequently seen as life-giving, even setting Phoebe's flesh 'tingling' (357) (there is a hint of sexual ambiguity about her). Unlike Coleridge's pale-featured, 'white as leprosy' undead figure, the female 'Life-in-Death', she vivifies rather than 'thicks man's blood with cold'.[34] This interplay is more than just wit; resurrecting lovers will become central to the plot and in the sequels, *Kiss of Life* (whose title makes this clear), and *Passing Strange*, which focuses on Karen (and whose title is a triple play on the idiom itself, on 'passing' as a euphemism for death, and on 'passing' as hiding a deviant identity behind a 'normal' one). This destabilising of life/death is part of the critique of essences which makes *Generation Dead* a sympathetic, but critical, view on identity politics.

This linguistic display of anti-essentialism is paralleled by the way Waters fervently asserts the agency of human subjects through a critique of mechanism. Alish Hunter, of the apparently humane Hunter Foundation, claims he 'enjoys wearing a lab coat and conducting experiments like a mad scientist' (129); a movie reference which is prophetic. Waters directs much of his satire against the narrow instrumental use of reason that treats human beings as thing-like and justifies their oppression.

In what is still a predominately scientific age, twentieth- and twenty-first-century undead fiction often proffers materialist causal explanations for the state of undeadness: viruses are posited in Richard Matheson's *I Am Legend* (1954), and more tentatively in the Sookie Stackhouse books. One would-be scientific explanation of the returning teenagers that circulates in *Generation Dead* is of a 'mold spore or something living in their brains' (300); this is a Gothic image in itself, one of possession, however much 'spore' makes it seem physiological. In one of his many cinematic references, Waters invokes a 'Frankenstein Formula theory', where 'a certain mixture of teenage hormones and fast food preservatives' is posited as a cause of the new teenage condition (7). Again, Waters identifies anxieties, contemporary and longer-term, over the threatening difference of youth and over modernity and consumption, and projects them on to the Other – but in a very knowing way.

But, without necessarily being anti-rationalist, Waters wants to see the creation of undeadness – and thus identity – as outside the realm of mechanical causality. Waters destabilises any kind of naturalism, with a certain sacrifice of verisimilitude perhaps, in order to further his attack on the reification of human beings. Resurrection is not presented as particularly uncanny; the supernatural is not invoked. It simply happens; inexplicably and as contingently as life itself. Other causes are offered by various characters, all signifying contemporary anxieties: inoculations, junk food, radioactivity – even alien abduction and the Apocalypse. New media are also blamed; such innovations have persistently summoned up mechanistic ideas of causality on young people's behaviour since the growth of novels and literacy in the eighteenth century. This is against the grain, of course, of Waters's existentialist stance. For example, one proffered cause of the young people's undead state has been the malign influence of 'First-person shooter games' where, as Karen dryly points out, the target is 'Usually zombies' (320–1). Waters's cultural references are always witty and never pointless. Because – and here lies the dialectical complexity – perhaps in some ways the dehumanising of the other in videogames *does* sanction violence towards the different, without invoking a mechanically causal power, just as the imagery of that earlier source of cultural anxiety, the cinema, is portrayed as legitimating bigotry throughout this narrative.

Yet Waters does not let such a position appear without presenting, dialectically, a counter position. Thus the bigots' rumours portray zombies as automata; Pete's uncritical absorption of myth posing as science shows how scientistic explanations of difference dehumanise people and strip them of agency, rendering them objects: 'I saw on the news that they think some kind of parasite crawls into their brains and controls their bodies after death' (342). This is a horror movie plot in itself, illustrating the ideological power of Gothic imagery when coupled with mechanical materialism. But Pete applies a similar reification to himself. Unlike Adam, he is unable to reject the bad faith of clinging to an essential nature and define an existential project of his own.[35] Waters continually challenges the objectification of human beings in his work, whether this is performed by characters on themselves or to others.

I have shown how Waters vividly articulates, through mimicry and parody, questions and arguments around identity politics as they have become appropriated or assimilated by contemporary Western culture. This is polyphonic, in Bakhtin's sense, with the latter's stress on the heteroglossal rendering of multiple voices as well as positions. The indeterminacy of the tenor in the zombie metaphor facilitates Waters's technique of shifting perspectives to build up this ensemble of arguments and ideologies of difference. And this parallels his refusal to countenance essences or the mechanical determination of human behaviour. This is a stance which also refuses to embrace an essential identity as the foundation of claims to autonomy, as in the varieties of identity politics that Eagleton identifies as '[t]he most uninspiring kind':

> those which claim that an already fully fledged identity is being repressed by others. The more inspiring forms are those in which you lay claim to an equality with others in being free to determine what you might wish to be. Any authentic affirmation of difference thus has a universal dimension.[36]

The existentialist strand in *Generation Dead* affirms precisely that freedom 'to determine what you might wish to be'.

The lack of subjectivity and autonomy that almost axiomatically define the zombie narrowly constrain its potential to elicit sympathy. Its abject repulsiveness is a further barrier and certainly bars it from the role of paranormal lover. Faeries and vampires have their glamour and hypnotic allure; even the werewolf or shape-shifter can be a lover in their human form (their bestial *alter ego* is, of course, highly effective in figuring human sexuality in these narratives). Therefore, Waters's portrayal of returning dead who, retaining their physical wounds and having the impeded consciousness and stumbling gait of the zombie, engage in love affairs and struggle for their rights, is a daring and tricky narrative move. Through this, he is able to explore identity politics with great depth and flexibility. What Waters does is, I think, unique: these Undead are humans, despite their shambling gait and mutilated bodies and absence of a pulse, engaged in dialogue with others. Contrast, too, his zombies with the revenants of Yvonne Woon's *Dead Beautiful*: 'When we reanimate, we're born into the best version of ourselves [...] The strongest. The smartest. The most beautiful' (424). This is far from Romeroesque; it is simply a different embodiment of the utopian transcendence that makes Meyer's vampires marvellously intense lovers, scintillating and super-strong. There is more to Woon's fine novel than just that, but I want to emphasise just how original Waters's concept is.

The Gothic mode, of which dark fantasy or paranormal romance novels are a contemporary reincarnation (though a 'romancing' of it),[37] has always had some kind of relationship to Enlightenment thought, whether reacting against it or siding with rationalism against dark, archaic forces. In the Enlightenment project, rights have to be fought and argued over; they arise out of the contestation of powers and are conceived through unconstrained dialogue as theorised by Jürgen Habermas;[38] this dialogism, in itself, dissolves identity boundaries. This process presupposes autonomous agents who are not thinglike, not deterministically constrained by their essences. Habermas explicitly connects the discursive activity of human subjects with both their claiming of rights and their agency:

> What raises us out of nature is the only thing whose nature we can know: *language*. Through its structure autonomy and responsibility are posited for us. Our first sentence expresses unequivocally the intention of universal and unconstrained consensus.[39]

Risen mysteriously out of death, Waters's Generation Dead articulate their claims to autonomy and responsibility, remaking and questioning the language that reifies them. In his humane, literate and witty novels, Waters shows these rights in formation and also, open-endedly, adumbrates a politics of active subjects claiming their common humanity against the forces that would objectify them and reduce them to dead things.

Notes

1 Heyes, 'Identity Politics'. For a full account of the rise of identity politics, see Nicholson, *Identity before Identity Politics*. Nicholson is broadly sympathetic; for a liberal and a radical left critique of identity politics in favour of universalism, see respectively Gitling, *The Twilight of Common Dreams* and Eagleton, *The Idea of Culture*.

2 As described in our introductory chapter above and explored in other chapters throughout this book.

3 See Clive Bloom's entertaining account, 'Day of the Dead'.

4 See, in particular, Lindsey Scott's Chapter 7, but other chapters engage with this too.

5 See Conrad Aquilina's Chapter 2 above.

6 And as performed by Yarbro in the Saint-Germain series, then on a grand scale by Coppola and, later, subtly explored from various angles in Joss Whedon's *Buffy* and *Angel*. These generic labels originate from retailers and publishers; it would be worthwhile to explore the relationship between such commercially motivated taxonomies and the more rigorous classification that could emanate from genre theory. The genres, or subgenres, overlap somewhat: Waterstone's, the booksellers, have applied 'dark romance' to young adult fiction and 'dark fantasy' to books for older readers, though both seem to intend predominately female readerships. Fred Botting's conjunction of Gothic and Romance in *Gothic Romanced* is a promising approach to these texts. It places it more precisely in a context and it avoids the now all-too broad category of simply 'Gothic'. On the problems of an all-encompassing, ahistorical use of the term, see Warwick, 'Feeling Gothicky?'

7 The vampiric subcultures in these two films are, Nicola Nixon argues, '"bad" families who represent the potential decay' of American ideals of 'normalized family values', and they 'conclude with a retrenchment of the good family unit' ('When Hollywood Sucks', pp. 127, 126).

8 Eagleton, *The Idea of Culture*, pp. 126–7. All ellipses in this chapter which represent editorial deletions are enclosed in square brackets.

9 Two essays from Stacey Abbot's collection illuminate the way that Caritas is an arena for the politics of difference: Abbott, 'Kicking Ass and Singing "Mandy"', and Beeler, 'Outing Lorne', in Abbott (ed.), *Reading Angel*.

10 Charlaine Harris, *Dead Until Dark* (2001), p. 1. The HBO TV series based on these novels, Alan Ball's *True Blood* (2008–), raises issues of race and sexuality more explicitly; Michelle Smith explores this in Chapter 12 above.

11 Hence the USA is 'the only country in the world' where 'vampirism' is legal, but vampires do not have the vote (*The Laughing Corpse* (1994), p. 12).

12 Hamilton, *The Laughing Corpse*, p. 90.

13 This is in addition to the more recent sympathetic portrayals of them; Dracula and Carmilla already had hints of sex appeal in the novels and their cinematic adaptations developed this. Now, alongside the humanisation of the monster there has been

the immense growth of 'paranormal romance', where supernatural creatures and humans become lovers.

14 Note 'faeries' rather than the more mundane 'fairies'; the former spelling is always used in these texts to signify the mythological authenticity and dark strangeness of these beings as opposed to twee little Victorians with butterfly wings.

15 Bond, 'When Love Is Strange'.

16 Christie and Lauro, Introduction, *Better Off Dead*, p. 2.

17 As Angela Tenga and Elizabeth Zimmerman argue in their forthcoming article, 'Vampire Gentlemen and Zombie Beasts'.

18 Maguire, *Jonas*, p. 2.

19 As, for example, in the HBO series *Walking Dead* and in a powerful story by Jonathan Maberry, 'Family Business', in the excellent 2010 collection edited by Christopher Golden, *Zombie*, pp. 177–249.

20 For the enslaved consciousness, see David Liss, 'What Maisie Knew', in Golden, pp. 11–55, and Caine's *Working Stiff*. For the onset of the loss of autonomy, see Rick Hautala, 'Ghost Trap', in Golden, pp. 349–70.

21 'Abjection' in Kristeva's sense, which accounts for the power and dubious pleasure of the zombie narrative (Kristeva, *The Powers of Horror*).

22 With the possible exception of the Marc Fratto film, *Zombies Anonymous* (2006) – a comedy in which zombies fight for legal identity and recognition.

23 Linda Nicholson suggests a like accommodation of identity politics to universalism, where there are 'degrees of commonality interspersed with difference' and where 'particular identities will both vary among members of any particular identity grouping while also expressing elements of similarity', p. 185.

24 All references to *Generation Dead* are to the cited edition and are in parentheses.

25 The parallels of racist registration acts in Nazi Germany and apartheid South Africa (as well as voter registration in the Southern USA) hardly need pointing out, but there are fictional parallels and precedents in Hamilton, Harris, and, more distantly, with the Mutant Registration acts in Marvel Comics's *Uncanny X-Men* (from the 1980s onwards) and associated films. For the details of popular cultural artefacts, Wikipedia is often an authoritative source, and the history of various Registration Acts in the Marvel universe is documented thoroughly in the article 'Registration Acts (Comics)'.

26 Waters's ellipses indicate the struggle to form speech that afflicts the risen dead.

27 Catherine Spooner in Chapter 9 above explores the intriguing links between vampire texts and Goth subculture; her emphasis on assimilation is of interest here, too.

28 *Passing Strange* will develop Waters's fluid exploration of otherness and strangeness into lesbian romance.

29 Waters, *Kiss of Life*, p. 407. And is there a deliberate allusion in *Passing Strange* to *Soul on Ice*, Eldridge Cleaver's Black Panther manifesto of 1968? Tak, the radical zombie leader, wants to persuade 'his people' away from Tommy's Luther King-like

'philosophy of civil disobedience'; he thinks of them as '"souls" under the ice' (where they are literally hiding) (p. 306).

30 Eagleton, *The Idea of Culture*, p. 111.

31 After the process famously described by Jürgen Habermas in *The Structural Transformation of the Public Sphere*.

32 Tommy's blog has been reproduced on line by Waters as *My So-Called Undeath*. Note how this paratext supplements the central narrative by suggesting further the dialogic struggle for Undead rights; here, in the arena of the internet.

33 Tak and his allies form their own group identity, labelling themselves 'The Lost Boys' (312); compare J. M. Barrie's Lost Boys, echoed by Schumacher's *The Lost Boys*.

34 Coleridge, *The Rime of the Ancient Mariner* (1834), lines 167–86 (*Complete Poems*, pp. 167–86).

35 Bad faith is 'the view that we are what we are in the way *things* or *objects* are what *they* are; that a man is a father or a waiter or a homosexual the way "an oak tree is an oak tree", instead of being radically free and inescapably contingent beings, creatures whose being is their freedom' (Danto, *Sartre*, p. 33).

36 Eagleton, *The Idea of Culture*, p. 66.

37 'Romance,' according to Fred Botting, 'as it frames Gothic, seems to clean up its darker counterpart'; he has Coppola particularly in mind. And recent representations of the vampire, particularly in fiction for young adults, do seem to lose their unsettling and potentially subversive danger; here, romance, as Botting puts it, 'recuperates gothic excesses in the name of the heterosexual couple' (*Gothic Romanced*, p. 1). Yet not all 'dark romance' does so, and in *Generation Dead* the two genres presided over by Eros and Thanatos mate fruitfully, bringing forth their vivaciously undead progeny in a way that retains its critical bite.

38 In his later work; see, for example, 'Towards a Theory of Communicative Competence'.

39 Habermas, *Knowledge and Human Interests*, p. 314.

16

The elusive vampire:
folklore and fiction —
writing *My Swordhand Is Singing*

Marcus Sedgwick

EVER SINCE I BECAME a published author, in 2000, it was my strong ambition to write a vampire novel. Why? Well, simply, I thought it would be enormously good fun to do so. I grew up as a fan of vampire cinema and fiction. One summer in the early 1980s the BBC screened a series of classic horror double bills every Saturday night, beginning with Tod Browning's 1931 *Dracula*, and running through every sequel not only of that film but the Karloff Frankenstein series, *The Mummy*, and so on and so on. I was hooked. Not much later I started to read classic vampire fiction; Stoker, Le Fanu – the usual suspects.

So why, after the publication of my first book, when I got a contract to write another book, didn't I leap straight into writing a vampire novel? The answer lies in the above – there are thousands of vampire stories already. This, to any author not just wanting to climb on a bandwagon, is off-putting to say the least. What right do you have to add another vampire novel to the genre when there are so many already? And not just books: Stacey Abbott has since told me there are over two thousand vampire movies. If I had known that, I probably would never have written *My Swordhand Is Singing*.

To finish on this subject, I was writing *My Swordhand Is Singing* in 2005, before the days of *Twilight*. If *Twilight* had already happened, I would never have written *any* vampire novel. I'm not alone in this John Ajvide Lindqvist, author of *Låt den rätte romma in*, or *Let the Right One In*, told me the same thing; he wouldn't have gone near the subject if the *Twilight* phenomenon had already been under way.

What I said to myself, then, was that I couldn't write a vampire novel unless there was some point in doing so, by which I meant something a bit different, a new take on an old theme, something that hadn't, at least to my knowledge, been done before.

Finally, and rather ironically, the idea which came was this: in order to do something 'new', I would go back to the old. At the time I was preparing my book, although *Twilight* had not yet emerged from its grave, the trend for contemporary vampire fiction was very much leaning towards the vampire in modern settings; Charlaine Harris would be a perfect example for the adult market, Darren Shan for the Young Adult. I decided to retreat from this position, and return to the oldest European vampire stories I could find. I thought it would be interesting to read the vampire through folktales, predominantly from Eastern Europe, and see what those creatures were like, and make a book out of that world. If I had known at the time the implications of that idea, I might again have been deterred from writing my vampire novel, because the vampires I ended up reading about were very different from the ones I thought I knew.

Before going further, it seems wise to summarise the book for those unfamiliar with it. The story's hero is a young man called Peter, and the emotional centre of the book revolves around his relationship with his father, Tomas, an irascible drunk, and two teenage girls: first, Agnes, a local girl, and, secondly, Sofia, a newcomer, a gypsy. Peter and his father have spent their lives on the move, as itinerant workers, but finally seem to have settled in the village of Chust, where they are working as woodcutters. They've built a hut just out of the village, in a river fork, which Tomas has turned into an island by digging a long channel. Peter has no idea why, just as he fails to understand certain other strange goings on around the village: the strange events that surround the funeral of a local man named Radu only provoke great curiosity in Peter, and increasing tension with his father.

Very soon, however, the truth of what is occurring in the village cannot be hidden, as Peter learns that the villagers of Chust suspect the dead are not keeping to their graves, and are 'coming back'. As tensions rise not only between Tomas and Peter and the village but between father and son as well, Peter learns that his father has a hidden past, from before he was born, in which he was a vampire hunter, working alongside Sofia's father, and other gypsies.

As the novel progresses, the power of the vampires increases, owing to the influence of a figure Peter believed only to be fairy tale, the Shadow Queen, bringing matters to a violent conclusion as Peter learns about, and uses, a magical sword his father has kept hidden from him to free the village of the vampire threat.

That's probably enough of the plot to give context to what follows, suffice only to add that all this is taking place in 'The Land Beyond The

Figures 16.1 and 16.2.   The appearance of the vampire has come a long way since
Thomas Hutter (*in loco* Jonathan Harker) met Orlok (Dracula).
Angel's usual outward appearance gives no hint of his vampiric nature – *opposite*

Forest'; that is, Transylvania, in the early seventeenth century. The only other
thing I would like to say at this point is that at no point is the word 'vampire'
used in the novel (aside from the publisher's blurb, an unavoidable necessity).
The reasons for this I will return to later.

I'd been reading through the usual early vampire 'sources': Calmet,
Summers and so on, and then, one day in 2004, my brother, an academic
bookseller at the time, put into my hands a small plain blue hardback book
called *Vampires in the Carpathians*.[1] He wrote on a compliment slip, placed inside
for me to find: 'Another award may be hidden in this tome?! See you soon.'

So I read the book, by Pëtr Bogatyrëv, expecting it to be a thrilling account
of vampire lore. It wasn't. Not that it wasn't interesting, more that its title
belied its true content. The subtitle, *Magical Acts, Rites and Beliefs on the Subcarpathian Rus'*, was a more accurate description of the contents. Bogatyrëv's final
chapter, 'Apparitions and Supernatural Beings', does, however, contain some
folk stories of vampires. It was at this point that my 'belief system' about
vampires began to wobble, though I was a long way yet from realising how it
would, almost completely, be destroyed.

I think it would be worth stating at this point what was in my head. I now
clearly see the folly of my way of thinking, but hindsight is indeed a gift. I
was working away under the belief that somewhere, back in the dim and
unrecorded past, was a proto-vampire, from some early folktale. The original

vampire, the true monster, purest in form and deed. The one that had given rise, eventually, to all the others. I didn't expect to find it, but I thought I might get close, get close in the shape of a fairly coherent and unified system of beliefs, as evidenced through oral storytelling, in the region of the world that we fairly rightly describe as being the home of the vampire.

The vampire, under other names of course, is a creature found in the folktales of many different cultures, from across the world. I'm not going to be foolish enough to try and define the vampire here, but I would like to simplify matters with this two-point lay person's definition. First, a vampire is a human who returns from the grave after their own death, and second, because the first point can also apply to ghosts and zombies, a vampire drinks the blood of the living.

With this as a working definition, I was aware that there are vampires to be found in many corners of the world, but, since the genre of vampire fiction I was hoping to work within stems from the Eastern European tradition, I wanted to make that the subject of my search back in time, for what turned out to be a very elusive vampire indeed.

Let's spend five minutes brain-storming what more we know about the vampire, and by this I mean again what a lay person's knowledge of the vampire might cover. Our list of results might look something like this:

A: First, as above, the vampire is undead, and therefore immortal

B: Vampires drink the blood of the living

C: They are hurt or destroyed by sunlight, and thus:

D: They sleep in coffins by day, usually filled with earth from their homeland

E: They are killed by staking through the heart

F: They are afraid of holy things: holy water, crosses, etc.

G: They are repelled by garlic

H: They cannot cross running water

I: They have no reflection in a mirror

J: A new vampire is made by a vampire biting a human

K: They cannot enter your home unless invited

L: They can transform into bats, wolves and sometimes mist

There are other features we might mention here, but the list above will suffice to demonstrate how mistaken I was in my apparent knowledge of the vampire, because when I returned to the original vampire from Eastern European folklore, I discovered that almost every single thing I knew about the vampire turned out not to be 'true'.

A few examples from the folktales should illustrate. Selecting from the above list, let's begin:

B: The vampire drinks blood. Well, sometimes it does, as Emil Petrovici tells us: 'A dead person becomes a pricolici and he feeds on his relatives. When he is exhumed his rump is pointing upwards and there is blood on his lips.'[2]

But in many of the folk tales, there is no drinking of blood. Sometimes they take something a bit more solid: 'They say that a corpse leaves his grave as a moroi and feeds on his relatives. He prefers their hearts.'[3]

And then again, very often they consume nothing on their nocturnal outings, spending time quarrelling with each other at crossroads instead or, in the case of one particular variety from Mihalcea, whose peasants believe that it is mostly women who are vampires, they 'take' milk, from cows, or even from nursing mothers, removing the power of the beast or mother to produce.[4]

C/D: Sunlight. While many of these folktales take place at night, typically at evening gatherings and parties in the villages of Romania, I found no single mention of a vampire being destroyed or even damaged by sunlight, and while vampires are frequently described in their graves, there seems to be no reason to infer from this that they *have* to rest in their own soil every night. It appears that Murnau's *Nosferatu* was the moment that the notion of the destructive power of sunlight on the vampire entered the canon, even though, owing to technical limitations, Orlok skips about in Wisborg in what is clearly bright sunshine.

E: Staking the body is something that sometimes appears in the folklore, though more often the heart is removed and burned, as in the very recent case from Marotinul de Sus in 2005 that made international headlines.[5] What does seem to happen to the body a lot in the folklore is that the body is pierced with a small needle or other object suitable for making a small hole in it. Paul Barber is very convincing on the reasons for this activity.[6]

F: Holy things. The peasant of Eastern Europe seems to prefer a belt and braces approach to dealing with the vampire, and so they resort to both the use of apparently folkloric, superstitious methods of attack, such as the use of charcoal, nets or seeds in the grave as well as the recitation of the Gospel by the grave of a suspected vampire.

H: Contrary to the belief that a vampire cannot cross running water, witness this story from Kryve: 'When he meets people at the waterside, he kills them. People run away when they see him. I have often seen how he shines. Oh, does he shine! He goes to the waterside. He passes through the water.'[7]

I: Mirrors provide an interesting subject – once again I could find no reference to reflections anywhere. There is some talk of mirrors; however, all related to the many ways in which a vampire can be created.

J: Curiously enough, the one way in which we currently understand a vampire to be made, through an existing monster biting a human, does not appear in the folklore. But if that makes one feel safer, the 'truth' is more terrible: there are a myriad ways in which one may become a vampire. Petrovici gives a worrying list, including dying unmarried, dying unforgiven by one's parents, dying a suicide, a murder victim, having a breeze blow across a corpse before burial, having a dog or cat walk under or over a corpse before burial, or leaving a mirror facing into the room, not turned to the wall at this precarious time, or even, simply, being a bad person.[8]

No wonder then, that according to one tale from Botoşani: 'There was once a time when vampires were as common as leaves of grass, or berries in a pail ...'[9]

L: Bats. While Perkowski claims mention of bats in the folklore,[10] these accounts are acknowledged to be relatively late, and would seem to have become cemented in our modern view of the vampire by Rymer (pictorially at least on the frontispiece to *Varney the Vampire*) and Stoker, particularly when *Dracula* was adapted for the stage. But vampires in the older folklore do indeed turn into a rather bewildering array of creatures: horses, dogs, men,[11] pigs, sheep and moths.[12]

This seems a reasonable place to point out that by now I was thoroughly confused, and somewhat disappointed. I was looking for good, by which I mean frightening and/or horrific, things to base my story on, and so far I had had to unlearn almost everything I knew about the creature, and was instead left with talk of vampires drinking milk, vampires squabbling at crossroads, vampire sheep and garlic. Lots of garlic.

Furthermore, what 'facts' there did seem to be in the folklore were often contradictory, and I began to feel that, rather as the tale from Botoşani said, there were as many *types* of vampire as leaves of grass in the meadow.

To be honest, I was more than a little dispirited at this point. My great idea about returning to the vampire 'source' material seemed to have backfired. I assayed what I had: zombie-like creatures, not at all suave, nothing charismatic about them at all, and, as I said, garlic. The reason for the preponderance of garlic in these stories has been, I think, nicely explained by Paul Barber's pathological approach to the origin of the vampire: the smell of a corpse pre-burial signifying evil and requiring the scent of garlic flowers to overpower it.[13] But for my purposes, it was not a particularly riveting or indeed scary vegetable to write about.

Determining not to give up, I decided on a new strategy. First, I took a look at what else the folklore research had thrown up, aside from garlic and sheep, and, secondly, I decided to broaden my look at Romanian folklore from just that of vampires to other areas of folklore too.

Once I had got used to the idea that I no longer knew what a vampire was, which I concede, after thirty years of film lore, took a bit of doing, I began to realise there were other interesting things I could potentially use.

The accounts of vampire deterrents, for example. Millet seed, strewn on the ground, slowing a vampire down, or, in his coffin, slowing his exit until he has counted or picked up every seed.[14] Likewise, a net placed in a coffin requires the vampire to unpick each knot, sometimes at the rate of one a year, or a stick of charcoal, which must be used up by writing before the vampire can emerge to do his worst.

These things were fascinating to me – their seeming mundanity appeared to me to be a subtle gift, the chance to turn each one into something more sinister. Readers of *My Swordhand Is Singing* will be aware of how each of these things became evident in the final novel. And even a small detail like the transformation into the moth; when Tomas squashes a Death's Head moth beneath his fist at the start of the book, his son Peter doesn't know the significance of that, but Tomas does.

A story from Murgoci, 'The Girl and the Vampire', in which a girl gains proof that her nocturnal visitor is indeed a vampire by secretly attaching a thread to the back of his coat and following him to his grave after he leaves her house, was particularly useful to me. It reminded me of Theseus in the Minotaur's maze, but in reverse; the thread he follows brings him out to safety – the thread followed in the vampire tale takes our hero towards death itself.

In this way I began to amass some nice ingredients after all for my vampire novel from the very folklore on which I wanted it to be based. Next I came across something with only a tangential relation to vampires, but which nonetheless I found intriguing.

I'm talking here about the Shadow Queen. In the fourth part of James Frazer's *The Golden Bough*, *The Dying God*, he relates accounts of this figure from the gypsies of south-eastern Europe. Palm Sunday is known as Shadow Day, and it's then that certain ceremonies are observed in relation to the Shadow Queen, a figure of evil, an effigy of whom is burnt at this time. I'll quote the passage at length from the third edition (1906–1915):

> This Shadow Queen ... vanishes underground at the appearance of Spring, but comes forth again the beginning of Winter to plague mankind during that inclement season with sickness, hunger, and death ... In Transylvania the gypsies who live in tents clothe the puppet in the cast off garments of the woman who has last became a widow. The widow herself gives the clothes gladly for this purpose, because she thinks that being burnt they will pass into the possession of her departed husband, who will thus have no excuse for returning from the spirit-land to visit her.[15]

Note that while no mention of vampires is made at this point, my reading of the psychological or folkloric interpretation made by the Transylvanian peasant was enough to convince me that 'returning from the sprit-land' meant nothing other than the reappearance of a deceased family member in the unfortunate guise of a vampire.

Once again then, we see how 'unfinished business' on the mortal plane, even something so trivial as the want of clothing, is enough to make the dead return to the world of the living.

There is little more than the passage quoted above on the Shadow Queen, but it was enough to imagine an evil force, whose powers are at the greatest between the end of November, St Andrew's Eve, and the return of Spring symbolised in the first growth of holy basil around St George's Eve.

As a noble counterforce to the Shadow Queen, I then created the legend of the Winter King. For some time, I had been interested in the way in which history can turn into legend, and, sometimes, just how quickly this can happen. Reading accounts of Vlad Tepes's (Vlad III Dracula's) campaigns against the Turkish forces of the Sultan Mehmed, in co-operation with the Hungarian ruler Matthew Corvinus in the winter of 1461–1462, I created a legend of a 'Winter King'. The story, as presented in the novel, is of a 'real' figure, King Michael, whose defeat of the Turks in the winter forests has very rapidly turned into the stuff of legend. Now known as the Winter King, it is almost the spirit of the forest itself that has defeated the struggling enemy armies, lost and waylaid in the frozen and endless forests of Transylvania.

As McNally and Florescu state: 'According to Romanian tradition, the "mad" forest and the mountains were "brothers of the people" that ensured survival of the nation through the ages.'[16]

At this point, I had decided to do something I'd done with other books, namely to go to the place I was writing about. Most often, this just helps set a mood in your own mind as a writer, and can provide good local colour so that details are accurate and vivid. These things are hopefully true with *My Swordhand Is Singing*, and a short trip to the Maramures was enough to fill my mind with images and sounds of a very beautiful country, but also, to learn about a couple of other fascinating things.

As in all good vampire films, a conversation in a bar about what I was doing in the country led me to hear about the first of these: the *Nunta Mortului* – as documented in Gail Kligman's account of a particularly peculiar ritual from Transylvania – The Wedding of the Dead.

The *Nunta Mortului* is fully accounted for in Kligman's book, so I won't go into detail here, but in brief it is an ancient and still current ceremony from Transylvania in which, upon the death of a young unmarried person of the community, a living bride or groom is chosen to marry the deceased at the graveside. The reasoning behind the ceremony seems to lie in the belief, as mentioned above, that the time between death and burial is a perilous one for the deceased.

According to Stahl: 'To die unmarried is to die perilously, because the most important aspect of life has not been realised. Therefore, a symbolic wedding is performed for the deceased.'[17]

What is Stahl saying here? What is in peril after death, but the soul? Kligman clarifies: 'it is believed that individuals who leave behind a mortal enemy, an unresolved love affair, or other unfinished matters will return in the forms of their bodies that they no longer inhabit. These "beings" are generally known as "strigoi" (spirits, ghosts, the living dead).'[18]

Don't die unmarried: you'll become a vampire. That's the message.

Kligman quotes from the lament sung on such occasions:

Figure 16.3.   The Wedding of the Dead, or *Nunta Mortului*: here, a young bridesmaid
watches over the deceased 'bride'

> I've never seen such a bride
> That the priest comes to the house
> And crowns you on the table
> Bride in a coffin,
> Groom is with God.[19]

The nature of the death-wedding is both moving and unnerving, to say the
least, and I decided I wanted it to occur in my book. I left the details of the
ceremony itself as they are, but added, for the sake of tension on the story, the
addendum that the living party, in this case a teenage girl called Agnes, must
spend forty days in isolation, in a locked hut, away from the rest of the village.

The second thing I learned about on my trip is a song, a well-known song
to anyone in Romania, known as *The Miorița*.

This song is old and with many variants, and almost as many interpretations as variants; people argue as to the precise meaning of the strange story
contained in the lyrics, which goes as follows.

A young shepherd is working high in the mountains with two friends. One
day, a lamb (the Miorița) comes to the shepherd to warn him that his two
colleagues mean to kill him, jealous of his youth and beauty.

What the shepherd does at this point is what gives this ballad its mystery,
and ultimately, I believe, its power. Rather than use this information to run
away and save himself, the young shepherd accepts his fate and meets his death

at the hands of his jealous friends. The only thing he does before he dies is to ask of the lamb that she should tell his mother that he has not died, but has gone to marry a princess of the heavens.

There is more to the tale, but this is the essence of it. Opinions differ as to its meaning, but I chose the meaning which suited the story I was trying to tell; not just a story about vampires, *My Swordhand Is Singing* is actually, for me, a story about two other things: redemption, and mortality. I was trying to tell a story in which the protagonist, a young man, has to face what we all do at some point, usually first during our teenage years, that death is inevitable, and that we have to find meaning in life beyond this realisation.

The young shepherd in the ballad accepts that death is inevitable, and therefore is nothing to be afraid of. Only through this realisation is one freed to live life to the full, until the moment of death. But not all the villagers of Chust in the novel have reached the same conclusion, and it is this reluctance to die, again, this unfinished relationship to life, that precipitates the return of the dead from beyond to the grave, empowered by the influence of the Shadow Queen.

Given that the vampires I had 'discovered' were so very different from the creature of mythology, I began to feel I didn't want to call them by this name, as I hinted at before. Furthermore, in the various folktales I had been reading, their names are many and varied, but the idea behind one name struck me in particular: hostages. The idea behind that is that people do not willingly become vampires, that they are held in this state against their will because of this unfinished business, and to let them free of it would be, therefore, some kind of blessing. So 'hostages' they are in my book, and those that free them, the 'ancestors', again a name taken from the folklore.

From that point on, I was on my own, by which I mean it was down to me to use an author's techniques to weave a story together, but I think it's safe to say that this would not have been the book it was without these simple delvings into the folklore of Transylvania – one of the more unusual and mysterious corners of Europe.

Notes

1 Bogatyrëv, *Vampires in the Carpathians*.
2 Cited in Perkowski, 'The Romanian Folkloric Vampire', p. 40.
3 *Ibid.*, p. 40.
4 Murgoci, 'The Vampire in Romania', p. 21.
5 Petrescu, 'The Long Shadow of Dracula'.
6 Barber, *Vampires*, pp. 52–3.

7 Bogatyrëv, *Vampires in the Carpathians*, p. 133.

8 Petrovici, 'The Romanian Folkloric Vampire', pp. 36–40.

9 Pamfile (ed.), *Ion Creangă*, p. 202.

10 Perkowski, *Vampires of the Slavs*, p. 272.

11 Bogatyrëv, *Vampires in the Carpathians*, p. 132.

12 Krauss, 'Vampyre in südslawischen Volksglauben', p. 68.

13 Barber, *Vampires*, p. 63.

14 Murgoci, 'The Vampire in Romania', p. 23.

15 Frazer, *The Golden Bough*, III: *The Dying God*, p. 243.

16 McNally and Florescu, *In Search of Dracula*, p. 51.

17 Stahl, *Eseuri Critice*, p. 160.

18 Kligman, *The Wedding of the Dead*, p. 216.

19 *Ibid.*, p. 222.

References

Printed and internet sources

'10 Questions for Stephenie Meyer', *Time* (21 August 2008), (online) www.time.com/time/magazine/article/0,9171,1834663,00.html [accessed 10 January 2012].

'The Absorptive Nature of Genius: Review of *The House of the Vampire* by George Sylvester Viereck', *Current Literature*, 44 (1908), 53–4.

'The Goth Phenomenon', *ABC News 20/20* (21 April 1999), transcript at *Columbine Links and Resources*, http://acolumbinesite.com/links/goth.html [accessed 27 September 2011].

Gothic Liberation Front – Central Kommand, www.myspace.com/gothicliberationfront [accessed 27 September 2011].

'History of Kodak', *Kodak*, www.kodak.com/ek/US/en/Our_Company/History_of_Kodak/Imaging-_the_basics.htm [accessed 2 April 2012].

'Luna Park First Night', *New York Times* (17 March 1903), (online) http://query.nytimes.com/gst/abstract.html?res=F00D1FF6345412738DDDAE0994DD405B838CF1D3.

'Registration Acts (Comics)', *Wikipedia*, http://en.wikipedia.org/wiki/Registration_acts_%28comics%29 [accessed 9 September 2012].

'Review of *Dracula*', *Athenaeum*, 109 (1897), 835; reprinted in Carol A. Senf (ed.), *The Critical Response to Bram Stoker* (Westport: Greenwood Press, 1993), pp. 59–60.

'Silver Bullet', *Wikipedia*, http://en.wikipedia.org/wiki/Silver_bullet [accessed 3 April 2012].

The Sophie Lancaster Foundation, www.sophielancasterfoundation.com [accessed 27 September 2011].

'Terrorist Novel Writing', in E. J. Clery and Robert Miles (eds), *Gothic Documents: A Sourcebook 1700–1820* (Manchester: Manchester University Press, 2000), pp. 182–4.

'Vampire', *Wikipedia*, http://en.wikipedia.org/wiki/Vampire [accessed 1 August 2011].

'Vampires', *Encyclopaedia Britannica* [1888 edn], Appendix V, in Stoker, *Bram Stoker's Notes*, ed. Eighteen-Bisang and Miller, pp. 306–8.

'Vampires in New England', *New York World* (2 February 1896), in Stoker, *Bram Stoker's Notes*, ed. Eighteen-Bisang and Miller, pp. 186–93.

'Viereck Got $2000 from Nazi Consul', *New York Times* (11 July 1938), p. 11.

'Viereck Kisses the Rod', *The Nation* (25 April 1934), p. 460.

'Why Does Silver Kill Werewolves?', http://au.answers.yahoo.com/question/index?qid=20080606150325AAqErX2 [accessed 3 April 2012].

Aaron, Michele, *Spectatorship: The Power of Looking On* (London: Wallflower, 2007).

Abbott, Stacey, 'From Madman in the Basement to Self-sacrificing Champion: The Multiple Faces of Spike', *European Journal of Cultural Studies*, 8:3 (2005), 329–44.

—— *Celluloid Vampires: Life after Death in the Modern World* (Austin: University of Texas Press, 2007).

—— *Angel* (Detroit: Wayne State University Press, 2009).

—— 'Walking the Fine Line between Angel and Angelus', *Slayage: The Journal of the Whedon Studies Association*, 9, http://slayageonline.com/PDF/abbott2.pdf [accessed 16 July 2011].

Abbott, Stacey (ed.), *Reading Angel: The TV Spin-off with a Soul* (London and New York: I. B. Tauris, 2005).

Adams, Michael, *Slayer Slang: A Buffy the Vampire Slayer Lexicon* (New York: Oxford University Press, 2003).

Ames, Melissa, 'Twilight Follows Tradition: Analysing "Biting" Critiques of Vampire Narratives for Their Portrayals of Gender and Sexuality', in Click, Aubrey and Behm-Morawitz (eds), *Bitten by Twilight*, pp. 37–54.

Annwn, David (ed.), *Dracula's Precursors: The Mysterious Stranger and Other Stories* (Hastings: ReScript Books, 2011).

Arata, Stephen D., 'The Occidental Tourist: *Dracula* and the Anxiety of Reverse Colonization', *Victorian Studies*, 33:4 (Summer 1990), 621–45; repr. in Byron (ed.), *Dracula: Contemporary Critical Essays*, pp. 119–44.

Arnheim, Rudolf, *Film as Art* (Berkeley and Los Angeles: University of California Press, 1957).

Assmus, Alexi, 'The Early History of X-rays', www.slac.stanford.edu/pubs/beamline/25/2/25-2-assmus.pdf [accessed 2 April 2012].

Auerbach, Nina, *Our Vampires, Ourselves* (Chicago and London: The University of Chicago Press, 1995).

Austin, Thomas, *Hollywood, Hype and Audiences: Selling and Watching Popular Film in the 1990s* (Manchester: Manchester University Press, 2002).

Bakhtin, Mikhail, *Rabelais and His World*, trans. Hélène Iswolsky (Bloomington and Indianapolis: Indiana University Press, 1984).

—— *Speech Genres and Other Late Essays*, trans. Vern W. McGee, ed. Caryl Emerson and Michael Holquist, University of Texas Press Slavic Series, 8 (Austin: University of Texas Press, 1986).

Bainbridge, Caroline, *A Feminine Cinematics: Luce Irigaray, Women and Film* (Basingstoke: Palgrave, 2007).

Barber, Paul, 'Forensic Pathology and the European Vampire', in Dundes (ed.), *Vampire*, pp. 109–42.

—— *Vampires, Burial and Death: Folklore and Reality*, new edn (1988; New Haven: Yale University Press, 2010).

Baring-Gould, Sabine, *The Book of Werewolves* (Dublin: Nonsuch Publishing, n.d.).

Barnard, Francis Pierrepont, *Strongbow's Conquest of Ireland*, English History from Contemporary Writers, 4, ed. F. York Powell (London: D. Nutt; New York: G. P. Putnam's Sons, 1888).

Barnes, Jennifer Lynn, 'Sweet Caroline', in Cordova (ed.), *A Visitor's Guide*, pp. 143–57.

Barreca, Regina, 'Five Reasons a Smart Middle Aged Woman Loathes TWILIGHT', *Psychology Today* (March 2009), www.psychologytoday.com/blog/snow-white-doesnt-live-here-anymore/200903/five-reasons-smart-middle-aged-woman-loathes-twiligh [accessed 20 December 2009].

Barthes, Roland, *Mythologies* (1957), trans. Annette Lavers (London: Paladin, 1972).

Basinger, Jeanine, *Silent Stars* (New York: Alfred A. Knopf, 2000).

Baudrillard, Jean, 'The Precession of Simulacra', in *Selected Writings*, ed. Mark Poster (Cambridge: Polity, 1988), pp. 1–79.

Beal, Timothy K., *Religion and Its Monsters* (New York: Routledge, 2002).

Benjamin, Walter, 'The Work of Art in the Age of Mechanical Reproduction' [1936], in *Illuminations*, trans. Harry Zohn, ed. and intr. Hannah Arendt (London; Fontana, 1973), pp. 219–53.

—— 'A Small History of Photography' [1931], in *One-Way Street and Other Writings*, trans. Edmund Jephcott and Kingsley Shorter, Verso Classics, 8 (London: Verso, 1997), pp. 240–57.

Bennett, Andrew, and Nicholas Royle, *Introduction to Literature, Criticism and Theory*, 3rd edn (Harlow: Pearson Longman, 2004).

Bentham, Jeremy, *Panopticon: or, The Inspection-House* (Dublin: Thomas Byrne, 1791).

Beresford, Matthew, *From Demons to Dracula: The Creation of the Modern Vampire Myth* (London: Reaktion, 2008).

Berg, Stephen, 'Technicolor Vampires', in Reed, *You Look Good*, pp. 58–68.

Biale, David, *Blood and Belief: The Circulation of a Symbol between Jews and Christians* (Berkeley: University of California Press, 2007).

Blickle, Peter, *Heimat: A Critical Theory of the German Idea of Homeland* (Rochester, New York: Camden House, 2002).

Bloom, Clive, 'Day of the Dead', *Times Higher Education* (24–30 June 2010), pp. 38–41.

Bode, Lisa, 'From Shadow Citizens to Teflon Stars: Reception of the Transfiguring Effects of New Moving Image Technologies', *Animation: An Interdisciplinary Journal*, 1:2 (2006), 173–89.

Bogatyrëv, Pëtr, *Vampires in the Carpathians: Magical Acts, Rites and Beliefs on the Subcarpathian Rus'*, trans. Stephen Reynolds and Patricia A. Krafcig, intr. Svetlana P. Sorokina, East European Monographs, 492 (New York: Columbia University Press, 1998).

Bolter, Jay David, and Diane Gromola, *Windows and Mirrors: Interaction Design, Digital Art and the Myth of Transparency* (London and Cambridge, MA: MIT Press, 2003).

Bolter, Jay David, and Richard Grusin, *Remediation: Understanding New Media* (London and Cambridge, MA: MIT Press, 1999).

Bond, Gwenda, 'When Love is Strange: Romance Continues Its Affair with the Supernatural', www.publishersweekly.com/pw/print/20090525/12458-when-love-is-strange-romance-continues-its-affair-with-the-supernatural-.html [accessed 22 September 2010].

Boone, Troy, 'Mark of the Vampire: Arnod Paole, Sade, Polidori', *Nineteenth-Century Contexts: An Interdisciplinary Journal*, 18:4 (1995), 349–66.

Botting, Fred, *Gothic*, New Critical Idiom (London and New York: Routledge, 1996).

——— 'Hypocrite Vampire …', *Gothic Studies*, 9:1 (2007), 16–34.

——— *Gothic Romanced: Consumption, Gender and Technology in Contemporary Fictions* (London and New York: Routledge, 2008).

Braddon, Elizabeth, 'Good Lady Ducayne' [1896], in Ryan (ed.), *The Penguin Book of Vampire Stories*, pp. 138–62.

Branch, Lori, 'Carlisle's Cross: Locating the Post-Secular Gothic', in Clarke and Osborn (eds), *The Twilight Mystique*, pp. 60–79.

Brandenburg, Ulrike, *Hanns Heinz Ewers (1871–1943): Von Der Jahrhundertwende zum Dritten Reich: Erzählungen, Dramen, Romane 1903–1932* (Frankfurt am Main and New York: Lang, 2003).

Brav, Stanley R., 'Jews and Judaism in *The Jewish Spy*', *Studies in Bibliography and Booklore*, 4 (1960), 133–41.

Brennan, Sarah Rees, 'Women Who Love Vampires Who Eat Women', in Cordova (ed.), *A Visitor's Guide*, pp. 1–20.

Brite, Poppy Z., *Lost Souls* (1992; Harmondsworth: Penguin, 1994).

Brownell, M. R., 'Pope and the Vampires in Germany', *Eighteenth-Century Life*, 2 (1976), 96–7.

Burley, Stephanie, 'The Death of Zofloya, or, the Moor as Epistemological Limit', in Ruth Bienstock Anolik and Douglas L. Howard (eds), *The Gothic Other: Racial and Social Constructions in the Literary Imagination* (Jefferson: McFarland, 2004), pp. 197–211.

Bush, George, 'Transcript of President Bush's address', *CNN* (21 September 2001), http://articles.cnn.com/2001-09-20/us/gen.bush.transcript_1_joint-session-national-anthem-citizens?_s=PM:US [accessed 13 July 2011].

Butler, Andrew, *Solar Flares: Science Fiction in the 1970s* (Liverpool: Liverpool University Press, forthcoming).

Butler, Erik, *Metamorphoses of the Vampire in Literature and Film: Cultural Transformations in Europe, 1732–1933* (Rochester, NY: Camden House, 2010).

Byron, Lord George, *The Works of Lord Byron*, 13 vols, ed. Rowland E. Prothero (London: John Murray, 1899), IV: *Letters and Journals*.

——— *Byron's Letters and Journals*, 12 vols, ed. Leslie Marchand (London: John Murray, 1973–1982), I: *In My Hot Youth* (1973).

——— *Lord Byron: The Complete Poetical Works*, 7 vols, ed. Jerome J. McGann and Barry Weller (Oxford: Clarendon Press, 1980–1993).

——— *Lord Byron: Selected Letters and Journals*, ed. Leslie Marchand (London: Picador, 1984).

——— *Byron's Letters and Journals. Supplementary Volume: What Comes Uppermost*, ed. Leslie Marchand (London: John Murray, 1994).

Caine, Rachel, *Walking Stiff*, Revivalist series, 1 (London: Allison and Busby, 2011).

Calarco, Joyce, 'An Historical Overview of the Discovery of the X-Ray', www.yale.edu/ynhti/curriculum/units/1983/7/83.07.01.x.html [accessed 10 April 2012].

Callahan, Vicki, *Zones of Anxiety: Movement, Musidora, and the Crimes Serials of Louis Feuillade* (Detroit: Wayne State University Press, 2005).

Calmet, Dom Augustin, *Dissertations upon the apparitions of angels, dæmons, and ghosts, and concerning the vampires of Hungary, Bohemia, Moravia, and Silesia* (*Dissertations sur les apparitions des anges, des démons & des esprits* (Paris, 1746); London: printed for M. Cooper, at the Globe in Pater-Noster-Row, 1759).

Canby, Vincent, 'Review: Coppola's Dizzying Vision of Dracula', *The New York Times* (13 November 1992), (online) http://movies.nytimes.com/movie/review?res=9E0CE2D61539F930A25752C1A964958260 [accessed 1 August 2011].

Carter, Margaret L., 'The Vampire as Alien in Contemporary Fiction', in Gordon and Hollinger (eds), *Blood Read*, pp. 27–44.

Cartmell, Deborah, and Imelda Whelehan, *Impure Cinema* (Basingstoke: Palgrave, 2010).

Charnas, McKee Suzy, *The Vampire Tapestry* (1980; St Albans: Granada, 1983).

Cherry, Brigid, *Horror*, Routledge Film Guidebooks (Abingdon and New York: Routledge, 2009).

Child, Francis J., *The English and Scottish Popular Ballads* (1882; New York: Dover, 1965).

Christie, Deborah, and Sarah Juliet Lauro (eds), *Better Off Dead: The Evolution of the Zombie as Post-Human* (New York: Fordham University Press, 2011).

Clarke, Amy M., and Marijane Osborn (eds), *The Twilight Mystique: Critical Essays on the Novel and the Films* (Jefferson: McFarland, 2010).

Clarke, John, et al., 'Subcultures, Cultures and Class: A Theoretical Overview', in Stuart Hall and Tony Jefferson (eds), *Resistance Through Rituals: Youth Subcultures in Post-war Britain* (London: Routledge, 2003), pp. 9–74.

Clements, Susannah, *The Vampire Defanged: How the Embodiment of Evil Became a Romantic Hero* (Grand Rapids: Brazos Press, 2011).

Clery, Emma, *The Rise of Supernatural Fiction 1762–1800*, Cambridge Studies in Romanticism, 12 (Cambridge: Cambridge University Press, 1999).

Click, Melissa, 'Rabid, Obsessed and Frenzied: Understanding *Twilight* Fangirls and the Gendered Politics of Fandom', *FLOW*, 11:4 (18 December 2009), http://flowtv.org/2009/12/rabid-obsessed-and-frenzied-understanding-twilight-fangirls-and-the-gendered-politics-of-fandom-melissa-click-university-of-missouri/ [accessed 18 January 2010].

Click, Melissa A., Jennifer Stevens Aubrey and Elizabeth Behm-Morawitz (eds), *Bitten by Twilight: Youth Culture, Media, and the Vampire Franchise* (New York: Peter Lang, 2010).

Cohen, Jeffrey J., 'Monster Culture (Seven Theses)', in J. J. Cohen (ed.), *Monster Theory: Reading Culture* (Minneapolis: University of Minnesota Press, 1996), pp. 3–25.

Coleridge, Samuel Taylor, *The Complete Poems*, ed. William Keach (London: Penguin, 1997).

—— 'Review of *The Monk*', in E. J. Clery and Robert Miles (eds), *Gothic Documents: A Sourcebook 1700–1820* (Manchester: Manchester University Press, 2000), pp. 185–9.

Comaroff, Jean, and John L. Comaroff, 'Alien-nation: Zombies, Immigrants, and Millennial Capitalism', *South Atlantic Quarterly*, 101:4 (Fall 2002), 779–805.

Cordova, Heather (ed.), *A Visitor's Guide to Mystic Falls* (Dallas: SmartPop Books, 2010).

Craft, Christopher, '"Kiss Me with Those Red Lips": Gender and Inversion in Bram Stoker's *Dracula*', *Representations*, 8 (1984), 107–30.

—— 'Come See about Me: Enchantment of the Double in *The Picture of Dorian Gray*', *Representations*, 91:1 (Summer 2005), 109–36.

Creed, Barbara, 'Horror and the Monstrous-Feminine: An Imaginary Abjection', in James Donald (ed.), *Fantasy and the Cinema* (London: BFI, 1989), pp. 63–89.

—— *Phallic Panic: Film, Horror and the Primal Uncanny* (Victoria: Melbourne University Press, 2005).

Creet, Julia, 'Daughter of the Movement: The Psychodynamics of Lesbian S/M Fantasy', *Differences: A Journal of Feminist Cultural Studies*, 3:2 (Summer 1991), 135–59.

Czech, Jan, 'Bella Swan – A Feminist's Nightmare', *Suite 101* (20 July 2009), http://teen-fiction-series.suite101.com/article.cfm/bella_swan_a_feminists_nightmare [accessed 20 December 2009].

Dain, Stephen J., 'Sunglasses and Sunglass Standards', *Clinical and Experimental Optometry*, 86:2 (March 2003), 77–90, (online) http://onlinelibrary.wiley.com/doi/10.1111/j.1444-0938.2003.tb03066.x/abstract [accessed 28 July 2011].

Daniels, Les, *The Don Sebastian Vampire Chronicles* (London: Robinson Publishing, 1994).

Danto, Arthur C., *Sartre*, Modern Masters (London: Fontana, 1975).

D'Argens, Jean-Baptiste de Boyer, Marquis, *The Jewish Spy: being a philosophical, historical and critical correspondence, by letters which lately pass'd between certain Jews in Turkey, Italy, France, &c.* (Lettres Juives (1738–42); London: printed for D. Browne, at the Black Swan without Temple-Bar; and R. Hett, at the Bible and Crown in the Poultry, 1739).

Darwin, Erasmus, *The Botanic Garden, Part II. Containing The Loves of the Plants, a Poem* (Lichfield: printed by J. Jackson. Sold by J. Johnson, St Paul's Church Yard, London: 1789).

Day, William Patrick, *Vampire Legends in Contemporary Culture: What Becomes a Legend Most* (Lexington: The University Press of Kentucky, 2002).

Deane, Seamus, *Strange Country: Modernity and Nationhood in Irish Writing since 1790* (Oxford: Clarendon Press, 1997).

Deaville, James, 'The Beauty of Horror: Kilar, Coppola, and Dracula', in Neil Lerner (ed.), *Music in the Horror Film: Listening to Fear* (London and New York: Routledge, 2010), pp. 187–205.

Deleuze, Gilles, 'Coldness and Cruelty', in *Masochism* (1967; New York: Zone, 1991), pp. 9–138.

Derrida, Jacques, *Of Grammatology*, trans. Gayatri Chakravorty Spivak, corrected edn (Baltimore: The Johns Hopkins University Press, 1998).

Dicks, Terrance, *Doctor Who and the State of Decay* (London: Target Books, 1981).

Dijkstra, Bram, *Idols of Perversity: Fantasies of Feminine Evil in Fin-de-siècle Culture* (New York and Oxford: Oxford University Press, 1986).

—— *Evil Sisters: The Threat of Female Sexuality and the Cult of Manhood* (New York: Knopf, 1996).

Dimic, Milan V., 'Vampiromania in the Eighteenth Century: The Other Side of Enlightenment', in *Man and Nature / L'Homme et la Nature: proceedings of the Canadian Society for Eighteenth-Century Studies*, 3, ed. by R. J. Merrett (Edmonton: The Society, 1984), pp. 1–22.

Doane, Mary Ann, *The Desire to Desire: The Woman's Film of the 1940s* (Bloomington: Indiana University Press, 1987).

Drewry, Richard D., 'What Man Devised That He Might See' (1997), (online) www.eye.uthsc.edu/history/WhatManDevised.pdf [accessed 28 July 2011].

Drum, Jean, and Dale Drum, *My Only Great Passion: The Life and Films of Carl Th. Dreyer* (Lanham: Scarecrow Press, 2000).

—— 'Film-Production Carl Dreyer', in the book accompanying *Vampyr: The Strange Adventures of Allan Gray*, dir. Carl Dreyer, 1932 (Eureka!, 2008) [on DVD].

Dundes, Alan (ed.), *The Vampire: A Casebook* (Madison: University of Wisconsin Press, 1998).

Dyer, Richard, 'Children of the Night: Vampirism as Homosexuality, Homosexuality as Vampirism', in Susannah Radstone (ed.), *Sweet Dreams: Sexuality, Gender and Popular Culture* (London: Lawrence and Wishart, 1988), pp. 47–72.

—— *White* (London: Routledge, 1997).

Eagleton, Terry, *The Idea of Culture*, Blackwell Manifestos (Oxford: Blackwell, 2000).

Empson, William, *Seven Types of Ambiguity* (1930; repr. London: Peregrine Books, 1961).

Ewers, Hanns H., 'Die Lösung der Judenfrage', in Julius Moses (ed.), *Die Lösung der Judenfrage: eine Rundfrage* (Berlin: Wigand, 1907), pp. 34–41.

—— 'Judentaufen', in Werner Sombart and Artur Landsberger (eds), *Judentaufen* (Munich: Müller, 1912), pp. 36–43.

—— 'Der Tod des Barons Jesus Maria Von Friedel', in *Die Bessessenen: seltsame Geschichten* (Leipzig: Müller, 1914), 223–9.

—— *Alraune: Die Geschichte eines lebenden Wesens* (Munich: Müller, 1919).

—— *Der Zauberlehrling: oder, die Teufelsjäger: Roman* (Munich: Müller, 1920).

—— *Vampir: Ein verwilderter Roman in Fetzen und Farben* (Berlin: Sieben Stäbe, 1928).

Ferrier, John, 'Of Popular Illusions, and Particularly of Medical Demonology' [1786], in *Memoirs of the Literary and Philosophical Society of Manchester* (Warrington: printed by W. Eyres, for T. Cadel in the Strand, London, 1785–), III, pp. 31–105.

Flanagan, Caitlin, 'What Girls Want', *The Atlantic* (December 2008), www.theatlantic.com/magazine/print/2008/12/what-girls-want/7161/ [accessed 10 January 2012].

Forman, Charles, *A Second Letter to the Right Honourable Sir Robert Walpole* ... (London: printed for J. Wilford, behind the Chapter-House, in St. Paul's Church-Yard, 1733).

Fortis, Alberto, *Travels into Dalmatia; ... Translated from the Italian Under the Author's Inspection ...* (*Viaggio in Dalmazia dell' Abate Alberto Fortis* (1774); London: printed for J. Robson, 1778).

Foster, Star, and Daniel Ravipinto, *Slouching Towards Bedlam* (self-published, 2003) [interactive fiction for the Z-machine platform].

Foucault, Michel, *Discipline and Punish: The Birth of the Prison*, trans. Alan Sheridan (Harmondsworth: Penguin, 1991).

Frayling, Christopher, *Vampyres: Lord Byron to Count Dracula*, new edn (1978; London and Boston: Faber and Faber, 1991).

—— 'Bram Stoker's Working Papers for *Dracula*', in Stoker, *Dracula*, ed. Auerbach and Skal, pp. 339–50.

Frayling, Christopher, and Robert Wokler, 'From the Orang-utan to the Vampire: Towards an Anthropology of Rousseau', in *Rousseau after 200 Years*, ed. R. A. Leigh (Cambridge: Cambridge University Press, 1982).

Frazer, Sir James, *The Golden Bough*, 12 vols (London: Macmillan, 1906–15), III: *The Dying God* (1911).

Frenschkowski, Marco, 'Von Schemajah Hillel zu Aaron Wassertrum: Juden und Judentum in der deutschsprachigen Phantastischen Literatur', in Thomas Le Blanc and Bettina Twrsnick (eds), *Traumreich und Nachtseite: die deutschsprachige Phantastik zwischen Décadence und Faschismus; Tagungsband 1995 Schriftenreihe und Materialien der Phantastischen Bibliothek Wetzlar* (Wetzlar: Förderkreis Phantastik 1995), pp. 126–57.

Freud, Sigmund, 'Three Essays on the Theory of Sexuality' [1905], in *The Penguin Freud Library*, ed. Angela Richards, trans. James Strachey, 15 vols (Harmondsworth: Penguin, 1977), VII: *On Sexuality*, pp. 31–169.

—— '"A Child Is Being Beaten": A Contribution to the Study of the Origin of Sexual Perversions' [1919], in *The Penguin Freud Library*, ed. Angela Richards, trans. James Strachey, 15 vols (Harmondsworth: Penguin, 1979), X: *On Psychopathology*, pp. 163–93.

—— 'The Uncanny' [1919], in *The Pelican Freud Library*, ed. Angela Richards, trans. James Strachey, 15 vols (Harmondsworth: Penguin, 1985), XIV: *Art and Literature*, pp. 335–76.

Friedberg, Anne, *The Virtual Window: From Alberti To Microsoft* (London and Cambridge, MA: MIT Press, 2006).

Gay and Lesbian Alliance against Defamation, 'Where We Are on TV Report, 2010–2011', www.glaad.org/document.doc?id=145 [accessed 13 July 2011].

Gelder, Ken, *Reading the Vampire* (London and New York: Routledge, 1994).

—— Introduction, in Gelder (ed.), *The Horror Reader*, pp. 1–7.

Gelder, Ken (ed.), *The Horror Reader* (London and New York: Routledge, 2000).

Genette, Gérard, *Narrative Discourse: An Essay in Method*, trans. Jane E, Lewin (Ithaca: Cornell University Press, 1980).

—— *Palimpsests: Literature in the Second Degree*, trans. C. Newman and C. Doubinsky (Lincoln: University of Nebraska Press, 1997).

Genz, Stéphanie, *Postfemininities in Popular Culture* (Basingstoke: Palgrave Macmillan, 2009).

Gerard, Emily, *The Land Beyond the Forest*, 2 vols (Edinburgh and London: William Blackwood and Sons, 1888).

Gibson, Matthew, *Dracula and the Eastern Question: British and French Vampire Narratives of the Nineteenth-Century Near East* (Basingstoke: Palgrave Macmillan, 2006).

Giraldus, Cambrensis, et al., *The Historical Works of Giraldus Cambrensis: Containing the Topography of Ireland, and the History of the Conquest of Ireland* (London: H. G. Bohn, 1863).

Gitling, Todd, *The Twilight of Common Dreams: Why America Is Wracked by Culture Wars* (New York: Henry Holt, 1995).

Glover, David, 'Bram Stoker and the Crisis of the Liberal Subject', *New Literary History*, 23:4, Papers from the Commonwealth Center for Literary and Cultural Change (Autumn 1992), 983–1002.

—— *Vampires, Mummies, and Liberals: Bram Stoker and the Politics of Popular Fiction* (Durham, NC: Duke University Press, 1996).

Goddu, Teresa A., *Gothic America: Narrative, History, and Nation* (New York: Columbia University Press, 1997).

Golden, Christopher (ed.), *Zombie: An Anthology of the Undead* (London: Piatkus, 2010).

Gordon, Joan, and Veronica Hollinger, 'Introduction: The Shape of Vampires', in Gordon and Hollinger (eds), *Blood Read*, pp. 1–7.

Gordon, Joan, and Veronica Hollinger (eds), *Blood Read: The Vampire as Metaphor in Contemporary Culture* (Philadelphia: University of Pennsylvania Press, 1997).

Gorky, Maxim, newspaper review of Lumière programme at the Nizhni-Novgorod fair, *Nizhegorodski listok* (4 July 1896); repr. in Colin Harding and Simon Popple (eds), *In the Kingdom of Shadows: A Companion to Early Cinema* (London: Cygnus Arts, 1996), p. 5.

Goss, Sara, 'Dracula and the Spectre of Famine', in *Hungry Words: Images of Famine in the Irish Canon* (Dublin: Irish Academic Press, 2005), pp. 77–107.

Goya, Francisco, *Los Caprichos*, intr. Philip Hoper (New York: Dover, 1969).

Greenburg, Louis, 'Sins of the Blood: Rewriting the Family in Two Postmodern Vampire Novels', *Journal of Literary Studies*, 26:1 (2010), 163–78.

Greenway, John, 'Seward's Folly: *Dracula* as a Critique of "Normal Science"', *Stanford Literary Review*, 3 (1986), 213–30.

Grossman, Lev, 'Zombies Are the New Vampires', *Time* (9 April 2009), (online) www.time.com/time/magazine/article/0,9171,1890384,00.html [accessed 24 July 2011].

Habermas, Jürgen, 'Towards a Theory of Communicative Competence', *Inquiry*, 13 (1970), 360–75.

—— *Knowledge and Human Interests*, trans. Jeremy J. Shapiro (Oxford: Polity, 1986).

—— *The Structural Transformation of the Public Sphere: An Inquiry into a Category of Bourgeois Society*, trans. Thomas Burger and Frederick Lawrence (Cambridge, MA: MIT Press, 1989).

Halberstam, Judith, *Skin Shows: Gothic Horror and the Technology of Monsters* (Durham, NC and London: Duke University Press, 1995).

Halualani, Rona Tamiko, 'Abstracting and De-racializing Diversity: The Articulation of Diversity in the Post-race Era', in Michael Lacy and Kent A. Ono (eds), *Critical Rhetorics of Race* (New York and London: New York University Press, 2011), pp. 247–64.

Hamilton, Laurell K., *The Laughing Corpse*, Anita Blake: Vampire Hunter, 2 (1994; London: Headline, 2009).

Hamrick, Craig, *Barnabas and Company* (New York: iUniverse Publishing, 2003).

Hanson, Helen, *Hollywood Heroines: Women in Film Noir and the Female Gothic Film* (London: I. B. Tauris: 2007).

Harris, Charlaine, *Dead Until Dark*, Southern Vampire (Sookie Stackhouse), 1 (London: Gollancz, 2004).

Hayles, N., Katherine, *Writing Machines* (London and Cambridge, MA: MIT Press, 2002).

Hebdige, Dick, *Subculture: The Meaning of Style* (London: Routledge, 1988).

Herbert, Christopher, 'Vampire Religion', *Representations*, 79 (Summer 2002), 100–21.

Heyes, Cressida, 'Identity Politics (Stanford Encyclopedia of Philosophy)', *The Stanford Encyclopedia of Philosophy*, ed. Edward N. Zalta (2002), http://plato.stanford.edu/entries/identity-politics [accessed 24 September 2010].

Holcroft, Thomas, *The Deserted Daughter: A Comedy* (London: Printed for … Robinson, Pater-Noster-Row, 1795).

Holland, Tom, *The Vampyre: The Secret History of Lord Byron* (1995; London: Warner Books, 1996).

—— *Supping with Panthers* (1996; London: Warner Books, 1997).

—— 'Undead Byron', in Wilson (ed.), *Byromania*, pp. 154–65.

Hollinger, Veronica, 'Fantasies of Absence: The Postmodern Vampire', in Gordon and Hollinger, *Blood Read*, pp. 199–212.

Hoy, David Couzens, and Thomas McCarthy, *Critical Theory* (Oxford and Cambridge, MA: Blackwell, 1994).

Hudders, Anthony, 'The Southern Vampire in American Popular Fiction' (unpublished Master's dissertation, Ghent University, 2010).

Huet, Marie-Hélène, 'Deadly Fears: Dom Augustin Calmet's Vampires and the Rule over Death', *Eighteenth-Century Life*, 21:2 (1997), 222–32.

Hughes, William, *Bram Stoker – Dracula: A Reader's Guide to Essential Criticism* (Basingstoke: Palgrave Macmillan, 2008).

Hughes, William, David Punter and Andrew Smith (eds), *The Encyclopedia of the Gothic*, Wiley-Blackwell Encyclopedia of Literature (Oxford: Wiley-Blackwell, 2012).

Hume, David, 'Of Miracles', in *Enquiries Concerning Human Understanding and Concerning the Principles of Morals*, ed. L. A. Selby-Bigge, revd. P. H. Nidditch, 3rd edn (1777 edn; Oxford: Clarendon Press, 1975), pp. 109–31.

Hutchings, Peter, *Dracula* (London: I. B. Tauris, 1988).

—— *Terence Fisher: British Film Makers* (Manchester and New York: Manchester University Press, 2001).

Ingelbien, Raphael, 'Gothic Genealogies: Dracula, Bowen's Court, and Anglo-Irish Psychology', *ELH*, 70:4 (Winter 2003), 1089–105.

Jameson, Fredric, 'Postmodernism and Consumer Society', in Hal Foster (ed.), *The Anti-Aesthetic: Essays on Postmodern Culture* (New York: New Press, 1983), pp. 111–25.

—— 'Conclusion: The Dialectic of Utopia and Ideology', in *The Political Unconscious: Narrative as a Socially Symbolic Act* (London: Routledge, 1989), pp. 281–99.

—— *Postmodernism, or, The Cultural Logic of Late Capitalism* (London: Verso, 1991).

Jann, Rosemary, 'Saved by Science? The Mixed Messages of Stoker's *Dracula*', *Texas Studies in Literature and Language*, 31:2 (1989), 273–87.

Johnson, Laurie R., *Aesthetic Anxiety: Uncanny Symptoms in German Literature and Culture* (Amsterdam: Rodopi, 2010).

Johnson, Neil M., 'Pro-Freud and pro-Nazi: The Paradox of George S. Viereck', *Psycho-analytic Review*, 58 (1971), 553–62.

—— *George Sylvester Viereck: German-American Propagandist* (Urbana: University of Illinois Press, 1972).

Johnson, Steven, *Interface Culture: How New Technology Transforms the Way We Create and Communicate* (San Francisco: Harper Edge, 1997).

Jordan, David, *Regionalism Reconsidered: New Approaches to the Field* (New York: Routledge, 1994).

Kalogridis, Jeanne, *The Diaries of the Family Dracul* (London: Headline, 1996).

Kane, Kathryn, 'A Very Queer Refusal: The Chilling Effect of the Cullens' Heteronor-mative Embrace', in Click, Aubrey and Behm-Morawitz (eds), *Bitten by Twilight*, pp. 103–8.

Kaveney, Roz (ed.), *Reading the Vampire Slayer* (London and New York: Tauris Parke Paperbacks, 2001).

Keller, Phyllis, 'George Sylvester Viereck: The Psychology of a German-American Militant', *Journal of Interdisciplinary History*, 2 (1971), 59–108.

—— *States of Belonging: German-American Intellectuals and the First World War* (Cambridge, MA: Harvard University Press, 1979).

Keyworth, G. David, 'Was the Vampire of the Eighteenth Century a Unique Type of Undead-corpse?', *Folklore*, 117:3 (December 2006), 241–60.

Kilfeather, Siobhán, 'The Gothic Novel', in John Wilson Foster (ed.), *The Cambridge Companion to the Irish Novel* (Cambridge: Cambridge University Press, 2006), pp. 78–96.

Kindinger, Evangelia, 'Reading Supernatural Fiction as Regional Fiction: of "Vamps," "Supes" and Places that "Suck"', *Kultur und Geschlecht*, 1:8 (2011), 1–29.

King, Stephen, *Salem's Lot* (London: New English Library, 1976).

King, Stephen, Scott Snyder and Rafael Albuquerque, *American Vampire: Volume 1* (New York: DC Comics, 2010).

Kipling, Rudyard, *A Choice of Kipling's Verse*, ed. T. S. Eliot (London: Faber and Faber, 1941).

Kittler, Friedrich, 'Dracula's Legacy', *Stanford Humanities Review*, 1 (1989), 143–73.

Klein, Melanie, *The Selected Melanie Klein*, ed. Juliet Mitchell (New York: Free Press, 1986).

Kligman, Gail, *The Wedding of the Dead* (Berkeley: University of California Press, 1988).

Knight, Deborah, and George McKnight, '*American Psycho*: Horror, Satire, Aesthetics, and Identification', in Steven Jay Schneider and Daniel Shaw (eds), *Dark Thoughts: Philosophic Reflections on Cinematic Horror* (Lanham, MD: The Scarecrow Press, 2003), pp. 212–29.

Krauss, Friedrich S., 'Vampyre in südslawischen Volksglauben', *Globus*, 62 (1892); repr. as 'South Slavic Countermeasures against Vampires', in Dundes (ed.), *The Vampire*, pp. 67–71.

Krauss, Rosalind, 'Reinventing the Medium', *Critical Inquiry*, 25:2 (Winter 1999), 289–305.

Kristeva, Julia, *The Powers of Horror: An Essay on Abjection*, trans. Leon S. Roudiez (New York: Columbia University Press, 1982).

Kugel, Wilfried, *Der Unverantwortliche: Das Leben des Hanns Heinz Ewers* (Düsseldorf: Grupello, 1992).

Kupsky, Gregory J., '"The True Spirit of the German People" German-Americans and National Socialism, 1919–1955' (unpublished PhD dissertation, Ohio State University, 2010).

Lamb, Lady Caroline, *Glenarvon*, Revolution and Romanticism 1789–1834 (London, Printed for H. Colburn, 1816; facs. repr. Oxford and New York: Woodstock Books, 1993).

Lampert, Lisa, '"O My Daughter!": "die schöne Jüdin" and "der neue Jude", in Hermann Sinsheimer's *Maria Nunnez*', *The German Quarterly*, 71 (1998), 254–70.

Landers, Jessica M., 'The Modern Vampire Phenomenon Paradox: Simultaneous Contradictions and Unlimited Limits' (MA dissertation, State University of New Jersey, 2011).

Laplanche, Jean, and J.-B. Pontalis, *The Language of Psycho-Analysis*, trans. Donald Nicholson-Smith (1967; New York: Norton, 1973).

Latham, Rob, *Consuming Youth: Vampires, Cyborgs and the Culture of Consumption* (Chicago: University of Chicago Press, 2002).

Layne, Jay M., 'Uncanny Collapse: Sexual Violence and Unsettled Rhetoric in German-Language Lustmord Representations, 1900–1933' (unpublished PhD dissertation, University of Michigan, 2009).

Leatherdale, Clive, *Dracula: The Novel and the Legend* (Brighton: Desert Island, 1993).

Leavenworth, Van, 'The Gothic in Contemporary Interactive Fictions' (unpublished doctoral thesis, Umea University, 2010), *SwePub*, (online) http://swepub.kb.se [accessed 13 July 2011].

Le Blanc, Thomas, and Bettina Twrsnick (eds), *Traumreich und Nachtseite: die deutschsprachige Phantastik zwischen Décadence und Faschismus; Tagungsband 1995 Schriftenreihe und Materialien der Phantastischen Bibliothek Wetzlar* (Wetzlar: Förderkreis Phantastik 1995).

Leech, Geoffrey, and Mick Short, *Style in Fiction* (Harlow: Pearson Longman, 2007).

Le Fanu, Sheridan, 'The Quare Gander', *The Dublin University Magazine. Literary and Political Journal*, 16 (July–December 1840), 390.

—— *Ghost Stories and Mysteries*, ed. E. F. Bleiler (New York: Dover Publications, 1975).

—— *In a Glass Darkly*, ed. Robert Tracey (1872; Oxford and New York: Oxford University Press, 1993).

Lindvqist, John Ajvide, *Let the Right One In*, trans. Ebba Segerberg (2004; London: Quercus, 2007).

Longhauser, Elsa, Foreword, in Reed, 'Painting/Vampire', n.p.

Loreck, Hanne, 'Some Reflections on David Reed's Paintings and How They Fail to Come About', in Reed, *New Paintings*, pp. 56–62.

MacCarthy, Fiona, *Byron: Life and Legend* (2002; London: Faber, 2004).

McCarthy, Thomas, 'A Theory of Communicative Competence', *Philosophy of the Social Sciences*, 3 (1973), 135–56.

McCormack, W. J., *Sheridan Le Fanu and Victorian Ireland* (Oxford: Clarendon Press, 1980).

—— 'Irish Gothic and After', in *The Field Day Anthology of Irish Writing*, ed. Seamus Deane, 3 vols (Derry: W. W. Norton, 1991), II, pp. 831–54.

—— *Sheridan Le Fanu* (Phoenix Mill: Sutton Publishing, 1997).

McCulloch, Sandra, 'Twilight Relationship Unhealthy, Professor Says', *Vancouver Sun* (16 November 2009), (online) www.vancouversun.com/entertainment/movie-guide/Twilight+relationship+unhealthy+professor+says/2227415/story.html [accessed 20 December 2009].

McDayter, Ghislaine, 'Conjuring Byron: Byromania, Literary Commodification and the Birth of Celebrity', in Wilson (ed.), *Byromania*, pp. 43–62.

—— Introduction, in Ghislaine McDayter (ed.), *Byromania and the Birth of Celebrity Culture* (Albany: State University of New York Press, 2009), pp. 1–28.

MacDonald, David Lorne, *Poor Polidori: A Critical Biography of the Author of The Vampyre* (Toronto: University of Toronto Press, 1991).

McElroy, James, and Emma Catherine McElroy, 'Eco-Gothics for the Twenty-first Century', in Clarke and Osborn (eds), *The Twilight Mystique*, pp. 80–91.

McFarland, Ronald E., 'The Vampire on Stage', *Comparative Drama*, 21 (1987), 19–33.

MacKenzie, Carina Adley, '*Vampire Diaries*' Star Nina Dobrev on Elena's Look-alike', *LA Times Entertainment* (21 January 2010), http://latimesblogs.latimes.com/showtracker/2010/01/vampire-diaries-star-nina-dobrev.html [accessed 10 January 2011].

McLuhan, Marshall, *Understanding Media: The Extensions of Man* (1964; repr. London and Cambridge, MA: The MIT Press, 1994).

McMahon-Coleman, Kimberley, and Roslyn Weaver, *Werewolves and Other Shapeshifters in Popular Culture* (Jefferson: McFarland, 2012).

McNally, Raymond, *A Clutch of Vampires* (London: New English Library, 1976).

McNally, Raymond T., and Radu Florescu, *In Search of Dracula: The History of Dracula and Vampires* (New York: Houghton Mifflin Harcourt, 1994).

Madore, Michael, 'Sixty Fractions of Wegohn', in Reed, *New Paintings*, pp. 4–11.

Maerz, Melissa, 'The Vampire', *Rolling Stone* (16 September 2010), pp. 58–9.

Maguire, Eden, *Jonas*, Beautiful Dead, 1 (London: Hodder Children's Books, 2009).

Malchow, H. L., *Gothic Images of Race in Nineteenth-Century Britain* (Stanford: Stanford University Press, 1996).

Manovich, Lev, *The Language of New Media* (London and Cambridge, MA: MIT Press, 2002).

—— 'Image Future', *Animation: An Interdisciplinary Journal*, 1:1 (2006), (online) http://manovich.net/ [accessed 31 July 2011], 25–44.

—— 'After Effects, or Velvet Revolution', *Artifact*, 1:2 (2007), (online) http://scholarworks.iu.edu/journals/index.php/artifact/article/view/1357 [accessed 8 March 2012].

Marcuse, Herbert, 'The Struggle Against Liberalism in the Totalitarian View of the State', in *Negations: Essays in Critical Theory*, trans. Jeremy J. Shapiro (Harmondsworth: Penguin, 1968), pp. 3–42.

Marryat, Florence, *The Blood of the Vampire* (1897; Kansas City, MO: Valancourt Books, 2009).

Martin, Philip, 'The Vampire in the Looking Glass: Projection and Reflection in Stoker's *Dracula*', in Clive Bloom et al (eds), *Nineteenth-Century Suspense* (London: Macmillan, 1988), pp. 80–92.

Marx, Karl, *Capital*, vol. 1, trans. Ben Fowkes (1867; Harmondsworth: Penguin, 1990).

Matheson, Richard, *I Am Legend*, SF Masterworks (1954; London: Millennium, 1999).

Melada, Ivan, *Sheridan Le Fanu*, Twayne's English Authors Series, 438 (Boston: Twayne Publishers, 1987).

Mellins, Maria, 'Fashioning the Vampire: A Qualitative Study Investigating Issues of Dress and Performance within the Female Vampire Fan Community in Both Online and Face-to-face Social Contexts' (unpublished doctoral thesis, St. Mary's University College, 2009).

Merritt, Henry, '"Dead Many Times": Cathleen ni Houlihan, Yeats, Two Old Women, and a Vampire', *Modern Language Review*, 96:3 (July 2001), 644–53.

Meyer, Stephenie, *Twilight* (2005; London: Atom, 2007).

—— *New Moon* (2006; London: Atom, 2007).

—— *Eclipse* (2007; London: Atom, 2008).

—— *Breaking Dawn* (2008; London: Atom, 2010).

—— *Midnight Sun: Partial Draft*, unpublished ms. available on Meyer's website (2008), www.stepheniemeyer.com/pdf/midnightsun_partial_draft4.pdf [accessed 23 March 2009].

Milbanke, Ralph, Earl of Lovelace, *Astarte: A Fragment of Truth Concerning George Gordon Byron, Sixth Lord Byron*, www.archive.org/stream/astartefragmentooooloveuof t#page/116/mode/2up/search/delusion [accessed 31 August 2011].

Milton, John, *Paradise Lost*, ed. Gordon Teskey (New York and London: Norton Critical Edition, 2005).

Moretti, Franco, 'The Dialectic of Fear', *New Left Review*, 136 (Nov.–Dec. 1982), 67–85.

—— 'A Capital *Dracula*', in *Signs Taken for Wonders: Essays in the Sociology of Literary Forms*, trans. Susan Fischer, David Forgacs and David Miller (New York: Verso, 1988), pp. 90–104.

Moses, Michael Valdez, 'The Irish Vampire: Dracula, Parnell, and the Troubled Dreams of Nationhood', *Journal x: A Journal in Culture and Criticism*, 2:1 (Autumn 1997), 67–111.

Mosse, George L., *The Crisis of German Ideology; Intellectual Origins of the Third Reich* (New York: Grosset & Dunlap, 1964).

Mulvey, Laura, 'Visual Pleasure and Narrative Cinema', *Screen*, 16:3 (Autumn 1975), 6–18.

Murgoci, Agnes, 'The Vampire in Romania', *Folklore*, 37:4 (1926), 320–49; repr. in Dundes (ed.), *The Vampire: A Casebook*, pp. 12–34.

Neale, Steve, *Cinema and Technology: Image, Sound, and Colour* (London: Macmillan Education, 1985).

—— 'Masculinity as Spectacle: Reflections on Men and Mainstream Cinema', in Steven Cohan and Ina Rae Hark (eds), *Screening the Male: Exploring Masculinities in the Hollywood Cinema* (Abingdon and New York: Routledge, 1993), pp. 9–22.

Nedeau, Jen, 'Twilight: A Feminist Nightmare', *Change.org* (22 November 2009), http://womensrights.change.org/blog/view/twilight_a_feminist_nightmare [accessed 20 December 2009].

Newman, Kim, *Anno Dracula*, new edn (1992; London, Titan Books, 2011).

——'Why Don't Vampires Cast Reflections?', *Empire* (23 May 2011), (online) www.empireonline.com/empireblogs/empire-states/post/p1040 [accessed 1 April 2012].

Nicholson, Linda, *Identity before Identity Politics*, Cambridge Cultural Social Studies (Cambridge: Cambridge University Press, 2008).

Nietzsche, Friedrich, *Also sprach Zarathustra* (Munich: Goldmann, 1960).

Nikkigassley, 'Feminism Doesn't Sparkle: What Twilight Teaches Young Girls', *Amplify YourVoice.org* (13 August 2009), www.amplifyyourvoice.org/u/nikkigassley/2009/8/13/Feminism-Doesnt-Sparkle-What-Twilight-Teaches-Young-Girls [accessed 20 December 2009].

Nixon, Nicola, 'When Hollywood Sucks, or, Hungry Girls, Lost Boys, and Vampirism in the Age of Reagan', in Gordon and Hollinger (eds), *Blood Read*, pp. 115–28.

Ó Buachalla, Breandán, *Aisling Ghéar: Na Stíobhartaigh Agus an Taos Léinn 1603–1788* (Leabhair Thaighde; Baile Átha Cliath: An Clóchomhar Tta, 1996).

O'Flinn, Paul, '"Leaving the West and Entering the East": Refiguring the Alien, from Stoker to Coppola', in Deborah Cartmell et al. (eds), *Alien Identities: Exploring Differences in Film and Fiction* (London: Pluto Press, 1999), pp. 66–86.

Ono, Kent A., 'To Be a Vampire on *Buffy the Vampire Slayer*: Race and ("Other") Socially Marginalizing Positions on Horror TV', in Elyce Rae Helford (ed.), *Fantasy Girls: Gender in the New Universe of Science Fiction and Fantasy Television* (Lanham, MD: Rowman and Littlefield, 2000), pp. 163–86.

Overbey, Karen E., and Lahney Preston-Matto, 'Staking in Tongues: Speech Act as Weapon in *Buffy*', in Wilcox and Lavery (eds), *Fighting the Forces*, pp. 73–84.

Pamfile, Tudor (ed.), *Ion Creangă*, 4 (Bucharest, 1911).

Park, Jennifer, 'Melancholy and the Macabre: Gothic Rock and Fashion', in Steele and Park (eds), *Gothic*, pp. 115–63.

Pateman, Matthew, '"You Say Tomato": Englishness in Buffy the Vampire Slayer', *Cercles*, 8 (2003), 103–13.

Pater, Walter, 'Leonardo Da Vinci', in *The Renaissance*, ed. Adam Phillips (Oxford: Oxford University Press, 1986), pp. 63–82.

Penzo, Giorgio, 'Zur Frage der "Entnazifizierung" Friedrich Nietzsches', *Vierteljahrshefte für Zeitgeschichte*, 34 (1986), 105–16.

Perkowski, Jan Louis, *Vampires of the Slavs* (Cambridge, MA: Slavica Publishers, 1976).

——— 'The Romanian Folkloric Vampire', in Dundes (ed.), *The Vampire*, pp. 35–46.

Petrescu, Monica, 'The Long Shadow of Dracula', *Daily Telegraph* (6 February 2005), (online) www.telegraph.co.uk/news/worldnews/europe/romania/1482941/The-long-shadow-of-Dracula.html.

Petrovici, Emil, *Texte Dialectale* (Leipzig: Muzeul Limbii Române, 1943).

Platt, Carrie Ann, 'Cullen Family Values: Gender and Sexual Politics in the *Twilight* Series', in Click, Aubrey and Behm-Morawitz (eds), *Bitten by Twilight*, pp. 71–86.

Pliny, *Natural History*, trans. H. Rackham, 10 vols, Loeb Classical Library, 394 (Cambridge, MA, and London: Harvard University Press, 1938–1962), XXV: Books 33–5 (1952).

Poley, Jared C., 'Ant People and Voodoo Queens: Hanns Heinz Ewers, the Occupied Rhineland, and German Decolonization' (unpublished doctoral dissertation, University of California, Los Angeles, 2001).

Polidori, John, *The Vampyre*, ed. Chris Baldick (Oxford: Oxford University Press, 1997).

——— *The Vampyre and Ernestus Berchtold; or, The Modern Œdipus*, ed. D. L. Macdonald and Kathleen Scherf (Calgary: Broadview Editions, 2007).

Potts, Donna L., 'Convents, Claddagh Rings, and Even the Book of Kells: Representing the Irish in *Buffy the Vampire Slayer*', *Simile: Studies in Media & Information Literacy Education*, 3:2 (May 2003), [n.p.].

Priest, Hannah, 'What's Wrong with Sparkly Vampires?', *The Gothic Imagination*, 20 July 2011, www.gothic.stir.ac.uk/guestblog/whats-wrong-with-sparkly-vampires/ [accessed 27 September 2011].

Prince, Stephen (ed.), *The Horror Film* (New Brunswick: Rutgers University Press, 2004).

Punter, David, *The Literature of Terror: A History of Gothic Fiction from 1765 to the Present Day*, 2 vols (London: Longman, 1996), I: *The Gothic Tradition*.

Punter, David (ed.), *A Companion to the Gothic* (Oxford: Blackwell, 2001).

Punter, David, and Glennis Byron, *The Gothic* (Oxford: Blackwell, 2004).

'Rastajay93' and 'Bladepaw18', dated October 2010, 'Dracula, 1931 (part 1/8)', *YouTube*, www.youtube.com/all_comments?v=i9qtivRryDM&page=2 [accessed 27 July 2011].

Rebelliouspixels, 'Buffy vs Edward: *Twilight* Remixed', *YouTube* (19 June 2009), www.youtube.com/watch?v=RZwM3GvaTRM&feature=player_embedded [accessed 20 December 2009].

Reed, David, *New Paintings for the Mirror Room and Archive in a Studio off a Courtyard* (Graz: Neue Galerie, 1996).

——— 'Painting/Vampire Study Center', Goldie Paley Gallery, Moore College of Art and Design, 10 September–17 October, 1999.

——— *You Look Good in Blue* (Nuremberg: Verlag für moderne Kunst, 2001).

Reimann, Hans, *Ewers. Ein Garantiert Verwahrloster Schundroman in Lumpen, Fetzchen, Mätzchen und Unterhosen* (Hanover: P. Steegemann, 1922).

Rhodes, Gary R., 'Drakula halála (1921): The Cinema's First Dracula', *Horror Studies*, 1:1 (January 2010), 25–47.

Rice, Anne, *Interview with the Vampire*, The Vampire Chronicles, 1 (New York: Knopf, 1976; London: Futura, 1977).

—— *The Vampire Lestat*, The Vampire Chronicles, 2 (1986; London: Futura, 1990).

Rose, Jacqueline, *Sexuality in the Field of Vision* (London: Verso, 1987).

Rudkin, David, *Vampyr* (London: BFI Publishing, 2005).

Ruthner, Clemens, *Unheimliche Wiederkehr: Interpretationen zu den gespenstischen Romanfiguren bei Ewers, Meyrink, Soyka, Spunda und Strobl* (Meitingen: Corian-Verlag, 1993).

—— 'Andererseits: Die deutschsprachige Phantastik des frühen zwanzigsten Jahrhunderts in ihrem kulturhistorischen Kontext', in Winfried Freund, Johann Lachinger and Clemens Ruthner (eds), *Der Demiurg ist ein Zwitter: Alfred Kubin und die deutschsprachige Phantastik* (Munich: Fink, 1999), 165–80.

Ryan, Alan (ed.), *The Penguin Book of Vampire Stories* (Harmondsworth: Penguin, 1987).

Rymer, James Malcolm, *Varney, the Vampyre, or, The Feast of Blood* (1845–1847; Ware: Wordsworth Editions, 2010).

Saberhagen, Fred, *The Dracula Tape* (New York: Baen, 1975).

Sanders, Julie, *Adaptation and Appropriation* (London: Routledge, 2006).

Sands, Sarah, 'EMO Cult Warning for Parents', *Mail Online* (16 August 2006), www.dailymail.co.uk/news/article–400953/EMO-cult-warning-parents.html [accessed 27 September 2011].

Schaffer, Talia, '"A Wilde Desire Took Me": The Homoerotic History of *Dracula*', *ELH*, 61:2 (Summer 1994), 381–425.

Scott, Walter, *Ivanhoe*, ed. Graham Tulloch (1819; Edinburgh: Edinburgh University Press, 1998).

Sedgwick, Eve Kosofsky, *The Coherence of Gothic Conventions* (New York: Methuen, 1986).

Sedgwick, Marcus, *My Swordhand Is Singing* (London: Orion, 2006).

—— *The Kiss of Death* (London: Orion, 2008).

—— *Midwinterblood* (London: Indigo, 2011).

Selzter, Sarah, 'A Feminist's Guide to Curing Yourself of Twilight-Mania', *RH RealityCheck.org* (26 November 2009), www.rhrealitycheck.org/blog/2009/11/25/a-feminists-guide-to-curing-yourself-twilightmania [accessed 20 December 2009].

Senf, Carol, 'Dracula: The Unseen Face in the Mirror', *Journal of Narrative Technique*, 9:9 (1979), 160–70.

—— *The Vampire in Nineteenth-Century English Literature* (Bowling Green, OH: Bowling Green State University Popular Press, 1988).

Shakespeare, William, *The Merchant of Venice: Authoritative Text, Sources and Contexts, Criticism, Rewritings and Appropriations*, ed. Leah Marcus (New York: W. W. Norton, 2006).

Shary, Timothy. 'Buying Me Love: 1980s Class-clash Teen Romances', *The Journal of Popular Culture*, 44:3 (2011), 563–82.

Shelley, Mary, *Frankenstein*, ed. J. Paul Hunter (New York and London: Norton Critical Edition, 1996).

Shwartzman, Sarah, 'Is *Twilight* Mormon?', in Clarke and Osborn (eds), *The Twilight Mystique*, pp. 121–36.

Silver, Alain, and James Ursini, *The Vampire Film: From Nosferatu to Twilight*, 4th edn (Milwaukee: Limelight, 2010).

Silver, Anna, '*Twilight* Is Not Good for Maidens: Gender, Sexuality, and the Family in Stephenie Meyer's *Twilight* Series', *Studies in the Novel*, 42:1/2 (Spring/Summer 2010), 121–38.

Sims, Michael (ed.), *Dracula's Guest: A Connoisseur's Collection of Victorian Vampire Stories* (London: Bloomsbury, 2010).

Sinclair, Upton, 'To George Viereck (Personal)', *The Nation* (29 November 1941), p. 551.

Skal, David J., *Hollywood Gothic: The Tangled Web of 'Dracula' from Novel to Stage to Screen* (New York and London: W. W. Norton, 1990).

Skal, David J. (ed.), *Vampires: Encounters with the Undead* (New York: Black Dog & Leventhal, 2001).

Skovron, Jon, 'Ladies of the Night, Unite!', in Cordova (ed.), *A Visitor's Guide*, pp. 51–66.

Smirnoff, Victor, 'The Masochistic Contract', *International Journal of Psychoanalysis*, 50 (1969), 665–71.

Smith, L. J., *The Awakening*, The Vampire Diaries, 1 (1991; New York: HarperTeen, 2009).

—— *The Struggle*, The Vampire Diaries, 2 (1991; New York: HarperTeen, 2009).

—— *The Fury & Dark Reunion*, The Vampire Diaries, 3 & 4 (1991; New York: HarperTeen, 2007).

—— *Nightfall*, The Vampire Diaries: The Return, 1 (New York: HarperTeen, 2009).

Smith, Philip E., 'Protoplasmic Hierarchy and Philosophical Harmony: Science and Hegelian Aesthetics in Oscar Wilde's Notebooks', *The Victorian Newsletter*, 74 (Fall 1988), 30–3.

Soergel, Albert, 'Siebentes Kapitel: Hanns Heinz Ewers', in *Dichtung und Dichter der Zeit: eine Schilderung der deutschen Literatur der letzten Jahrzehnte*, 7th edn (Leipzig: Voigtländer, 1911), pp. 817–21.

Sombart, Werner, and Artur Landsberger, *Judentaufen* (Munich: Müller, 1912).

Southey, Robert, *Thalaba the Destroyer, Volume the Second* (London: Longman, Hurst, Rees and Orme, 1809).

Spooner, Catherine, '"Forget Nu Rave, We're Into Nu Grave!": Styling Gothic in the Twenty-first Century', in Justin D. Edwards and Agnieszka Soltysik Monnet (eds), *The Gothic in Contemporary Literature and Culture: Pop Goth* (London: Routledge, 2012).

Spooner, Catherine, and Emma McEvoy (eds), *The Routledge Companion to Gothic* (London: Routledge, 2007).

Stagg, John, 'The Vampire', www.simplysupernatural-vampire.com/thevampire-john-stagg-poem.html [accessed 27 August 2011].

Stahl, H., *Eseuri Critice* (Bucharest: Minerva, 1983).

Staiger, Janet, *Bad Women: Regulating Sexuality in Early American Cinema* (Minneapolis and London: University of Minnesota Press, 1995).

Stam, Robert, and Alessandra Raengo (eds), *Literature and Film: A Guide to the Theory and Practice of Film Adaptation* (Malden: Blackwell, 2005).

Steele, Valerie, and Jennifer Park, *Gothic: Dark Glamour* (New Haven: Yale University Press, 2008).

Stoichita, Victor I., *A Short History of the Shadow*, Essays in Art and Culture (London: Reaktion Books, 1997).

Stoker, Bram, *Dracula*, ed. Maud Ellman (1897; Oxford: Oxford World's Classics, Oxford University Press, 1996).

—— *Dracula*, ed. Nina Auerbach and David J. Skal (1897; New York and London: W. W. Norton, 1997).

—— *Dracula*, ed. Roger Luckhurst (1897; Oxford: Oxford World's Classics, Oxford University Press, 2011).

—— *Bram Stoker's Notes for Dracula: A Facsimile Edition*, ed. Robert Eighteen-Bisang and Elizabeth Miller (Jefferson: McFarland, 2008).

Stone, Allucquère Rosanne, *The War of Desire and Technology at the Close of the Mechanical Age* (London and Cambridge, MA: MIT Press, 1995).

Stuart, Roxana, *Stage Blood: Vampires of the Nineteenth-Century Stage* (Bowling Green, OH: Bowling Green State University Press, 1994)

Studlar, Gaylyn, 'Masochism and the Perverse Pleasures of the Cinema', *Quarterly Review of Film Studies*, 9:4 (1984), 267–78.

—— 'Visual Pleasure and the Masochistic Aesthetic', *Journal of Film and Video*, 37:2 (Spring 1985), 5–27.

—— 'Midnight S/excess: Cult Configurations of "Femininity" and the Perverse', *Journal of Popular Film and Television*, 17:1 (Spring 1989), 2–14.

—— 'Masochistic Performance and Female Subjectivity in *Letter from an Unknown Woman*', *Cinema Journal*, 33:3 (Spring 1994), 35–57.

Summers, Montague, *The Vampire: His Kith and Kin* (London: K. Paul, 1928); *The Vampire in Europe* (London: K. Paul, 1929); repr. as *Vampires and Vampirism* (New York: Dover, 2005).

Sweeney, Emily, 'Dark Days for Goths', *The Boston Globe* (15 October 2004), (online) www.azcentral.com/ent/pop/articles/1015teengoth15.html [accessed 27 September 2011].

Sweeney, Ken, '*Dracula* Creator Bram Stoker Also Had Painting in His Blood', *Irish Independent* (7 April 2012), (online) www.independent.ie/national-news/dracula-creator-bram-stoker-also-had-painting-in-his-blood–3073837.html [accessed 7 April 2012].

Taubin, Amy, 'Bloody Tales', *Sight and Sound*, 5:1 (January 1995), 8–11.

Tenga, Angela, and Elizabeth Zimmerman, 'Vampire Gentlemen and Zombie Beasts: A Rendering of True Monstrosity', *Gothic Studies*, 3:24, Open Graves, Open Minds special issue (May 2013).

Teukolsky, Rachel, 'Picture Language: The Invention of Photography', in *The Literate Eye* (Oxford: Oxford University Press, 2009), pp. 42–7.

Theweleit, Klaus, *Male Fantasies*, trans. by Stephen Conway (Minneapolis: University of Minnesota Press, 1987).

Thomas, Dylan, *Under Milk Wood: A Play for Voices* (1954; London: Dent, 1977).

Thornton, Sarah, *Club Cultures: Music, Media and Subcultural Capital* (Cambridge: Polity Press, 1995).

Thurber, Ann, 'Bite Me: Desire and the Female Spectator in *Twilight*, *The Vampire Diaries*, and *True Blood*' (MA dissertation, Emory University, 2011).

Todorov, Tzvetan, *The Fantastic: A Structural Approach to a Literary Genre* (Ithaca, NY: Cornell University Press, 1975).

Tomlinson, Janis, *Francisco Goya y Lucientes 1746–1828* (London and New York: Phaidon, 1994).

Toscano, Margaret M., 'Mormon Morality and Immortality in Stephenie Meyer's Twilight Series', in Click, Aubrey and Behm-Morawitz (eds), *Bitten by Twilight*, pp. 21–36.

Tournefort, Joseph Pitton de, *A Voyage into the Levant (Relation d'un voyage du Levant)* (1717; London: printed for D. Browne et al, 1718).

Tudor, Andrew, 'Unruly Bodies, Unquiet Minds', *Body and Society*, 1:1 (March 1995), 25–41.

Twitchell, James B., *The Living Dead: A Study of the Vampire in Romantic Literature* (Durham, NC: Duke University Press, 1981).

Tyree, J. M., 'Warm-blooded: *True Blood* and *Let the Right One In*', *Film Quarterly*, 63:2 (2009), 31–7.

UWMKatie, 'A Significant Step Down from Buffy', *Community Feministing* (8 August 2009), http://community.feministing.com/2008/08/a-significant-step-down-from-b.html [accessed 20 December 2009].

Valente, Joseph, *Dracula's Crypt: Bram Stoker, Irishness, and the Question of Blood* (Chicago: University of Illinois Press, 2002).

Venters, Jillian, *Gothic Charm School: An Essential Guide for Goths and Those Who Love Them* (New York: Harper Collins 2009).

Viereck, George S., *The House of the Vampire* (New York: Moffat, Yard, 1907).

—— *Confessions of a Barbarian* (New York: Moffat, Yard, 1910).

—— 'No Room for the Alien, No Use for the Wastrel' [1923], *Guardian*, Great Interviews Online, www.guardian.co.uk/theguardian/2007/sep/17/greatinterviews1 [accessed 5 May 2011].

—— *Spreading Germs of Hate* (New York: Liveright, 1930).

—— *Glimpses of the Great* (New York: The Macaulay Company, 1930).

—— 'Letter to the Editor', *New York Times* (7 June 1934), 13.

—— *The Temptation of Jonathan* (Boston: Christopher, 1938).

—— 'Letter to Elmer Gertz', Library of Congress, Gertz papers, Box 443, 5 November 1938.

—— 'Letter to Elmer Gertz', Library of Congress, Gertz papers, Box 443, 29 March 1939.

—— 'Mr. Viereck Protests (Letter to the Editor)', *Forum and Century* (1939), 111–12.

—— 'Hitler or Chaos', University of Iowa, George Sylvester Viereck Papers, Box 4.

—— What I Saw in Hitler's Germany', University of Iowa, George Sylvester Viereck Papers, University of Iowa, Box 4.

—— 'The German-Jewish War', University of Iowa, George Sylvester Viereck Papers, University of Iowa, Box 4, Item 4.

Viereck, George S., and Paul Eldridge, *My First Two Thousand Years: The Autobiography of the Wandering Jew* (New York: Macaulay, 1928).

Voltaire, François-Marie Arouet de, 'Vampires', in T*he Works of Voltaire, A Contemporary Version*, A Critique and Biography by John Morley, notes by Tobias Smollett, trans. William F. Fleming, 21 vols (New York: E. R. DuMont, 1901), VII: *Philosophical Dictionary*, Part 5 [1764], (online) http://oll.libertyfund.org/title/1660 [accessed 11 May 2012].

Wadler, Joyce, and Johnny Greene, 'Anne Rice's Imagination May Roam Among Vampires and Erotica, but Her Heart Is Right at Home', *People*, 30:23 (5 December 1988), (online) www.people.com/people/archive/article/0,,20100681,00.html [accessed 11 May 2012].

Waller, Gregory, *The Living and the Undead: Slaying Vampires, Exterminating Zombies* (Urbana: University of Illinois Press, 2010).

Walton, James, *Vision and Vacancy: The Fictions of J. S. Le Fanu* (Dublin: University College Dublin Press, 2007).

Warchol, Tomasz, 'How Coppola Killed Dracula', in Carla T. Kungl (ed.), *Vampires: Myths and Metaphors of Enduring Evil* (Oxford: Inter-Disciplinary Press, 2003), pp. 7–10.

Warwick, Alexandra, 'Feeling Gothicky?', *Gothic Studies*, 9:1 (May 2007), 5–15.

Waters, Daniel, *Generation Dead* (New York: Hyperion Books; London: Simon and Schuster, 2008).

—— *Kiss of Life* (New York: Hyperion Books; London: Simon and Schuster, 2009).

—— 'My So-Called Undeath', http://mysocalledundeath.blogspot.com [accessed 3 September 2010].

—— *Passing Strange* (New York: Hyperion Books; London: Simon and Schuster, 2010).

Weibel, Peter, 'Phantom Painting: Reading Reed: Painting Between Autopsy and Autoscopy', in Reed, *New Paintings*, pp. 49–55.

Wicke, Jennifer, 'Vampiric Typewriting: *Dracula* and Its Media', *ELH*, 59:2 (Summer 1992), 467–93.

Wikoff, Karin E., 'Hanns Heinz Ewers' *Vampir*' (MA thesis, Cornell University, 1995).

Wilcox, Rhonda V., 'There Will Never Be a "Very Special" Buffy', *Journal of Popular Film and Television*, 27:2 (1999), 16–23.

—— *Why Buffy Matters: The Art of Buffy the Vampire Slayer* (London and New York: I. B. Tauris, 2005).

Wilcox, Rhonda V., and David Lavery (eds), *Fighting the Forces: What's at Stake in Buffy the Vampire Slayer* (Lanham, Boulder, New York and Oxford: Rowman & Littlefield, 2002).

Wilde, Oscar, 'The Critic as Artist', Part 1, in *The Soul of Man Under Socialism and Select Critical Prose*, ed. Linda Dowling (London: Penguin, 2001), pp. 213–43.

—— *The Picture of Dorian Gray*, ed. Joseph Bristow (1891; Oxford: Oxford University Press, 2006).

Williams, Linda, 'When the Woman Looks', in Marc Jancovich (ed.), *The Horror Film Reader* (London: Routledge, 2001), pp. 61–6.

Williamson, Milly, *The Lure of the Vampire: Gender, Fiction and Fandom from Bram Stoker to 'Buffy'* (London: Wallflower, 2005).

Willis, Martin, 'Le Fanu's "Carmilla", Ireland, and Diseased Vision', in Sharon Ruston (ed.), *Literature and Science*, Essays and Studies, 61 (Cambridge: D. S. Brewer, 2008), pp. 111–30.

Wilson, Frances (ed.), *Byromania: Portraits of the Artist in Nineteenth- and Twentieth-Century Culture* (Basingstoke: Macmillan, 1999).

Wilson, Katharina M., 'The History of the Word "Vampire"', *Journal of the History of Ideas*, 46:4 (October–December 1985), 577–83.

Wilson, Natalie, *Seduced by Twilight: The Allure and Contradictory Messages of the Popular Saga* (Jefferson, NC: McFarland, 2011).

Wolfman, Marv, and Gene Colan, *The Tomb of Dracula* (New York: Marvel Comics, 1972–1979).

Woolley, Benjamin, *The Bride of Science: Romance, Reason and Byron's Daughter* (New York: McGraw-Hill, 1999).

Woon, Yvonne, *Dead Beautiful* (2010; London: Usborne, 2011).

Worland, Rick, *The Horror Film: An Introduction* (Malden, MA: Blackwell, 2007).

Wright, Jonathan, 'Southern Lady', *SFX*, 195 (June 2010), pp. 72–4.

Wynne, Catherine, *Bram Stoker and the Stage: Reviews, Reminiscences, Essays and Fiction*, 2 vols (London: Pickering and Chatto, 2012).

Yarbro, Chelsea Quinn, *Hôtel Transylvania: A Novel of Forbidden Love* (New York: St Martin's Press, 1978).

Zanger, Jules, 'Metaphor into Metonymy: The Vampire Next Door' in Gordon and Hollinger (eds), *Blood Read*, pp. 17–26.

Film

The American Nightmare, dir. Adam Simon (USA: Minerva Pictures, 2000).

Bram Stoker's Dracula, dir. Francis Ford Coppola (USA: Columbia Pictures, 1992: DVD).

Breaking Dawn, dir. Bill Condon (USA: Summit, 2011).

Dracula, dir. Tod Browning (USA: Universal Pictures, 1931).

Eclipse, dir. David Slade (USA: Summit Entertainment, 2010).

The Hunger, dir. Tony Scott (USA: Metro-Goldwyn-Mayer, 1983).

Let Me In, dir. Matt Reeves (UK: Hammer Films, 2010).

Let the Right One In [*Låt den rätte komma in*], dir. Tomas Alfredson (Sweden: Sandrew Metronome, 2008).

The Lost Boys, dir. Joel Schumacher (USA: Warner Bros. Pictures, 1987).

Nosferatu: eine Symphonie des Grauens, dir. F. W. Murnau (Germany: Film Arts Guild, 1922).

Salem's Lot, dir. Tobe Hooper (USA: Warner Brothers, 1979).

Teen Wolf, dir. Rod Daniel (USA: Atlantic, 1985).

Twilight, dir. Catherine Hardwicke, perf. Kristen Stewart, Robert Pattinson, Billy Burke. (USA: Summit Entertainment, 2008).

Twilight: New Moon, dir. Chris Weitz (USA: Summit Entertainment, 2009).

Underworld, dir. Len Wiseman (USA: Lakeshore Entertainment, 2003).

Vampyr: Der Traum des Allan Grey, dir. Carl Theodor Dreyer (Germany: Vereinigte Star-Film GmbH, 1932).

Television

Being Human, created Toby Whithouse (UK: BBC, 2009–).

Buffy the Vampire Slayer, created Joss Whedon (USA: Warner Bros/UPN, 1997–2003).

    'Afterlife', dir. David Solomon, writ. Jane Espenson, 6.03 (first broadcast 9 October 2001 by UPN).

    'Anne', dir. and writ. Joss Whedon, 3.01 (first broadcast 29 September 1998 by WB).

    'Bargaining Part 1', dir. David Grossman, writ. Marti Noxon, 6.01 (first broadcast 2 October 2001 by UPN).

    'Bargaining Part 2', dir. David Grossman, writ. David Fury, 6.02 (first broadcast 2 October 2001 by UPN).

    'Becoming Part 1', dir. and writ. Joss Whedon, 2.21 (first broadcast 12 May 1998 by WB).

    'Becoming Part 2', dir. and writ. Joss Whedon, 2.22 (first broadcast 19 May 1998 by WB).

    'Buffy vs. Dracula', dir. David Solomon, writ. Marti Noxon, 5.1 (first broadcast 6 September 2000 by WB).

    'Doppelgangland', dir. and writ. Joss Whedon, 3.16 (first broadcast 23 February 1999 by WB).

    'Fool for Love', dir. Nick Marck, writ. Douglas Petrie, 5.07 (first broadcast 14 November 2000 by WB).

    'Grave', dir. James A. Contner, writ. David Fury, 6.22 (first broadcast 21 May 2002 by UPN).

    'The Harvest', dir. John T. Kretchmer, writ. Joss Whedon, 1.02 (first broadcast 10 March 1997 by WB).

    'Innocence', dir. and writ. Joss Whedon, 2.14 (first broadcast 20 January 1998 by WB).

    'Lessons', dir. David Solomon, writ. Joss Whedon, 7.01 (first broadcast 24 September 2002 by UPN).

    'Lies My Parents Told Me', dir. David Fury, writ. David Fury and Drew Goddard, 7.17 (first broadcast 25 March 2003 by UPN).

    'Once More, with Feeling', dir. and writ. Joss Whedon, 6.07 (first broadcast 6 November 2001 by UPN).

'Nightmares', dir. Bruce Seth Green, story Joss Whedon, teleplay David Greenwalt, 1.10 (first broadcast 12 May 1997 by WB).

'Prophecy Girl', dir. and writ. Joss Whedon, 1.12 (first broadcast 2 June 1997 by WB).

'Surprise', dir. Michael Lange, writ. Marti Noxon, 2.13 (first broadcast 19 January 1998 by WB).

'Villains', dir. David Solomon, writ. Marti Noxon, 6.20 (first broadcast 14 May 2002 by UPN).

'Welcome to the Hellmouth', dir. and writ. Joss Whedon, 1.01 (first broadcast 10 March 1997 by WB).

'The Wish', dir. David Greenwalt, writ. Marti Noxon, 3.09 (first broadcast 8 December 1998 by WB).

'State of Decay', dir. Peter Moffatt, writ. Terrance Dicks, *Doctor Who* (UK: BBC TV, 1980; DVD box set *Doctor Who: The E-Space Trilogy* (2 Entertain, 2009)).

True Blood, created Alan Ball, based on the novels by Charlaine Harris (USA: HBO, 2008–).

'I Will Rise Up', dir. Scott Winant, writ. Alan Ball, 2.9 (first broadcast 16 August 2009 by HBO; DVD: HBO Home Video, 2010).

'Shedding Light on Vampires in America', Season 1 extra (DVD: Warner Home Video, 2009).

'Sparks Fly Out', dir. Daniel Minahan, writ. Alexander Woo, 1.5 (first broadcast 14 August 2009 by HBO; DVD: Warner Home Video, 2009).

'Strange Love', dir. Alan Ball, writ. Alan Ball, 1.1 (first broadcast 17 July 2009 by HBO; DVD: Warner Home Video, 2009).

'Timebomb', dir. John Dahl, dor. Alexander Woo, 2.8 (first broadcast 9 August 2009 by HBO; DVD: Warner Home Video, 2009).

The Vampire Diaries, created Kevin Williamson and Julie Plec, based on the novels by L. J. Smith (USA: CW Network, 2009–).

'As I Lay Dying', dir. John Behring, writ. Turi Meyer, Al Septien and Michael Narducci, 2.22 (first broadcast 12 May 2011).

'Bad Moon Rising', dir. Patrick Norris, writ. Andrew Chambliss, 2.3 (first broadcast 23 September 2010 by the CW Network).

'Blood Brothers', dir. Liz Friedlander, writ. Kevin Williamson and Julie Plec, 1.20 (first broadcast 29 April 2010 by CW; DVD: Warner Bros 2010).

'Bloodlines', dir. David Barrett, writ. Kevin Williamson, Julie Plec and Sean Reycraft, 1.11 (first broadcast 21 January 2010 by CW; DVD: Warner Bros, 2010).

'Daddy Issues', dir. Joshua Butler, writ. Kevin Williamon and Julie Plec, 2.13 (first broadcast 3 February, 2011 by CW, DVD: Warner Bros, 2010).

'The Dinner Party', dir. Marcos Siega, writ. Andrew Chambliss, 2.15 (first broadcast 17 February 2011 by CW, DVD: Warner Bros, 2010).

'Fool Me Once', dir. Marcos Siega, writ. Brett Conrad, 1.14 (first broadcast 11 February 2010 by CW; DVD: Warner Bros, 2010).

'Founder's Day', dir. Marcos Siega, writ. Bryan Oh and Andrew Chambliss, 1.22 (first broadcast 13 May 2010 by CW; DVD: Warner Bros, 2010).

'Masquerade', dir. Charles Beeson, writ. Kevin Williamson and Julie Plec, 2.7 (first broadcast 28 October, 2010 by CW, DVD: Warner Bros, 2010).

'Miss Mystic Falls', dir. Marcos Siega, writ Bryan Oh and Caroline Dries, 1.19 (first broadcast 22 April 2010 by CW; DVD: Warner Bros, 2010).

'The Night of the Comet', dir. Marcos Siega, writ. Kevin Williamson and Julie Plec, 1.2 (first broadcast 17 September 2009 by CW; DVD: Warner Bros, 2010).

'The Pilot', dir. Marcos Siega, writ. Kevin Williamson and Julie Plec, 1.1 (first broadcast 10 September 2009 by CW; DVD: Warner Bros, 2010).

'The Return', dir. J. Miller Tobin, writ. Kevin Williamson and Julie Plec, 2.1 (USA: first broadcast 9 September 2010 by CW, DVD: Warner Bros, 2010).

'The Sun Also Rises', dir. Paul Sommers, writ. Caroline Dries and Mark Daniels, 2.21 (USA: first broadcast 5 May 2011 by CW, DVD: Warner Bros, 2010).

'There Goes the Neighbourhood', dir. Kevin Bray, writ. Bryan Oh and Andrew Chambliss, 1.16 (USA: first broadcast April 1, 2010 by CW; DVD: Warner Bros 2010).

'You're Undead to me', dir. Kevin Bray, writ. Sean Reycraft and Gabrielle Stanton, 1.5 (USA: first broadcast 8 October 2009 by CW, DVD: Warner Bros, 2010).

Video games

Vampire Rush (A-Steroids/Chillingo, 2011) [videogame for iOS and Bada platforms].

Adams, Scott, *The Count* (Adventure International, 1981) [text-based computer game for Apple II Plus, Atari 400, Atari 800, Commodore PET, TI 99/4a, TRS–80, Vic 20, and ZX Spectrum platforms].

Index

Note: literary works can be found under author's names. Page numbers in *italics* refer to illustrations.

Lightning Source UK Ltd.
Milton Keynes UK
UKHW02f2152280218

318665UK00005B/432/P

9 781784 993627